OLD LONDON
Covent Garden and the Thames to Whitehall

THE
'VILLAGE LONDON'
SERIES
from
THE ALDERMAN PRESS

THE VILLAGE LONDON SERIES

Other titles already published in hard back are:

VILLAGE LONDON Volume I
VILLAGE LONDON Volume II
LONDON RECOLLECTED Volume I
LONDON RECOLLECTED Volume II
LONDON RECOLLECTED Volume III
LONDON RECOLLECTED Volume IV
LONDON RECOLLECTED Volume V

Other titles already published in paperback:

VILLAGE LONDON Pt. 1 West and North
VILLAGE LONDON Pt. 2 North and East
VILLAGE LONDON Pt. 3 South-East
VILLAGE LONDON Pt. 4 South-West

OLD FLEET STREET
CHEAPSIDE AND ST. PAUL'S
THE TOWER AND EAST END
SHOREDITCH to SMITHFIELD
CHARTERHOUSE to HOLBORN
STRAND to SOHO
COVENT GARDEN and the THAMES to WHITEHALL

*The above seven titles are extracts from the
hardback edition of London Recollected.*

OLD LONDON

Covent Garden and the Thames to Whitehall

by

EDWARD WALFORD

THE ALDERMAN PRESS

British Library Cataloguing in Publication Data.

Walford, Edward.
    Old London: Covent Garden and the Thames
    to Whitehall.
    1. London (England)_____History
    I. Title II. Walford, Edward. Old and
    new London
    942.1   DA677

ISBN 0-946619-30-1

This edition published 1987.

The Alderman Press, 1/7 Church Street,
Edmonton, London, N9 9DR

Printed and bound in Great Britain
by Robert Hartnoll (1985) Ltd., Bodmin.

CONTENTS.

———◆———

CONTENTS.

CONTENTS.

CHAPTER XLVIII.
WHITEHALL.—THE WESTERN SIDE.

LIST OF ILLUSTRATIONS.

CHAPTER XXVI.

ST. GILES'S IN THE FIELDS.

"On Newgate steps Jack Chance was found,
And bred up near St. Giles's Pound."—*Old Song.*

St. Giles, the Patron Saint of Lepers—The Lepers' Hospital founded here—The Village of St. Giles in the Time of the Plantagenets, Tudors, and Stuarts—Executions at St. Giles's—The "Half-way House" on the Road to Tyburn—The Cage and the Pound—St. Giles's Church —Church Lane—Monmouth Court and the Catnatch Press—The Seven Dials—Shaved by a Woman—The Prince and the Beggars.

ST. GILES, the patron saint of this and of so many other outlying parishes in English towns and cities, is said, by Alban Butler in his "Lives of the Saints," to have been of noble birth at Athens. He flourished in the seventh and eighth centuries, and combined with his piety a marked love of solitude. Quitting his own country he found a retreat in France, and passed many years of his life in the recesses of a forest in the neighbourhood of Nismes. It is said that the French king and a troop of hunters pursued a hind, which fled for protection to the saint. An arrow, intended for the hind, wounded the saint, who, however, continued his devotions, and refused all recompense for the injury done to his body. The hind, it appeared, had long nourished him with its milk, and had strayed into danger in one of the glades. This incident made Giles a great favourite with the king, but nothing could induce him to quit his forest for the atmosphere of a court. Towards the end of his life, however, he so far abandoned his solitude as to admit several disciples and found a monastery, which afterwards became a Benedictine abbey. The saint is commemorated in the Martyrologies of St. Bede and others, and St. Giles and the hind have often afforded a subject for the artist's pencil. St. Giles is the patron saint of lepers, and is styled in the calendar of the Roman Church "Abbot and Confessor."

It is very doubtful whether this manor and village, of which we now come to treat, was dedicated to St. Giles before the erection of the lepers' hospital by Queen Matilda, for there is no mention of it by any such name in "Domesday Book." The hospital consisted of a house or principal mansion, with an oratory and offices; but the "oratory" appears to have been only a chapel added on to the village church. "Private charity, however," says Newton, "augmented it in after times, and the brotherhood seem to have become subsequently possessed of other lands, as the Spital croft, consisting of sixteen acres, lying on the north side of the highway, opposite the great gate of the hospital, and also two estates called Newlands and Lelane, the exact situations of which, though probably contiguous, we are unable to point out."

According to existing records, the earliest notice of this district tells us that a hospital for lepers was founded here, about the year 1118, by Queen Matilda, the good wife of Henry I., and that it was attached as a "cell," or subordinate house, to a larger institution at Burton Lazars, in Leicestershire, then recently founded. Grants of royalty were confirmed by a bull of Pope Alexander VI. (1240). The hospital here stood on land belonging to the Crown, and not very far from the present parish church. Its grounds were enclosed with a wall, and formed almost a triangle, embracing between seven and eight acres. On the north it was bounded by High Street, on the west by Crown Street, and on the east by Dudley (formerly Monmouth) Street. The conventual buildings do not appear to have been of any great size, and, so far as we know, there is no print of their extent. The foundation, however, as we happen to know, was for "forty lepers, one clerk, and one messenger, besides matrons, the master, and other members of the establishment." Mr. Newton tells us that the grant from the Crown expressly stipulated that the hospital should be built "on the spot where 'John, of good memory,' was chaplain;" and hence he argues that the village church formed part of the grant along with the ancient manor.

Carew, in his "Survey of Cornwall," says that leprosy was common in the far west in his own day (James I.), and attributes it to the "disorderly eating of sea-fish newly taken, and principally the livers of them, not well prepared, soused, pickled, or condited." St. James's, St. Giles's, and Burton Lazars, in Leicestershire, were the three oldest houses for lepers in the kingdom.

At the Reformation St. Giles's Hospital was dissolved, and granted by Henry VIII. to John Dudley, Viscount Lisle, whom the king graciously allowed to alienate it to John or Wymond Carew, in 1547. Belonging to the hospital was a Grange at Edmonton (Edelmston). At the time of this alienation (1547) Dr. Andrew Borde, "the first of Merry Andrews," was the tenant of a messuage, with an orchard and garden, adjoining the said dissolved hospital. Mr. Parton identifies this with the site of the residence afterwards given to the rector by the Duchess of Dudley, and later known as Dudley Court. The hospital was endowed with lands at Feltham and Isleworth, and by an annual rent from St. Clement's parish. Lord Lisle fitted up the chief part of the building, and lived here two years. Mr. Parton publishes the list of masters and wardens of the hospital, with accounts, &c. Cotterell Garden, in St. Giles's parish, was confirmed to the hospital in 1186.

The hospital chapel and the parish church of

liament was passed, ordering the "western road" of London, from "Holborne Bars" to St. Giles-in-the-Fields, to be paved, "as far as there was any habitation of both sides of the street." The village of St. Giles had its ancient stone cross, which seems to have stood near what is now the north end of Endell Street.

In 1413 there was in London a conspiracy of the sect called the Lollards. They met in the fields adjoining St. Giles's Hospital, headed by Sir John

SEVEN DIALS, 1870. (*From an Original Sketch.*)

St. Giles would appear to have been two distinct structures under a single roof, much like the arrangement still to be seen in St. Helen's Church, Bishopsgate. Before the high altar in the chapel burnt St. Giles's light. There was a second altar and chapel of St. Michael.

The chief part of the village of St. Giles, in the days of our Plantagenet kings, was composed of houses standing on the north of the highway which led westward from Holborn to Tyburn, and whose gardens stretched behind them to St. Blemund's Dyke. In Ralph Aggas' map it figures as a small village, or rather a small group of cottages, with their respective garden-plots nestling around the walls of the hospital. In 1541 an Act of Par-

Oldcastle, who afterwards was executed on the spot, being hung in chains over a slow fire.

In the days of Elizabeth it was not so easy either for lepers or for ordinary people to find their way from St. Giles's to St. James's, as there were no continuous rows of houses in that south-west direction. But at the point where Tottenham Court Road now intersects Oxford Street, there was a notice, at the top of a narrow lane running across where is now Soho, "The Road to Reading." It led, however, by a somewhat singular bend, no further than the top of the Haymarket and a narrow lane parallel to it, which bore the rural name of Hedge Lane, not far from the corner of Leicester Fields.

The first era of building began a little before

VIEWS IN THE ROOKERY, ST. GILES'S, 1860.

1600, at which date Holborn and St. Giles's were nearly connected together. On the wall of the hospital being pulled down, houses began to be built on the east, west, and south sides of the church, and on both sides of St. Giles's Street new dwellings multiplied. Ten years later saw the commencement of Great Queen Street, and a continuation of the houses down both sides of Drury Lane. And so great was the increase that in 1623 no less than 897 houses were rated. Indeed, in Elizabeth's time, the parish was very largely built on, and distinguished by the rank of its inhabitants. (Both Elizabeth and James, it will be remembered, forbade building in the suburbs.) At the end of Charles II.'s reign there were more than 2,000; in Anne's, more than 3,000; in 1812, nearly 5,000 houses rated in the parish books.

A second great era of building came in with the Restoration. After the Revocation of the Edict of Nantes, large numbers of poor French emigrants took up their quarters about this part.

In this parish, unfortunately, the earlier volumes of the rate-books have perished, so that it is not possible to obtain such accurate information as to its inhabitants in the Tudor and Stuart times as we find in those of St. Martin's, and of St. Paul's, Covent Garden.

Although the parish of St. Giles is reckoned, as indeed it is, a poor and third-rate neighbourhood, and its very name has passed into a by-word as the very antipodes of fashionable St. James's, still it is richer in its materials for history than many districts inhabited by a class-higher in the social scale. It is observed in "Haunted London" that "the story of St. Giles's parish should properly embrace the whole records of London vagrancy."

When criminals ceased to be executed at the Elms in Smithfield, or, as some say, at a much earlier date, a gallows was set up near the north-west corner of the wall of the hospital; and it soon became a regular custom to present every male-factor, as he passed the hospital gate in the fatal cart on his way to the gallows, with a glass of ale. When the hospital was dissolved, the custom was still kept up; and there is scarcely an execution at "Tyburn Tree," recorded in the "Newgate Calendar," in which the fact is not mentioned that the culprit called at a public-house *en route* for a parting draught.

The memory of this last drink given to criminals on their way was long preserved by Bowl Yard or Alley, on the south side of the High Street, over against Dyott Street, *alias* George Street; and Parton, in his "History of the Parish," published in 1822, makes mention of a public-house bearing the sign of "The Bowl," which stood between the end of St. Giles's, High Street, and Hog Lane.

"A like custom," writes Pennant, "obtained anciently at York, which gave rise to the saying, that the saddler of Bawtry was hanged for leaving his liquor: had he stopped, as was usual with other criminals, to drink his bowl of ale, his reprieve, which was actually on its way, would have arrived in time enough to have saved his life."

The "Bowl" would appear to have been succeeded by the "Angel," or to have had a rival in that inn. At all events, in 1873, the *City Press* reported that another memorial of ancient London was about to pass away, namely, the "Angel" Inn, at St. Giles's, the "half-way house" on the road to Tyburn—the house at which Jack Ketch and the criminal who was about to expiate his offence on the scaffold were wont to stop on their way to the gallows for a "last glass." The proprietor, however, was prevailed upon to stay the work of demolition for a time; but the house has since been rebuilt.

When Lord Cobham was executed at St. Giles's, it is said that a new gallows was put up for that special occasion. But Lord Cobham was not the only distinguished person who here paid the last penalty of the law. St. Giles's Pound is also memorable as the scene of the execution of some of the accomplices in Babington's plot against Queen Elizabeth, though Babington himself suffered at Lincoln's Inn Fields, "even in the place where they used to meet and conferre of their traytorous practices."

The Cage and the Pound originally stood close together in the middle of the High Street, but they were removed in 1656 to make room for alms-houses. The Pound, too, occupied, as we learn casually, a space of thirty feet near the same site, but it was removed about the same time to the corner of Tottenham Court Road, where it stood till 1765 on the site of the isolated block of houses opposite the entrance to Messrs. Meux's Brewery.

The immediate neighbourhood of this Pound bore none of the highest characters, if we may draw any inference on the subject from the words of a popular song by Mr. Thompson, an actor at Drury Lane Theatre, which we have prefixed as a motto to this chapter.

In the High Street, on the left-hand side going towards Tottenham Court Road, the late Mr. J. T. Smith remembered four large and handsome houses, "with grotesque masques on the key-stones above the first-floor windows." He also tells us that just where Oxford Street and Tottenham Court Road meet there was a large circular boundary-stone let into the pavement. "When," he adds, "the charity boys of St. Giles's parish walk the boundaries, those who have deserved flogging are whipped at this stone, in order that when they grow up they may remember the place, and be competent to give evidence should any dispute arise with the neighbouring parishes."

Mr. Smith also tells us, in his "Book for a Rainy Day," that he remembered a row of six small almshouses, surrounded by a dwarf brick wall, standing in the middle of High Street. They were pulled down about the year 1780, and rebuilt near the coal-yard at the north-east end of Drury Lane. There was formerly a vineyard here, as there was on the slope of the hill near to Hatton Garden.

It is remarkable that in almost every ancient town in England, the church of St. Giles stands either outside the walls, or, at all events, near its outlying parts, in allusion, doubtless, to the arrangements of the Israelites of old, who placed their lepers outside the camp.

St. Giles's Church stands on the south side of High Street, at the junction of Broad Street, and was erected between the years 1730 and 1734. It is a large and stately edifice, built entirely of Portland stone, and is vaulted beneath. The steeple, which rises to a height of about 160 feet, consists of a rustic pedestal, supporting a range of Doric pilasters; whilst above the clock is an octangular tower, with three-quarter Ionic columns, supporting a balustrade with vases, on which stands the spire, which is also octangular and belted. The interior of the church is bold and effective; the roof is supported by rows of Ionic pillars of Portland stone, and the semicircular-headed windows are mostly filled with coloured glass.

There was here a previous structure of red brick, consecrated by Laud, whilst Bishop of London, in 1623, and towards the building of which the poor "players of the Cockpit," so cruelly persecuted by the Puritan party, gave £20. This church was pulled down to make room for the present edifice, which was opened for worship in 1734. It had for its architect one Henry Flitcroft, the same who built the church of St. Olave, Southwark; and Mr. Peter Cunningham draws attention to the fact that it bears a close resemblance to that of St. Martin's-in-the-Fields. The first church of all on this spot appears to have had a round tower, not unlike those to be seen in the small parishes in the eastern parts of Norfolk and Suffolk.

Strype gives an account of several of the monuments in the church and churchyard, but we shall notice only a few. One of these was put up in 1611, by John Thornton to his wife, who died in childbed. He probably was the builder of Thornton's Alley, and that he was from the north country is more than probable from the legend round the family tomb :—

> "Full south this stone four foot doth lie,
>   His father John and grandsire Harvey;
> Thornton of Thornton in Yorkshire bred,
>   Where lives the fame of Thornton being dead."

Another stone in the churchyard records the death of one Eleanor Stewart, an old resident in the parish, who died in 1725, at the age, according to the inscription, of 123 and five months, an age which we bring here under the notice of those who deny centenarianism.

In the churchyard are tombs to the memory of Richard Pendrill, to whom Charles II. owed his escape after the fatal battle of Worcester, and of George Chapman, the earliest translator of Homer's "Iliad;" the latter is said to have been the work of Inigo Jones. The following bombastic epitaph on Pendrill's tomb will amuse our readers :—

> "Hold, passenger, here's shrouded in his hearse,
> Unparallel'd Pendrill through the universe;
> Like whom the Eastern star from heaven gave light
> To three lost kings, so he in such dark night
> To Britain's Monarch, toss'd by adverse war,
> On earth appear'd, a second Eastern star;
> A pole, a stem in her rebellious main,
> A pilot to her royal sovereign.
> Now to triumph in heaven's eternal sphere
> He's hence advanced for his just steerage here;
> Whilst Albion's chronicles with matchless fame
> Embalm the story of great Pendrill's name."

Chapman deserves more particular mention here, as the intimate friend of Ben Jonson, who thus speaks of his translation of Homer :—

> "Whose work could this be, Chapman, to refine
>   Old Hesiod's ore, and give it thus, but thine,
> Who hadst before wrought in rich Homer's mine?
>
> "What treasure hast thou brought us, and what store
>   Still, still dost thou arrive with at our shore,
> To make thy honour and our wealth the more?
>
> "If all the vulgar tongues that speak this day
>   Were asked of thy discoveries, they must say,
> To the Greek coast thine only knew the way.
>
> "Such passage hast thou found, such returns made,
>   As now of all men it is called the trade;
> And who make thither else, rob or invade."

He translated Hesiod's "Works and Days," as well as Homer, and was even better known as a play-writer; and was more than once imprisoned, along with Ben Jonson, for the freedom of his pen. Chapman and Fletcher, indeed, were Jonson's most intimate friends. He told Drummond of Hawthornden that he loved them both, and that "next to himself, they were the only poets who could make a masque." Chapman died in 1634, at the age of nearly eighty. The inscription was re-cut in 1891, but the tomb itself sadly needs repair.

Elsewhere is a stone which a few years ago had upon it some faint vestiges of what was once a coat of arms and some appearance of an inscription; but the most expert of heralds would fail to describe the one, and eyes, however penetrating, might be baffled to decipher the other. Yet this marked a grave without its dead—a mockery of the tomb—a cheating of the sexton; for hither were brought the decapitated remains of one who was among the brightest and most popular young noblemen of his time, and hence were they afterwards disinterred and privately conveyed to Dilston, in Northumberland, and deposited in the family vault, amid the ashes of his forefathers. Here, in fact, was first deposited the body of the amiable and unfortunate James Radcliffe, Earl of Derwentwater, whose fatal connection with the fortunes of the Pretender, and untimely death on Tower Hill, are matters of history, and reveal a sad tragedy, in which he was at once the hero and the victim. The body of the earl was again removed from its grave in Northumberland, and carried to Thorndon, Lord Petre's seat in Essex, for re-interment, in October, 1874.

In the church and in the churchyard adjoining repose several other persons known to history. Among them Lord Herbert of Cherbury; Shirley, the dramatic writer; Andrew Marvell, of whom we have already spoken; the notorious Countess of Shrewsbury; Sir Roger L'Estrange, the celebrated political writer; Michael Mohun, the actor; and Oliver Plunkett, the Roman Catholic Archbishop of Armagh, who was executed at Tyburn on the charge of high treason in 1681.

The only monument of interest in the church is to be seen in the first window in the north aisle. It is a recumbent figure of the Duchess of Dudley, who was created a duchess in her own right by Charles I., and who died in 1669. "This monument," Mr. P. Cunningham tells us, "was preserved when the church was rebuilt, as a piece of parochial gratitude to one whose benefactions to the parish in which she had resided had been both frequent and liberal." Among other matters, she had contributed very largely to the interior decoration of the church, but had the mortification of seeing her gifts condemned as Popish, cast out of the sacred edifice, and sold by order of the hypocritical Puritans. The duchess, who was also in other ways a benefactor to the parish of St. Giles, was buried at Stoneleigh, Warwickshire.

The gate at the entrance of the churchyard, which dates from the days of Charles II., is much admired. It is adorned with a bas-relief of the Day of Judgment. It formerly stood on the north side of the churchyard, but in 1865, being unsafe, it was taken down and carefully re-erected opposite the western entrance, in the idea that it would adorn the new street that was destined sooner or later to be opened from Tottenham Court Road to St. Martin's Lane.

Mr. J. T. Smith, in his "Book for a Rainy Day," speaks of this "Resurrection Gateway" as being of red and brown brick: he says of the carving above it that it was "borrowed, not from Michael Angelo, but from the workings of the brain of some ship-carver." Rowland Dobie, in his "History of St. Giles'," states that "the composition is, with various alterations, taken from Michael Angelo's 'Last Judgment.'" Mr. E. L. Blanchard, in his "London Guide Book," informs us that the carving is "an elaborate and curious specimen of bronze sculpture," and that it was "brought from Florence." But a better authority, Bishop Thorold, tells us, in his "Yearly Report on the parish, in 1865," that "*it is carved in oak, of the date of 1658.*"

The lich-gate was erected from the designs of William Leverton, Esq., and cost altogether the sum of £185 14s. 6d., as may be seen in the parish records. Out of this sum "Love, the carver," received the miserable stipend of £27, showing the estimation in which sacred art was held under our Stuart kings. At the time of the removal of the gate, the tombstones were levelled in the churchyard, young trees were planted, the footway outside widened, and an ornamental railing placed by the kerb-stone instead of a dead wall.

Of all the dark and dismal thoroughfares in the parish of St. Giles's, or, indeed, in the great wilderness of London, few could be compared with that known as Church Lane, which ran between High Street and New Oxford Street. During the last half-century, while the metropolis has been undergoing the pressure of progress consequent upon the quick march of civilisation, what remained of the Church Lane of our early days was left with its little colony of Arabs as completely sequestered from London society as if it were part of Arabia Petræa. Few passed through Church Lane who were not members of its own select society. None else had any business there; and if they had, they would find it to their interest to get out of it as soon as possible. Its condition was a disgrace to the great city. It was pulled down in 1878-9.

The mansion house inhabited by Lord Lisle,

and afterwards by the Carews and the Duchess of Dudley, stood a little to the west of the church. It was demolished in order to build Denmark Street. Its site is marked by Lloyd's Court.

In Monmouth Court, off Little Earl Street, used to be, until its removal to Great St. Andrew Street, the printing and publishing office named after the late James Catnach, by whom it was founded in 1813. From it has been issued by far the largest store of ballads, songs, broadsides, "last dying speeches," &c., that has ever appeared in London, even in this most prolific age. Catnach was a native of Alnwick, in Northumberland, and, coming to London when a lad to fight the battle of life, was apprenticed as a compositor in the office of the *Courier* newspaper. He deserves the credit of having been the first who, availing himself of larger capital and greater mechanical skill than his precursors and rivals, substituted white paper and real printer's ink for the execrable tea-paper, blotched with lamp-black and oil, which had marked the old broadside and ballad printing. He also first conceived and carried out the idea of publishing collections of songs by the yard, and giving for one penny (formerly the price of a single ballad) strings of poetry. He was the patron of much original talent among the bards of St. Giles's and Drury Lane; and in the quarter of a century which elapsed between the establishment of his press and his death, he had literally made a name in literature—of a particular kind. Among the events of the day which he turned to the best and most profitable account, were the trial of Queen Caroline, the Cato Street conspiracy, and the murder of Weare by Thurtell. On the last-named occasion, when the excitement about the execution was about to die out, he brought out a second penny broadside, headed "WE ARE alive again," which the public read as "WEARE." The public did not like the trick, and called it a "catchpenny;" hence arose the set phrase, which for a long time afterwards stuck to the issues of the Seven Dials' press, though they sold as well as ever. All sorts of stories are told to show the fertility of Catnach's resources. He received such large sums in coppers, that he used to take them to the Bank of England in a hackney-coach; and when his neighbours in Seven Dials refused to take them, for fear of catching a fever which was said to have spread through their contact with low cadgers and hawkers, he boiled them *en masse* with a decoction of potash and vinegar, to make them bright, and his coppers recovered their popularity. He had also a knack of carving rough and rude illustrations on the backs of music-blocks, which he nailed on to pieces of

wood. Probably through his connection with Northumberland, he next fortunately picked up some of the wood blocks of Thomas Bewick, which raised at once the character of his printing-press. His next step was to increase the quantity which he gave for a penny, embodying his generosity to the public in a phrase which soon was in everybody's mouth, "Songs, three yards a penny! Songs, beautiful songs!" He next employed his talents on cheap Christmas carols and broadsheets of a higher class; and having realised something more than a competency, retired, in 1839, to the neighbourhood of South Mimms, on the borders of Hertfordshire, where he died about two years afterwards. The business of the "Seven Dials' Printing Office" he left to his sister, Mrs. Ryle, by whom it was carried on for a time, in conjunction with a Mr. Paul. It is now managed by Mr. W. S. Fortey, who, as a boy, was employed by Mr. Catnach. The press is still as busy as ever, and though rivals have arisen, it enjoys a literary *prestige* which will not soon pass away, if we may judge from the fact that it still turns out and sells yearly no less than a million of cheap fly-sheets of the various kinds mentioned above.

Some idea of the Catnach literature may be formed from the two items here following, taken from the catalogue of a second-hand bookseller:—

"BROADSIDES.—A Collection of 9 Curious Old Broadsides and Christmas Carols, printed at Seven Dials and elsewhere. On rough folio paper, *and illustrated with quaint and rude woodcuts, in their original condition, with rough edges, neatly mounted on white paper and bound in half roxburghe.* Contents:—Letter written by Jesus Christ—6 Carols for Christmas—Messenger of Mortality, or Life and Death Contrasted—Massacre of the French King, by which the unfortunate Louis XVI. suffered on the scaffold, with a large woodcut of his execution.

"OLD SONGS AND BALLADS.—A Collection of 35 most Curious Old Songs and Ballads, printed at Seven Dials, on rough old straw paper, and *illustrated with quaint and rude woodcuts or engravings.* In their original condition with rough edges, *very neatly mounted on fine paper, and bound in half roxburghe.* This collection embraces a most varied series of old Ballads, commencing with the Wanton Wife of Bath, Woful Lamentation of Mrs. Jane Shore, Unhappy Lady of Hackney, Kentish Garland, Dorsetshire Garland, or Beggar's Wedding, Faithless Captain, and similar pieces. It next has 16 ballads with large engravings, illustrative of the pieces, bacchanalian, humorous, &c. &c.; and concludes with Liston's Drolleries (with a character portrait), the Paul Pry Songster (with woodcut of Liston as 'Paul Pry'), and the Harp of Ossian, &c."

The central space in this neighbourhood, called Seven Dials, was so named on account of the plan upon which the neighbourhood was laid out for building, seven streets being made to converge at a centre, where there was a pillar adorned with, or at all events, intended to be adorned with, seven dial faces. Till this column was put up, it was called "the Seven Streets," according to the "New View of London," which tells us that at the time of its publication (1708) only four of the seven streets had been actually built. The locality is

ducer of the late lotteries, in imitation of those at Venice." Gay, in his "Trivia," sings :—

" Here to seven streets Seven Dials count their day,
    And from each other catch the circling ray."

It appears that the dial-stone had but six faces, two of the seven streets opening into one angle.

THE GATEWAY OF ST. GILES'S, IN ITS ORIGINAL POSITION. (*See page* 202.)

built on what was formerly known as the Marsh-lands, and also as Cock and Pie Fields. These were surrounded by a ditch, which ran down to St. Martin's and so into the Thames, but was blotted out when the Seven Dials was built. Evelyn thus mentions the work in his "Diary," under date 5th October, 1694 :—" I went to see the building near St. Giles, where seven streets made a star, from a Doric pillar placed in the middle of a cir-cular area, said to be built by Mr. Neale, intro-

The column and dials were removed in June, 1774, to search for a treasure supposed to be concealed beneath the base ; they were never replaced, but in 1822 were purchased of a stonemason, and the column was surmounted with a ducal coronet, and set up on Weybridge Green as a memorial to the late Duchess of York, who died at Oatlands, in 1820. The dial-stone formed a stepping-stone at the adjoining "Ship" inn. The angular direction of each street renders the spot rather embarrassing to a pedestrian who crosses this maze of buildings unexpectedly, and frequently causes him to diverge from the road that would lead him to his destination.

The business carried on in Seven Dials seems to be of a very heterogeneous character. It is the boots and shoes, &c.; ginger-beer, green-grocery, and theatrical stores. Cheap picture-frame makers also abound here. In many of the houses, in some of these streets, whole families seem to live and thrive in a single room. In Charles Knight's "London" we read that "cellars serving whole

QUEEN ANNE'S BATH. (*From a View taken in* 1851.)

great haunt of bird and bird-cage sellers, also of the sellers of rabbits, cats, dogs, &c.; and as some of the houses, being of an old fashion, have broad ledges of lead over the shop windows, these are frequently found converted into miniature gardens, which help, in some degree, to counterbalance the squalor and misery still to be seen in some of the courts and lanes hard by. In certain of the streets close by not a few of the shops are devoted to the sale of old clothes, second-hand families for 'kitchen, and parlour, and bed-room, and all,' are to be found in other streets of London, but not so numerous and near to each other. Here they cluster like cells in a convent of the order of La Trappe, or like onions on a rope. It is curious and interesting to watch the habits of these human moles when they emerge, or half emerge, from their cavities. Their infants seem exempt from the dangers which haunt those of other people: at an age when most babies are not trusted alone on a level floor, these urchins stand secure on the upmost round of a trap-ladder, studying the different conformations of the shoes of the passers-by. The mode of ingress of the adults is curious: they turn their backs to the entry, and, inserting first one foot and then the other, disappear by degrees. The process is not unlike (were such a thing conceivable) a sword sheathing itself. They appear a short-winded generation, often coming, like the otter, to the surface to breathe. In the twilight, which reigns at the bottom of their dens, you can sometimes discern the male busily cobbling shoes on one side of the entrance, and the female repairing all sorts of rent garments on the other. They seem to be free traders: at certain periods of the day tea-cups and saucers may be seen arranged on their boards; at others, plates and pewter pots. They have the appearance of being on the whole a contented race."

"On one occasion," says Mr. J. Smith, in his "Topography of London," "that I might indulge the humour of being shaved by a woman, I repaired to the Seven Dials, where, in Great St. Andrew's Street, a slender female performed the operation, whilst her husband, a strapping soldier in the Horse Guards, sat smoking his pipe. There was a famous woman in Swallow Street, who shaved; and I recollect a black woman in Butcher Row, a street formerly standing by the side of St. Clement's Church, near Temple Bar, who is said to have shaved with ease and dexterity. Mr. Batrick informs me that he has read of the five barberesses of Drury Lane, who shamefully maltreated a woman in the reign of Charles II."

Considering the class of the inhabitants, it is not surprising that many lodging-houses are to be met with here. Diprose, in his "Book about London," tells us that perhaps the most celebrated and notorious of those in St. Giles's was kept by "Mother Cummins."

It is related that Major Hanger accompanied George IV. to a beggars' carnival in St. Giles's. He had not been there long when the chairman, Sir Jeffery Dunstan, addressing the company, and pointing to the then Prince of Wales, said, "I call upon that ere gemman with a shirt for a song." The prince, as well as he could, got excused upon his friend promising to sing for him, and he chanted a ballad called "The Beggar's Wedding, or the Jovial Crew," with great applause. The major's health having been drank with nine times nine, and responded to by him, wishing them "good luck till they were tired of it," he departed with the prince, to afford the company time to fix their different routes for the ensuing day's business. At that period they used to have a general meeting in the course of the year, and each day they were divided into companies, each company having its particular walk; their earnings varied much, some getting as much as five shillings per day.

Monmouth (afterwards Dudley) Street, which will now be looked for in vain, is the street to which Daniel Burgess referred when preaching on the subject of a "robe of righteousness." "If any one of you, my brethren," he said, "would have a suit to last a twelvemonth, let him go to Monmouth Street; if for his lifetime, let him apply to the Court of Chancery; but if for eternity, let him put on the Saviour's robe of righteousness."

CHAPTER XXVII.

THE PARISH OF ST. GILES'S-IN-THE-FIELDS (continued).

"Rure ego viventem, tu dicis in urbe beatum."—*Horace.*

The Poor of St. Giles's – Curious Parish Regulations—"Old Simon," the Beggar—Denmark Street—Etymology of Brownlow and Belton Streets—Endell Street – Queen Anne's Bath—British Lying-in Hospital—Baths and Washhouses—French Protestant Episcopal Church—Bloomsbury Chapel– Bedford Chapel—Outbreak of the Plague of 1665 in St. Giles's—Lewknor's Lane, and its Character in the Reign of Queen Anne—Nell Gwynne's Reputed Birthplace—St. Giles's Almshouses—The Old Round House and Jack Sheppard's Escape—The Cockpit and Phœnix Theatres—The "White Lion" in Drury Lane—"The Flash Coves' Parliament"—Great Queen Street and its Fashionable Residents—The Gordon Riots—Opie's Popularity—James Hoole's Residence—The Freemasons' Hall and Tavern—The Wesleyan Chapel—The Marriage Register of David Garrick—Benjamin Franklin's Printing-press—Gate Street—The Great and Little Turnstiles—Tichborne Court—Religious Persecutions.

THE parish of St. Giles, with its nests of close and narrow alleys and courts inhabited by the lowest class of Irish costermongers, has passed into a byword as the synonym of filth and squalor. But now New Oxford Street and the Charing Cross Road have been carried through the worst part of its slums—"the Rookery" and Hog Lane––and though the work of improvement is not yet complete, much has been done to redeem the neighbourhood from reproach. Time was, as Peter Cunningham remarks, when "the parish could show its pound, its cage, its round-house and watch-house, its stocks, its whipping-post, and at one time its gallows," as our readers are already aware. The locality, nevertheless, is not without its historic or romantic interest, for "a redoubt with two flanks near St. Giles's Pound," and a small fort at the east end of Tyburn Road, are mentioned among the forts ordered to be raised round London by the Parliament in 1642.

According to the "London Spy" (1725), St. Giles's was in the days of the two first Georges a wealthy and populous parish, and one "said to furnish his Majesty's plantations in America with more souls than all the rest of the kingdom besides." It was also remarkable for producing the "Jack Ketches" of that day, as well as a fair proportion of the malefactors who suffered at Tyburn. The same authority quotes an old saying—

> "St. Giles' breed,
> Better hang than seed."

They were a noisy and riotous lot, fond of street brawls, equally "fat, ragged and saucy;" and the courts abounded in pedlars, fish-women, news-criers, and corn-cutters.

Parton, in his "History of St. Giles's," tells us that in remote times this parish "contained no greater proportion of poor than other parishes of a similar extent and population; the introduction of Irish mendicants, and other poor of that description, for which it afterwards became so noted, is not to be traced further back than the time of Queen Elizabeth." Strype, too, remarks that "when London began to increase in population, there was observed to be a confluence here out of the countries of such persons as were of the poorer sorts of trades and occupations; who, because they could not exercise them within the jurisdiction of the City, followed them within the suburbs; therefore the Queen, as well as forbidding the further erection of new buildings, ordered all persons within three miles of the gates of the City to forbear from letting or settling, or suffering any more than one family only to be placed in one house."

In 1637 it was ordered that, "to prevent the great influx of poor people into this parish, the beadles do present every fortnight, on the Sunday, the names of all *new-comers, under-setters, inmates, divided tenements, persons that have families in cellars,* and other abuses." "This," says Parton, "is the first mention of *cellars* as places of residence, and for which the parish afterwards became so noted that the expression of 'a cellar in St. Giles's' used to designate the lowest poverty, became afterwards proverbial, and is still used, though most of these subterranean dwellings are now gone."

Speaking of the beggars of St. Giles's, we should not omit to mention Simon Edy, who lived there in the middle of the last century. "Old Simon," as he was commonly named, lodged, with his dog, under a staircase in an old shattered building called "Rat's Castle," in Dyot Street.* He is thus described by Mr. J. T. Smith in his "Book for a Rainy Day:"—"He wore several hats, and suffered his beard to grow, which was of a dirty yellow-white. Upon his fingers were numerous brass rings. He had several waistcoats, and as many coats, increasing in size, so that he was enabled by the extent of the uppermost garment to cover the greater part of the bundles, containing rags of various colours, and distinct parcels with which he was girded about, consisting of books, canisters containing bread, cheese, and other articles of food; matches, a tinder-box, and meat for his dog; cuttings of curious events from old newspapers, scraps from Foxe's 'Book of Martyrs,' and three or four dogs'-eared and grease-thumbed numbers of the *Gentleman's Magazine*. From these and such-like productions he gained a great part of the information with which he sometimes entertained those persons who stopped to look at him." This eccentric character (perhaps the original of the "Simple Simon" of our nursery rhymes) stood for many years at the gate of St. Giles's Church, and a portrait of him is to be found in Mr. J. T. Smith's well-known book, "Sketches from the London Streets."

Denmark Street is described by Strype as "a fair, broad street, with good houses, and well inhabited by gentry." Near it is Lloyd's Court or Alley, to which Hogarth has given a celebrity by making it and the adjoining Hog Lane the scene of one of his series of sketches, "The Four Times of the Day." Lord Wharton's residence stood at the corner of this thoroughfare.

In Brownlow (now Betterton) Street died, in 1684, Michael Mohun, the actor. The street, and the adjoining one of Belton (now Endell) Street, derived their names from Sir John Brownlow, Bart., of Belton, whose name occurs constantly in the parish rate-books as a resident in the reign of Charles II. His town mansion and gardens stood on this site, but the former was pulled down before the year 1682. The noble estate of Belton, in Lincolnshire, passed by marriage to the Custs, the head of whom is now Earl Brownlow.

At No. 25, Endell Street (formerly Old Belton Street), in the rear of the premises occupied by Messrs. King, ironmongers, is an ancient bath, said

---

* This street, once so squalid, has been reconstructed.

by local tradition to have been used by Queen Anne, which for the most part has escaped the notice of antiquaries. It was fed by a fine spring of clear water, which was said to have medicinal qualities. Whether it was the favourite bagnio of Queen Anne or not, it certainly is a curious relic of other days, though shorn of its ancient glories. Descending a dark and narrow staircase, we find ourselves in a low apartment, about twelve or fourteen feet square, its walls inlaid with Dutch tiles, white, with blue patterns—clearly of the sixteenth century. It once had "a lofty French groined dome roof," but the upper part of the chamber is now cut off by a modern flooring, and formed into a blacksmith's forge.

In a "View of Old London" published in 1851, the bath is said to be "supplied direct from the spring, which is perpetually running; the water," adds the writer, "is always fresh, and is much used in the neighbourhood, where it is considered a good cure for rheumatism and other disorders. It is a powerful tonic, and evidently contains a considerable trace of iron." Some of the Dutch tiles have been taken away, and the lower part is now filled with lumber and rubbish instead of clear water, and the spring no longer flows; in this respect presenting a marked contrast to the "old Roman bath" of which we have spoken in our account of the Strand.*

There are one or two buildings in Endell Street deserving of mention, not only on account of their architectural merits, but for their beneficial effects on the humble class of the inhabitants for whom they are specially intended. The first of these is the British Lying-in Hospital, a picturesque Elizabethan structure, erected in 1849, with all the improvements of modern science. This institution was originally established in Brownlow Street, in 1749, but was removed in the above year to its new quarters. It is the oldest lying-in hospital in London. It is solely for affording medical and surgical treatment to married women, who are either admitted into the hospital as in-patients, or are attended at their own homes. Down to the year 1896 some 65,000 in-patients have received the benefits of this institution. The hospital is supported mainly by voluntary subscriptions and donations. The number of patients annually benefited is about 600, and the yearly receipts amount to about £1,500.

Then there are the Baths and Washhouses, a handsome edifice of Italian architecture, opened in 1852, not far from the site of Queen Anne's Bath; and close by are Christ Church, in the

Early English style, erected in 1845, and the St. Giles Workhouse. The Protestant Swiss Church should also be mentioned.

In what used to be the southern part of Bloomsbury Street, now merged in Shaftesbury Avenue, are two chapels side by side. The first is the French Protestant Episcopal Church, built in the Early Pointed style, in 1845. This church was founded by Charles II., in the Savoy. Next is Bloomsbury Chapel, built by Sir Morton Peto for the Baptists. Adjoining this stood Bedford Chapel until, in 1896, it was pulled down. It was built, or at all events remodelled, in 1844, and here for some time the late Rev. J. C. M. Bellew officiated, and afterwards the Rev. Stopford Brooke.

St. Giles's Parish enjoys the distinction of having originated the Great Plague of 1665. It is on record that the first persons seized were members of a family living near the top of Drury Lane, where two men, said to have been Frenchmen, were attacked by it, and speedily carried off. The havoc caused by the plague in this parish alone, in the above-named year, amounted to 3,216 deaths, "its malignity," as Dr. Sydenham observes, "being mostly discovered among the poorer sort of people in St. Giles's." The parish registers and rate-books contain many curious entries relating to this sad year; amongst them, the receipt of £50 from Sir Edmundbury Godfrey, and of nearly £500 from Lord Craven, for visiting and relieving the poor.

What used to be Lewknor's Lane, opposite Short's Gardens, near the top of Drury Lane, derived its name from Sir Lewis Lewknor, who owned property here in the reign of James I. From an early date it bore a bad character, and in it Jonathan Wild kept "a house of ill-fame." Constant allusions to its residents occur in the plays of the time of Queen Anne; and Gay, in the *Beggar's Opera*, alludes to it as one of the three places in which ladies of easy virtue might be found. If we may judge from a passage in "Instructions how to find Mr. Curll's Authors," published in Swift's and Pope's Miscellanies, it was also the residence of hack-writers for the press. "At Mr. Summer's, a thief-catcher, in Lewknor's Lane, a man that wrote against the impiety of Mr. Rowe's plays." The thoroughfare (called Lutnor's Lane by Strype) was down to our own day, as it was two hundred years ago, "a very ordinary place." Immorality in the distant past is further indicated by Samuel Butler, who speaks—satirically, of course—of

"The nymphs of chaste Diana's train,
    The same with those of Lewknor's Lane."

To which passage Sir Roger L'Estrange adds a note to the effect that it was a "rendezvous and nursery for lewd women, first resorted to by the Roundheads."

The Coal or Cole Yard, on the eastern side of Drury Lane, near its Holborn end, a row of miserable tenements, has of late years been rebuilt, and now rejoices in the name of Goldsmith Street. Here stood the old "Round House," in which highwaymen and other dangerous personages were confined until they could be brought before the sitting magistrates and formally committed to prison. In one of the cells, it is said, Jack Sheppard was ordered to be confined for a night, but before the morning he had made his escape. Other prisoners, however, remained here long enough to cut their names or initials on the walls and window-sills. The Coal Yard is also associated by tradition with another notorious person, for here, according to some, Nell Gwynne was born. The tradition is at best a doubtful one, for "pretty witty Nell" is also said to have first seen the light in Wales.

In Goldsmith Street are the Casual Wards of the St. Giles District Board of Works, which represents the united parishes of St. Giles-in-the-Fields and St. George, Bloomsbury, and in convenient contiguity is the Stone Yard, where those who have enjoyed the hospitality of the ratepayers during the night perform their allotted task before sallying forth to see what Fortune has in store for them. Here also are the Coroner's Court and Mortuary of the united parishes, and an industrial day school of the London School Board. The parish almshouses are in Smart's Buildings, close by.

A part of Oldwick Close, between Lincoln's Inn Fields and Drury Lane, was in possession of the celebrated Sir Kenelm Digby. In 1632 it was bounded on the western side by a ditch and a mud wall, intermixed with a few scattered buildings, among which was the Cockpit Theatre, erected about 1615, but pulled down by the mob in 1617, and all the apparel of the players torn to pieces. On its site arose a second theatre, called the Phœnix, but this again, after a few years, gave way to Drury Lane Theatre, of which we shall have more to say presently. In 1651 most of the property had passed into the possession of the ancient and worthy family of the Welds, of Lulworth Castle, Dorsetshire, the head of which, Mr. Humphrey Weld, built here a handsome residence, the site of which is marked by Wild (formerly Weld) Court and Little Wild Street.

In Parker Street, or Parker's Lane, which runs eastwards from Drury Lane to Little Queen Street, Holborn, were formerly situated the premises and stables of the Dutch ambassador. Here the London County Council has built a Municipal Lodging-house, which quickly became a very popular institution.

The "White Lion," in Drury Lane, in former years, was a place of resort late at night for "swells" of the upper class, and also for market-gardeners and other persons, who resorted to the neighbouring market. As may be imagined, it bore no very good reputation.

At the "Crown Coffee House," in this lane, was held, in former times, an evening assembly called "The Flash Coves' Parliament"—a loose sort of gathering of members of the bar, small tradesmen, and "men about town," each of whom bore the title of some member or other of the Upper House of Parliament: e.g., one would be "Lord Brougham," another "the Duke of Wellington," another "Lord Grey," and so forth. This, however, has long since passed away.

Great Queen Street, which connects Drury Lane with Lincoln's Inn Fields, in a line with Long Acre, was so named in honour of Queen Elizabeth, and stands on the site of the common footpath which anciently separated the south part, or Aldewych Close (properly so called) from the northern division—latterly termed White Hart Close—which extended to Holborn. In the reign of Elizabeth this footpath appears to have become a roadway, but no houses were built on it up to that time. In a map of Westminster, by Norden, dated 1593, no houses are shown eastward of Drury Lane; but building must have commenced very shortly after this, for in Speed's Map of Westminster, in his "Great Britain," the commencement of Great Queen Street is indicated, together with a continuation of the houses on both sides of Drury Lane. In 1623 only fifteen houses appear to have existed on the south side of Great Queen Street, which was then open to the country, and the north side is of later date. Shortly after the Restoration, a new era of building having set in, the houses were finished on the south side of the street, from the designs, it is said, of Inigo Jones and his pupil Webbe. It was at one time called Henrietta Street, in compliment to Henrietta Maria, Queen of Charles I.

. "According to one authority," says the author of "Haunted London," "Inigo Jones built Queen Street at the cost of the Jesuits, designing it for a square, and leaving in the middle a niche for the statue of Queen Henrietta. The 'stately and magnificent houses' begun on the north side, near Little Queen Street, were not continued. There were fleurs-de-luce placed on the walls in honour of the queen."

"Great Queen Street, in the time of the Stuarts," says Leigh Hunt, "was one of the grandest and most fashionable parts of the town. The famous Lord Herbert of Cherbury died there. Lord Bristol had a house in it, as also did Lord Chancellor Finch, and the Conway and Paulet families." Mr. Parton, the author of the topographical work on St. Giles's, mentions Paulet House, Cherbury House, and Conway House among the fine mansions still (1822) standing in this street.

The house of Lord Herbert of Cherbury—"the Sir Edward Herbert, the all-virtuous Herbert" of

priation of each house to its respective inhabitant is, however, a matter of uncertainty, no clue whatever being to be found among our parish records, nor, indeed, any mention made of them to guide our inquiries."

Sir Thomas Fairfax dated a printed proclamation from Great Queen Street, February 12th, 1648, and is supposed, on that account, to have lived in the street. George Digby, second Earl of Bristol, lived in Great Queen Street, says Evelyn (1671);

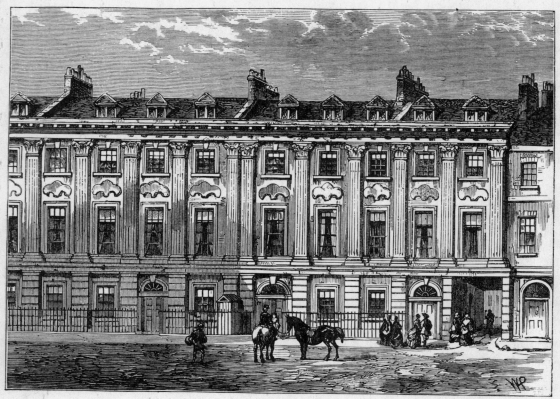

OLD HOUSES IN GREAT QUEEN STREET, SOUTH SIDE, 1850.

Ben Jonson—was a few doors from Great Wild Street. Here he wrote a part of his celebrated treatise, " De Veritate," and here he died, in 1648, aged seventy-seven, and was buried in St. Giles's Churchyard. The Lord Chancellor Finch mentioned above was the famous Royalist, Sir Heneage Finch, afterwards Earl of Nottingham, who died in 1682. He presided at Lord Stafford's trial, in 1680, and pronounced judgment on that unfortunate nobleman in a speech of great ability. He was the " Omri" of Dryden's "Absalom and Achitophel"—

" To whom the double blessing does belong,
    With Moses' inspiration, Aaron's tongue."

Many other distinguished personages lived here about this time; "but," says Parton, "the appro-

his house was taken by the Commissioners of Trade and Plantations. The Duke of Buckingham, the Earl of Lauderdale, Sir John Finch, Waller the poet, and Colonel Titus (author of " Killing no Murder "), were among its new occupants. At Conway House, in this street, lived Lord Conway, an able soldier, defeated by the Scotch at Newburn. In the year 1733 the Earl of Rochford lived in Great Queen Street; here, too, about that time, lived Lady Dinely Goodyer, and Mrs. Kitty Clive the actress. It would be difficult, at this distant date, to fix upon the exact house in which any of these notabilities resided, for the practice of numbering was not in use till 1764; Burlington Street having been the first and Lincoln's Inn Fields the

MIDDLE ROW, ST. GILES'S, ABOUT 1838.

second place in London where it was adopted. Sir Martin Ffolkes, an eminent scholar and antiquary, was born in Great Queen Street in 1690. He was a great numismatist, and the first President of the Royal Society of Antiquaries. He died in 1784.

In 1780 the Gordon Riots may be said to have had their rise in Great Queen Street, the first meeting in favour of the petition presented by Lord George Gordon to Parliament, asking for the repeal of a measure of relief granted to the Roman Catholics, having been held in Coachmakers' Hall, in this street, on the 29th of May. On the rejection of the petition, on the 2nd of June, the mob burnt the Roman Catholic chapels in Duke Street, Lincoln's Inn Fields, and Welbeck Street. On the following days they proceeded to further excesses, and on the 6th of June the house of Mr. Justice Cox, in Great Queen Street, was burned, together with the houses of other magistrates who had become obnoxious. The rest of the story of the Gordon Riots is told in its proper place.

It is recorded that in 1735 Ryan the comedian, whose name was well known in connection with "Bartlemy Fair," was attacked in this street at midnight by a footpad, who fired a pistol in his face, severely wounding him in the jaw, and robbed him of his sword. He was hurt so badly that a performance was given at Covent Garden for his benefit, when the Prince of Wales sent him a purse of a hundred guineas.

No. 51 was until recently the office of Messrs. Kelly and Co., the well-known printers and publishers of the Post Office London and County Directories. Messrs. Kelly removed here from Old Boswell Court, on the demolition of that neighbourhood to clear a space for the new Law Courts; their offices are now at High Holborn.

In this street used to be one of those Homes for Homeless and Destitute Children which have done, of late years, such good service to the State. It was commenced in St. Giles's, in a loft over a cow-shed, about the year 1843, its originator being a Mr. Williams. It then gradually grew into a school, and was located for a time in Arthur Street, St. Giles's, whence it was removed hither in 1860. The premises which were occupied by the boys were formerly a carriage-maker's; they held from 120 to 130 boys, most of whom were gradually drafted off to the *Chichester* and *Arethusa* training-vessels, or to farm-work in the country, chiefly with a view to emigration, the rest being taught various trades and employments. A few years ago the head-quarters of this excellent charity were removed to Shaftesbury Avenue. In addition to the boys' refuge and working boys' home in the Avenue, there are a boys' home at Twickenham, a farm-school at Bisley, girls' homes at Sudbury and Ealing, and a sailors' home in East India Dock Road.

At No. 52 lived Sir Robert Strange, the eminent historical engraver, and adherent of Prince Charles Edward, "the Young Pretender." Strange died in 1792, and here his widow resided for some years afterwards.

Another artist of renown who resided in this street was Opie. He was living here in 1791, when his popularity was at its highest. In Opie's "Memoirs" we get a glimpse of the condition of Great Queen Street, when the roadway was sometimes blocked up with the carriages of his sitters. The great painter removed in 1792, and by the end of the century the street was no longer fashionable, the polite world having migrated westward.

At No. 56 in this street, in a large house, part of which is over the entrance to New Yard, lived James Hoole, the translator of Tasso, Metastasio, and Ariosto, who died in 1803. Born in London in 1727, he devoted his leisure hours to literary pursuits, especially to the study of the Italian language, of which he made himself a perfect master. He was the author of three original tragedies— *Cyrus, Timanthes,* and *Cleonice*—which were acted at Covent Garden, and also of some poems, and of a life of John Scott, of Amwell, the Quaker poet. With Hoole lived Hudson the painter, Sir Joshua Reynolds' master.

This house, now a steam pencil-factory, is the only one in the street which retains its original architectural features, all the rest having been either rebuilt or modernised. Worlidge, an artist of some celebrity, who was famous for his etchings in the manner of Rembrandt, died in this house in 1766. Richard Brinsley Sheridan lived in it for some years; many of the letters in Moore's "Life" are addressed to him here. How long Sheridan remained is not known, but it is related that he passed the day in seclusion at his house in Great Queen Street on the occasion of Garrick's funeral, in 1779. The "beautiful Perdita," Mrs. Robinson, the unfortunate favourite of George IV., appears to have lived in this same house shortly after her marriage in 1773; she describes the house in her "Memoirs" as "a large, old-fashioned mansion, the property of the widow of Mr. Worlidge."

Like the seven towns which claim to have given birth to Homer, Great Queen Street is claimed by some writers to have been the locality of the "scene" between Sir Godfrey Kneller and Dr. Radcliffe, which we have already described in our account of the Royal College of Physicians;*

---

* See Chap. XXI., p. 143.

others, however, fix the abodes of the great physician and Sir Godfrey in Bow Street, Covent Garden.

The most important buildings in Great Queen Street are the Freemasons' Hall and Tavern. These stand on the south side of the street, and present a noble and elegant appearance. The Hall was first built by an architect named Sandby —one of the original members of the Royal Academy—in 1775-6, as its name implies, for the purpose of furnishing one central place for the several lodges of Loyal Masons to hold their meetings and dinners, instead of borrowing, as up to that time had been the custom, the halls of the City companies. Freemasons' Hall, as we are told by Hunter, in his "History of London," was "dedicated" in May, 1776. The Tavern was built in 1786, by William Tyler.

The original Hall, at the back of the Tavern, was built at a cost of about £5,000, which was raised by a tontine. "It was the first house," says Elmes, "built in this country with the appropriate symbols of masonry, and with the suitable apartments for the holding of lodges, the initiating, passing, raising, and exalting of brethren." It was a noble room, although not so large as the present hall. Above the principal entrance was a gallery, with an organ ; and at the opposite end was a coved recess, flanked by a pair of fluted Ionic columns, containing a marble statue of the late Duke of Sussex, executed for the Grand Lodge by Mr. E. H. Baily, R.A. Here very many public meetings —political, charitable, and religious—were held ; but the last-named have mostly migrated to Exeter Hall, in the Strand.

Among the most important public meetings held at Freemasons' Tavern was one in June, 1824, at which Lords Liverpool, Brougham, Sir J. Mackintosh, Sir Robert Peel, Sir Humphry Davy, Mr. Huskisson, and Mr. Wilberforce, bore public testimony to the services of James Watt as the inventor of the steam-engine, and resolved that a national monument should be erected in his honour in Westminster Abbey. It was on this occasion that Peel frankly and generously acknowledged the debt of gratitude which was due to Watt from himself and his own family, as owing to him their prosperity and wealth. Here public dinners were given to John Philip Kemble, to James Hogg ("the Ettrick Shepherd"), and to many others who, either in the ranks of bravery, science, or literature, have won a name which shall last as long as the English language is spoken.

Of late years the Freemasons' Hall and Tavern have been considerably altered, and in part rebuilt, and now occupy a very much larger area than the original erection. The work was carried out, about the year 1866, under the direction of Mr. F. P. Cockerell, son of the late accomplished Professor of Architecture in the Royal Academy, and the illustrator of the Æginetan Marbles. The Grand Lodge buildings and the Freemasons' Tavern are now entirely separate establishments, although they join ; the former, which stands on the west side of the Tavern, contains offices for all the Masonic charities, Grand Secretary's office, and lodge-rooms entirely for the use of the craft. These rooms, as it were, form the frontage of the large hall—a magnificent room, of noble proportions, which, from its internal fittings, may be truly termed the temple of Masonic rites. The room is beautifully decorated, and lit from above. Here have been held the balls and dinners of the Royal Scottish Humane, Artists', and other benevolent societies and institutions.

Mr. Timbs, in his "Curiosities of London," tells us how that St. Paul's, in 604, and St. Peter's, Westminster, in 605, were built by Freemasons ; that Gundulph, Bishop of Rochester, who is said to have built the White Tower, governed the Freemasons. Peter of Colechurch, architect of Old London Bridge, was Grand Master. Henry VII., in a lodge of master Masons, founded his chapel at Westminster Abbey. Sir Thomas Gresham, who planned the Royal Exchange, was Grand Master ; as was also Inigo Jones, the architect. Sir Christopher Wren, Grand Master, founded St. Paul's with his Lodge of Masons, and the trowel and mallet then used are preserved; and Covent Garden Theatre was founded, in 1808, by the Prince of Wales, in his capacity as Grand Master, assisted by the Grand Lodge. For some reason or other, however, Freemasonry has latterly been under the ban of the Roman Catholic Church.

Two doors eastward of Freemasons' Tavern is a Wesleyan Chapel ; and it may be interesting to record here the fact, "not generally known," that at a place of worship on or near this spot on the 22nd of June, 1748, one "David Garrick, of St. Paul's, Covent Garden," was married by his friend, the celebrated Dr. Franklin, to "Eva Maria Violette, of St. James's, Westminster, a celebrated dancer." According, however, to her own statement to Mr. J. T. Smith, when within a few months of her death, Mrs. Garrick was married at the parish church of St. Giles's, and afterwards in the Chapel of the Portuguese Ambassador, in South Audley Street. She also said that she was born at Vienna, on the 29th of February, 1724. If so, at her death she must have been only three months short of entering on her hundredth year. She was buried beside her husband, in Poet's Corner, Westminster Abbey.

Although Mrs. Garrick's maiden name (apparently) is given in the above record of her marriage, there has always been a mystery about her birth. Lee Lewis asserted that she was a natural daughter of Lord Burlington. When Mrs. Garrick heard this, she replied with indignation, "Lee is a liar; Lord Burlington was not my father: but still, I am of noble birth." It was also said that Lord Burlington gave Garrick £10,000 to marry her. This, too, she denied, adding that she had only the interest on £6,000, which was paid to her by the Duke of Devonshire. She died at an advanced age, in October, 1822, in her arm-chair, in the front drawing-room of her house in the Adelphi, having survived her husband forty-three years. She had just ordered her servants to put out on chairs two or three dresses, in order to choose one in which to appear that evening at Drury Lane, it being a private view of Elliston's improvements for the coming season. Mr. J. T. Smith, who knew her personally, speaks thus of her in his "Book for a Rainy Day:"—"Perhaps no lady in public or private life held a more unexceptionable character. She was visited by persons of the first rank; even our late Queen Charlotte, who had honoured her with a visit at Hampton, found her peeling onions for pickling. The gracious queen commanded a knife to be brought, saying, 'I will peel some onions too.' The late King George IV. and King William IV., as well as other branches of the royal family, frequently honoured her with visits." In addressing her servants, however, she was in the habit of using more expletives than would now be thought ladylike in any circle, high or low.

Great Queen Street seems to have been a favourite locality for the residence of actors. Miss Pope, a celebrated actress of the last century, lived for forty years "two doors west of Freemasons' Tavern." She died at Hadley, in 1801. In a house on the south side, occupied before 1830 by Messrs. Allman, the booksellers, died Lewis, the comedian; and at No. 74, now part of Messrs. Wyman and Sons' premises, and known in these days as the "Lincoln's Inn Steam Printing Works," died, in 1826, Edward Prescott Holdway Knight, the comedian, commonly called "Little Knight." Within the walls of Messrs. Wymans' establishment (then Messrs. Cox and Co.'s) Laman Blanchard discharged the duties of a printer's reader side by side with his friend, Douglas Jerrold, who at that time (about the year 1825) was the editor

of a periodical called *La Belle Assemblée;* and many other interesting literary traditions cling to the place.

Benjamin Franklin has been described by some writers to have worked at Messrs. Wymans' printing-office as a journeyman printer. This is an error, Franklin having been employed at Mr. Watts's, which was on the south side of Wild Court, a turning out of Great Wild Street, near the western end of Great Queen Street. The press which Franklin recognised as that at which he had worked as a journeyman pressman in London in the years 1723-6, stood in Messrs. Wymans' office, however, for many years. In course of time it was taken down, and passed into the hands of Messrs. Harrild and Sons, who in 1840 parted with it to Mr. J. V. Murray, of New York, on condition that he would secure for them in return a donation to the Printers' Pension Society of London—a highly-deserving institution (its object being the support of aged and decayed printers and widows of printers), and of which they were active members. By Mr. Murray the press was exhibited in Liverpool, and afterwards taken to America. So great was the interest excited by the exhibition of the press, that it was ultimately arranged to have a lecture delivered on "The Life of Benjamin Franklin" during its exhibition. This was accordingly done, and with such success as to enable the committee of the Printers' Pension Society to initiate the "Franklin Pension," amounting to ten guineas per year; and it is interesting to record that one of the early recipients of this small bounty was a very old servant of the firm in whose office he and the press had so long done duty together.

The following inscription is engraved upon the plate affixed to the front of the press :—

"DR. FRANKLIN's Remarks relative to this Press, made when he came to England as Agent of the Massachusetts, in the year 1768. The Doctor at this time visited the Printing-office of Mr. Watts, of Wild Street, Lincoln's Inn Fields, and, going up to this particular Press (afterwards in the possession of Messrs. Cox and Son, of Great Queen Street, of whom it was purchased), thus addressed the men who were working at it :—'Come, my friends, we will drink together. It is now forty years since I worked like you, at this Press, as a journeyman Printer." The Doctor then sent out for a gallon of Porter, and he drank with them—

'SUCCESS TO PRINTING.'

" From the above it will appear that it is 108 years since DR. FRANKLIN worked at this identical Press.

"June, 1833."

In 1863 the authorities of the South Kensington Museum of Patents, being engaged in collecting some early memorials relating to the art of printing, made application to Messrs. Wyman for the loan of a companion press to that above described, and which was then in daily use. After being photographed *in situ*, the press was removed to the Museum of Patents, it having been presented to the trustees by Mr. Wyman. This press, of which we here give an engraving, is a fac-simile of the

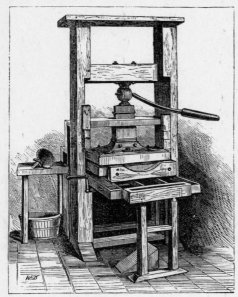

DUPLICATE OF FRANKLIN'S PRESS.

Franklin press, and there is strong reason to suppose that the celebrated American philosopher worked at it as well as at that which is now a venerated relic in the public museum of Philadelphia.

It may be added that at this printing-office in Great Queen Street, for nearly a century, was executed all the printing relating to our possessions in the East, for the once famous East India Company.

In Great Queen Street also is the Novelty Theatre, opened in 1882 under its present name, which, however, was afterwards changed to Folies Dramatiques, and this to the Jodrell Theatre. Its career has been a somewhat chequered one.

At the eastern end of Great Queen Street, where it debouches upon Lincoln's Inn Fields, now happily, as we have already had occasion to say, dedicated to the public use and enjoyment for ever, is Gate Street, the name of which is very significant of its origin, as being at the top of a lane out of which the horses would have strayed into the high road towards St. Giles's if it had not been for a gate. This thoroughfare leads to a narrow passage called Little Turnstile, which, with another known as the Great Turnstile, at the northeast corner of Lincoln's Inn Fields, opens up a communication between the "Fields" and High Holborn, the continuation of New Oxford Street.

The Great Turnstile, according to Strype, in 1720 was "a great thoroughfare, and a place inhabited by sempsters, shoemakers, and milliners, for which it is of considerable trade and well noted."

Of Whetstone Park, the connecting thoroughfare between the two Turnstiles, we have already spoken in our chapter on Lincoln's Inn Fields. We may, however, add that it was a resort of profligate persons some two centuries since, and that its character at that time is commemorated in the plays of Shadwell, Dryden, and Wycherley :—

"Where ladies ply, as many tell us,
Like brimstones in a Whetstone alehouse."

But, if we may believe Strype, its infamous and vicious inhabitants had been banished previous to the year 1720.

One of the small courts between Lincoln's Inn Fields and Holborn, near the eastern end of Whetstone Park, is called Tichborne Court ; over the Holborn entrance were, until 1882, when the archway was rebuilt, the arms of the Tichbornes. This property came to the Tichborne family early in the seventeenth century, by the marriage of White Tichborne, Esq., of Aldershot (grandfather of the sixth baronet), with Ann, the daughter and heiress of Richard (or James) Supple, Esq , a member of the Vintners' Company.

ANNO DNI. 1685.

THE ARMS OF TICHBORNE.

Among the more celebrated inhabitants of the parish of St. Giles's are, Andrew Marvell, whom we have already mentioned, and the profligate Countess of Shrewsbury, concerning whom Horace Walpole tells us that she held the horse of Villiers, Duke of Buckingham, while the latter killed her husband in a duel.

Among the old families in St. Giles's, Parton names the Spencers, or De Spencers, after whom the great ditch which ran along the southern side of the parish was called Spencer's Ditch or "Dig."

The name of this drain in more recent times was Cock and Pie Ditch.

The "History of St. Giles's-in-the-Fields," by Mr. Parton, contains a variety of curious and interesting matter, and we have drawn largely upon it in these pages. But we have not adopted all his statements, having our confidence in him as a topographer and historian a little shaken by the fact that he gives in it a plan or map of the parish as it was in the thirteenth century—in other words, two centuries and a half, at the least, earlier than the map of London by Ralph Aggas, which is the oldest authority known to antiquaries, and from which, it is clear, on a close inspection, that he has borrowed many of his details. It is, indeed, made

out so minutely as to show each man's possession in the parish, and every garden-plot delineated, with flower-beds, parterres, and bordered walks, just as if the gardener of William III. or Queen Anne had been alive in the Wars of the Roses! Mr. Parton gives no authority for these details; and it is to be feared that he allowed his antiquarian zeal to carry him in this one matter—like Herodotus of old—out of the domain of fact into the airy regions of fiction. In other respects, however, he would appear to have been a trusty chronicler, and his work from first to last is full of interest.

We may conclude our notice of St. Giles's with the following paragraph from a publication which does not often mislead, or misrepresent facts:—

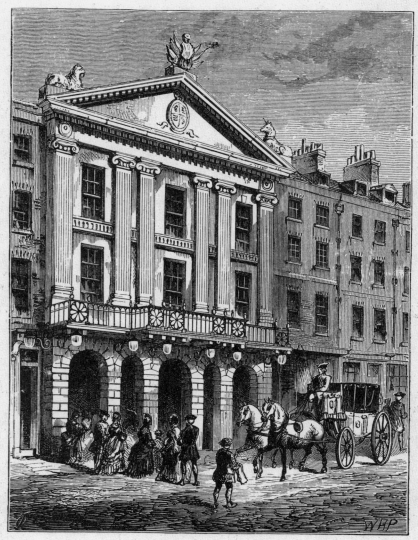

FRONT OF OLD DRURY LANE THEATRE.

DRURY LANE CELEBRITIES.

BETTERTON.   GARRICK.   MACKLIN.
MRS. PRITCHARD.   MRS. ROBINSON.

"As lately as the year 1767," says a writer in the *Gentleman's Magazine*, "another mass-house was discovered in Hog Lane, near the Seven Dials," and the officiating priest was "condemned to perpetual imprisonment"—simply for saying mass and giving the communion to a sick person. After four years' imprisonment his sentence was "commuted into exile for life." At the end of the last century, if not early in the present, Dr. Archer, a well-known Roman Catholic divine, and the author of several volumes of sermons, said mass in the garret of a small public-house in St. Giles's, kept by an Irishman who was not ashamed of his religion. This sounds strange in our ears in the present state of general toleration and liberty; but more than a century before, in 1663, Pepys records the fact that "a priest was taken in his vestments officiating somewhere in Holborn the other day, and was committed [to prison] by Mr. Secretary Morris, according to law."

CHAPTER XXVIII.

DRURY LANE THEATRE.

"I sing of the singe of Miss Drury the First,
And the birth of Miss Drury the Second."—*Rejected Addresses.*

The Original Playhouse in Covent Garden—The Players Imprisoned in the Gate House—The Cockpit Theatre—Ki'ligrew's Theatre in Drury Lane—Betterton's Early Triumphs—The Players first styled "His Majesty's Servants"—Testimonial to Mrs. Bracegirdle—Lovely "Nancy" Oldfield—Colley Cibber as Manager and Dramatist—Garrick at Drury Lane—Kitty Clive, the Comic Actress—A Batch of Fortunate Actresses – Edmund and Charles Kean—Mrs. Nisbet, Macready, and Madame Celeste—Anecdote of Madame Malibran—Michael Balfe, and the Statue erected to his Honour—Salaries of Celebrated Players—Changes and Vicissitudes of "Old Drury"—The New Theatre closed by Order of the Lord Chamberlain—Mrs. Siddons' *Début*—The Kembles—Sheridan's Habit of Procrastination—The Theatre again destroyed by Fire—Coolness of Sheridan—The "Rejected Addresses"—Mr. Whitbread and the Colonnade – Rebuilding and Opening of the New Theatre—Its subsequent Vicissitudes—Van Amburgh and his Wild Beasts—The Theatre opened as an Opera-house.

IN speaking of Drury Lane Theatre there arises a frequent source of confusion in the fact that it had no especial name till the middle of the eighteenth century; being in the neighbourhood of Covent Garden, where the quality then resided, it was often styled "The Covent Garden Theatre." Thus Pepys, writing under date 1662: "To Lincoln's Inn Fields, and, it being too soon to go to dinner, I walked up and down, and looked upon the outside of the new theatre building in Covent Garden, which will be very fine." The late Mr. Richardson, of coffee-house celebrity, was in possession of a ticket inscribed, "For the Music at the Play House in Covent Garden, Tuesday, March 6, 1704"—nearly thirty years before Covent Garden Theatre, properly so called, was opened. It was also styled "The King's Theatre," and "The King's House;" Killigrew and his company being "His Majesty's Servants," while Davenant and his rival company were known by the name of "The Duke's Servants."

Guest writes, "I have not met with any play which is said on its title-page to have been acted in the Theatre Royal Drury Lane till after the division of the company in 1695; nor am I aware that the theatre is called 'Drury Lane' in any preface of the time. Even in 1704, *Love the Leveller* is said on its title-page to have been acted at the Theatre Royal in Brydges Street, Covent Garden. In 1719-20, an order from the Lord Chamberlain's office is addressed to 'The Managers of the Theatre in Drury Lane, in Covent Garden.'"

It is worthy of note that, although there were other theatres in London at an earlier date, there was, according to Guest, in the time of Shakespeare one at least outside the walls—namely, the Phœnix or Cockpit, on the eastern side of Drury Lane, the site of which was afterwards defined by Pitt Court—formerly Cockpit Alley. The company who acted there were styled "The Queen's Servants." In 1647, when an act was passed for the suppression of stage plays, the Cockpit was converted from the error of its ways into a school-room, but, in spite of the supremacy of the Puritans, its existence as a seat of learning was brief; it backslided, and again became a place of profane amusement, until in 1649, when the Puritan soldiers broke into the playhouse during a performance, routed the audience, and broke up the seats and stage. Nor was this all. Dr. Doran says that "the players, some of them the most accomplished of their day, were paraded through the streets in all their stage finery, and clapped into the Gate-house and other prisons, whence they were only too glad to escape, after much unseemly treatment, at the cost of all the theatrical property which they had carried on their backs." They had already experienced similar treatment in 1617, in a popular outbreak, when their clothes and properties were torn up by the mob, for what cause is not apparent.

Subsequently, after General Monk's arrival in London, the theatrical standard was raised again, and the drama commenced its new career at the Cockpit, with Rhodes for its "master"—managers being not then known—and Betterton as his pupil and apprentice.

Pepys thus writes in his "Diary," November 20th, 1660: "This morning I found my lord in bed late, he having been with the king, queen, and princesses at the Cockpit all night, where General Monk treated them, and after supper a play." It may be added that the original name of the "pit" in our theatres was the "cock-pit"—a word strongly corroborating the fact that our earliest places of such entertainment were used for lower sports before being applied to the purposes of the dramatic muse.

The principal actors at the Cockpit were Betterton and the beautiful youth, Edward Kynaston, who generally performed women's parts, before female actresses were permitted on the stage. Of Kynaston Pepys writes, Aug. 18: "Capt. Ferrers took me and Creed to the Cockpitt play—the first that I have had time to see since my coming from sea. *The Loyall Subject*, where one Kynaston, a boy, acted the duke's sister, but made the loveliest lady that ever I saw in my life." "Jan. 7. Tom and I and my wife to the theatre, and there saw *The Silent Woman*. Among other things here Kynaston, the boy, had the good turn to appear in three shapes: first as a poor woman, in ordinary clothes, to please 'Morose;' then in fine clothes, as a gallant, and in them was clearly the prettiest woman in the whole house; and lastly as a man, and then likewise did appear the handsomest man in the whole house."

Pepys tells us that the old actors were in possession of the Cockpit in August, 1660; also that he saw *The Cardinal* acted there, October 2, 1662; but the theatre was small, and seems to have soon been superseded. At all events, nothing further is known of its history. There is a chance allusion to it in *The Muse's Looking-glass* of Randolphe, wherein the following dialogue occurs:—

"*Mrs. Flowerdew.* It was a zealous prayer
I heard a brother make concerning playhouses.
  Bird. For charity, what is it?
      F. That the Globe,
Wherein (quoth he) reigns a whole world of vice,
Had been consum'd; the Phœnix burnt to ashes."

We hear very little of the other actors of the Cockpit, save that one Allen became a major in Charles's army, and acted as quartermaster-general at Oxford; and that two others, named Perkins and Sumner, finding their occupation gone, "kept house together at Clerkenwell, where they died some years before the Restoration."

Soon after the Restoration Thomas Killigrew, Page of Honour, and subsequently Master of the Revels, to Charles I., purchased from the Earl of Bedford a lease for forty-one years of a piece of ground situated in the two parishes of St. Martin's-in-the-Fields and St. Paul's, Covent Garden. On this site, until then known as the "Riding Yard," he erected, we are told, at a cost of £1,500, a theatre, the dimensions of which were 112 feet by 59 feet, and which was opened in 1663. The following is a copy of the first playbill issued:—

"By His Majesty his company of Comedians, at the New Theatre in Drury Lane. This day, being Thursday, April 8th, 1663, will be acted a comedy called *The Humorous Lieutenant*. The King, Mr. Wintersell; Demetrius, Mr. Hart; Seleucus, Mr. Burt; Leontius, Major Mohun; Lieutenant, Mr. Clun; Celia, Mrs. Marshall. The Play will begin at Three o'clock exactly. Boxes, 4s.; Pit, 2s. 6d.; Middle Gallery, 1s. 6d.; Upper Gallery, 1s."

This comedy (by Beaumont and Fletcher) is mentioned in Pepys' "Diary," in the following terms:—"To the King's House, and there saw *The Humorous Lieutenant*—a silly play, I think—only the spirit in it that grows very tall, and then sinks again to nothing, having two heads breeding upon one, and then Knipp's singing, did please us. Here, in a box above, we spied Mrs. Pierce; and going out, they called us, and so we staid for them; and Knipp took us all in, and brought us to Nelly, a most pretty woman, who acted the great part, 'Cœlia,' to-day, very fine, and did it pretty well. I kissed her, and so did my wife; and a mighty pretty soul she is."

Of Killigrew it is recorded by Pepys that "when a boy he would go to the 'Red Bull,' and when the man cried to the boys, 'Who will go to be a devil, and he shall see the play for nothing?' then would he go in, and be a devil on the stage, and so get to see plays." It may here be remarked by way of parenthesis that the "Red Bull" which stood at the end of St. John Street, Clerkenwell, was, according to tradition, the playhouse before which Shakespeare held gentlemen's horses.

Dr. Doran writes:—"In December, 1661, there is a crowded house at the theatre in Lincoln's Inn Fields, to see young Mr. Betterton play the Dane's part in *Hamlet*; charming Mistress Saunderson acting 'Ophelia.' Old ladies and gentlemen flock in crowds to witness it, and the streets are fairly blocked with the lumbering carriages; among the carriage folk being Mrs. Palmer, destined to become, next year, Countess of Castlemaine." "It's beyond imagination," whispers Mr. Pepys to his neighbour, who answers only with a long-drawn " Hush !" " Mr. Betterton," rejoins Pepys, in the complacent tone of one qualified to judge, " is the best actor in the world, and Miss Saunderson is the best lady on the stage. It is a pity they are not married."

Fifty years after these early triumphs Mr. and Mrs. Betterton, having made their fortune as well as their fame, are living in Great Russell Street, Covent Garden, in a well-appointed house. In April, 1710, the former retired from the stage, fixing the 13th as his benefit-night at the Haymarket Theatre, then newly built. He died within forty-eight hours afterwards.

Actors were first known as " His Majesty's Servants" in 1603, having been previously styled "The Servants of the Lord Chamberlain." It may be mentioned here that as " His Majesty's Servants" the actors were entitled to wear, and did wear, the royal livery of scarlet. The last actor who wore it was Baddeley, who gave the annual " cake " to the green-room of Drury Lane. He was, we believe, the original " Moses " in *The School for Scandal.* A portrait of Baddeley, in his red waistcoat, used to be seen in poor old " Paddy " Green's collection at " Evans's." At this period dramatic entertainments began at one and terminated at three o'clock in the afternoon.

In 1663, as we see by the playbill before quoted, fashion had altered the hour of commencement to three p.m. ; in 1667 it had crept on to four o'clock, until by degrees the evening came to be recognised as the most appropriate time for such amusements. Mohun and Hart had both held commissions in the army, and excelled in tragic and heroic parts. The former was a boon companion and favourite of Rochester. " Becky Marshal " is frequently mentioned by Pepys, and always with praise, as also is Mrs. Knipp, of whom Killigrew told him, " Knipp is like to make the best actor that ever come upon the stage, she understanding so well, that they are going to give her thirty pounds a year more."

Time and space alike, however, would be wanting to enumerate all the dramatic celebrities who have immortalised themselves upon the boards of " Old Drury ; " their name is " Legion." As they pass in review before our imagination we can only briefly particularise a few of the most remarkable.

Here Thomas Betterton, who, as we have seen, served his apprenticeship at the Cockpit, and was long the chief attraction of the theatre in Lincoln's Inn Fields, took a farewell benefit in 1709, preliminary to the one before mentioned, being then in his seventy-fifth year. As admirable in his private as in his professional character ; a devoted husband to a wife who, herself an actress, was as virtuous as she was beautiful ; generous and charitable to excess to his poorer "brethren of the buskin ; " the son of the cook of Charles I. fairly earned the universal esteem in which he was held, and which procured him a royal funeral in Westminster Abbey. Here Mrs. Bracegirdle, equally celebrated for her beauty and her coldness, drove troops of scented fops to distraction.

There seems little doubt of her attachment to the unfortunate Mountford, who acted "Alexander" to her "Statira," and who was murdered by Captain Hill, one of her many rejected suitors. Hill and Lord Mohun having made an abortive attempt to carry off Mrs. Bracegirdle, the former (as we have seen) vowed vengeance upon Mountford, whom he regarded as the cause of the lady's coldness. He accordingly laid wait for the actor in the street, and struck him. Mountford demanded " what that was for ; " upon which (according to the dying man's deposition) Hill drew his sword and ran it through the actor's body.

At Drury Lane flourished the lovely " Nancy " Oldfield, who quitted the bar of the " Mitre " for the stage, and whose notorious intimacy with General Churchill, cousin of the great Duke of Marlborough, obtained for her a grave in Westminster Abbey. Persons of rank and distinction contended for the honour of bearing her pall, and her remains lay in state for three days in the Jerusalem Chamber !

Here, too, Barton Booth stimulated the rival parties of Whigs and Tories in Addison's famous tragedy of *Cato.* Of this piece Johnson remarks, in his " Life of Addison :" " The whole nation was at that time on fire with faction. The Whigs applauded every line in which liberty was mentioned as a satire on the Tories, and the Tories echoed every clap, to show that the satire was unfelt. The story of Bolingbroke is well known. He called Booth to his box, and gave him fifty guineas for defending the cause of liberty so well against a perpetual dictator."

Is not Drury Lane Theatre also intimately associated with the name of Colley Cibber, successful manager and dramatist, and for twenty-seven years Poet Laureate ? His annual birthday and New Year odes, all religiously preserved in the *Gentleman's Magazine*, are so invariably bad that his friends asserted that he wrote them as so many jokes. The *London Magazine* for 1737 contains the following epigram :—

" ON SEEING TOBACCO-PIPES LIT WITH ONE OF THE LAUREATE'S ODES.

" While the soft song that warbles George's praise
From pipe to pipe the living flame conveys,
Critics who long have scorn'd must now admire ;
For who can say his ode now wants its fire ? "

Drury Lane at this time exhibited a perfect constellation of talent. Quin, Macklin, Garrick, Mrs. Clive, and Mrs. Pritchard, with others of subordinate merit, formed a company which has rarely been equalled. It must have been a cruel blow to Quin, long the favourite tragedian of the town, to see himself rivalled by Macklin, and subsequently surpassed by Garrick. In spite of the contempt with which he affected to regard the latter, he expressed his own secret misgivings in his first burst of indignation at the rapid success of the rising actor :—" If this young fellow be right, then *we* have all been wrong."

From 1747 to 1776 Drury Lane owned the sway of David Garrick, the English Roscius, of whom Horace Walpole says : " All the run is now after Garrick, a wine-merchant who is turned player. The Duke of Argyll says he is superior to Betterton." This, however, was not the opinion of the cynical Horace, although Alexander Pope's verdict on Garrick was, " That young man never had his equal as an actor, and he will never have a rival." And Dr. Johnson awarded him a still higher meed of praise in saying : " Here is a man who has advanced the dignity of his profession. Garrick has made a player a higher character."

Drury Lane made the fortune of the ugly, witty, and most popular comic actress, Kitty Clive, thus celebrated by Horace Walpole—

" Here liv'd the laughter-loving dame—
A matchless actress—Clive her name ;
The comic muse with her retir'd,
And shed a tear when she expir'd."

To which Peter Pindar (Dr. Wolcot), who was a devoted admirer of Mrs. Jordan, retorted—

" Know Comedy is hearty—all alive ;
Truth and thy trumpet seem not to agree ;
The sprightly lass no more expir'd with Clive
Than Dame Humility will do with thee."

Here the silver-toned Mrs. Billington appeared in the opera of *Rosetta*. Haydn the composer, who admired this lady greatly, observed of Sir Joshua Reynolds' celebrated picture of her—where she is represented as " St. Cecilia " listening to the heavenly choir—" It is a very fine likeness, but there is a strange mistake in the picture. You have painted her listening to the angels ; you ought to have represented the angels listening to her."

Old Drury witnessed the farewell performance of Miss Farren (Countess of Derby) in 1797, just before she exchanged the buskin for a coronet ; witnessed, too, the first appearance of Harriet Mellon, in 1795, and her last, in February, 1815—for in the previous month she had wedded Mr. Coutts, the banker. In 1827, Mrs. Coutts having been then five years a widow, married the Duke of St. Albans, at that time in his twenty-seventh year. Drury Lane saw the rise of the long and devoted attachment of the Duke of Clarence to Mrs. Jordan, and the short-lived passion of George, Prince of Wales, for the lovely Mrs. Robinson, better known as " Perdita," the character in which she appeared on the evening when she captivated her royal admirer.

Here, in the present century, Edmund Kean ran his brilliant but erratic career, and his more estimable, although less highly gifted, son Charles made his *début* as " Young Norval." Here, in 1828, Joe Grimaldi, prince of clowns and of good fellows, took his farewell of the stage, where, the following year, Mrs. Nisbet (subsequently Lady Boothby), made her first curtsey to a London audience ; and there for several years the imperious Macready rode roughshod over supers, brother-actors, and managers, until, after a personal assault upon the lessee, he transferred his services to the rival house. Neither must the name of Madame Celeste be omitted from the list ; for, although it was not Drury Lane Theatre to which she owed her reputation as an actress, it was nevertheless there that she made her first appearance in London, in the ballad of *La Bayadere* in 1830. This lady may fairly be ranked among the wonders of her age, for in 1874 we find her performing the part of the Indian huntress in *The Green Bushes* with all the vigour and pathos and much of the freshness of her youth. During those four-and-forty years generations of great actresses had arisen, shone as stars for a score of years, and passed away into oblivion, marriage, or death ; but Celeste still survived and flourished—half a century after her *début*—bidding defiance alike to old Time and new fashions, as if warranted, like Tennyson's brook, to " go on for ever."

The two first operas of Michael Balfe—*The Siege of Rochelle* and *The Maid of Artois*—were produced at Drury Lane in 1835-6. The gifted and ill-fated Madame Malibran sustained the principal part in *The Maid of Artois* a few months before her premature death. In Bunn's " History of the Stage " we are told an amusing anecdote of the famous vocalist in this character. She was supposed in the last act to be perishing with thirst in the desert ; the scene was long and exhausting, the lady in delicate health. She therefore proposed to Bunn that he should somehow convey a pint of porter to her in the desert, promising him in that case an *encore* to the finale. " So," says Bunn, " I arranged that behind the pile of drifted sand on which she sinks exhausted a small aperture should be made in the stage, and through that aperture a pewter-pint of porter was conveyed to the parched lips of this rare child of song, which so revived her, after the terrible exertion of the scene, that she electrified the audience, and had strength to repeat the finale."

quent triumphs as a successful composer of English, French, and Italian opera. The works of Michael Balfe are appreciated not only in England, but in France, Germany, and Italy. The statue erected to his honour in the vestibule of this temple,

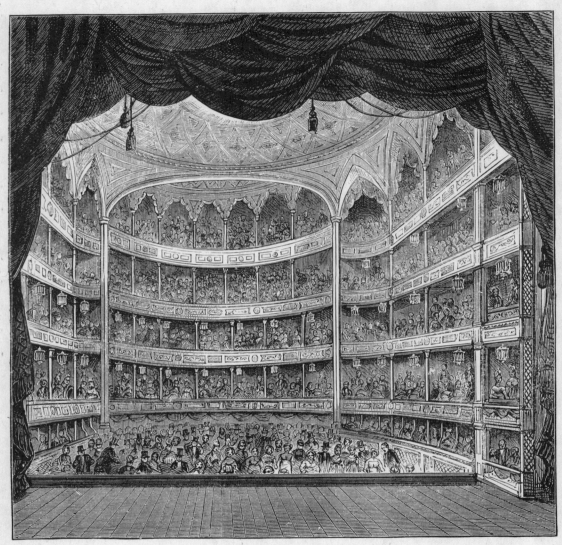

INTERIOR OF DRURY LANE THEATRE, 1804.

Bunn having paid Malibran £125 for each of fifteen performances in one month, she, after much persuasion, consented to sing for him throughout the next month for the sum of £1,000, but added, "For goodness' sake, do not let any one know I am singing on such terms!"

The name of Balfe, not the least eminent of British composers, is intimately associated with Drury Lane, from the time of the young Irishman's unassuming *début* in the orchestra to his subse-

where so many of his triumphs have been achieved —a memorial to which numbers of the most distinguished patrons and professors of music, literature, and the drama, both native and foreign, added their quota—will be a lasting proof of the estimation in which he has been held both at home and abroad.

It is worth while to notice how the salaries of actors have been steadily rising during the last two centuries. We have Pepys' authority that Mrs.

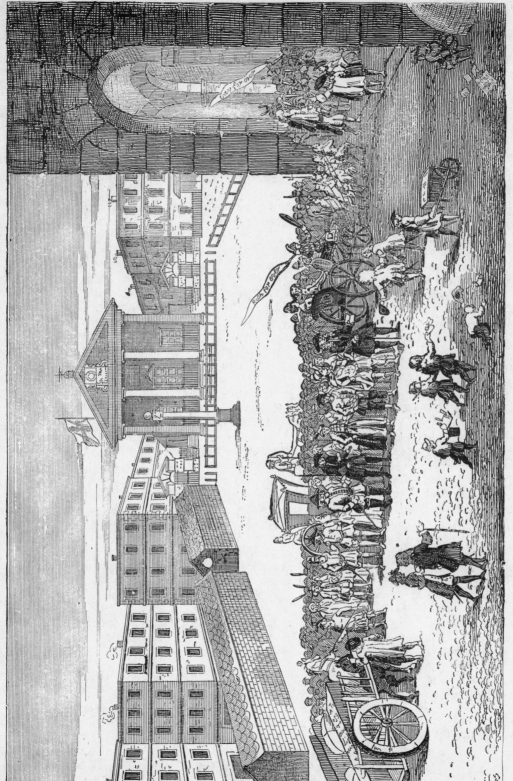

"RICH'S GLORY." *After the Original Caricature.* (*See page 227.*)

Knipp, "who was like to make the best actor of her time," had her salary increased £30 a year. A century later Garrick, as head of his company, drew the highest salary—i.e., £16 16s. a week. Yet fifty years, and Miss Farren, "the Oldfield of her day," is receiving £31 10s. a week, while scarcely a decade afterwards we find Edmund Kean drawing double that sum nightly.

It was remarked about fifty years ago by a well-known writer "that Malibran drew five times the salary of the Colonial Secretary, the President of America was not so well paid as Ellen Tree, or the Premier of Great Britain as Mr. Macready." What would he have said in 1874, when Madame Christine Nilsson received £200 a night at Drury Lane, and Madame Patti demanded and was paid £800 for singing six songs at the Liverpool Musical Festival?

"Old Drury," viewed simply as a building, has experienced many changes and vicissitudes. In 1672 it was burnt to the ground, and the company migrated to the theatre in Lincoln's Inn Fields, until the completion of a new building, designed by Sir Christopher Wren.

The new theatre was opened in 1674, with a prologue and epilogue by Dryden, who, as shown by Mr. R. P. Collier, in Vol. IV. of the Shakespeare Society's Papers, was joined with Killigrew, Mohun, &c., in the speculation of what was then colloquially termed "the New Play House."

In 1707 this theatre, of which Christopher Rich was then the patentee, was temporarily closed, by order of the Lord Chamberlain, in consequence of the violent quarrels between the proprietors and the actors. It subsequently passed into the hands of Willer, Dogget, Cibber, and Booth. In 1714 a life patent was granted to Sir R. Steele, which five years afterwards was revoked. In 1747, when Lacy and Garrick entered into partnership, the latter revived here the performance of Shakespeare's plays; the prologue on that occasion being written, as every Englishman knows, by Dr. Johnson.

In 1780, during the Gordon Riots, a "No Popery" mob got up a row in the theatre, to which they did considerable damage. The objects of their fury were "the papists and Frenchmen" whom Garrick had engaged to dance in a grand spectacular piece entitled *The Chinese Festival*. His Majesty George III., who happened to be present the night of the riot, seemed, it is said, rather amused than otherwise!

In 1775 the afterwards famous Mrs. Siddons, then in her twentieth year, made her first appearance at Drury Lane, in the character of "Portia," in *The Merchant of Venice*. She seems to have excited but little notice at this time, and retired to the provinces the following year. It was not until 1782, when her performance at the Bath Theatre had excited general admiration, that she obtained a re-engagement at Drury Lane—which she used often to call "the wilderness"—and where her brother, John Kemble, made his *début* as Hamlet, in 1783. In 1776, when Garrick retired from the profession, Messrs. Sheridan, Linley, and Ford became the proprietors of the theatre which he had rendered so justly celebrated. It was pulled down in 1791, and rebuilt, the company meanwhile performing at the Haymarket. In 1794 the new theatre—which was designed by Mr. Holland, and is said to have been a model of elegance and beauty—opened, with every prospect of a long and brilliant career. For some years subsequently the gifted Kemble family—John and Charles, with their unapproachable sister, Mrs. Siddons—were the principal attraction at Drury Lane, and the fortunes of the theatre were seriously affected by their withdrawal, in 1803.

We are told in the "Memoirs" of Sheridan that his translation of *The Death of Rolla*, under the title of *Pizarro*, brought him in £25,000 in five weeks. The *Era Almanack* mentions a curious instance of Sheridan's inveterate habit of procrastination:—"At the time the house was overflowing, on the first night's performance of *Pizarro*, all that was written of the play was actually rehearsing; and, incredible as it may appear, until the end of the fourth act, neither Mrs. Siddons, nor Charles Kemble, nor Barrymore, had all their speeches for the fifth. Mr. Sheridan was up-stairs in the prompter's-room, where he was writing the last part of the play while the earlier parts were acting, and every ten minutes he brought down as much of the dialogue as he had done, piecemeal, into the green-room, abusing himself and his negligence, and making a thousand winning and soothing apologies for having kept the performers so long in such painful suspense."

In 1809 Drury Lane Theatre was again destroyed by fire. Sheridan, at the time of the conflagration, was at the House of Commons, which voted an immediate adjournment when the disastrous news arrived; though Sheridan himself protested against such an interruption of public business on account of his own or any other private interests. He went thither, however, in all haste, and whilst seeing his own property in flames, sat down with his friend Barry in a coffee-house opposite, to a bottle of port, coolly remarking, in answer to some friendly expostulation, that it was "hard if a man could not drink a glass of wine by his own fire!"

The fire which burnt down "Old Drury" was

not altogether profitless to the world of poetry, though so heavy a blow to the dramatic muse, for it proved the immediate cause of the appearance of the "Rejected Addresses"—the joint production of Horace and James Smith—one of the most popular contributions to modern light literature. The history of the book was as follows:—In the month of August, 1812, there appeared in the daily newspapers an advertisement to the effect that the committee for rebuilding Drury Lane Theatre were anxious to promote a "free and fair competition" for an address to be spoken upon the re-opening of the theatre on the 10th of October ensuing, and that they had therefore announced to the public that they would be glad to receive such compositions, addressed to their secretary. Some hundred and twelve compositions were sent in—good, bad, and indifferent; and the two Smiths, seizing on the occasion, put together and published in a small volume twenty-one such imaginary addresses or prologues, imitating in the most delicate and graceful manner the styles of the chief writers of the day. The book, as soon as published, sold like wild-fire, and ran through very many editions before the end of the year, and soon established itself as an English classic. Among those writers who were thus travestied were Lord Byron, Scott, Crabbe, Wordsworth, Thomas Moore, Dr. Johnson, "Monk" Lewis, Fitzgerald, William Cobbett, and Samuel T. Coleridge. Of all the imitations, however, that of Sir Walter was universally pronounced the best; and as it contains a vivid description of the scene of conflagration, though in mock-heroic style, we may be pardoned for drawing upon it here rather largely.

First we have a picturesque description of London in darkness; next, we are thus introduced to the outbreak of the fire in the early morning—by a poetical licence, of course, since it happened, in fact, in the evening:—

> " As Chaos, which, by heavenly doom,
>   Had slept in everlasting gloom,
>   Started with terror and surprise
> When light first flashed upon her eyes:
> So London's sons in nightcap woke,
>   In bedgown woke her dames;
> For shouts were heard 'mid fire and smoke,
> And twice ten thousand voices spoke—
>   ' The Playhouse is in flames!'
> And, lo! where Catherine Street extends,
> A fiery tail its lustre lends
>   To every window-pane;
> Blushes each spout in Martlet Court,
> And Barbican, moth-eaten fort,
> And Covent Garden kennels sport
>   A bright ensanguined drain."

Then follows the description of the arrival of the fire-engines, quite in the style of Sir Walter Scott in "Marmion" or "The Lady of the Lake:"—

> " The summoned firemen woke at call,
>   And hied them to their stations all;
> *   *   *   *   *
>   The engines thundered through the street,
>   Fire-hook, pipe, bucket, all complete,
>   And torches glared, and clattering feet
>   Along the pavement paced.
>   And one, the leader of the band,
>   From Charing Cross along the Strand,
>   Like stag by beagles hunted hard,
>   Ran till he stopped at Vinegar Yard.
>   The burning badge his shoulder bore,
>   The belt and oilskin cap he wore,
>   The cane he had his men to bang,
>   Showed foreman of the British gang.
>   His name was Higginbottom: now
>   'Tis meet that I should tell you how
>   The others came in view:
>   The Hand in Hand the race begun,
>   Then came the Phœnix and the Sun,
>   The Exchange, where old insurers run,
>   The Eagle, where the new."

And then we have the fire itself brought before us in all its sensational details:—

> " A sadder scene was ne'er disclosed;
>   Without, within, in hideous show,
>   Devouring flames resistless glow,
>   And blazing rafters downwards go.
>   And never halloo, ' Heads below!'
>   Nor notice give at all.
>   The firemen, terrified, are slow
>   To bid the pumping torrent flow,
>   For fear the roof should fall.
>   Back, Robins, back! Crump, stand aloof!
>   Whitford, keep near the walls!
>   Huggins, regard your own behoof!
>   For, lo! the blazing, rocking roof
>   Down, down, in thunder, falls.
>   An awful pause succeeds the stroke,
>   And o'er the ruins volumed smoke,
>   Rolling around its pitchy shroud,
>   Concealed them from the astonished crowd.
>   At length the mist awhile was cleared,
>   When, lo! amidst the wreck upreared,
>   Gradual a moving head appeared,
>   And Eagle firemen knew
>   'Twas Joseph Muggins—name revered!—
>   The foreman of their crew.
>   Loud shouted all, in signs of woe,
>   ' A Muggins! to the rescue, ho!'
>   And poured the hissing tide.
>   Meanwhile, Joe Muggins fought amain,
>   And strove and struggled, all in vain
>   For, rallying but to fall again,
>   He tottered, stink, and died."

Last follows a picture, too often seen in other and lesser conflagrations, of the death of a gallant fireman, told with a mock-heroic power which never certainly has been surpassed.

Of the brothers Smith, the authors of these charming parodies, we have already spoken in our description of Craven Street, Strand. It will be therefore enough to add here the fact that, having shone as wits in London society for more than a quarter of a century, they died, James in 1839, and Horace ten years later. Lord Byron himself, in spite of being one of the authors so pleasantly satirised in the volume, called the "Rejected Addresses" by far the best thing of the kind since the "Rolliad." Slight and small as was the volume, it was reviewed at considerable length by Lord Jeffrey in the *Edinburgh Review,* while the *Quarterly* criticised it in company with forty of the "Addresses" which had really been "rejected" on the occasion, pronouncing it a model of "humour, good-humour, discrimination, and good taste." It may be of interest, and an encouragement to young authors, to learn that the copyright, which in the first instance Murray refused to buy for twenty, was sold by the brothers for upwards of a thousand pounds! The book has been republished in America, and is read with delight wherever the English language is known. The imitations of Wordsworth ("The Baby's Début"), Cobbett ("The Hampshire Farmer's Address"), Southey ("The Rebuilding"), Coleridge ("Play House Musings"), Crabbe ("The Theatre"), Lord Byron (the first stanzas of "Cui Bono?"), the songs entitled "Drury Lane Hustings" and "The Theatrical Alarm Bell" (imitations of the then editor of the *Morning Post*), and the travesties of *Macbeth, George Barnwell,* and *The Stranger,* were all written by James Smith; the rest, including the parody of Sir Walter Scott, by Horace.

The present edifice—the fourth erected on the site—modelled upon the plan of the great theatre at Bordeaux, by Mr. Wyatt, the architect, was opened in 1812, with a prologue written by Lord Byron. In 1831 the Doric portico in Catherine Street, and the colonnade in Little Russell Street, were added to the structure. It is not a little singular that the necessity of such a colonnade had been thus humorously brought under the notice of the Building Committee as far back as the year 1812, in one of the "Rejected Addresses," in the following lines, in imitation of S. T. Coleridge:—

"Oh, Mr. Whitbread! fie upon you, sir!
I think you should have built a colonnade.
When tender beauty, looking for her coach,
Protrudes her gloveless hand, perceives the shower,
And draws the tippet closer round her throat,
And ere she mount the step, the oozing mud
'Sinks through her pale kid slipper.
                          On the morrow
She coughs at breakfast, and her gruff papa

Cries, 'There you go! this comes of playhouses!'
To build no portico is penny wise;
Heaven grant it prove not in the end pound foolish!"

The new building was pronounced by the imitators of Mr. Cobbett, in the "Rejected Addresses," "not a gimcrack palace, not a Solomon's temple, not a frost-work of Brobdingnag filagree, but a plain, honest, homely, industrious, wholesome, brown-brick playhouse"—a "large, comfortable house, thanks to Mr. Whitbread." The theatre, in 1818, was under a committee of noblemen and gentlemen, among whom were Lord Yarmouth (afterwards Marquis of Hertford) and Lord Byron, the latter of whom, however, soon after being appointed, left England, never to return.

For many years after that date the great national theatre ran an erratic and, for the most part, disastrous career, having been not inaptly compared to a syren luring adventurous lessees to ruin and bankruptcy. In the agony of desperation it has worn "motley," caught eagerly at every *bizarre* attraction, and been—

"Everything by turns, and nothing long;"

a monster concert-hall, a French hippodrome, and even an arena for the sports of Van Amburgh and his wild beasts, with spasmodic intervals of pantomime and legitimate drama. Sad to relate, we have it on the authority of Mr. Bunn, the lessee, that Van Amburgh was a greater success, in a pecuniary point of view, than Mr. Macready.

For several seasons it was the home of English opera, a class of entertainment which has never been appreciated as it deserves among our countrymen, though frequent attempts have been made to give it a position equal to that enjoyed by Italian opera. It may be observed here that Clara Novello, later the Countess Gugliucci, made a brilliant *début* at Drury Lane, in 1843, as "Sappho."

After the destruction by fire of Her Majesty's Theatre, in 1867, "Old Drury" rose greatly in the social scale, having been advanced to the dignity of the opposition opera-house to Covent Garden. This, however, was only a temporary arrangement until the new opera-house should be built. In 1879 the lesseeship of the theatre passed into the hands of Mr. (afterwards Sir) Augustus Harris, under whose management "Old Drury" has fully maintained its claim to be styled the "National Theatre." Sir Augustus, one of the greatest of theatrical managers, died in 1896.

Apart from the interest attaching to the theatre as a place of dramatic entertainment, some details of the present building may be placed on record here. The general form of the edifice is that of a parallelogram : its extent from north to south being 131 feet, and from east to west 237 feet, independently of the painting and scene-rooms, which are partially detached, extending 93 feet further eastward. The chief entrance is approached by a flight of steps, protected by a porch. The entrance-hall communicates, eastward, with the rotunda and the staircases to the boxes ; on the north and south, with the pit-lobbies ; and from the latter, by circuitous passages, with the pit itself. The rotunda and grand staircase form very beautiful portions of the theatre. The rotunda, 30 feet in diameter, is surrounded by a circular gallery, and crowned by an elegant dome. Here, among other statues of famous poets and actors, is the bust of Balfe already alluded to.

The auditory has a most imposing effect, and is built nearly in the form of a horse-shoe ; it is 46 feet wide at the stage, 52 feet across the centre of the pit, and 48 feet from the front of the stage to the centre of the dress-circle. The height from the floor of the pit to the ceiling is 47 feet. There are three tiers of boxes, and an upper and lower gallery ; and the house is calculated to accommodate upwards of 3,000 persons.

The proscenium, being as it were the portico of the stage, has less of imitative art in its decoration than the other parts of the house. On each side are two demi-columns of the Corinthian order, supporting a rich entablature, a coved ceiling, and, spanning the stage, an elliptical arch, the whole being very rich in gilding. Down to about the year 1860, when the theatre underwent extensive renovation, the proscenium bore above it the royal arms, together with the well-known classical motto "*Veluti in speculum.*" In its original state the interior of the theatre was circular, but it was altered to its present form during the management of Mr. Elliston, at a cost of not less than £21,000. The interior has several times been renovated and beautified at considerable expense, and now presents an aspect of uncommon splendour.

The stage is of great extent, being 96 feet from the orchestra to the back wall, and upwards of 77 feet in width from wall to wall. The manager's room, actress' dressing-rooms, and various other apartments, are on the north side of the stage ; and on the south are the green-rooms, the prompter's-room, the actors' dressing-rooms, and a range of stabling for twenty horses. Above the auditory are the carpenters' shops and store-rooms ; whilst the gas-fitters' and property-rooms are in the immediate vicinity of the stage. The painting-room is over the eastern extremity of the stage, and measures nearly 80 feet in length by 36 in height and width. An opening has been made through the original back wall of the stage, whereby the space below the painting-room can be made available for scenic effects, thus giving to the stage an entire depth of 125 feet, the largest of any stage in Europe.

CHAPTER XXIX.

COVENT GARDEN THEATRE.

"The houses twain
Of Covent Garden and of Drury Lane."—*Rejec'ed Addresses.*

The Building of the Theatre—"Rich's Glory"—The First Performance at Covent Garden—Ladies at the Theatre—Receipts of the House—Performance of Handel's "Messiah"—Royalty flock to the Haymarket, and Horace Walpole's Remarks upon the Subject—First Appearance of "Peg" Woffington—Death of Rich, and Sale of Covent Garden Theatre—Charles Macklin, the Comedian and Centenarian—Stephen Kemble—Incledon—George Frederick Cooke—John Philip Kemble—"The Young Roscius'—The Theatre burnt in 1808—The Duke of Northumberland's Generosity to Kemble—The Theatre rebuilt and opened—The "O. P." Riots, succeeded by a run of uninterrupted Prosperity—Poetic Effusions upon Actresses wedded to Noblemen.

WE have seen that "the new playhouse in Drury Lane" was frequently spoken of as "Covent Garden Theatre," and naturally enough, for the theatre in Bow Street was not built until the year 1731. The latter was a speculation of John Rich, the celebrated harlequin, and patentee of the theatre in Lincoln's Inn Fields, who removed hither with his company in 1732.

Hogarth's caricature of "Rich's Glory ; or, His Triumphal Entry into Covent Garden," of which we give a copy on page 223, refers to this removal.

The progress of the building was thus commented on in the *Daily Advertiser* for March 2, 1730 :—"We hear the new theatre which is to be built in Covent Garden will be after the model of the opera-house in the Haymarket ; and by the draught that has been approved of for the same, it's said it will exceed the opera-house in magnificence of structure."

The same paper for August 4, 1731, states:—"The new theatre building in Covent Garden for Mr. Rich is carrying on with such expedition and diligence (there being a great number of hands employed therein) that it's thought it will be completely finished and ready to receive his audience next winter. Several persons of distinction resort thither daily to view the said work, and seem much pleased at the performance."

The first performance at Covent Garden Theatre was advertised in the following manner :—

the boxes, the young married women compose the second row, while the rear is generally made up of mothers of long standing, undesigning maids, and contented widows. Whoever will cast his eye upon them under this view, during the representation of a play, will find me so far in the right, that a *double entendre* strikes the first row into an affected gravity or careless indolence, the second will venture

COVENT GARDEN THEATRE : FRONT IN 1850.

"By the Company of Comedians.—At the Theatre Royal in Covent Garden, on Thursday next, being the 7th day of December, 1732, will be revived a comedy called *The Way of the World*, written by Mr. Congreve. The cloathes, scenes, and decorations entirely new, and, on account of the great demand for places, the pit and boxes, by desire, will be laid together at 5s.; gallery, 2s ; upper gallery, 1s.; and to prevent the scenes being crowded, the stage half-a-guinea. N.B.—All persons who want places are desired to send to the stage-door (the passage from Bow Street leading to it), where attendance will be given and places kept for the following night as usual."

It was doubtless *àpropos* of some such comedy as the one just mentioned that the *Guardian* remarks :—"As the playhouse affords us the most occasions of observing upon the behaviour of the face, it may be useful (for the direction of those who would be critics this way) to remark that the virgin ladies usually dispose themselves in front of

at a smile, but the third take the conceit entirely and express their mirth in a downright laugh."

Here, as Mr. Timbs reminds us, Rich and Lambert, in 1735, founded the Beefsteak Club ; and here, in 1746, Garrick played for the season.

The site of the theatre was leased to Rich for a term of years by the Duke of Bedford, at a yearly rental of £100. It held before the curtain £200, which was at that time reckoned a good receipt. In Shakespeare's day £20 was considered profitable ; and "in 1747," says Colley Cibber, in his "Apology," "Mrs. Rich said she was always contented if the receipts reached three figures." In 1750, further to increase the profits, seats were built on the stage sufficient to accommodate a large number of persons ; but this arrangement was such an obstruction to the actors that it was abolished by

Garrick. At the time of the death of John Rich in 1761, the ground-rent had been raised from £100 to £300 per annum, and the property was estimated at £60,000. In 1792, when the Duke of Bedford, as ground-landlord, granted a new lease, it was at the rate of £940 a year.

It was at Covent Garden that Handel, in 1741, produced his great oratorio, the *Messiah*. The fashion of the day was against him, though he was

royalties went to the Haymarket when it was the fashion to frequent the other opera in Lincoln's Inn Fields. Lord Chesterfield one night came into the latter, and was asked if he had been at the other house. 'Yes,' said he; 'but there was no one there but the king and queen; and as I thought they might be talking business, I came straight away.'"

It was at Covent Garden that the fascinating

INTERIOR OF COVENT GARDEN THEATRE IN 1804.

supported by the court, the mob, and the poet of common sense, Alexander Pope, who records in his "Dunciad" how, on finding it impossible to hold his own against the Italian faction, Handel quietly withdrew to Ireland for a year or so, till the tide should turn in his favour. "Handel has set up an oratorio," writes Horace Walpole in 1742, "against the operas, and it succeeds." And well was Handel avenged. In a few years the Italian Opera House in the Haymarket went out of fashion, and the nobility set up their own rival house in Lincoln's Inn Fields. "What the Court then patronised," observes Charles Knight, "the aristocracy rejected." As usual, Horace Walpole has a cynical story to tell upon the subject. He writes thus to Mr. Conway, in 1761 :—"The late

Irish actress, Margaret Woffington, made her first appearance upon a London and her last upon any stage. Her choice of a character for her *début*, in 1738, excited the surprise of the public, being that of "Sir Harry Wildair;" but so captivating did she appear in it that Garrick, with whom it had been a favourite part, gave it up from that time. Her best *rôle* was that of "Rosalind," in *As You Like It*, to which, in 1757, she was speaking the epilogue with all the saucy piquancy peculiarly her own, when she was suddenly stricken with paralysis, and carried off the stage never to return to it. According to Dr. Doran, a bitter source of jealousy existed between "Peg" Woffington and the beautiful and notorious George Anne Bellamy, whose "Memoirs," written by herself with an astonishing absence of reserve, were formerly read and quoted by every lady of fashion. "The charming Bellamy," says Dr. Doran, "had procured from Paris two gorgeous dresses wherein to enact 'Statira' in the *Rival Queens*. 'Roxana' was played by Woffington, and she was so overcome by malice when she saw herself eclipsed by the dazzling glories of the resplendent Bellamy, that she rolled 'Statira' and her spangled sack in the dust, pommelling her the while with the handle of her stage dagger, as she declaimed, Alexander standing by :—

'Nor he, nor heaven shall shield thee from my justice !
Die, sorceress, die ! and all my wrongs die with thee !'"

Rich lies buried in Hillingdon churchyard, near Uxbridge. A vignette of his tomb, and a fac-simile of his autograph, attached to an agreement with Charles Fleetwood respecting the receipts of Covent Garden Theatre, will be found in "Smith's Historical and Literary Curiosities."

A few years after the death of Rich the theatre, having been sold by his heirs for £60,000, was opened in 1767 by Messrs. Harris, Colman, Powell, and Rutherford. In 1774 Mr. Colman sold his share, and from this time the theatre was virtually under the management of Mr. Harris, who had by far the largest interest in the property. In 1787 it was almost wholly rebuilt, and was further altered and enlarged in 1792.

Covent Garden is rich in names famous in histrionic annals, each of which is a landmark to point out the progress of the drama during the last century and a half. Among the earliest of these is that of Charles Macklin, the comedian and centenarian, who frequently performed on its boards, and unless absent from London on engagements at Dublin, lived constantly almost under its shadow —mostly under its piazza; or hard by, in James Street, Hart Street, or Tavistock Row. Having once retired from the stage in middle life, in the hope of making a fortune by establishing a tavern and coffee-house in Hart Street, he returned to it after the failure of his scheme and his consequent bankruptcy, and for many years, whilst quite an old man, played leading parts with some of the fire of youth. His last appearance at Covent Garden was on May 7th, 1789, he being then eighty-nine years of age, when he attempted the part of "Shylock" for his "benefit," but was unable to proceed with the performance. But in spite of his loss of memory he still lived much abroad as usual, haunting the scene of his former triumphs, telling his stock of anecdotes over and over again, and, evening after evening, frequenting a public-house in Duke's Court, close by, where a large concourse would repair in order to hear the anecdotes of so aged and remark-

able a person, who remembered the days of the dramatic giants of an earlier generation. "As the infirmities of age increased on him, he would wander feebly about the neighbourhood of Covent Garden, sometimes looking in at the theatre, though he went thither rather more from the force of habit than from any gratification that he could receive, except, perhaps, from the music between the acts. On these occasions the audience, it is said, would always venerate his age, and compassionate his condition; for on his entrance into the pit, however full the house might be, room was always made for him in his accustomed seat—the centre of the last row next to the orchestra; and when the performance was over he would walk home leisurely by himself across the square of Covent Garden to Tavistock Row, where he lived and where he died, a veritable centenarian, in 1797. His "Memoirs," which originally appeared in the *European Magazine*, but were subsequently re-published in a volume, furnish us with some curious information respecting society in London and the manners and habits of the gentry and professional classes a century ago.

Macklin does not say much for the morality of Covent Garden and its neighbourhood, or of the taverns and public-houses by which it was surrounded, or of the still lower public-houses near Clare Market, which were the resort of second-rate actors, and theatrical critics of Grub Street or Drury Lane, who "lived from hand to mouth." The ordinaries of the time, it appears, were charged from sixpence to a shilling a head—in the latter case being supplied with two courses, and attended by a superior sort of mixed company; though there were private rooms besides for wits of the higher order, and for such of the nobility as liked to frequent such places, where conviviality was often carried to excess. Macklin says also that the habits and manners of the dramatic as well as of other professions were very different from those which now prevail. The merchant, at that time, scarcely ever lived out of the City, his residence being always attached to his counting-house, and, indeed, his credit being in a great degree dependent on his observance of the established practice. According to Macklin, the first migration of the London merchants to the westward dates only from 1747, when a few of those who had already made large fortunes removed to Hatton Garden. The lawyers, too, he used to tell his hearers, used at that time to live mostly in their inns of court, or else about Westminster Hall; and in like manner the actors "did mostly congregate" around the two great theatres. Thus, as we know, Quin, Booth, and Wilks lived almost constantly in or about Bow

Street, Colley Cibber in Charles Street, Billy Howard in Henrietta Street, and Garrick, for a considerable portion of his life, in Southampton Street. The inferior players lodged in and about Vinegar Yard, Little Russell Street, and the lesser courts round the theatres; "so that," says Macklin, "we could all be mustered by beat of drum, could attend rehearsals without any inconvenience, and yet save coach-hire—no inconsiderable part, let me tell you, of a former player's annual expenses. I do not know how the change has been effected, but we are now all looking out for high ground—squares and genteel neighbourhoods—no matter how far distant from the theatre, which should be the great scene of business; as if, forsooth, local situations could give rhythm to the profession, or genteel neighbourhoods instinctively produce good manners." What he would have said on this subject if he had lived on into our own days may be easily inferred from these last remarks of the father of the theatrical world a century ago. But we must return from this digression to the theatre itself, from which we are in danger of wandering with the actors.

Stephen Kemble made his first appearance here, as "Othello," in 1783. Possessed, like all of his family, of considerable dramatic capabilities, his talents were unhappily obscured under a load of personal obesity, which had, however, the advantage of enabling him to enact the part of "Falstaff" (his best character) without stuffing! Charles Incledon—"The Ballad-singer—" as he loved to be termed—made his *début* as "Dermot," in *The Poor Soldier*, in 1790. His voice is said to have been the most melodious, as well as powerful, of his time; and his manner of singing such songs as "Black-eyed Susan," "The Soldier tired," and "The Storm," has never since been surpassed. In 1794 Charles Kemble, and in 1797 Mrs. Glover, made their first appearances here. In 1800 George Frederick Cooke achieved a great success as " Richard III." —a performance spoken of as " the best since Garrick." In 1803 John Philip Kemble purchased a sixth part of the property of the Covent Garden patent, transferring his own services, with those of his sister, Mrs. Siddons, and his brother Charles, from Drury Lane to Covent Garden. In 1804 " The Young Roscius," William Henry Betty, at twelve years of age was filling the theatre to overflowing, and a detachment of the Guards was posted outside, with a large body of constables inside, to preserve order amongst the thousands who had assembled hours before the opening of the doors. His salary was at first £50 a night, but, after three performances, was increased to £100; and at sixteen years of age he quitted the profession with a handsome fortune. Twelve years later he returned to the stage; but the performance of his maturer years was not considered to fulfil the promise of his youth; and disappointed at the coldness with which he was received, he again retired into private life. He died in August, 1874, aged eighty-two.

On the morning of the 30th of September, 1808, Covent Garden Theatre was totally destroyed by fire; a calamity which involved a fearful loss of human life—twenty-three firemen being killed by the unexpected fall of a part of the ruins. The splendid organ left by Handel, and the stock of wine belonging to the Beefsteak Club, shared the fate of the whole building. The loss of property was estimated at £150,000, of which £50,000 were covered by insurances.

John Kemble, who had invested his all in the share so recently purchased, met with universal sympathy, which, in some notable instances, did not confine itself to words. The Prince of Wales, afterwards George IV., presented him with £1,000; and the Duke of Northumberland with £10,000, which Kemble declined as a gift, but accepted as a loan, giving the duke his bond for the amount. On the 31st of December, 1808, the Prince of Wales laid the first stone of the new theatre, and the Duke of Northumberland sent Kemble back his bond, enclosed in a letter, saying that, " it being a day of rejoicing, he concluded there would be a bonfire, and he therefore requested that the enclosed obligation might be thrown in, to heighten the flames." The architect was Sir Robert Smirke, and the model selected, the Temple of Minerva in the Acropolis at Athens. The Doric portico in Bow Street, with its four fluted columns, and statues of Tragedy and Comedy, were by Flaxman, and the two long panels in the upper part, with representations in basso-relievo of ancient and modern drama, were by Flaxman and Rossi. Some £50,000 of the cost of the construction was received from the insurance offices, and the remaining £100,000 was raised by subscription shares of £500 each.

On the 18th of September, 1809, the splendid edifice was opened at " new prices," a proceeding which the management considered necessary on account of the enormous cost of the building. These new prices were by no means approved by the public, and led to the well-known " O.P." riots. On the opening night of the new theatre, a cry of " Old prices!" (afterwards diminished to "O.P.") burst from every part of the house. This continued and increased in violence till the 23rd, when rattles, drums, whistles, and cat-calls having completely drowned the voices of the actors, Mr. Kemble, the stage-manager, came forward and said "that a committee of gentlemen had undertaken to examine the finances of the concern, and that until they were prepared with their report the theatre would be closed." "Name them!" was shouted from all sides. Their names were declared. "All shareholders!" bawled a wag from the gallery. In a few days the theatre re-opened; the public paid no attention to the report of the referees, and the tumult was renewed for several weeks with even increased violence. The proprietors sent in hired bruisers to mill the refractory into subjection. This irritated most of their former friends, and amongst the rest the annotator, who accordingly wrote the song of "Heigh-ho, says Kemble," which was caught up by the ballad-singers, and sung under Mr. Kemble's house windows in Great Russell Street. In the end Kemble was obliged to give way, and after a humble apology, which was graciously accepted by a crowded audience, peace and the "old prices" were simultaneously restored.

For many years after this inauspicious commencement Covent Garden enjoyed a run of uninterrupted prosperity, the receipts between 1809 and 1821 averaging £80,000 each season. The largest annual amount taken at the theatre was in the year 1810-11, when the sum of £100,000 was received at the doors! The annual expenses during this period averaged £40,000—an outlay which required a skilful and liberal management to insure the large amounts just mentioned. It will be sufficient to mention the names of the principal performers at Covent Garden between 1809 and 1822 to show how powerful was the dramatic force there assembled:—In tragedy, Messrs. Kemble, Cooke, Macready, Young, &c. &c.; Mrs. Siddons, Miss O'Neill, &c. In comedy, Messrs. Liston, Munden, Charles Mathews, sen., W. Farren, &c.; Mesdames Jordan, Brunton, Foote, C. Kemble, &c. In opera, Messrs. Incledon, Braham, Pyne, and Mesdames Catalani, Bolton, Stephens, and Tree. "Kitty" Stephens made her first appearance here in 1812; Miss O'Neill, in 1814; Macready, in 1816; and Farren, in 1818. Several of these actresses and singers afterwards married noblemen; and the "Memoirs" of the late James Smith, published in 1840, contain various poetic effusions upon those ladies. We will quote a few, which will interest our readers :—

The first, in allusion to Miss Farren, Countess of Derby, runs thus :—

> "Farren, Thalia's dear delight,
> Can I forget the fatal night,
> Of grief unstain'd by fiction,
> (E'en now the recollection damps)
> When Wroughton led thee to the lamps,
> In graceful valediction?"

Another verse is in honour of Miss Brunton, Countess of Craven :—

> "The Derby prize by Hymen won,
> Again the god made bold to run
> Beneath Thalia's steerage ;
> Sent forth a second earl to woo,
> And captivating Brunton too,
> Exalted to the peerage."

Of Miss Bolton, Lady Thurlow, whose celebrated part was "Polly" in *The Beggar's Opera*, the poet says—

> "Thrice vanquished thus on Thespian soil,
> Heart-whole from Cupid's toil
> I caught a fleeting furlough :
> Gay's Newgate *Opera* charmed me then ,
> But 'Polly' sang her requiem when
> Fair Bolton turned to Thurlow."

Of Miss O'Neill, who made prize of a baronet in the matrimonial lottery, he writes :—

> "These wounds some substitute might heal ;
> But what bold mortal bade O'Neill
> Renounce her tragic station—
> Taste, talent, beauty to trepan?
> By Heaven! I wonder how the man
> Escaped assassination!"

Appended to these verses is one from another pen, written some years later, immortalising the lady who afterwards became Countess of Essex :—

> "Last of this dear, delightful list—
> Most followed, wondered at, and missed
> In Hymen's odds and evens—
> Old Essex caged our nightingale,
> And finished thy theatric tale,
> Enchanting Kitty Stephens."

Miss Foote, although not celebrated in verse by the author of "The Rejected Addresses," was another actress of this period who was elevated from the stage to the peerage. She made her first appearance at Covent Garden, in 1814, as "Amanthis," in Mrs. Inchbald's comedy of *The Child of Nature;* and became Countess of Harrington in 1831. She died in 1867.

Among the many good stories and anecdotes relating to Drury Lane and Covent Garden Theatres to be found in abundance in the anecdote biography of the two last centuries, the following, relating as it does to Miss Farren, may be repeated here :—Lord Derby once applied in the green-room to Sheridan for the arrears of Lady Derby's (Miss Farren's) salary, averring that he would not leave the room until it was paid. "My dear lord," said Sheridan, "this is too bad; you have taken from us the brightest star in our little world, and now you quarrel with us for a little dust which she has left behind her."

Mrs. Siddons retired from the stage in 1812; her brother, John Kemble, followed her example in 1816, presenting his share of the theatre (one-sixth) to his brother Charles.   In 1820 Mr. Harris, who owned seven-twelfths of the property, died, and from this time the fortunes of the theatre declined. Differences arose between Mr. Henry Harris (who had succeeded to his father's share) and Mr. Charles Kemble, resulting in legal proceedings.

In 1822 Mr. Henry Harris resigned his management, and the property was thrown into Chancery. Nevertheless, the Shakespearian play of *King John* was put upon the stage here in 1823, though Mr. Kemble was doubtful how far any attempt to improve the costume would succeed, being afraid lest he should be considered an "antiquary." But in this matter he listened to the advice of Mr. Planché, and the introduction of appropriate mail-armour and helmets of the thirteenth century was thoroughly appreciated by the public, "receipts of from £400 to £600 nightly soon reimbursed the management for the production; and a complete reformation of dramatic costume became from that moment inevitable upon the English stage."

In spite, however, of these and other undisputed successes, the theatre, in 1829, was seized by the parochial authorities, advertised for sale, and was only rescued by public subscriptions and voluntary contributions of the company.   Charles Kemble's administration was not so fortunate as that of his brother, although the last three years of his management were brightened by the triumphs of his daughter, Miss Fanny Kemble, afterwards Mrs. Butler. Here was performed, in January, 1832, Lord Francis Egerton's tragedy of *Catharine of Cleves*.   In 1833 Edmund Kean made his last appearance on these boards. In the same year the two great theatres of Drury Lane and Covent Garden were united under the management of Mr. Bunn, but the union was of short duration. In 1835 Covent Garden was leased to Mr. Osbaldistone, and the experiment tried of reducing the prices. Charles Kemble, Macready, and Miss Helen Faucit were the principal stars under this management, which only lasted two years, when the theatre passed into the hands of Macready. A Shakespearian revival now took place, and *The Tempest, Coriolanus, Henry V.*, and *King Lear* were produced in a style of gorgeous and appropriate magnificence. The profits were, however, by no means commensurate with the expenses, and within two years Mr. Macready retired from the management a considerable loser.

In 1839 Covent Garden Theatre was taken by Madame Vestris, the most fascinating actress of her time; Mr. Planché, as he tells us in his agreeable "Recollections," acting as superintendent of the decorative department, and introducing great

reforms in the matter of costume, and acting also as "reader" of plays submitted to the manager by unknown authors; but in spite of the almost unrivalled attractions afforded by a company which, in addition to the talented lessee and her no less talented husband, Charles Mathews—including Messrs. Harley and Keeley, and Mesdames Nisbet, Humby, and Keeley, &c.—the speculation was a losing one, and was resigned at the end of the third season. About this time Dickens wrote for Covent Garden Theatre, by way of helping the manager, a farce about which the actors could not agree, and which he afterwards turned into his story of "The Lamplighter."

In April, 1842, Mr. Charles Kemble again essayed the direction of the theatre, which opened with the opera of *Norma*, Miss Adelaide Kemble being the prima donna; but Mr. C. Kemble, in spite of the prestige of his name, and his great success as an actor, was not destined to be fortunate as a manager, and the smallness of the receipts obliged him to withdraw the following November. The Christmas of the same year found the indomitable Mr. Bunn in possession, the entertainment offered being a curious olla-podrida, compounded of Shakespeare, English opera, and pantomime. Mr. Bunn's brief management ended in May, 1843, and the theatre was then let to the Anti-Corn-Law League, who used it for the purpose of a bazaar. Next, M. Jullien installed himself there for a season of winter promenade concerts, which were highly successful; and on March 4th, 1844, the first *bal-masqué* given in England during the present century took place at Covent Garden, under his auspices. During the spring of the same year *Antigone* was performed, the theatre being under the direction of M. Laurent.   M. Jullien's concerts and *bal-masqué* again attracted large crowds during the season of 1845-6.

Mr. Planché, in his "Recollections," in contrasting Covent Garden with Drury Lane at this period, speaks of the former as "strong in comedy, and superior to its rival in spectacular entertainments."   To a certain extent this remark held true long after it was made; and in proof of the latter part of the assertion, it may be said, without fear of contradiction, that Covent Garden was until recently celebrated for the gorgeousness and brilliancy of its pantomimes. In fact, so gorgeous were the spectacular entertainments here, that on one occasion we find Mr. Planché complaining to Mr. Kemble, the manager, that a thousand pounds were often lavished on a Christmas pantomime or an Easter spectacle, whilst the plays of Shakespeare were put upon the stage with "makeshift scenery,

44*

and old and second-rate dresses." *Apropos* of the degeneracy of the drama (proper), and of the rising taste for "spectacle," Byron writes—

"Gods! on those boards shall Folly rear her head,
Where Garrick trod and Kemble loves to tread."

It was at this time the project was formed of opening a rival opera-house to the one in the Haymarket; and in April, 1847, after undergoing important alterations and additions, Covent Garden

Italian opera." That this exclusive right was no dead letter had been proved by Mr. Bunn in 1835, when the entire company of "The King's Theatre" had performed for one night only in *La Gazza Ladra* at Drury Lane—a performance immediately followed by a dignified protest from the Lord Chamberlain. A period of a dozen years, however, produces a change both of times and of Lords Chamberlains, and Mr. Lumley found out, as he

BURNING OF COVENT GARDEN THEATRE IN 1856.

Theatre commenced its new career as "The Royal Italian Opera House." The company consisted principally of seceders from Her Majesty's—hitherto the only Italian opera-house in London—and comprised the famous names of Giulia Grisi, Persiani, Mario, Tamburini, and even the great leader of the orchestra—Michael Costa himself. No wonder the alarmed lessee of Her Majesty's made strenuous efforts to prevent the threatened rivalry, in virtue of a privilege having been of old granted to the "King's Theatre" (the name by which it was known previously to her Majesty's accession) "for the exclusive production in perpetuity of Italian opera;" the same document containing a stipulation that "the patents of Drury Lane and Covent Garden should never be used for the purpose of

tells us in his "Reminiscences," that he was under a government which discouraged monopolies of all kinds; and, his opposition notwithstanding, the Royal Italian Opera House, Covent Garden, was duly opened, "without let or hindrance."

The *Era* of June 13th, 1847, remarks:—"It has been said that London cannot support two operatic companies; but while the house at the Haymarket was filled to overflowing by the presence of Jenny Lind, that at Covent Garden was crammed to suffocation by Grisi." Yet, although Grisi, so long the popular idol, still held her own, in spite of the Jenny Lind mania, and, supported by Alboni—who made a triumphant *début* during this year—insured a full house every night, the expenses were frightfully in excess of the receipts. Two years

COVENT GARDEN IN 1660.

sufficed to involve Mr. Delafield, the lessee, in bankruptcy, although he had commenced his speculation with £100,000. The reconstruction of the interior, by Albano, had cost £40,000; the vocal department, in 1848, cost £33,349, of which Alboni drew £4,000, and Grisi £3,106. The orchestra cost £10,048; the ballet, £8,105; gas and gasmen, £1,927; properties, £1,920; carpenters' work, £1,858; advertisements, £2,376; wardrobes, £3,100; printing, £982; bills of performance, £885; hairdressers, £100; salaries of officials, £2,118; law expenses, £2,100; and fireworks, £27! The whole expenditure in 1848 was £78,765; the aggregate receipts, including cloak-room, saloon, &c., £44,008.

A curious contrast to this lavish outlay is to be found in the modest charges of a play acted in the year 1511, on the Feast of St. Margaret, of which the expenses were as follow :—

		£	s.	d.
For Players	... ...	1	4	0
,, Musicians	... ...	0	5	6
,, John Hobbard, Priest, and Author of Play	... ...	0	2	8
,, Decorations, Dresses, and Play-books	...	0	1	0
,, Hire of Place of Performance	... ...	0	1	0
,, Furniture	... ...	0	1	4
,, Painting Three Phantoms and Three Devils	... ...	0	0	6
,, Fish, Bread, and Ale for Players	...	0	3	5
,, Four Chickens for the Hero	... ...	0	0	4
Sum total	... ...	£1	19	9

In 1850 Covent Garden passed into the hands of Mr. Gye. At the commencement of 1856 Mr. Gye let the theatre for a few weeks to Professor Anderson, the "Wizard of the North," whose short lease terminated on the 4th of March with a masked ball, for which Mr. Gye's reluctant consent had been extorted, after repeated refusals. It was not, as we have seen, the first or the second time that Covent Garden Theatre had been employed for the same purpose; but Mr. Gye's objections were in this instance unfortunately prophetic. The festivities were just concluding with the performance of the "National Anthem," at five a.m., there being then only about 200 of the vast crowd of revellers left in the building, when the alarm of fire was given, and in a few hours nothing remained of the splendid structure but a heap of smoking ruins. Happily no lives were lost, although little else was saved in the general destruction, except the façade, and Flaxman's statues and bassi-relievi. The origin of the fire was never ascertained. Such a catastrophe, occurring at a period when the preparations and engagements for the coming season were on the point of completion, was calculated to daunt the stoutest heart; but Mr. Gye's courage and fertility of resource were equal even to an emergency like this. He at once engaged the Lyceum for the season, made a manly appeal to the public to support him, and opened his temporary opera-house on the 15th of April to a brilliant and crowded audience. Early in the following year Mr. Gye obtained from the Duke of Bedford a lease of the site for a new theatre, at a rent of £850 for ninety years. This site included not only the ground on which the late theatre stood, but also that occupied by the "Piazza" Hotel, together with other tenements, the whole being equivalent to more than an acre. The funds for the new building were raised by loans; amongst the contributors being the Duke of Bedford, £15,000; Messrs. Lucas, £10,000; Colonel Meyrick, £5,000; Mr. Billings, £5,000; Mr. Maynard, £5,000; Sir E. Majoribanks and Mr. Antrobus, £5,000; besides Sir George Armytage, Mr. E. M. Barry, Mr. Turner, and others.

The yearly interest upon this large capital is necessarily considerable, and the securities contain a proviso that if the interest be in arrear over three months, or the premiums of fire insurance be not paid, the lessee is to be considered as a tenant at a rental of £4,000 per annum.

These preliminaries arranged, the work of rebuilding the theatre commenced, and progressed with extraordinary rapidity, and with every improvement in the way of lighting, ventilation, decoration, comfort, and precaution against fire which modern science and taste could suggest. In contemplating this, one of the largest and most magnificent theatres in Europe, it is difficult to realise that it was begun and completed within the short space of six months.

The edifice occupies a space of ground measuring 219 feet on the south side, next the Floral Hall, 210 feet on the Hart Street side, and 127 feet along the Bow Street end, where there is an enclosed portico projecting about 17 feet. The portico is about one-fifth larger than that of its predecessor, adorned by Corinthian columns 36 feet high, and by the figures and basso-relievos of Flaxman from the old building, which were cleverly adapted to the new theatre, and were insured by the Duke of Bedford for £1,000. The area of the stage, exclusive of the bow in advance of the proscenium, measures 90 feet by 88, and the cost of the stage-machinery and various appurtenances was nearly £2,500. There are eight main staircases, besides six minor ones, all of which are fireproof. In addition to the usual entrances there is a private one in Hart Street, with a staircase attached, leading to the royal box, and also a separate entrance and staircase leading to the box of the Duke of Bedford. The architect of this splendid structure was Mr. E. M. Barry; the contractors Messrs. Lucas; and the sum originally calculated, £60,000, but the estimate was greatly exceeded, and the actual cost has been computed at more than £70,000.

The new theatre is said to be of the same size as La Scala at Milan, which up to that time had the reputation of being the largest theatre in Europe, or perhaps in the world. The interior decorations are of a very chaste and elegant design.

It was opened on the 15th of May, 1858, by Mr. Harrison, in conjunction with Miss Louisa Pyne, with Meyerbeer's opera of *Les Huguenots*, which was performed to an overflowing audience, the numbers present on that occasion being 300 in excess of the estimate of a "full house;" and it was under their management that Balfe's celebrated opera of *Satanella* was produced with the greatest success. It was called by the critics of the time Balfe's "happy inspiration."

It would be a work of supererogation to mention the names of the great artists who within the last forty years have made their world-wide reputation upon these boards. Who of the present generation needs to be reminded of Adelina Patti, who rose upon the horizon of the musical world in 1861, and has reigned ever since queen of song and of hearts; of Pauline Lucca, equally fascinating and capricious; of the stately Titiens, always in splendid song, the only soprano that recalls to the connoisseur the singing of Pasta, Malibran, or Grisi; of Trebelli or Albani; of Nordica, Calvé, or Melba; of Santley, Faure, Nicolini, or Tamberlik; of the de Reszkes, Maurel, or Alvary?

For ten years after the opening of the new theatre in Covent Garden, the lessees of the rival opera-houses were fully occupied in endeavouring to solve the vexed question whether two such establishments simultaneously carried on, in opposition to one another, could be made to pay. In 1869 the belligerents, believing that the solution of the problem was to be found only in a coalition of forces, entered into partnership; but difficulties beset them from the very commencement, and the ultimate result was far from satisfactory, and, to begin with, Sir Michael Costa, the dignified *chef d'orchestre* at Covent Garden, declined to countenance the scheme, and withdrew his august services; Signors Arditi and Li Calsi being thereupon appointed to conduct by turns. Next, differences of opinion (to speak very mildly) arose among the "bright, particular stars" of the amalgamated companies, and terminated with the secession of Mdlles. Nilsson and Di Murska, and Signors Foli, Santley, Arditi, and others. Finally, the general public began to be dissatisfied, for a brisk competition between those who cater for its amusement is always an advantage, and monopoly of any sort invariably ends in mediocrity. Before the conclusion of the year 1870 the fusion had terminated in "confusion worse confounded;" Messrs. Mapleson and Gye had dissolved their brief partnership, and the season of 1871 saw them again in rivalry. But in the end the Covent Garden house triumphed, and its chief competitor has now given place to Mr. Beerbohm Tree's new theatre. A few years ago Covent Garden came into the hands of the late Sir Augustus Harris, the lessee of Drury Lane, under whose spirited management it enjoyed several brilliant seasons of opera, mainly German and modern Italian. A marked change has come over the taste of the English public in regard to opera, due mainly to the growing influence of Wagner, whose music-dramas are now appreciated hardly less in this country than in Germany.

Adjoining the theatre, on the southern side, is the Floral Hall, erected about the year 1860, somewhat on the plan of the original Crystal Palace in Hyde Park; but of this we shall have more to say in a subsequent chapter.

It may be interesting here to make a note of the fact recorded in Forster's "Life of Dickens," that when he was about twenty years old he applied to Mr. Bartley, the then manager of Covent Garden, for an engagement at that theatre, and that a day was fixed for him to make trial of his powers. When the day came he was laid up with a bad cold, and could not appear; his trial was therefore postponed till the next season. In the meantime he had made himself famous by his pen, and so he took to literature instead. Possibly to that "bad cold" we owe "Pickwick," "Nicholas Nickleby," and "Oliver Twist."

We have thus endeavoured to compress into a few pages an outline of the history of the two leading theatres, and, indeed, for many years, the only theatres of London. But the whole neighbourhood around Covent Garden teems with theatrical reminiscences, for which a volume, in reality, would scarcely suffice. We will, however, endeavour, in the following chapters, to skim lightly over the ground, yet carefully, and as exhaustively as possible, rambling about from street to street, as the bee flits from flower to flower, and sipping here and there from the stores of past history of the Stuart and Hanoverian ages.

CHAPTER XXX.

COVENT GARDEN:—GENERAL DESCRIPTION.

"Hail, market, hail, to all Megarians dear !"—*Aristophanes, "Acharnians."*

Extent of the District—Covent Garden in the Fourteenth Century—The Site passes into the hands of the Duke of Somerset, and afterwards the Earls of Bedford—Origin of the Market—Annals of Covent Garden—The Fashionable Days of Covent Garden—The Piazzas as a Promenade—History of the Market—The Sun-dial—The Hackney-coach Stands—The Mohocks and other Marauders.

THE region which we intend to embrace in this and the following chapter, extending, to speak roughly, from St. Martin's Lane on the west to Drury Lane on the east, and from Long Acre on the north to the Strand on the south—in other words, considerably less than half a mile the one way and a quarter of a mile the other—is remarkable as including in its circuit more of literary, and, indeed, of human interest, than any other spot in modern or ancient London. That interest belongs chiefly, if not wholly, to the last two centuries ; and the memorials of it are scattered on every side of us in such thick profusion, that one can almost fancy we can see the *genius loci* standing there and pointing around him with his wand, and exclaiming, "Si monumentum requiris, circumspice ;" like Sir Christopher Wren in the cathedral church of St. Paul. In the well-known words of the " Connoisseur," the neighbourhood of Covent Garden was in the last century—though it is no longer— "the acknowledged region of gallantry, wit, and criticism." And doubtless it was as a frequenter of this neighbourhood, and in love with the good literary society which its coffee-houses afforded, that Johnson assented with a " Why yes, sir," to Boswell's frank avowal that "the vicinity of the Strand was much better than Blackheath Park."

The latter half of the seventeenth century formed an important epoch in the growth of western London. We see from the Plan of London, published by Aggas in 1562, that it was then comparatively a small place, almost entirely confined to the limits of the City proper. But our capital "found itself so secure in the glorious government of Elizabeth," that by the year 1600 very considerable additions were made to the north of the long line of street now known as the Strand, and the gap between London proper and Westminster was nearly filled up.

Covent Garden—a corruption, we need hardly say, of "the Convent Garden"—was an enclosure belonging, as far back as the first quarter of the thirteenth century, to the abbots of Westminster, who it is supposed used the site as the burial-place for the convent, as being at a convenient distance for "burying their dead out of sight." Here were "fair spreading pastures" seven acres in extent, now all swallowed up in the general name of "Long Acre ;" the present Long Acre, which was built in the reign of Charles I., being carried from the north-east towards the south-west—from the middle of St. Martin's Lane and the top of Drury Lane. It is said that where Long Acre runs there was once an avenue of stately elms, whose shade was grateful to the citizens of London when they walked out on holydays ; and that there were country lanes with green fields on either side.

In the map of Ralph Aggas above alluded to, Covent Garden is shown as enclosed by a brick wall, which runs straight on the north side, parallel with these shady elms ; whilst the southern side is bounded by the houses and small inclosures abutting upon the Strand highway. Nearly in the middle of the old garden there appear to be some small buildings, probably the dwellings of gardeners and other workmen, and the trees are scattered up and down the place so thick as to give it the appearance almost of a wilderness. "A large pond," writes Newton in his " London in the Olden Time," "is said to have existed near the middle of Covent Garden two centuries ago. It was fed partly by a running stream from the higher grounds, and partly by a local spring which still supplies a pump near the modern parish church. The overflow from this pond would pass by Ivy Bridge Lane down to the Thames."

Stow himself makes no mention of Covent Garden ; but Strype tells us that it probably had the name of the Convent Garden, " because it was the garden and field of that large convent and monastery where Exeter House formerly stood." But here, no doubt, Strype is in error, for there are no traces of a " convent" or "monastery" on that site ; and according to general tradition this convent garden belonged to the abbot and monks of Westminster, by whom it was used partly as their kitchen garden, supplying, no doubt, not only the wants of that religious community, but also the public markets, and so bringing in an income to the abbey, and partly as a burial-ground, as already stated. This supposition is confirmed by the fact that in digging for the foundations of the new market in 1829, a quantity of human bones was exhumed on the north side of the area.

Walter Savage Landor thus quaintly and pointedly describes the change which came over the Convent Garden of the monks of Westminster :—" The Convent becomes a playhouse ; monks and nuns turn actors and actresses. The garden, formal and quiet, where a salad was cut for a lady abbess, and flowers were gathered to adorn images, becomes a market, noisy and full of life, distributing thousands of fruits and flowers to a vicious metropolis." It is to be feared, from the turn of his expressions here, that Landor did not remember that the Latin *conventus*, and its French equivalent, *couvent*, is strictly applied to the houses of religious men as well as women ; if so, it is more probable that a salad cut on this spot was destined for the Abbot of St. Peter's, Westminster, and not for an abbess. But this is a matter of no great moment.

At the dissolution of the religious houses this property came into the hands of the Duke of Somerset, on whose attainder in 1552 it was given by the Crown to John Russell, Earl of Bedford, under the description of " Covent Garden, lying in the parish of St. Martin's-in-the-Fields next Charing Cross, with seven acres called Long Acre, of the yearly value of six pounds six shillings and eight pence."

It is probable that for a very long time after the Russells became possessed of this property, it still remained a garden, or at all events consisted of open fields ; for in 1627, as Mr. P. Cunningham tells us, " only two persons were rated to the poor of the parish of St. Martin's-in-the-Fields under the head of ' Covent Garden.' "

" If we add an ' n ' to ' Covent,' and say Convent Garden," observes a writer in the *City Press*, " we shall go back to the old days when nuns or friars studied their missals in the church orchard, and then we shall think of Henry VIII., and the Bedford family with their slice of consecrated ground. It was then, and long after, in the country, and was probably used for pasture until the growing population made it an object to possess a market." How the work prospered may be gathered in some measure from the fragmentary accounts which have reached us. The *Spectator* speaks of daily prayer at the Garden Church, and tells us how fine ladies, with black pages carrying their books, walked across the market to their pews. Even at the beginning of the century the arrangements were very primitive. " The middle walk consisted of odd, tumble-down shed shops, though the fruit, flowers, and vegetables were excellent. Crockery-ware was sold in several of them. There were two medical herb-shops, where you could purchase leeches ; and snails, then employed to make broth for con-

sumptive patients, were vended. Also a well-known itinerant bird-dealer had a stall, where he sold larks, canaries, owls, and, if you desired it, could get you a talking parrot, or manufacture you a love-bird, on the shortest notice. ' Quality folks ' often walked in the centre avenue, but there was no accommodation for choice plants on the roof. The ducal proprietor improved the market into its present state ; but of course far more might be done with the present site. Covent Garden was used for many years as a pasture-ground, and was subsequently let on a building lease. Then the square was planned, and Inigo Jones designed it. The piazza, which runs round a part of it, was also his work. The market originated casually. Vendors of vegetables and fruit from the neighbouring villages used the centre of the square as a market ; and, in lapse of time, the market grew into a recognised institution. It was strangely unsightly, being but a rude combination of stalls and sheds. But in 1831 the present market buildings were erected at the Duke of Bedford's expense ; and, a few years later, open-air accommodation was obtained on the roof, at the entrance, for the sale of plants, &c. The duke derives a considerable revenue from the rents and tolls. It is quite a problem to what the tolls amount. Those who occupy shops or stands by the week or year, and who sell the greater part of the produce brought in, merely pay their rents as for ordinary shops. Some of them, though held only from week to week, have continued in the same families through two or even three generations.

" The early morning at Covent Garden affords a curious sight. From 3.30 to 4.30 there is little bustle in the market, though business goes on rapidly. Early risers of both sexes—a class of ' higglers ' who indorse the old proverb that ' the early bird catches the worm '—flock to the market. They form a medium between the grower and the small dealer, buying the whole stock from the former, and seeking to sell portions of it to the latter at a higher price. The crowd and bustle increase from five o'clock up to seven or eight. Porters, with baskets, offer their help to buyers. The piazzas become very lively with their clamour. Against every post and pillar are small tables, where coffee, tea, bread and butter may be purchased. Hawkers parade in every direction with cakes, buns, knives, and pocket-books for sale. Many customers seek for stimulants, and consume gin or hot spirits-and-water with avidity.

" In our climate piazzas were a novelty—we seldom need to exclude the sun—yet those in Covent Garden became popular. Long afterwards two piazzas were erected in Regent Street, and termed the 'Colonnade,' but they were not a success and have been removed. Those in Covent Garden, though much dishonoured, still (1870) remain; and are, perhaps, the only buildings in that style in England." Thus Byron says in "Beppo"—

June 24 following. The poet Dryden was assaulted in Covent Garden, on account of some verses in his 'Hind and Panther.' 1687, April 14. A soldier, William Grant, hanged in the market for running from his colours. 1636. This date is cut in a stone let into the brickwork of No. 23, King

ENTRANCE TO COVENT GARDEN MARKET, 1870.

" For, bating Covent Garden, I can hit on
     No place that's called 'Piazza' in Great Britain."

The following is given by the same authority as a brief epitome of the annals of Covent Garden. We shall enlarge upon it as we proceed in our survey :— " The market buildings were commenced in 1632 by the Earl of Bedford. 1650, April 26. Col. Poyse was shot to death in the market. 1675, December 29. A proclamation issued against coffee-houses. 1679, January 8. To allow their continuance till

Street, of Evans's Hotel, we are told. It formed a prominent object in Hogarth's print, 'Morning.' And here lodged Sir William Alexander, Earl of Stirling, 1637; Thomas Killigrew, 1640; Denzil Hollis, 1644; and in 1647, Sir Harry Vane, and also Sir Kenelm Digby, 1662. Of Hollis this anecdote is told :—In a hot debate in Parliament, Ireton offended Hollis, upon which he persuaded him to walk out of the House, and told him he must fight to justify his words. Ireton pleaded that 'his conscience would not suffer him to fight a duel;' upon which Hollis pulled him by the nose, saying, ' If his conscience forbade his giving men satisfaction, it should also keep him from provoking them.' We are assured that nearly all the foundlings of St. Paul, Covent Garden, were laid at the door of Nathaniel, Lord Crewe, Bishop of Durham."

Covent Garden was made into a separate parish in 1645, and the patronage of it vested in the Russell family; the district which it comprises

son, Sir R. Steele, Otway, Dryden, Pope, Warburton, Cibber, Fielding, Churchill, Bolingbroke, and Dr. Johnson; Rich, Woodward, Booth, Wilkes, Garrick, and Macklin; Kitty Clive, "Peg" Woffington, Mrs. Pritchard, the Duchess of Bolton, Lady Derby, Lady Thurlow, and the Duchess of St. Alban's; Sir Peter Lely, Sir Godfrey Kneller, and Sir James Thornhill; Vandevelde, Zincke, Lambert, Hogarth, Hayman, Wilson, Dance, Meyer, and Samuel Foote. But even to this list it would be possible to make many additions.

COVENT GARDEN MARKET, LOOKING EASTWARD.   (*From a Print of* 1786.)

being cut off under the provisions of a special Act of Parliament from that of St. Martin's-in-the-Fields. The parish church was dedicated to St. Paul.

In the days of the first two Georges the parish was, if not the fashionable part of the town, at all events a fashionable district, and the residence of a great number of persons of title and high rank, as well as of men known in the world of art and literature. "A concourse of arts, literary characters and other men of genius frequented the numerous coffee-houses, wine and cider-cellars, &c., within the boundaries of Covent Garden," says Mr. Timbs, who adds the following formidable list of persons whose names are connected with the place:—Butler, Addi-

Strange as it may appear, Covent Garden was for a long period fashionable as a residence and a promenade. From 1666 down to 1700 the following noble persons tenanted the Piazzas:—Lords Hollis, Brownlow, Lucas, Newport, Barkham; Crewe, Bishop of Durham, Duke of Richmond, Earl of Oxford, Sir Godfrey Kneller, Sir Edward Flood, Sir Kenelm Digby, Earl of Bedford, Hon. Colonel Russell, Bishop of St. David's, Marquis of Winchester, Earl of Sussex, and the Earl of Peterborough, in the house where the auctioneer Robins afterwards flourished.

Earl Ferrers, who was executed in 1760 for the murder of his steward, was living in Covent Garden in 1722. Even so lately as the reign of George II.

Covent Garden retained much of its fashionable character. At all events, in the March of 1730 the *Daily Advertiser* gravely tells its readers that "the Lady Mary Wortley Montague, who has been greatly indisposed at her house in Covent Garden for some time, is now perfectly recovered, and takes the benefit of the air in Hyde Park every morning, by advice of her physicians." The same journal for June 10, 1731, tells us that, "A few days ago the Right Hon. the Lady Mary Wortley Montague set out from her house in Covent Garden for Bath."

The Piazzas attracted many remarkable literary and scientific persons. In addition to Sir Godfrey Kneller, several gifted painters chose them for their studios—viz., John Zoffany, Aggas, Sir Peter Lely, Peter Roestraten, Mrs. S. P. Rose (a famous water-colourist), and John Mortimer Hamilton. Benjamin West, too, when he first came from America, resided in Covent Garden. The neighbouring streets also—King Street, Henrietta Street, &c.—were crowded with "persons of quality" and artists.

The area of Covent Garden, when as yet it had not been set aside for the worship of the goddess Pomona, was a fine open space, which served as a playground for the youths of London and Westminster, lying as it did half-way between each city. To this fact Gay alludes in his "Trivia," every line obviously being a sketch drawn from the life :—

"Where Covent Garden's famous temple stands,
That boasts the work of Jones' immortal hands,
Columns with plain magnificence appear,
And graceful porches lead along the square.
Here oft my course I bend, when, lo ! from far
I spy the furies of the football war.
The 'prentice quits his shop to join the crew ;
Increasing crowds the flying game pursue.
O whither shall I run ? the throng draws nigh,
The ball now skims the street, now soars on high ;
The dext'rous glazier strong returns the bound,
And jingling sashes on the penthouse sound."

But it is time to enter into a more detailed account of the district. The large square, with the fruit and vegetable market in its centre, which is known to every Londoner and to most Englishmen as "Covent Garden," was laid out during 1630-31 by Francis, fourth Earl of Bedford, from the designs of Inigo Jones. In all probability the Square was never completed, its sides being built at different times ; and Peter Cunningham was of opinion that they may not have been even "designed in full." The Arcade or Piazza, however, ran along not only the north but the whole of the eastern side. That part to the south of Russell Street, however, was burnt down, and the Piazza was never replaced, probably from motives of economy.

The church of St. Paul, erected between the years 1631 and 1638, also from the design of Inigo Jones, formed, as it still forms, the western side of "the Garden," whilst its southern side for many years was formed by a blank wall which bounded the garden of Bedford House. Along this ran a row of trees, under the shade of which the market was originally held, and afterwards in a few temporary stalls and sheds.

The Square, or "Market-place," as it is often called in books and documents of the date of the Rebellion and of Charles II., seems to have grown gradually in importance as a place of business. Its inhabitants doubtless were proud of it, and foresaw that in the course of time it would prove a source of income and profit. Accordingly we find the parishioners of St. Paul's, in 1656, taxing themselves for painting the benches and seats there, and ten years later for planting a new row of trees ; and between 1665 and 1668 the wealthier residents subscribed various sums towards setting up the column and dial mentioned below. It was not, however, until 1671 that the market was formally established under a charter granted by the king to the Earl of Bedford ; and Mr. Cunningham tells us that eight years later, when the market was the first time actually rated to the poor, there were twenty-three salesmen amenable to the rate. For a contemporary description of the market as it was in 1689, we fortunately have Strype to refer to. He writes :—

"The south side of Covent Garden Square lieth open to Bedford Garden, where there is a small grotto of trees, most pleasant in the summer season ; and on this side there is kept a market for fruits, herbs, roots, and flowers every Tuesday, Thursday, and Saturday ; which is grown to a considerable account, and well served with choice goods, which makes it much resorted to." It would appear, however, from another passage in Strype, that at this time it was inferior as a market to the "Stocks' Market" in the City—of which we have already spoken *—afterwards transferred to the west side of Farringdon Street. In 1710, as we can see by a print published in that year, the market was still restricted to a few stalls and sheds on the south side.

Before the middle of the century, however, a great change had come over the place : the streets around being largely inhabited by well-to-do persons and their dependents, the market gradually increased ; and the small hucksters and retail dealers began to erect sleeping apartments

* See Vol. I., p. 436 ; Vol. II., p. 497.

over their stalls to such an extent as to provoke a memorial from the inhabitants in vestry assembled to the Duke of Bedford, complaining of this encroachment as prejudicial to the tradesmen and fair dealers.

The prints of the square, at the time of which we write, show the inclosure as gravelled, and fenced in with rows of low posts and chains. In its centre was a fluted column of the Corinthian order, with a sun-dial on the top, which would appear by an inscription to have been erected in 1668. Thornton, in his "Survey of London and Westminster" (1786), speaks of the column as surrounded by *four* sun-dials, and informs us that the inner portion of the Square at that time was surrounded by light wooden rails.

The column, as we learn from another source, stood on a pedestal, which was raised upon six steps of black marble. The capital was very much enriched; it supported a square stone, *three* sides of which served as sun-dials. Upon this stone stood a globe, supported by four scrolls. It was removed in June, 1790.

Upon the steps of this column sat sundry old women who sold milk, porridge, barley-broth, &c., and to whom allusion is thus made in a *brochure* entitled "The Humours of Covent Garden," published in 1738:—

> "High in the midst of this most happy land
> A well-built marble pyramid does stand,
> By which spectators know the time o' th' day
> From beams reflecting of the solar ray ;
> Its basis with ascending steps is grac'd,
> Around whose area cleanly matrons plac'd
> Vend their most wholesome food, by Nature good,
> To cheer the spirits and enrich the blood."

Mr. Peter Cunningham reminds us that the scene of Dryden's *Sir Martin Mar-all* is laid in this once fashionable quarter of the town, and that allusions to the Square, the Church, and the Piazza are of constant occurrence in the dramas of the reigns of Charles II., James II., William and Mary, and Anne. Thus the Piazza is the locality of a scene in *The Soldier's Fortune* of Otway, and also of one in *The Country Wife* of Wycherley.

There were plenty of stands for hackney coaches in and around Covent Garden at the commencement of the reign of George III., and Voltaire probably often used them in passing backwards and forwards between the theatres and his lodgings in Maiden Lane. The forms and shapes of these lumbering vehicles are familiar to all who know Kip's prints of the period referred to.

Such, then, in its main and leading features, was and is the district which will occupy our attention during the next two or three chapters, a district most interesting in a literary point of view, though the coffee-house and theatrical elements will be found, we fear, to predominate very much over that of domestic life. In fact, with the exception of certain actresses, and a few grand ladies of "the quality," the feminine element is "conspicuous by its absence," the coffee-houses of the last century being the equivalent of the clubs and club-land of the present.

The vicinity, however, it is only fair to state here, bore scarcely a higher repute on quite another score. At night it was simply unsafe for pedestrians. For was not Dryden waylaid and beaten by Mohocks or Mohawks at the corner of Rose Street and King Street? In spite of this fact, however, and although it is well known that certain parts of London, Hyde Park for instance, a century ago were very unsafe thoroughfares, on account of footpads and highway robbers, we may raise a smile of incredulity on the faces of some of our readers when we quote the following remarks from Shenstone, in the reign of George II. :—

"London is really dangerous at this time ; the pickpockets, formerly content with mere filching, make no scruple to knock people down with bludgeons in Fleet Street and the Strand, and that at no later hour than eight o'clock at night ; but in the Piazzas, Covent Garden, they come in large bodies, armed with couteaus, and attack whole parties, so that the danger of coming out of the playhouses is of some weight in the opposite scale when I am disposed to go to them oftener than I ought." And in like manner, and with the same meaning, Shadwell in one of his plays makes a character remark : "They were brave fellows indeed ; for in those days a man could not go from the 'Rose' Tavern to the Piazza once but he must venture his life twice."

The Mohocks are well described in the *Spectator*, and in Swift's *Journal;* and Shadwell's comedy of *The Scourers* affords a striking picture of the dangerous state of the streets of London at night in the early part of the eighteenth century. In reference to this, Gay writes :—

> "Who has not heard the Scourers' midnight fame?
> Who has not trembled at the Mohocks' name?"

"These disorderly ruffians," observes Mr. Peter Cunningham, "seldom ventured within the City proper, where the watch was more efficient than in any other part; but took their stand about St. Clement Danes and Covent Garden, breaking the watchman's lantern and halbert, and frequently locking him up in his own stand-box." The curious reader may find much amusing information on this subject in the old ballad of "The Ranting

Rambler, or a Young Gentleman's Frolic through the City at night, and when he was taken by the Watch," printed in Mackay's "Songs of the London Prentices' and Traders;" and in Arthur Murphy's letters to David Garrick will be found a graphic sketch of one of the best of the race, known as

"Tiger Roach," the bully of the "Bedford Coffee-house" in 1769.

It is satisfactory to know that, thanks to the police, both the Piazza and King Street are to be traversed now-a-days with less danger to life and limb.

CHAPTER XXXI.

COVENT GARDEN (*continued*).

"Thames Street gives cheeses, Covent Garden fruits;
Moorfields old books, and Monmouth Street old suits."—*Gay's Trivia*.

The Market described—The Covent Garden of the Past and Present contrasted—Best Time to view the Market—The Flower Market—The Piazza—The Irish Society of Fortune-hunters—Pepys in the Piazza—Theodore Hook and Sheridan—The Puppet Show—The "Bedford Coffee House"—The Floral Hall—The "Hummums"—"Evans's Hotel"—The Old Supper Room—The New Hall—Famous Residents in Covent Garden—Auction Rooms—Marriage à-la-Mode.

IT is now, however, time to proceed to a more minute description of Covent Garden itself. The present market, which occupies all the centre of the square, consists of a central arcade and two side rows of shops, intersected in the centre by another thoroughfare at right angles. It was built, in 1830, by John, sixth Duke of Bedford, whose architect was Mr. William Fowler. The centre consists of an arch raised upon the entablature of two Tuscan columns, with a single-faced archivolt supported by two piers, which carry a lofty triangular pediment, the tympanum of which is embellished by the armorial bearings of the noble owner of the soil, his Grace the Duke of Bedford. On each side of this appropriate centre, which is high enough to admit a lofty loaded wagon into the central area, is a colonnade of the Tuscan order, projecting before the shops. The columns are of granite; and over the east end is the inscription, "JOHN, DUKE OF BEDFORD. Erected MDCCCXXX."

At each of the extreme angles of the four portions of this new market are raised quadrangular pavilions, which break the monotony of the composition in a very satisfactory and artistic manner, for they are at the same time useful and ornamental. The area of the market is about three acres, and it forms the principal mart of the metropolis for fruit, vegetables and flowers.

Those who wish to see the sight and smell the scent of fresh flowers in London in the summer should pay a visit to Covent Garden before, or, at the latest, soon after sunrise on Tuesday, Thursday, or Saturday; but the central arcade is a pretty sight at whatever time, and in whatever season, it may be visited.

"The contrast between the Covent Garden of fifty years ago and the present," says Mr. Diprose, in his "Book about London," "is as wide a one

as can possibly exist. The old watchman—helpless for good, and the most corrupt of public officers—the turbulent and drunken old women, the porters quarrelling over their morning potations, the jaded and neglected horse dropping beneath the cart-load of half-rotten turnips, the London rakes—(fast men of those days)—making, not the night, but morning, hideous by their obscene blasphemies, and deeming it conduct becoming of gentlemen to interrupt honest industry and to scoff at early labour;—all this has gone, and so also are the terrible lessons that it inculcated. Order is now preserved as well as it can be amongst a rude assemblage of women and men whose battle for existence begins when the civilisation of the great city slumbers."

"There is no *rus in urbe*," writes Charles Kenny, "like Covent Garden Market. Here Nature empties forth her teeming lap filled with the choicest of produce. . . . It is the metropolitan congress of the vegetable kingdom, where every department of the 'growing' and 'blowing' world has its representatives—the useful and the ornamental, the needful and the superfluous, the esculent and the medicinal. It is a twofold temple, dedicated to Pomona and Flora, in which daily devotion is paid to the productive divinities. Here, as in a very temple, all classes and grades, all denominations and distinctions of men jostle each other in the humility of a common dependence on the same appetites, the same instincts, the same organs of taste, sight, and smell—the fashionable lady, who has left her brougham at the entrance, in quest of some pampered nursling of the conservatory, and the wan needlewoman bent on the purchase of a bunch of wallflowers, or a root of pale primroses to keep her paler cheeks in countenance; the artisan's wife, purveying for her husband's meal, and the comfortable housekeeper, primed with the discriminating lore of Mrs. Glass, making provisions for her winter's preserves ; the bloated *gourmand*, in search of precocious peas, and the sickly hypochondriac eager to try the virtue of some healing herb.

"The priestesses who serve the temple form two distinct classes—those of Pomona and those of Flora—the basket-woman and the bouquet-girl. As to the former, hers is no finiking type of female beauty ; the taper waist and slender neck would ill befit the rude labours she is devoted to. Her portly figure is rather architectural than sculptural in its graces ; and with arms upraised, in support of the basket balanced on her head, she might serve as a model for the caryatids of a new temple to the deity she serves.

" He who would behold her in full activity must gratify his curiosity at some expense. He must voluntarily accomplish that which is enforced upon the vegetable visitor of the market—he must tear himself from his bed, foregoing the suavities of the morning's sleep to face the bleak air of dawning day : unless, indeed, he repair to the scene, as we have often done, as a sort of 'finish'—to use the language of antiquated fast men—after a round of evening parties, his temples throbbing with an unhallowed mixture of festive beverages, from the bland negus to the ice-bound fire of champagne punch ; his senses jaded with a thousand artificial and violent delights ; and, perhaps, a secret wound rankling at his heart—a wound that he has attempted to treat with light indifference, and to bury under a hecatomb of flirtations, but which now asserts itself with redoubled pangs, and mingles its reproaches to the many-voiced objurgations of conscience to sicken and disgust him with his existence. Under such circumstances is it that the most striking phase of Covent Garden—that which it presents on the morning of a market-day—will produce its fullest effect.

" Towards the afternoon another and very different phase of the market is presented. To the range of heavy-tilted carts and wagons has succeeded a line of brilliant and elegant equipages. The *utile* has given place to the *dulce*, and pleasure now shows itself almost as busy as need. Over this period of the day Flora more especially presides, and the bouquet-girl—her priestess—is in the height of her ministry. Her delicate fingers are now busily employed in tricking out the loveliness of Nature ; for even her loveliest daughters must be drilled and trained ere they can make their *début* in the world of artifice they are called upon to adorn. Their slender stems need a wiry support to prop

the head that else would droop in the oppressive atmosphere of the ball-room or the theatre. Art must draw fresh beauties from the contrast of each with the other ; nor will the self-complacent ingenuity that paints the lily and gilds refined gold be satisfied till it has completed their toilet by investing them in a white robe of broidered paper.

"The clients of the bouquet-girl consist almost exclusively of the sighing herd of lovers. These, with the exception of an occasional wholesale order from the manager of a theatre with a view to some triumphant *début*, form the staple consumers of her wares. But among the whole tribe she has no such insatiate customer as he who is struggling in the toils of a *danseuse*. 'If music be the food of love,' bouquets are certainly the very air upon the regular supply of which hangs its existence ; and on such air does the *danseuse*, chameleon-like, seem exclusively to live. They are the Alpha and Omega, the beginning and the end of her life— the symbols of her triumphs, public and domestic."

Covent Garden Market, it is true, is a limited arena, in comparison with its requirements, and consequently on market mornings the streets and avenues around, for half a mile, are thronged with merchants and traders, with heavy carts or wagons, from the elegantly painted light van to the hand-cart of the humble coster. "The apparent tumult of these occasions," says Mr. Diprose, in his "Book about London," "is all sober business, and the earnestness of all present is most remarkable to a stranger, who is apt to look upon the scene as one of the wildest uproar and confusion. The thousands of tons of vegetables and fruit are dispersed through every avenue and artery of the metropolis by nine o'clock, and the market is then apparently emptied ; excepting the many choice fruits and early vegetables to be found in the beautiful arcade, when the peaceable folks arrive on the exquisite mission of discovering delicacies for some poor cast-down invalid friend ; and it is in this long-continued arch that the bouquets are made for the evening exhibitions which do such terrible mischief in Cupid's calendar, at balls, theatre, opera, concert, and in the private boudoir of my 'ladye-love.' "

A visit to Covent Garden Market in the early morning in summer is a sight that should not be missed. Between the hours of one and five there is apparently little bustle in the market, though business goes on rapidly ; and the scene presented is curious in the extreme. It is one of those phases of life in which Charles Dickens delighted, and which would require the pen of Swift, or Sterne, or Fielding, to describe adequately and picturesquely, as it deserves. It has been sketched slightly by several hands, but by none perhaps as effectively as it might be. Nor can this be a matter of wonder; for in order to get a view of the scene an effort is required which would be too great a tax on the energies of a hard-worked man of letters in London, and would involve an amount of self-denial beyond his powers. But at all

stones, and scrambled for by porters, who die early through exhaustion and excessive labour at unseemly hours. Then it is that the citizen's dinner is tossed to and fro, smoking with the temperature it has attained by close packing and long confinement, and is at last consigned to an unclean cart, for the district where its destiny is to be completed. The citizens are happily ignorant of

POWELL'S PUPPET-SHOW. *From a Contemporary Print.* (*See page* 250.)

events, it is freely granted that "this *market*" is the most popular, not only in England, but throughout the world. "When I had no money," writes Charles Dickens, "I took a turn in Covent Garden, and stared at the pine-apples."

"People who know Covent Garden only in its quiet afternoon aspect," says a writer in the *City Press*, describing things as they were five-and-twenty years or so ago, "can form no idea of the vile den it is at the busy hour of daybreak. Then the cabbages and peas that have been fermenting in the wagons for some hours past are tilted out on the flag-

the copper used in cooking, and the preliminary cooking vegetables are subjected to on their way to and from the market. We are fully cognisant of the fact that Spitalfields and Farringdon absorb some portion of the trade in vegetables; but Covent Garden is *the* market, *par excellence*, and it is a disgrace to the metropolis to be compelled to rely on the capabilities of a place which, spacious as it may be, is fitted at the very utmost to serve as a market for a town of 60,000 inhabitants."

"The flower market of Covent Garden," observes a clever American writer, "is carried on in

COVENT GARDEN MARKET ABOUT 1820.

the open area opposite the church, and at the entrance of the grand row of shops which runs down the centre. The growers chiefly bring their productions into the market at or before midnight, and about one o'clock is the briskest period of the sale, the road being rendered almost impassable from the number of basket-women and others taking in their supply for the day of flowers in pots, as well as cut flowers. A more animated scene of the bustle of business, with the gay and varied hue of the flowers, and their delightful fragrance, it is scarcely possible to describe, than that which continues till about four or five o'clock, when the traders, having generally exhausted their stock, return home, and the dealers are on their way to supply their different walks and routes for the day. The peripatetic dealers having obtained their supply, the next who come in for their share are the various greengrocers of the metropolis, who take but a limited supply; whilst the remnants are left to salesmen for the day's demand of the market. The chief source of the costermonger's market is in the metropolis; and their supply being exhausted on other days but those of the market-days of Tuesday, Thursday, and Saturday, they replenish their stock from the nurserymen, who may be considered the manufacturers, in the neighbourhood of the metropolis, from whom the limited and humble flora of the metropolis is supplied. It is amusing likewise to contemplate the variety of persons who, at an early hour in the morning, are the visitants of the Market. There are the humble trader trafficking with the grower for his day's supply; the rake or the *roué*, and the unhappy companion of his night's frolic and dissipation, retiring to their unhallowed rest, whilst others are actively employed in the business of the day; the sot reeling home from his night's debauch, unfitted for the occupation which demands his exertion; the unfortunate, who, homeless, has wandered the streets, and contemplates luxuries in which he cannot indulge; and others induced to visit thus early this fac-simile, as it may be termed, of the most interesting of country enjoyments in the pursuit of health and pleasurable gratification. Such compose the motley group which we jostle against in an early visit to Covent Garden Market.

"The nature of the supply of flowers to the market of course depends upon the season; but it is surprising to what an extent *art* has beaten *nature* in the race for priority. In the midst of winter Covent Garden Market shows all the realities of advanced and advancing spring. In February we have primulas, mignonette, wallflowers, violets, tulips, hyacinths, narcissuses,

and other forced bulbs; in March, forced verbenas, camellias, epacrises, the heaths of Australia, lilacs, rhododendrons, azaleas, the honeysuckles of the American woods, and kalmias; in April these are more numerous, with a variety of hybrid heaths, acacias, forced roses, and pelargoniums; in May a greater variety of heaths are coming to perfection; and now also we have, in large and interesting variety, pelargoniums or geraniums, the standard flower of English ornament; mignonette, which has continued in perfection all through this artificial season, is now very abundant, and the beautiful China roses add a variety to the scene. In June the varieties of pelargoniums are in full perfection, and upwards of one hundred distinct sorts grace the show in the market; so great being the supply at this time of year that frequently from five to six hundred dozens are daily sent by growers. We have now the beautiful pendant fuchsias, many sorts of verbenas, cactuses, hydrangeas, cockscombs, balsams, stocks, heartsease; and pinks and picotees will soon be added to enliven the floral scene. Now, too, we have the pretty gardenia or Cape jasmine; and the sweet-scented lemon-plant. The flower-market is at the acme of its perfection, and the usual variety of supply continues, with little variation, till the autumnal months."

Some idea may be formed of the taste for flowers in London, and the extent of trade done in them, by reading a case of bankruptcy before Mr. Registrar Brougham, October 19th, 1871, at the hearing of which a proof was put in for £353 for flowers supplied in six months to one individual. Among the items were charges of 10s. 6d. for a moss-rose, and £150 for lilies of the valley and ferns.

A new building has been erected in the southeast corner of the market-place, in which the wholesale business of the flower-market is mainly carried on. The structure possesses little or nothing in the way of architectural pretensions, and has its principal entrance in Wellington Street.

At Wilton House, near Salisbury, the seat of the Earl of Pembroke, there is a fine picture of Covent Garden, painted by Inigo Jones himself. It represents the place in its original state, with a tree standing in the middle. A companion picture by the same artist, as already stated, it may be added, gives a view of Lincoln's Inn Fields when first built upon.

The houses on the north and east sides of the market inclosure, as already mentioned, were so built as to form a covered pathway before the shopfronts, which was commonly known as the Piazza. The name "piazza," as every scholar knows, means in the Italian simply "place," or "square;" but with us it denotes an open arcade of semi-cloistral appearance. Such an arcade, running round the north and part of the east side of the great Square of Covent Garden, came, we know not exactly how, to be called "The Piazza"—possibly an instance of the logical fallacy which puts the part for the whole—and thus the term in English has passed into quite a different signification; and so in Blount's "Glossographia" it is vaguely explained as "a market-place or chief street, such as that in Covent Garden."

The Piazza when first erected was a fashionable lounge, and generally regarded as a work of high artistic merit. Allusions are constantly made to it in the works of the dramatists of the time of the Stuarts and of the first half of the eighteenth century, as a place of appointments and assignations. Peter Cunningham tells us that the north side was called the Great, and the east the Little Piazza; and that so popular and fashionable did the place become, that for a century after its erection many of the female children baptised in the parish were christened "Piazza!"

Thornton, in his "Survey of London and Westminster," published in 1786, says of the Piazza, that if it had been carried around the Square, according to the plan of Inigo Jones, it would have rendered Covent Garden one of the finest squares in Europe. This is perhaps the language of exaggeration; but it certainly is much to be regretted that the design was not carried out in its entirety. Horace Walpole writes: "In the arcade there is nothing very remarkable; the pilasters are as errant and homely stripes as any plasterer could have made." On this Mr. Peter Cunningham very justly remarks: "This is very true now, though hardly true in Walpole's time, when the arcade remained as Inigo Jones had built it, with stone pilasters on a red-brick frontage. The pilasters, as we now see them, are lost in a mass of compo and white paint; the red bricks have been whitened over, and the pitched roof of red tile replaced with flat slates." It will be remembered by readers of the English drama, that in this same piazza Otway has laid one of the scenes in his play, *The Soldier of Fortune.*

In discoursing of this parish, the "London Spy" (1725) observes that "the vicissitude of all human affairs is pretty discernible in the lives of the gamesters who patrol the Piazza for about three hours generally in the afternoon." The writer adds sarcastically, with reference to the freaks of fortune often witnessed here, as now-a-days at Homburg or Baden, "I have known an inauspicious hand of cards or dice transmute a silver-hilted sword into a brass one. . . On the other hand, a pair of second-hand shoes has often here stepped at once into a chariot."

The same authority states that in this parish the Irish Society of Fortune-hunters are said to hold their quarterly meetings; but, as his account of their "transactions" on one of these occasions is clearly an exaggerated piece of satire, it is probable that the statement should be received *cum grano salis.* Little boys used to play a bat game—a sort of cricket—under the Piazza.

Pepys thus writes, in his "Diary," under date of January 2, 1664-5:—"To my Lord Brounker's by appointment, under the Piazza in Covent Garden, where I occasioned much mirth with a ballet [ballad] that I brought with me made from the seamen at sea to their ladies in town." This ballad, it would appear, was none other than the well-known song beginning—

"To all ye ladies now on land."

In the Piazza, close to the steps of Covent Garden Theatre, about 1704, lived Sir Godfrey Kneller, State-painter to five sovereigns of England in succession, and the painter of scores of the leaders of fashion, as well as of the portraits of the "Kit-cat Club."

Here too Wilson, "the English Claude," friend of Garrick and Dr. Arne, had rooms in his palmy days; poor unlucky Wilson, with his Bardolph nose and fondness for porter and skittles! Utter opposite of the courtly Reynolds, Wilson died neglected and forgotten in a little village in Denbighshire; still his fame among connoisseurs now is almost as great as that of the famous portrait-painter, and happy the possessor of one of his classic sunshiny landscapes.

The "Piazza" Hotel, which may now be looked for in vain, was long a favourite resort of Richard Brinsley Sheridan and his friends.

It was by an improvisation at the "Piazza" Tavern that Theodore Hook, when little more than a lad, made that favourable impression on Sheridan which led to his introduction to the gay West-end circles in which for many years he shone supreme as a wit and amateur singer.

Under the Piazza in Covent Garden, Powell, about 1710, set up his well-known Puppet Show, which had acquired great celebrity in the provinces at Bath, and which is immortalised in the *Spectator.* It was humorously announced by Steele that Powell would gratify the town with the performance of his drama on the story of the chaste Susannah, which would be graced by the addition of two new elders. In the fourteenth number of the *Spectator* is a bantering letter which purports to be written by the sexton of St. Paul's parish church, and in which the latter complains, " When I toll to prayers, I find my congregation take warning of my bell, morning and evening, to go to a puppet-show set forth by one Powell under the Piazza. By this means I have not only lost two of my best customers, whom I used to place, for sixpence a-piece, over against Mrs. Rachel Eyebright, but Mrs. Rachel herself has gone thither also. There now appear among us none but a few ordinary people, who come to church only to say their prayers, so that I have no work worth speaking of but on Sundays. I have placed my son at the Piazzas to acquaint the ladies that the bell rings for church, and that it stands on the other side of the garden; but they only laugh at the child. I desire that you would lay this before all the whole world, that I may not be made such a tool for the future, and that Punchinello may choose hours less canonical. As things are now, Mr. Powell has a full congregation, while we have a very thin house." So well known and popular was this place of amusement that Burnet asks, in "The Second Tale of a Tub," "What man or child that lives within the verge of Covent Garden, or what beau, belle, or visitant of Bath, knows not Mr. Powell?"

The "Bedford Coffee-house"—an establishment rendered famous in connection with the names of Garrick, Quin, Foote, Murphy, Sheridan, and other theatrical celebrities—stood at the north-east corner of the Piazza. "This coffee-house," observes a writer in the *Connoisseur* (in 1754), "affords every variety of character. This coffee-house is crowded every night with men of parts. Almost every one you meet is a polite scholar and a wit; jokes and *bon-mots* are echoed from box to box; every branch of literature is critically examined, and the merit of every production of the press, or performance at the theatres, weighed and determined. This school . . . . . has bred up many authors to the amazing entertainment and instruction of their readers." It appears to have been modelled on "Button's," but it never reached the fame of that coffee-house, frequented as it had been—even by the confession of its friends and supporters—by Addison, Steele, and Pope, in the previous generation. And yet the "Bedford" once attracted so much attention as a place of public resort as to have its history written. Nor is its history one of those "blanks" which, if the proverb be true, constitute the happiness of nations and peoples; for a search in the Library of the British Museum will convince even the most incredulous

that the "Memoirs of the 'Bedford' Coffee House," which were first published in 1751, reached a second edition twelve years afterwards.

The "Bedford" was Foote's favourite coffee-house. In 1754, when it was in the height of its fame, Foote would sit there, in his usual corner, a king among the critics and wits, like Addison and Steele at "Button's." "The regular frequenters of the room," says Mr. John Timbs, "strove to get admitted to his party at supper; and others got as near as they could to the table, as the only wit flowed from Foote's tongue." Everybody who knew this celebrated wit came early, in the hope of being one of his party during supper; and those who were not acquaintances had the same curiosity in engaging the boxes near him. Foote, in return, was no niggard in his conversation, but, on the contrary, was as generous as he was affluent. He talked upon most subjects with great knowledge and fluency; and whenever a flash of wit, a joke, or a pun came in his way, he gave it in such a style of genuine humour as was always sure to circulate a laugh, and this laugh was his glory and triumph.

Another frequenter of the "Bedford" was Garrick. One day he was leaving the house with Foote, when the latter let fall a guinea, and exclaimed as he looked about for it, "Why, where on earth has it gone to?" "Gone to the d——l!" replied Garrick, still, however, continuing the search. "Well said, David," was the quick and witty answer of Foote; "let you alone for making a guinea go further than any one else in the world."

It will be remembered that here, too, at the shilling rubber meeting, arose the sharp squabble between Hogarth and Churchill, when Hogarth used some insulting language towards Churchill, who resented it in "The Epistle." "Never," says Horace Walpole, "did two angry men of their abilities throw mud at each other with less dexterity."

It was at the "Bedford Coffee-house" that the Beefsteak Club, of which we have already spoken in connection with the Lyceum Theatre, was for some time held under date of 1814. Mr. J. T. Smith, in his "Book for a Rainy Day," writes:—"Mr. John Nixon, of Basinghall Street, gave me the following information respecting the Beefsteak Club. Mr. Nixon, as secretary, had possession of the original book. Lambert's Club was first held in Covent Garden Theatre, in the upper room, called the 'Thunder and Lightning;' then in one even with the two-shilling gallery; next in an apartment even with the boxes; and afterwards in a lower room, where they remained until the fire. After that time, Mr. Harris insisted upon it, as the playhouse was a new building, that the Club should not be held there. They then went to the 'Bedford Coffee-house' next door. Upon the ceiling of the dining-room they placed Lambert's original grid-iron, which had been saved from the fire. They had a kitchen, a cook, and a wine-cellar, &c, entirely independent of the 'Bedford Coffee-house.' The society held at Robins's room was called the 'Ad Libitum' Society, of which Mr. Nixon had the books, but it was quite unconnected with the Beef-steak Club." Previously to being called the "Bedford" the house had been held by Macklin, who then kept what Fielding calls a "Temple of Luxury."

In the north-east corner of the Piazza, and immediately adjoining the Opera House, with which it communicates, is the Floral Hall. This elegant building was intended as the realisation of a long-cherished scheme on the part of Mr. Gye, namely, to establish a vast central flower-market, for many years a growing desideratum in the metropolis. An opportunity was at last presented by the re-building of Covent Garden Theatre, after its destruction in 1856; and it was decided to carry out Mr. Gye's favourite plan, by erecting an arcade on the south side of the new Opera House. The ground-plan of the building may be described as resembling two sides of an unequal triangle, the principal entrance being by the side of the Opera House, in Bow Street, at the end of the longer side of the figure, while the other opens upon Covent Garden Market, on the side of the Piazza. The public footway of the Piazza is continued along the Covent Garden entrance, in the shape of a gallery roofed with glass and iron. The main arcades run in a direct line from the entrances, and are surmounted at the point of junction by a lofty dome of fifty feet span, which forms an imposing object in the view. This dome, as well as the roofs, are principally composed of wrought iron; the arches, columns, and piers are of cast iron; the frontage, both in Bow Street and the Piazza, is of iron and glass, of which the entire structure is principally composed, brickwork forming but a very small part of the composition. The utmost length of the arcade, from the Bow Street entrance to the west wall, is 227 feet; and the length of the shorter side, from Covent Garden Market to the wall of the theatre, nearly 100 feet. The total height, from the ground to the top of the arched dome, is rather over 90 feet. Each of the main arcades is 75 feet wide, and has a side-aisle between the main columns and the wall, 13 feet in width and 30 in height. The entrances are both elegant and simple, the doorways being so deeply

recessed as, in conjunction with the richly-designed iron arches which give admission to the interior, to obviate the flat appearance which generally characterises buildings of glass and iron. The interior is fully equal in lightness and grace of design to the exterior. The columns which support the roof are of cast iron, with richly ornamented capitals, the latter perforated, in order to ventilate the basement beneath, with which the hollow columns communicate. The ground having been excavated beneath, the principal floor forms a basement of the same area as the building above it, and sixteen feet in height, the floor of the arcade being supported by cast-iron columns. This building was, as its name implies, designed for a flower-market, and was expected to prove a boon to the many florists and nurserymen scattered among the outskirts of London, but has never fulfilled the purpose for which it was erected. It was opened on the 7th of March, 1860, with a Volunteer ball, under royal patronage, and for a time was employed principally for promenade concerts; in it is now held the wholesale market for foreign fruit.

In the south-east corner of the market-place, and occupying that portion which was destroyed by fire, stood two hotels, known by the strange names of the "Old Hummums" and the "New Hummums." The name is a corruption of the Eastern word "Humoum." Mr. Wright, in his "History of Domestic Manners of England," says, "Among the customs introduced from Italy was the hot sweating bath, which, under the name of the hot-house, became widely known in England for a considerable time." Sweating in those hot-houses is spoken of by Ben Jonson; and in the old play of *The Puritan*, a character, speaking of some laborious undertaking, says, "Marry, it will take me much sweat; 'twere better to go to sixteen hot-houses." These "Hummums," however, when established in London, seem to have been mostly frequented by women of doubtful repute, and they became, as in the East, favourite rendezvous for gossip and company of not the most moral kind. They soon came to be used for the purposes of intrigue, and were eventually suppressed.

The "Old Hummums" was the scene of what Dr. Johnson pronounced the best accredited ghost-story that he had ever heard. The individual whose ghost was said to have appeared here in a supernatural manner was a Mr. Ford, a relation or connection of the learned doctor, and said to have been the riotous parson of Hogarth's "Midnight Modern Conversations." The "Old Hummums" was pulled down in 1881; and the site is now occupied by a large hotel, styled "The Hummums."

In the north-west corner of Covent Garden is a large house once known as Evans's Music-hall. It is a fine specimen of a London mansion of the olden time. It was built originally in the reign of Charles II., and was for a time the residence of Sir Kenelm Digby, as we learn from Aubrey's "Lives:"—"Since the restoration of

and ruined the French fleet. From the Earl of Orford it passed to the Lords Archer. The house, which is said to have been the first family hotel established in London, is built of fine red brick, and down to about the year 1850, when considerable alterations were made in its appearance, the façade was thought to resemble the forecastle of

THE OLD ROOM AT "EVANS'S."

Charles II., he (Sir Kenelm Digby) lived in the last faire house westward in the north portion of Covent Garden, where my Lord Denzill Holles lived since. He had a laboratory there. I think he dyed (died) in this house."

The mansion was subsequently altered, if not rebuilt, for the Earl of Orford, better known by the name of Admiral Russell, the same who, in 1692, defeated Admiral de Tourville, near La Hogue,

a ship. The front of the house, still used as an hotel, is remarkable for its magnificent carved staircase, and for at least one elegantly painted ceiling, which remains in its original state.

At the end of the last, and during the early part of the present century, when used as a dinner and coffee-room only, it was called in the slang of the day, "The Star," from the number of men of rank by whom it was frequented. Indeed, it is said that

"MORNING." *From Hogarth's Print.* (*See page* 257.)

previous to the establishment of clubs, it was no unusual occurrence for nine dukes to dine there in one evening.

Part of the house was long used for the reception of the Savage Club, composed mainly of dramatists and dramatic authors.

"Evans's" is thus described by a writer in *Once a Week*, in 1867:—"About twenty years ago the list of metropolitan concert-rooms was headed by 'the Cyder Cellars' and 'Evans's.' The entertainments to be found in such places were not very select; but while the former has disappeared altogether, the latter has been altered and purged. The surviving establishment, half supper-room and half music-hall, and one of the 'lions of London,' is situated at the western extremity of Covent Garden Piazza. It is subject to peculiar and stringent regulations. Ladies are not admitted, except on giving their names and addresses, and then only enjoy the privilege of watching the proceedings from behind a screen. The whole of the performances are sustained by the male sex, and an efficient choir of men and boys sing glees, ballads, madrigals, and selections from operas, the accompaniments being supplied on the piano and harmonium. . . The new hall, one of the most elaborately ornamented in London, was erected from designs by Mr. Finch Hill. Its proportions are certainly fine, and the decorations cost about £5,000. On the occasion of our last visit to 'Evans's,' we heard standard music, English, German, and Italian, performed with admirable spirit, precision, and delicacy. The performances commence at eight o'clock; and we recommend 'Evans's' to the notice of steady young men who admire a high class of music, see no harm in a good supper, but avoid theatres and the ordinary run of music-halls. The so-called *café* is a spacious room, supported by pillars, and hung round with portraits of actresses. Previous to the erection of the new hall, the chamber thus adorned was used as the singing-room."

The music-hall, to which the *café* formed a sort of vestibule, was built in 1856, and ran out at the rear of the house, occupying a plot of ground which was formerly the garden of Sir Kenelm Digby. At a later period the site contained a cottage in which the Kemble family occasionally resided, when in the full tide of their popularity. According to tradition it was in this cottage that their talented daughter, Miss Fanny Kemble, was born. The hall was about 70 feet in length, by about 33 feet in width and height. The carved ceiling, richly painted in panels, was supported on either side by a row of substantial columns with ornamental capitals, from which sprang bold and massive arches; these columns helped also to support the gallery, which extended along the two sides and one end of the hall, and in which were the private screened boxes alluded to above. The hall was well ventilated, well conducted, well served, and therefore well patronised, particularly between the hours of ten and twelve, when visitors were continually dropping in to enjoy a hot supper and listen at the same time to the charming melodies provided for their delectation.

After enjoying for many years a fair share of popularity. "Evans's Music-hall" was closed in 1880, and soon after the building was converted into a club-house to be occupied by the Falstaff Club. It is now known as Lockhart's Coffee Rooms.

Sir William Alexander, Earl of Stirling, the poet, resided in 1637 in a house in the north-west corner of Covent Garden; here also Thomas Killigrew, the wit, was living between the years 1637 and 1662. The site was afterwards occupied by Denzil Holles, Sir Harry Vane, Sir Kenelm Digby; Lord Crewe, Bishop of Durham; and Russell, Earl of Orford. The house was subsequently taken by Lord Archer, who married Sarah, the daughter of Mr. West, some time President of the Royal Society. Mr. West's library and collection of prints, coins, and medals, were sold in this house, and occupied the auctioneer six weeks in the disposal of them. After the above sale in 1773, the mansion was converted into a family hotel, by a person named Low, and is said to have been the first of the kind established in London. About 1790, a Mrs. Hudson became proprietor. Her advertisements were curious; one ends thus — "Accommodation, with stabling, for one hundred noblemen and horses." After one or two more changes in the proprietorship, the hotel came into the hands of Mr. W. C. Evans, of Covent Garden Theatre, whose name henceforth became so closely associated with it. In 1844 he retired, and Mr. John Green became proprietor and manager. This gentleman, who was well known in the musical profession as "Paddy Green," was a man of rather eccentric character; he died in December, 1874.

It was in the north-western angle of the Piazza that Sir Peter Lely resided for many years. It is well known that names were sometimes adopted from sign-boards. That of Rothschild, the "Red Shield," is an example. Another instance is to be found in Sir Peter Lely. "His grandfather," says Mr. Larwood, "was a perfumer, named Van der Vaas, and lived at the sign of the 'Lily'— possibly a 'vase' of lilies. When his son entered the English army, he discarded his Dutch name, and for the paternal sign adopted the more euphonious name of Lilly or Lely." He died at the age of sixty-three, in 1680.

To the above list of notables who have resided here must be added the name of Dr. Berkeley, the philosopher, Bishop of Cloyne. Zoffany's house was the same which afterwards became the auction-room of George Robins, and Peter Cunningham identified " the second house eastward from James Street " as the abode of Sir James Thornhill.

The auction-rooms of George Robins were for many years one of the celebrities of London. They were formerly known as "Langford's and Cox's," and formed part of the mansion originally tenanted by Sir Peter Lely ; but more recently they were used by the owner of the Tavistock Hotel as breakfast-rooms. In these rooms, says Mr. Peter Cunningham, "Hogarth exhibited his 'Marriage à la Mode' gratis to the public." These are the same rooms which we have mentioned as subsequently tenanted by Richard Wilson, the landscape painter, if we may believe Mr. J. T. Smith, in his "Life of Nollekens."

It may be worth a passing note to record the fact that Covent Garden was the first place in London where a balcony or "belconey," as it was at first styled, was set up ; it was said to be an invention of the Lord Arundel of the time.

CHAPTER XXXII.

COVENT GARDEN AND ITS NEIGHBOURHOOD (continued).

ʾΑγορὰ ʾν ʾΑθήναις χαῖρε.
Aristoph., "Acharn."

St. Paul's Church first built—Destroyed by Fire and rebuilt—Dispute between the Earl of Bedford and the Vicar of St. Martin's-in-the-Fields— Horace Walpole's Criticism of the Building—Extracts from the Parish Register—Notabilities interred in the Churchyard—The Parish Rate-books and Church Registers—"King's" Coffee House—The Westminster Elections—The Duchess of Devonshire and Lady Duncannon's Patriotism—Fox "chaired" as the Man for the People—"Treasonable Practices" of the "Independent Electors"—Excitement consequent on the Westminster Elections—Morals of Covent Garden in the Seventeenth Century—Suicide of Mr. Damer—Arrest of the Muscovite Ambassador, and his Detention in the "Black Raven"—The "Finish"—The "Museum Minervæ."—The Marquis of Worcester and the Covent Garden—Noted Residents of Covent Garden—Tavistock Street—Tavistock Row—Charles Macklin's Residence—The Murder of Miss Ray.

THE parish church of St. Paul, Covent Garden, on the west side of the market, as we have said, was built by Inigo Jones, in 1633, at the expense of the ground-landlord, Francis, Earl of Bedford. It was consecrated by Juxon, Bishop of London, on the 27th of September, 1638 ; repaired, in 1727, by the Earl of Burlington ; totally destroyed by fire on the 17th of September, 1795 ; and rebuilt (John Hardwick, architect) on the plan and in the proportions of the original building. The great delay between the period of erection and that of consecration was owing to a dispute between the Earl of Bedford and Bray, the Vicar of St. Martin's-in-the-Fields, on the right of presentation ; the earl claiming it as his own, because he had built it at his own expense, and the vicar claiming it as his own, because, not being then parochial, it was nothing more than a chapel-of-ease to St. Martin's. The matter was heard by the King in Council on the 6th of April, 1638, and judgment given in favour of the earl.

The architecture of St. Paul's Church was not to the taste of Horace Walpole, who criticises it in his usual caustic style :—"The arcade of Covent Garden, and the church—two structures of which I want taste to see the beauties. In the arcade there is nothing remarkable ; the pilasters are as errant and homely stripes as any plasterer would make. The barn roof over the portico of the church strikes my eyes with as little idea of dignity or beauty as it could do if it covered nothing but a barn. In justice to Inigo, one must own that the defect is not in the architect, but in the order : who ever saw a beautiful Tuscan building ? Would the Romans have chosen that order for a temple ? Mr. Onslow, the late Speaker, told me an anecdote that corroborates my opinion of this building. When the Earl of Bedford sent for Inigo, he told him he wanted a chapel for the parishioners of Covent Garden, but added he would not go to any considerable expense. 'In short,' said he, 'I would have it not much better than a barn.' 'Well, then,' replied Jones, 'you shall have the handsomest barn in England.' The expense of building was £4,500."

The parish register records the baptism of Lady Mary Wortley Montague, and the marriage (1764) of Lady Susan Strangways to O'Brien, the handsome actor.

In the churchyard hard by lie buried many eminent persons : amongst others, Robert Carr, Earl of Somerset, who died in 1645 ; Sir Henry Herbert (whose "office book," as "Master of the Revels," throws so much light on the history of our stage and drama in the time of Charles I.), brother to Lord Herbert of Cherbury and George Herbert, who died in 1673. Not far off rests Samuel Butler, the author of "Hudibras." Butler died in Rose Street, of consumption, on the 25th of September, 1680, and was buried, "according to his owne appointment," as Aubrey tells us in his "Lives," "in the churchyard of Covent Garden ; sc. in the north part next the church at the east end. His feet touch the wall. His grave 2 yards distant from the pilaster of the dore (by his desire), 6 foot deepe. About 25 of his old acquaintance at his funerall : I myself being one." It is a "moot point" whether Samuel Butler was buried at the eastern or the western end of the north wall of the churchyard, the accounts of two individuals who might be presumed to be best acquainted with the exact spot where he lies being in conflict on this matter of detail. "Subsequently," says Mr. J. H. Jesse, "some persons unknown to fame erected a monument to the memory of the poet, in the churchyard, but apparently no trace of it now remains." Here, too, lies buried Sir Peter Lely, the painter, who died in the Piazza in 1680. His monument of white marble, which shared the fate of the church when destroyed by fire in 1795, was adorned with a bust of the great artist between two Cupids, as well as with fruit, foliage, and other devices, executed by Gibbons : the inscription alone has been preserved. Near him lie Dick Estcourt, the actor and wit, who died in 1711–12, and Edward Kynaston, the celebrated actor of female parts at the Restoration—a complete female stage-beauty, "that it has since been disputable among the judicious, whether any woman that succeeded him so sensibly touched the audience as he."* Here too rest William Wycherly, the dramatist, who died in Bow Street in 1715 ; Pierce Tempest, who drew the "Cries of London," known as "Tempest's Cries," and who died in 1717 ; and Grinling Gibbons, the sculptor and carver in wood, who died in 1721. Not far off are Mrs. Centlivre, author of *The Busybody* and *The Wonder*, and Robert Wilkes (the original "Sir Harry Wild-air," celebrated by Steele for acting with the easy frankness of a gentleman), who died in 1731. Near him are James Worsdale, the painter, who carried Pope's letters to Curll and, dying in 1767, was buried in the churchyard, with an inscription (removed in 1848) of his own composing ; also John Wolcot, the "Peter Pindar" of the reign of George III., whom he lashed, as well as his minister Pitt, with merciless vigour and persistency. He became the popular satirist of the day, and the fluency of his pen was equalled by its grossness and obscene vulgarity. Those who remember him when he lived in the neighbourhood say that he was a gross sensualist, in spite of his moral mission as a satirist, and that he whimsically lay in bed nearly all day because it was easier to exist when his body weighed only a few ounces than when he had to carry some

fifteen stone about. He died in January, 1819, and deserves mention here on account of his eccentricities, of which it were much to be wished that they could be called harmless ones. But he was the enemy of others as well as of himself, and no one cares to say a good word on his behalf. Here also may or might be seen a curious epitaph upon Mr. Button, who kept the noted coffee-house in Russell Street :—

> "Odds' fish, and fiery coals,
> Are graves become Button-holes !"

In St. Paul's Church is buried, in a nameless grave, a lady, who died in James Street, in this parish, in March, 1720, and who was described at the time simply as "the unknown." This mysterious person is described by Mr. J. Timbs, in his "Romance of London," as "middle-sized, with dark brown hair, and very beautiful features, and the mistress of every accomplishment of fashion. Her circumstances," he continues, "were affluent, and she possessed many rich trinkets set with diamonds. A Mr. John Ward, of Hackney, published several particulars of her in the newspapers, and amongst others said that a servant had been directed by her to deliver to him a letter after her death ; but, as no servant appeared, he felt himself required to notice those circumstances, in order to acquaint her relations that her death occurred suddenly after a masquerade, where she declared that she had conversed with the king ; and it was remembered that she had been seen in the private apartments of Queen Anne, though, after the queen's death, she lived in obscurity. 'The unknown' arrived in London in 1714 from Mansfield, in a carriage drawn by six horses. She frequently said that her brother was a nobleman, but that her elder brother dying unmarried, the title was extinct ; adding that she had an uncle living from whom she had expectations. It was conjectured," adds Mr. Timbs, though he does not tell us why, "that she was the daughter of a Roman Catholic, who had consigned her to a convent." But the rumours "lacks confirmation."

Mr. J. H. Jesse, in his "London," pronounces St. Paul's Church as "unquestionably the most interesting spot in Covent Garden ;" and possibly it might be so had not the old church been destroyed by fire at the end of the last century. "Few persons," he writes, "who are in the habit of passing by this heavy-looking building, are aware that, with the exception of Westminster Abbey, here lie the remains of more men of genius than, apparently, in any other church in London." He adds, however, that "except a small tablet to the memory of Macklin, the actor, it contains no

* Downe's "Roscius Anglicanus," 8vo. 1708.

monumental memorials of the dead;" a fact, we should have thought, which would have been very fatal to its claim to be the "most interesting spot" of the neighbourhood. We want to see these mute memorials with our eyes, and to read the names inscribed upon them, in order to realise, save in the faintest sense, the local and personal interest which clings to such places.

The rectory of St. Paul's, Covent Garden, is still in the patronage of the Duke of Bedford; and, curiously enough, the parish is entirely surrounded by that of St. Martin's-in-the-Fields, from which it was cut off.

The rate-books of this parish are kept carefully arranged in streets, like a Post-office Directory; and they contain the name of every householder from the first formation of the parish down to the present day. The church registers also are kept with scrupulous care.

Close under the portico of the church was a common kind of shed, "once well known," says Arthur Murphy, "to all gentlemen to whom beds are unknown," facetiously termed "King's Coffee House." "It was kept," writes Peter Cunningham, "by a person of the name of Tom King, and it forms a conspicuous feature in Hogarth's print of 'Morning.'" Of this print we give an engraving on page 253. The coffee-house has, however, long since been swept away.

As the hustings for the Westminster elections, from time immemorial to a recent date, have been fixed before the east end of St. Paul's Church, that side of Covent Garden has often witnessed the most exciting scenes. But never was witnessed, either there or elsewhere, an election more exciting than that of May, 1784, when the Tory party moved heaven and earth to exclude the Whig leader, Charles James Fox, from the representation of Westminster. As, day after day, the inhabitants of the metropolitan parishes had polled, and the numbers were nearly even, the task of beating up the outlying voters in the suburbs was undertaken with a heart and a will by Georgiana, Duchess of Devonshire, and her sister, Lady Duncannon. "These ladies," writes Sir N. W. Wraxall, "being furnished with lists of the outlying voters, drove in their carriages to their respective dwellings, sparing neither entreaties nor promises. In some instances even personal caresses were said to have been permitted in order to prevail on the sulky and inflexible; and there can be no doubt of common mechanics having been conveyed to the hustings by the Duchess in her own coach." The effect of such a powerful intervention soon showed itself. Fox was soon a hundred votes ahead of his

opponent, Sir Cecil Wrey, and in spite of the counter efforts of the Countess of Salisbury, at the close of the poll he had a clear majority of 235. It was on this occasion that an Irish costermonger, if we may believe the story, came up to Her Grace of Devonshire, who was one of the leading beauties of the day, and respectfully and wittily entreated to be allowed to "light his pipe at her ladyship's eye." It is on record that Her Grace of Devonshire used regularly, on the occasion of an election, to hire a first-floor in Henrietta Street in order that she might witness the proceedings, and lend at least her countenance to the Whig party. From the hustings at Covent Garden a procession was formed, and Fox was "chaired," as the man of the people, through the chief streets of Westminster to Carlton House, the gates of which were thrown open to the excited multitude; the ostrich plumes carried in front of him denoting the patronage of the Whig cause by the Prince of Wales; while another flag was inscribed with the words, "Sacred to Female Patriotism," in allusion to the Duchess of Devonshire. The intense feelings excited on this occasion are thus summed up by a contemporary writer:—"All minor interests were swallowed up in this struggle, which held not only the capital, but also the nation, in suspense, while it rendered Covent Garden and its neighbourhood, during three successive weeks, a scene of outrage and even of blood."

The Westminster elections would seem generally to have been conducted with very bitter feelings on both sides. We are told by Wright, in a foot-note to the letters of Horace Walpole, how the keeper of the "White Horse" in Piccadilly, being at a dinner among the "independent electors," taking notes in pencil, was beaten and cuffed by them, being supposed to be an informer against their treasonable practices. Among the more noteworthy persons who have figured upon the hustings here, have been Sir Francis Burdett ("Old Glory"), Sir John Hobhouse, Lord Cochrane, Mr. John Stuart Mill, and General Sir De Lacy Evans.

Down to the passing of the first Reform Bill the voting continued for fourteen days, during which the whole of London was kept in a state of violent excitement. Mr. H. C. Robinson, in his "Diary," speaks of a Westminster election as "a scene only ridiculous and disgusting. The vulgar abuse of the candidates from the vilest rabble," he adds, "is not rendered endurable by either wit or good temper."

"I saw," writes Cyrus Redding, "the election for Westminster, when Sheridan and Paull were rivals. Among other ridiculous things, a kind of stage was brought from Drury Lane Theatre, supported on men's shoulders; upon this there were four tailors busily at work, with a live goose and several huge cabbages; they came close up to the hustings, before Paull, amidst roars of laughing. The joke was, that Paull's father had been a tailor.

"This town two bargains has not worth one farthing,
  A Smithfield horse, and wife of Covent Garden."

And that the tastes of its inhabitants were alike loose and extravagant may be gathered from Wycherley, who speaks of "an ill-bred City dame, whose husband has been broke by living in Covent Garden."

MACKLIN'S HOUSE, TAVISTOCK ROW, 1870. (*See page* 260.)

A voter called out to Sheridan that he had long supported him, but should, after that, withdraw his countenance from him. 'Take it away at once—take it away at once,' cried Sheridan from the hustings; 'it is the most villainous-looking countenance I ever beheld!'"

As to the morals of Covent Garden in the seventeenth century, we may leave them to be inferred from the following couplet in the epilogue to Dryden's *Limberham* :—

In a tavern at Covent Garden, the husband of the exquisite sculptress, the Hon. Mrs. Damer, shot himself in 1776. Mr. Damer's suicide was hastened, and indeed provoked, by the refusal of his father, Lord Milton, to discharge his debts. Horace Walpole, after entering at length into this matter in a letter to Sir Horace Mann, in August, 1776, gives the following circumstantial account :— " On Thursday Mr. Damer supped at the 'Bedford Arms,' in Covent Garden, with four ladies and a blind fiddler. At three in the morning he dismissed his seraglio, ordering his Orpheus to come up again in half an hour. When he returned he found his master dead, and smelt gunpowder. He called: the master of the house came up; and they found Mr. Damer sitting in a

sion, are not, it would seem, sufficient for happiness, and cannot check a pistol."

The following curious circumstance is mentioned in the "Life of Queen Anne," where, under date of 1708, we read that "the Muscovite Ambassador having had his audience of leave of the Queen,

DINING-ROOM OF THE GARRICK CLUB. (*See page 263.*)

chair dead, with one pistol beside him and another in his pocket. The ball had not gone through his head or made any report. On the table lay a scrap of paper with these words,·'The people of the house are not to blame for what has happened; it was my own act . . . .' What a catastrophe for a man at thirty-two, heir to two-and-twenty thousand a year!" Horace Walpole remarks, with his usual cynicism on this affair, that "Five thousand a year in present, and £22,000 in rever-

Mr. Morton, a laceman in Covent Garden, and some others of his creditors, caused him to be arrested, on the 21st of July, as he was riding in his coach. The bailiffs thrust themselves into the coach, took away his sword and cane, and carried him to a sponging-house, called the 'Black Raven.' Here the Ambassador sent to one of the Secretaries of State to acquaint him with his being insulted in that manner, but no secretaries could be found; and only Mr. Walpole, an under-secretary, came to him (as the Czar observes in his letter) to be witness to his disgrace; for, instead being discharg'd, he was compell'd to put in bail to the action. It seems the debt was but £50, and all the debts he ow'd did not amount to £300, which still renders the crime more unpardonable; and after all, no punishment adequate to the offence either way or (as 'tis said) could be inflicted on the offender by the laws of this kingdom. The Imperial, and Prussian, and other Foreign Ministers, looking upon themselves concern'd in this affair, demanded satisfaction for the outrage. Indeed, Morton and some others of the creditors, with the attorney and bailiffs, were summoned before the Council, and committed to custody for the present, and an information ordered to be preferred against them; but when the case came to be argued, the Court could not discover any law they had offended."

Among the notorieties of "the Garden" was the well-known night house called "The Finish." It stood on the south side of the market sheds, and was kept at the beginning of the present century by a Mrs. Butler. There, according to "Tom Cribb's Memorial to Congress," the "gentlemen of the road" used to divide their spoil in the grey dawn of the morning, when it was time for the night birds to fly to their roost. Hence Tommy Moore, who frequented this place, whimsically says that the "Congress" is—

> "Some place that's like the 'Finish,' lads !
> Where all your high pedestrian pads
> That have been up and out all night
> Running their rigs among the rattlers,
> At morning meet, and, honour bright,
> Agree to share the blunt and tatters."

One of the earliest records of the artistic fame of Covent Garden is that of Charles I. establishing, in the house of Sir Francis Kynaston, an academy called the "Museum Minervæ," for the instruction of gentlemen in arts and sciences, knowledge of metals, antiquities, painting, architecture, and foreign languages. Was this the first faint foreshadowing of the Royal Academy?

An amusing story in connection with Covent Garden—more especially with reference to the derivation of its name from Convent Garden—is told respecting the old Marquis of Worcester. His lordship being made prisoner, was committed to the custody of the Black-Rod, who then lived in Covent Garden; the noble Marquis, says the historiographer, demanded of Dr. Bayly and others in his company, "What they thought of fortune-tellers?" It was answered, "That some of them spoke shrewdly." Whereupon the Marquis said,

"It was told me by some of them, before ever I was a Catholic, that I should die in a *Convent*, but I never believed them before now; yet I hope they will not bury me in a *Garden*."

Lady Muskerry, the Princess of Babylon of De Grammont's "Memoirs," was living here in 1676, according to Mr. P. Cunningham, in the north-west angle, at the corner of James Street. Nicholas Rowe, the dramatic poet, was residing in Covent Garden in 1716; and close by lived and died Thomas Southern, the author of *Oroonoko* and of the *Fatal Marriage*, whose remains are interred in the Church of St. Paul hard by. In Covent Garden there was, at all events, one auction-room for the sale of prints, &c., that of the elder Langford, the same who is introduced by Foote as "Mr. Puff" in his farce of *The Mirror*.

Of Tavistock Street, which adjoins the south side of Covent Garden, Mr. Walker writes thus in "The Original :"—" The standard of wealth is no less changed than the standard of society. Tavistock Street, Covent Garden, was once a street of fashionable shops, what Bond Street was till lately, and what Bond Street and Regent Street together are now. I remember hearing an old lady say that in her young days the crowd of handsome equipages in Tavistock Street was considered one of the sights of London. I have had the curiosity to stride it. It is about one hundred and sixty yards long, and, before the footways were widened, would have admitted three carriages abreast."

The only memory that Mr. Peter Cunningham recalls to us in his generally exhaustive "Handbook of London" concerning this street, is the fact that in it the celebrated singer, Leveridge, kept a public-house after retiring from the stage.

The house No. 4, in the corner of what used to be Tavistock Row, the same in which Miss Ray lived, was the last residence of Charles Macklin, the comedian and centenarian, who died here in July, 1797. And here, says Mr. Cunningham, "the elder Mathews was called upon to give the aged actor a taste of his boyish quality for the stage."

To Tavistock Row, now covered by the offices of the Strand District Board of Works, properly belongs the story of the murder of Miss Ray. Though referred to by Horace Walpole as "among the strangest that he had ever heard, and one which he could scarcely bring himself to believe," it has been often told, but by no one better than by Mr. John Timbs in his "Romance of London." It appears that the gay Earl of Sandwich, First Lord of the Admiralty under Lord North's administration, whilst passing through Covent Garden, espied one day a pretty milliner at No. 4, on the southern side, at the corner of Tavistock Street. Her name was Martha Ray; according to one account, her parents were labourers at Elstree, on the borders of Hertford-shire; though others say that they were staymakers in Holywell Street. Be this as it may, she had served her time as an apprentice with a mantua-maker in Clerkenwell Close; and when Lord Sandwich first saw her she was very young.* He removed her from the shop, had her education completed, and took her as his mistress, though he was old enough to be her father. In spite of his countess being alive, Lord Sandwich introduced her to his family circle at Hinchinbrooke, his seat in Huntingdonshire; and she charmed the county families around—especially the ladies, and even the bishop's wife—by her charming, yet modest, manners, and her beautiful voice. And we have the authority of Mr. Cradock for saying that in her situation she was a pattern of discretion; for when a lady of rank, between one of the acts of the oratorio, advanced to converse with her, she ex-pressed her embarrassment; and Lord Sandwich, turning privately to a friend, said, "As you are well acquainted with that lady, I wish you would give her a hint that there is a boundary line in my family that I do not wish to see exceeded." She was already the mother of a young family by the earl, when she made the acquaintance of a certain Captain Hackman, an officer in a foot regiment, then quartered at Huntingdon, whom she soon inspired with the same passion as that which had brought Lord Sandwich to her feet. Hackman (whom Mr. Cradock met at Hinchinbrooke, the hospitable seat of Lord Sandwich) at once pro-posed marriage to her, but she told him that "she did not choose to carry a knapsack." Her new admirer therefore resolved to exchange the army for the Church, and became vicar of Wyverton, in Norfolk. Half inclined, probably, to marry Hackman, she appears now to have complained that no settlement had been made upon her, adding that she was anxious to relieve his lordship of expense, and to have even thought of taking an engagement as a singer at the Italian Opera, where she had an offer of £3,000 and a free benefit. Lord Sandwich, in some doubt as to the real mind of his mistress, now placed Miss Ray under the charge of a duenna; while Hackman grew jealous, and appears to have resolved to destroy either himself or Miss Ray, or both. On the evening of the 7th of April, 1779, Miss Ray went, with a

female attendant, to Covent Garden Theatre, to see *Love in a Village.* She had declined to tell Mr. Hackman how she was engaged that evening; he appears, therefore, to have watched her move-ments, and saw her carriage drive by a coffee-house in Cockspur Street, where he had posted himself. As the carriage drove on, Hackman fol-lowed, at a quick pace, to the theatre. The ladies sat in a front box, and three gentlemen, all con-nected with the Admiralty, occasionally paid their compliments to them. Mr. Hackman, too, was sometimes in the lobby and sometimes in an upper side-box, and more than once called at the "Bedford Coffee-house" to take a glass of brandy and water, but still was unable, on returning to the theatre, to obtain an interview with Miss Ray. The upshot was that after the piece was over, when the crowd was beginning to pour out, Hackman rushed out of the door of the coffee-house, just opposite to that of the theatre, and as a gentleman was handing the lady into her carriage, drew forth a pistol and shot her through the head. He then drew another pistol to shoot himself; but the ball grazed with-out penetrating his head, and he then endeavoured to beat out his own brains with the butt-end of the pistol. In this attempt on his own life, however, he was prevented, and was carried off as a prisoner by the Bow Street "runners" to the Bridewell at Tothill Fields.

Horace Walpole gives us some additional parti-culars concerning the murder of Miss Ray in one of his letters to his acquaintance:—"Miss Ray, it appears, has been out of order, and abroad but twice all the winter. She went to the play on Wednesday night, for the second time, with Galli the singer. During the play the desperate lover was at the 'Bedford' Coffee-house, and behaved with great calmness, and drank a glass of capillaire. Towards the conclusion he sallied out into the Piazza, waiting till he saw his victim handed to her carriage by Mr. Macnamara, an Irish Templar, with whom she had been seen to coquet during the performance in the theatre. Hackman came behind her, pulled her by the gown, and, on her turning round, clapped the pistol to her forehead and shot her through the head. With another pistol he then attempted to shoot himself. . . . Now, is not the story full as strange as ever it was? Miss Ray has six children; the eldest son is fifteen; and she was at least three times as much."

The real fact, however, is that Miss Ray had borne to Lord Sandwich no less than nine chil-dren, five of whom were then living. One of these afterwards attained distinction, Mr. Basil Mon-

* Mr. Cradock, in his "Literary Memoirs," tells us that his lordship first saw her on going into a shop in this neighbourhood to buy a pair of gloves.

tague, Q.C., eminent both as a lawyer and as a man of letters, who died in 1851, and whose early success at the bar, it is said, was very greatly a result of his having contradicted the then Lord Chancellor on a point of law, and being told by his lordship next day that he was right in his view. But to return to Miss Ray's assassination. Hackman was tried at the Old Bailey for the murder, and the fact that he had two pistols instead of one compelled the jury to believe that it was not suicide only that he had contemplated as he sat that evening in the window of the hotel in Cockspur Street, but that his assassination of Miss Ray was a cool and deliberate act. Accordingly he was found guilty, sentenced to death and hanged at Tyburn, being accompanied in the coach by Lord Carlisle and by James Boswell, who, like George Selwyn, was fond of being present at executions.

A curious book, it may here be remarked before quitting the subject, arose out of this tragical story. In the following year was published an octavo volume pretending to contain the correspondence of Hackman and Miss Ray. It was entitled "Love and Madness; or a story too true, in a series of letters between parties whose names would perhaps be mentioned were they less known or less lamented." The book, appealing as it did to the sensational element in nature, soon ran through several editions. The real author of it was Sir Herbert Croft. Walpole, as if puzzled what to make of it, writes, "I doubt whether the letters are genuine; and yet, if fictitious, they are well executed, and enter into his character: hers appear less natural; and yet the editors were certainly more likely to be in possession of hers than of his. It is not probable that Lord Sandwich should have sent to the press what he found in her apartments; and no account is pretended to be given of how they came to light."

It was said that when Miss Ray's body was brought into the "Shakespeare" Tavern, George Selwyn put on a long black cloak, and sat in the room with the corpse, as a mourner; but the story "lacks confirmation."

CHAPTER XXXIII.

COVENT GARDEN AND ITS NEIGHBOURHOOD (continued).

Distinguished Inhabitants of James Street—Henrietta Street—Sir Robert Strange, the Historical Engraver—Duel between Sheridan and Mathews—Formation of the Society of Arts—King Street—D'Urfey's Allusion to the "Three Kings"—Hutchins' and Paterson's Auction Rooms—"The Essex Serpent"—Samuel Taylor Coleridge—The Garrick Club—Collection of Theatrical Portraits—Rose Street—Samuel Butler, the Author of "Hudibras"—Assault of Dryden—The "Pope's Head" and Curll the Bookseller—New Street—Dr. Johnson's Dinner—Artists in Long Acre—Wedgwood—Removal of Signboards—Bedford Street—An Old Tea Shop—Garrick in Southampton Street—The old Welsh Alehouse—Danby and Marvell—Voltaire—Turner—Quarrel between Hogarth and Churchill—The "Cider Cellars"—Chandos Street—Bedfordbury—Sir F. Kynaston and the Museum Minervæ.

CONTINUING our desultory tour, we next come to James Street, which runs out of Covent Garden on the north, and connects it with Long Acre: it shows the date of its erection by its name, being called after the Duke of York, afterwards James II. It is mentioned casually in the *Spectator*, No. 266, and has had at all events one distinguished inhabitant—Sir James Thornhill. In the *European Magazine* for 1804, the house is spoken of as situated on the eastern side of the street, with back offices and a painting-room abutting on Langford's (then Cock's) auction-rooms, in the Piazza; but since then the east side has been almost entirely rebuilt. Here, according to Mr. P. Cunningham, lived Sir Henry Herbert, the last Master of the Revels at the Stuart Court; and also the engraver, Charles Grignion. In other respects the street seems to have enjoyed but little celebrity in comparison with the neighbouring thoroughfares.

Henrietta Street, which connects the south-west corner of Covent Garden with Bedford Street, was built in 1637, and named after Henrietta Maria, queen of Charles I. Indeed, it may be said that all the streets around Covent Garden, except those named after the Russell family, bespeak by their names—all borrowed from our Stuart princes—the dates of their erection. Strafford, Lord Lieutenant of Ireland, was one of the earliest aristocratic inhabitants of this street. In 1640 Sir Robert Strange, the engraver, was living at the "Golden Head," in this street, when he published his proposals for engraving by subscription three historical prints. Two other interesting reminiscences belong to this street. It was at the "Castle" Tavern, in Henrietta Street, that Sheridan fought a duel with Mathews, his rival in the affections of Miss Linley; and at Rawthmell's Coffee-house that the Society of Arts was formed, in 1754.

King Street, the thoroughfare running parallel with Henrietta Street, and forming an outlet from the north-west corner of Covent Garden, was built at the same time as Henrietta Street. Lenthall, the Speaker of the House of Commons during the Commonwealth, lived in this street, in a house the site of which is now covered by the "Westminster Fire-office." Here was the residence of the three Indian kings mentioned in the *Tatler* and *Spectator*, and who lodged in the house of Mr. Arne, an upholsterer. This Mr. Arne was the father of the celebrated Dr. Arne, the composer. In after times an inn, called after these three Oriental sovereigns, would appear to have been established there; to it, probably, Tom D'Urfey alludes in his collection of songs, published in 1719:—

> " Farewell, ' Three Kings,' where I have spent
> 　　Full many an idle hour ;
> Where oft I won, but never lost,
> 　　If it were in my power.
> Farewell, my dearest Piccadill,
> 　　Notorious for great dinners ;
> Oh, what a tennis-court was there !
> 　　Alas ! too good for sinners.
> Now, God bless all that will be blest ;
> 　　God bless the Inns of Court,
> And God bless D'Avenant's Opera,
> 　　Which is the sport of sport."

From an early date King Street would appear to have been a favourite haunt for the auctioneers. Here were the sale-rooms of Hutchins, and of Paterson, to whose son Dr. Johnson stood as god-father, and for whom he wrote letters of recommendation to Sir Joshua Reynolds. In these two sale-rooms large collections of prints and pictures were constantly passing under the auctioneer's hammer ; and among the crowds of purchasers were such men as Gough, the editor of Camden's " Britannia," with his formal-cut coat and waist-coat, and high boots, and carrying in his hand a " swish-whip " instead of a walking-stick ; Dr. Lort, chaplain to the Duke of Devonshire, and the correspondent of " Old Cole," with his thick worsted stockings and " Busby " wig ; Caleb Whiteford, witty and well dressed, after the fashion of the Garrick school ; Dr. Gossett, Captain Baillie, Mr. Baker, Mr. Woodhouse, Mr. Musgrave, Mr. Pitt, and Mr. Woodhall—all of them keen-scented collectors of articles of *vertu*, and of prints by celebrated artists such as Hogarth, Cipriani, and Rowlandson.

In King Street there might still be seen, until a few years ago, " The Essex Serpent." Mr. Larwood suggests that this sign is an allusion to a fabulous monster recorded in a broadside of 1704, from which we learn that before Henry II. died a dragon of marvellous bigness was discovered at St. Osyth, in Essex. In the absence of any more probable hypothesis, we may accept this suggestion as plausible, if not as satisfactory.

In King Street also lived the philosophical poet, Samuel Taylor Coleridge, from 1799 down to 1802, whilst he was earning his livelihood as an unknown writer on political subjects for the *Morning Post*.

The Garrick Club was originally established in King Street, at No. 35, about the middle of the north side, in 1834 ; and here its fine gallery of theatrical and literary portraits remained until the opening of its new and permanent home in Garrick Street, in 1864.

Garrick Street is the name given to a wide and spacious thoroughfare which was driven about the year 1860 across the site of Rose Street and a nest of close and crowded alleys, between King Street and St. Martin's Lane. It takes its name from the Garrick Club, which occupies a noble building erected for its members by Mr. Marrable, and in which is to be seen the finest collection of theatrical portraits in the kingdom. It was first made by the elder Charles Mathews, at his residence in Kentish Town. It includes authentic likenesses of most of the theatrical celebrities of the past two centuries— Foote, Quin, Garrick, Nell Gwynne, Mrs. Billington, Nancy Dawson, Colley Cibber—some in costume, and others in private dress. The Club is allowed to be inspected on every Wednesday (except during September) by any one personally introduced by a member. Among the pictures, which cover nearly the whole of the walls of the various rooms set apart for the use of the members, may be specially mentioned the half-length portrait of Mrs. Oldfield, by Sir Godfrey Kneller ; Mrs. Siddons, by Harlow ; a fine picture of King ; and Mr. and Mrs. Baddeley in *The Clandestine Marriage*, by Zoffany ; Macklin as " Sir Pertinax Macsycophant," by De Wilde ; Mathews, in five characters, by Harlow ; Garrick between Tragedy and Comedy ; Mrs. Bracegirdle ; Mrs. Abington as " Lady Bab," by Hickey ; the screen scene from the *School for Scandal*, as originally cast ; Rich as harlequin (1753) ; King as " Touchstone," by Zoffany ; C. Kemble and Fawcett in *Charles II.*, by Clint ; Garrick as " Richard III.," by the elder Morland. Since the removal of the club to Garrick Street the number of pictures has been greatly augmented ; among the more recent additions being a choice collection of water-colour full-length portraits of theatrical celebrities painted by Mr. John Leech. Upon the walls of the smoking-room there are a few large paintings by Clarkson Stanfield, Louis Haigh, David Roberts, and others. In the coffee-room there are some objects of interest to the curious, independent of the paintings upon the walls—namely, the jewels, &c., presented to Garrick and worn by him upon the stage. Among the busts, of which there are several in the Club, especially in the library, may be particularly noticed one of Thackeray; one of Mrs. Siddons and her brother; and one of Shakespeare, which was formerly bricked up in a wall, but was discovered and brought again to light during the demolition of the old Lincoln's Inn Theatre, in 1848.

Old Rose Street, which ran north and south from the western end of King Street, has been so altered within the last few years by the advancing spirit of clearance and ventilation that its original aspect has been almost entirely swept away. Previous to the year 1859, when many of its old and dilapidated tenements were pulled down in order to form the broad thoroughfare of Garrick Street, which now crosses it, here might be seen low gambling-houses; floors let out to numerous families with fearful broods of children; sundry variations of the magisterial permission "to be drunk on the premises;" strange, chaotic trades, to which no one skilled contribution imparted a distinctive character; and, by way of a moral drawn from the far-off pure air of open fields and farm-yards, a London dairy, professing to be constantly supplied with fresh butter, cream, and new milk from the country: these were some of the special features of a thoroughfare which was marked by a tablet upon one of its houses bearing the super-scription, "This is Red Rose Street, 1623." If the appearance of the street as above indicated, were all it could boast of, Rose Street might go down into dust without a word by way of epitaph. But there are circumstances connected with it which will render it immortal in our annals, when its very site shall have become a matter of doubt hundreds of years hence; for Samuel Butler, the author of "Hudibras," died here in 1680, of a complication of ailments and miseries, the most urgent of which was want.

We may here say that in this dark and narrow alley, too—for Rose Street is, or rather was, scarcely anything better—Dryden the poet was attacked by three hired assailants, and beaten, to use the expressive phrase, "within an inch of his life." This attack has become almost historical. Some of his biographers tell us that when the ferocious assault was made upon him he was going home to his house in Gerrard Street, from "Will's Coffee-house" in Russell Street, Covent Garden, which he was in the habit of frequently attending. This statement has given rise to much controversy,

which the late Mr. Robert Bell, in the first volume of *Once a Week*, was at considerable pains to set at rest. The assault took place on the night of the 18th of December, 1679, so that the poet could not be making his way at the time to Gerrard Street, for that street, it is alleged, was not built till some two years later. Dryden is stated, on the authority of the rate-books of the parish, to have lived in Fleet Street from 1673 to 1682, when he removed to a house in Long Acre, exactly facing the dismal *embouchure* of Rose Street. Here he lived till 1686, when he went farther westward to the house 43, Gerrard Street, where he died on the 1st of May, 1700. "If these dates be correct," says the writer above referred to, "there would be no difficulty in determining where Dryden was living at the time; . . . for we find that while the rate-books of St. Bride's are quoted to show that in 1679 he was living in Fleet Street, the rate-books of St. Martin's are relied upon with equal confidence to prove that at the same time he was living in Long Acre. The biographers who have escaped the dilemma by sending him on to Gerrard Street at once may therefore turn out to be right, after all. Fleet Street, at all events, is put out of court. We know from the contemporary account of the circumstance that he was going from Covent Garden; and if he were going home, as must be inferred from the lateness of the hour, he could not have been going to Fleet Street, which would take him in the opposite direction, while the way both to Gerrard Street and Long Acre lay direct through this unsavoury Rose Avenue. To one or other of these places he must have been going. "Perhaps," the writer naïvely adds, "most readers will be of opinion that it is not very material which date is correct, or to what house he was wending his way at the time." The important event is the assault itself, and the circumstance that it occurred in Rose Street.

At the "Rose" Tavern, in or close to Rose Street, as Mr. John Timbs tells us, the "Treason Club" met, at the time of the Revolution, to consult with Lord Colchester, Mr. Thomas Wharton, and many others; and it was on this occasion resolved that the regiment under Lieutenant-Colonel Langdale's command should desert entire, as in fact it did in November, 1688.

In Rose Street lived the notorious bookseller, Edmund Curll, at the "Pope's Head," a sign which he had set up, not, certainly, out of affection for Alexander Pope, but rather from an opposite feeling. "After the quarrel which arose out of Curll's piratical publication of Pope's library correspondence," says Mr. Larwood, in his "History of Sign-

Boards," "Curll addressed, in May, 1735, a letter of thanks to the House of Lords, ending thus: 'I have engraved a new plate of Mr. Pope's head from Mr. Jervas's painting, and likewise intend to hang him up in effigy for a sign to all spectators of his falsehood and my **veracity,** which I will always

New Street, just by. Several of them had travelled. They expected to meet every day, but did not know one another's names. It used to cost the rest a shilling, for they drank wine; but I had a cut of meat for sixpence, and bread for a penny, and gave the waiter a penny; so that I was quite well served

INTERIOR OF ST. MARTIN'S HALL, 1850. (*See page* 269.)

maintain, under the Scotch motto, '*Nemo me impune lacesset.*'"

New Street, which forms the continuation from King Street to St. Martin's Lane, was a favourite resort of Dr. Johnson. His first lodgings were at the house of Mr. Norris, a staymaker, in Exeter Street, adjoining Catherine Street, in the Strand. "I dined," said he, "very well for eightpence, with very good company, at the 'Pine Apple,' in

—nay, better than the rest, for they gave the waiter nothing." In the reign of Charles II. New Street was very fashionably inhabited; for, as Mr. Peter Cunningham tells us, the Countess of Chesterfield, the lady with whom Van Dyck was in love, occupied a house on the south side in 1660. Flaxman, the famous sculptor, was living here in the years 1771 and 1772.

The neighbourhood to the east of St. Martin's

Lane up to Long Acre northwards a century ago formed the centre for artists of every class and their allies. The great Sir Joshua Reynolds, as we have seen in an earlier chapter, held his court in Leicester Square; the old Life Academy had been for years in a house at the top of a court in "the Lane," as it was at that time familiarly styled; and "in Long Acre itself were congregated the colour-makers, goldbeaters, artists' tool-makers, modellers, and journeymen of every kind," as Miss Meteyard tells us in her "Life of Wedgwood." Here, at the corner of Newport Street and of St. Martin's Lane, in a house with a double frontage into either thoroughfare, in 1768–74, were the show-rooms of Josiah Wedgwood's pottery-ware and porcelain, before he settled down in Greek Street, Soho, where we found him in a previous chapter. As Miss Meteyard remarks, "Newport Street and its neighbourhood have undergone, since then, so great an amount of alteration as to show at this day few, if any, vestiges of its old condition; but, judging by our present ideas relative to space, light, and accessibility, it must have been a gloomy and confined situation for such a shrine of the arts, and one so resorted to by the noblest in intellect and rank in the land." Although the house thus celebrated is no longer standing in its entirety, it may be of some interest to state, on the same authority, that whilst the ground-floor was a shop for the sale of ordinary goods, where "the public entered in and out at pleasure," the first-floor suite formed a gallery or repository into which only Mr. Wedgwood's wealthy and aristocratic patrons were admitted; and the second-floor formed the home of Mr. Wedgwood and his family when in town. Josiah himself thus describes the house in a letter to Bentley: "It is at the top of St. Martin's Lane, a corner house, 60 feet long; the streets are wide which lye to it, and carriages may come to it either from Westminster or the City without being incommoded with drays full of timber and coals, which are always pouring in from the various wharfs, and making stops in the Strand, very disagreeable and sometimes dangerous. The rent is . . . 100 guineas a year. My friends in town tell me that it is the best situation in London for my rooms."

Another fact relating to the neighbourhood of Covent Garden and St. Martin's Lane may as well be noticed here. It was the first in the West End of London to dispense with the old sign-boards which used to project over the pathways. A daily paper of November, 1762, tells us, as a piece of news, that "the signs in Duke Court, St. Martin's Lane, are all taken down, and affixed to the front of the houses." Thus the City of Westminster began the innovation by procuring an Act of Parliament with powers for that purpose. Other West-End parishes, including that of Marylebone, copied the example; the City of London in due course followed suit, and long before the end of the last century the picturesque signs were superseded by plain and prosaic numbers. Along with the signs, of course, went the sign-posts. Mr. J. Larwood tells us, in his "History of Sign-Boards," that this removal of the sign-posts, and the paving of the streets at the same time with Scotch granite, gave rise to the following epigram:—

"The Scottish new pavement deserves well our praise;
    To the Scotch we're obliged, too, for mending our ways:
    But this we can never forget, for they say
    As that they have taken our posts all away."

Bedford Street, which runs northwards from the Strand to the west of the churchyard of St. Paul's, Covent Garden, can at all events boast of some ancient memories. Strype describes it as "a handsome, broad street, with very good houses," adding that since the Fire of London the latter are generally taken up by tradesmen of the better class, such as mercers, drapers, and lacemen; but these have given way to newspaper and publishing offices. The houses on the western side, Strype remarks, are better than those on the east. The upper part of the street dates from 1637; in the lower part is the West End branch of the Civil Service Stores, a handsome building of red brick faced with terra-cotta. In this street resided Quin the actor; Chief Justice Richardson; Sir Francis Kynaston the poet; the Earl of Chesterfield; and Thomas Sheridan, the father of Richard Brinsley Sheridan. Whyte, in his "Miscellanea Nova," tells us how one day when there he looked out up Henrietta Street—opposite to which Mr. Sheridan lived—and saw Dr. Johnson walking "with a peculiar solemnity of deportment and an awkward sort of measured step, and laying his hands, as he went along, upon the top of each of the posts." No. 26 in this street, an old-established gold lace manufacturer's shop, retained its sign, "The Three Crowns," till the house was pulled down in 1875.

We find the following advertisement respecting the newly-introduced luxury of tea in the *Tatler* of March, 1710:—"The finest Imperial Tea, 18s.; Bohee, 12s., 16s., 20s., and 24s.; all sorts of Green, the lowest 12s. To be had of R. Tate, at the 'Star' in Bedford Court, near Bedford Street, Covent Garden." Tea had been introduced into England more than half a century before; but even at the date to which reference is here made it was evidently still a costly and rare article, if we may judge from the prices given in the above advertisement.

In consequence of the removal of house-signs (of which we have already spoken), the difficulty of finding out a house at night was greatly increased, and therefore other means were resorted to, as we learn from an advertisement of " Doctor James Tilbrough, a German doctor," who resided " over against the New Exchange in Bedford Street, at the sign of the Peacock, where you shall see at night two candles burning within one of the chambers before the balcony, and a lanthorn with a candle in it upon the balcony." We have mentioned in a preceding chapter that it is to Covent Garden that London is indebted for the introduction of " balconies."

Southampton Street is the name of the thoroughfare which connects the southern side of Covent Garden with the Strand. Garrick at one time lived in Southampton Street. Mr. Cradock, who knew him well, tells us several good stories about him. Garrick was a great mimic, and by his power of imitation could make Johnson seem extremely ridiculous. He could put on the doctor's rough and uncouth manners, and growl out four or five lines of Gray's " Bard," without, however, articulating the words. This he could do at his suppers to the entertainment of his friends, but not to the satisfaction of Dr. Johnson. Another anecdote, related likewise by Mr. Cradock, introduces Mrs. Garrick :—" My apartments," he tells us, " were at that time in Southampton Street, opposite to Mr. Garrick, who sometimes would divert a few friends with a ludicrous story at my expense, ' That I had stayed out so very late one night at the " Piazza " Coffee-house ; and that at my return I had disturbed Mrs. Garrick and his whole neighbourhood ; so much so, indeed, that he was afraid he must have called for the watch.' Part of this story might be correct ; but Mrs. Garrick owned to whom it was indebted for its embellishments. The whole truth was, that the lady of the house where I lodged was built on a very large scale, and in her hurry to let me in, by some accident or other fell down in the passage, and could not readily be got up again ; and I believe that, growing rather impatient, I possibly might call out very vociferously, till the lady could be safely removed ; and that the husband, who was seriously disturbed, became angry, and absolutely declared that his wife at no future time should sit up so late for a lodger." From Southampton Street Garrick removed to his house in Adelphi Terrace, at the solicitation of his friend Lord Mansfield. The houses on the Terrace, from

the beauty of their prospect, had been selected by his lordship for particular friends. The centre house was allotted to the great actor, but none of them, Mr. Cradock tells us, were quite suited to him, as his health was then declining, and the bleak situation was ill contrasted with the warm and sheltered apartments in Southampton Street which he had left. In Southampton Street lived and died old Gabriel Cibber, and here his son Colley Cibber was born.

Extending from Southampton Street to Bedford Street, about midway between the Strand and Henrietta Street, is Maiden Lane, on which we have already slightly touched in a previous chapter. We may add, however, that the well-known tavern here, called the " Old Welch Ale House," which stood on the site of the " Bedford Head," and which was pulled down in 1870, has risen, phœnix-like, in a new building, which has returned to its old designation, being now known as the " Bedford Head " hotel. It adjoins the site of the house of Andrew Marvell, poet and patriot, where he was lodging when Lord Danby climbed his stairs with a message and bribe from the king, but found him too honest and too proud to accept it. It is said that he was dining off the pickings of a mutton-bone when Lord Danby called, and that as soon as he was gone he was obliged to send to a friend to borrow a guinea. Two doors off, at an old French perruquier's, at the sign of the " White Peruke," Voltaire lodged when young, and when busy in publishing his " Henriade ;" he was a constant visitor at the " Bedford," where his bust still adorns a room. Voltaire had been imprisoned in the Bastile for a libel, and after his release came over to London, where he procured many subscriptions towards publishing his poem. He remained here several years, becoming acquainted with Pope, Congreve, Young, and other celebrated literary men of his time ; and tradition says that they frequently resorted to this tavern together of an evening. When J. M. W. Turner lived in this street (that is, before 1800) he would often spend an evening at the " Bedford." " In the parlour of the ' Bedford,' " says Mr. J. H. Jesse, in his " London," "met the ' Shilling Rubber Club,' of which Fielding, Hogarth, Goldsmith, and Churchill were members. It was at one of their meetings here that the quarrel arose between Hogarth and Churchill which induced the latter to satirise his friend, and the former to retaliate upon him with his unrivalled pencil. The ' Epistle to Hogarth ' is comparatively forgotten ; but Churchill will still live as ' Bruin ' when his verse shall have passed into oblivion." The present tavern, which has resumed its ancient name, is adjoined on the west by a large block styled "Sussex Mansions," and let out as offices and for residential purposes.

Exactly opposite, on the south side, was a part of the premises of Messrs. Godfrey and Cooke, of Southampton Street, the oldest chemists and druggists in London, having been established in 1680. A hundred years ago, or a little more, Mr. Ambrose Godfrey, one of the firm, proposed to extinguish fires by a "new method of explosion and suffocation," thereby anticipating the "Fire Extincteur" of our own day. But these premises have now been absorbed into a handsome Catholic church, with schools and presbytery attached, solemnly opened by the late Cardinal Manning in the autumn of 1874.

On the south side, nearer to the west end of the street, was a house which in 1864 became a "School of Arms and of Athletic Exercises." It was previously a place notoriously of bad reputation as the " Cider Cellars "—a place of low and not very moral amusement for the fast young "swells" of the City and West End after the theatres were closed, and rivalling the " Coal Hole " and the " Judge and Jury " in their special characteristics of immorality. It had been devoted to the muse of song for a century and a half at the least. On the same side of the street is the Maiden Lane Synagogue, and also the back of the Adelphi Theatre, which stretches thus far from the Strand.

Maiden Lane is said by Mr. Isaac D'Israeli, in his "Curiosities of Literature," to have received its name from a statue of the Virgin Mary, "which in Catholic days adorned the corner of the street, as Bagford writes to Hearne," who also says that the frequent sign of " the Maidenhead " denoted " Our Lady's Head." But this may be a fanciful conjecture, as the sober and honest chronicler, John Stow, tells us that its original designation was "Ingene" or "Ing" Lane.

Chandos Street, which leads from Maiden Lane towards the lower end of St. Martin's Lane, was so called after Brydges, Lord Chandos, the ancestor of the "princely" Duke of Chandos. It was built in the reign of Charles I., and of late years has been largely rebuilt. It now contains the Medical School of Charing Cross Hospital, and one of the two frontages of the West End branch of the Civil Service Stores, the other being in Bedford Street. In the *Harleian Miscellany* we are told that at the corner of Chandos Street was the sign of a Balcony, "which country people were wont much to gaze on."

At the "Three Tuns," a bagnio in this street,

the Honourable John Finch was stabbed, in a fit of jealousy, by a celebrated personage, Sally Pridden, whose portrait was painted by Sir Godfrey Kneller. She was called "Sally Salisbury," on account of a fancied resemblance to the then Countess of Salisbury. She died in Newgate whilst undergoing her sentence for the above deed of violence, "leaving behind her," says Caulfield, in his " Memoirs of Remarkable Persons," " the character of the most notorious woman that ever infested the Hundreds of Old Drury or Covent Garden either."

Bedfordbury is the name once given to a district containing a few small streets lying between St. Martin's Lane, on the West side, and Bedford Street, Covent Garden, on the east, but now confined to the narrow lane running southwards from New Street to Chandos Street. The district was built about the year 1635, and was once the residence of well-to-do families. It has, however, but few historical or literary associations; though Mr. Peter Cunningham records the fact that in 1636 Sir Francis Kynaston, the accomplished scholar and poet, was living hereabouts, "on the east side of the street towards Berrie," and he supposed that his name was perpetuated in Kynaston's Alley adjoining. All the eastern side of the lane was pulled down in 1880, and a block of model lodging-houses erected instead.

Of Sir Francis Kynaston some interesting details will be found in Faulkner's " History of Chelsea." It appears that during the prevalence of the plague in London, in 1636, Sir Francis, at that time Regent of the Museum Minervæ, presented to the king a petition requesting permission to remove his institute to Chelsea College, and the king granted his request. "The Museum Minervæ," adds Faulkner, "was an academy instituted in the eleventh year of King Charles I., and established at a house in or near Covent Garden, purchased for the purpose by Sir Francis Kynaston, and furnished by him with books, manuscripts, paintings, statues, musical and mathematical instruments, &c., and every requisite for a polite and liberal education. Only the nobility and gentry were admissible into the academy. Sir Francis Kynaston was chosen president or regent of the new institution, and professors were appointed to teach the various arts and sciences. The constitutions of the Museum Minervæ were published in London in 1626, in quarto." The authorities of Chelsea College, however, remonstrated against this royal concession, and so the grant never took effect. Sir Francis and his colleagues accordingly were obliged to content themselves with other quarters, at Little Chelsea. The subsequent history of the Museum

Minervæ we have not been able to trace; but it is worth mentioning here in connection with the borderland of Covent Garden and St. Martin's Lane, as in all probability it furnished some hints towards the first foundation—or, at all events, to the first rough outline—of the Royal Academy. It is supposed by Allibone that Sir Francis did not long survive the transaction here recorded, but died about the year 164-. He was the author of a Latin verse translation of Chaucer's "Troilus and Cressida," and of a poem entitled "Leoline and Sydanis, an Heroic Romance of the Adventures of two Amorous Princes," together with sundry affectionate addresses to his mistress under the name of "Cynthia." Sir Francis is mentioned in terms of appreciation in George Ellis's "Specimens of Early English Poets," and in the "Censura Literaria."

CHAPTER XXXIV.

COVENT GARDEN AND ITS NEIGHBOURHOOD (continued).

"Rus in urbe, urbs in rure."

Long Acre—Its Original Condition—The Head-quarters of Carriage-builders—Distinguished Residents—St. Martin's Hall—Mr. Hullah's Choral Classes—St. Martin's Hall destroyed by Fire and rebuilt—The Queen's Theatre—Messrs. Merryweather's Fire-engine Manufactory—Hanover Court, and Taylor the "Water-Poet"—Hart Street—Charles Macklin as a Tavern-keeper—Bow Street—The Police Office—Noted Residents—Fall of Grinling Gibbons' House—Dr. Radcliffe—The Poet Wycherley—The "Garrick's Head"—Exhibition of Sign-boards—The "Wrekin"—Wycherley's Dying Request to his Young Wife.

HAVING completed our desultory survey of the purlieus of Covent Garden lying westward as far as St. Martin's Lane, we once more turn our face towards the east, and wend our way through Long Acre. This fine thoroughfare, as already stated, was originally called "The Elms," and the "Elm Close;" then "The Seven Acres;" and in after times it got its present name from a long and narrow slip of ground belonging to the Abbot of Westminster, used as a pathway, which bordered the garden on the north. The pleasure-grounds behind the convent are said to have covered seven acres, and an avenue of tall elms is reported to have stood along the present line of road. Among the entries in the Council Books of the time of King Edward VI. mention is made of a grant from the king to the Earl of Bedford and his heirs male of "the Convent Garden" and of "the meadow-ground known as 'The Long Acre.'" It began to be built upon at the close of the sixteenth or early in the seventeenth century.

Probably from the time of Charles I., when coaches were first introduced into use in London, Long Acre became the head-quarters of carriage-builders, whose manufactories still exist there in considerable numbers, side by side with varnish-makers, coach-trimming makers, &c. Many of the other houses not so occupied were tenanted by persons of note; and others, again, by physicians and medical quacks. Stothard, the painter and Royal Academician, we are told, was the son of a carriage-maker in this street. John Dryden lived in it, on the north side, opposite to Rose Street;

and Oliver Cromwell on the southern side, from 1637 to 1643.

Long Acre has had many other distinguished residents. Here lived the beautiful "Chloe" with whom Prior has made us so familiar in his poems. Instead, however, of being young, elegant, and beautiful, we learn that she was the commonplace wife of a cobbler, or, according to other accounts, of a soldier or an alehouse-keeper. But whoever and whatever she may have been, Pope tells us that "Prior used to bury himself here for whole days and nights together with the poor mean creature." Let us hope that she had merits of her own and qualities unknown to the world outside.

At a corner on the north side of Long Acre, where it meets Endell Street, with entrances in Wilson Street, Charles Street, and Long Acre, stood the Queen's Theatre. This building passed through the first two stages of its existence under the name of "St. Martin's Hall." The first edifice bearing that name was built, in the year 1847, by William Cubitt, from a design by the younger Westmacott, on a site which was presented to Mr. John Hullah by one of the civic companies. It was of the Elizabethan style of architecture, with a domed iron roof of immense space. The music-hall, which was capable of easily accommodating 3,000 persons, was opened in 1850 by Mr. Hullah, the founder of a new school of choral harmony. Here Mr. Hullah held his singing-classes; and oratorios and concerts, both instrumental and vocal, of a high order of excellence, were given under his direction. Here, too, Mr. Charles Dickens first appeared as a public lecturer, in April, 1858, on behalf of the Hospital for Sick Children, in Great Ormond Street, and a week or two later on his own account.

St. Martin's Hall was not only used for musical purposes, but also sometimes echoed to far less harmonious sounds when occupied by noisy and crowded meetings where political and social ques-

promenade concerts by Mr. Strange, lessee of the Alhambra; but its career as a concert-hall was drawing to a close. On the 24th of October, 1867, after undergoing considerable alterations, it was opened as a theatre by Mr. Alfred Wigan, under the title of "The Queen's," a name that had just before been discarded by the theatre near Tottenham Court Road, afterwards styled the "Prince of Wales's." From that period it changed hands

AN OLD COACHMAKER'S SHOP IN LONG ACRE (1870).

tions were agitated. On August 26, 1860, a fire broke out early in the morning in the coach-factory of Messrs. Kesterton, at the corner of Long Acre and Endell Street, closely adjoining St. Martin's Hall, and from the inflammable nature of the contents of the workshops the flames spread with a rapidity which defied the efforts of the engines. The fire was not long in reaching the roof of St. Martin's Hall, and this noble concert-room shared the fate of the adjacent building; not a vestige of it remained, and with it perished the fine organ by which it was adorned.

St. Martin's Hall was rebuilt, and reopened as a concert-hall in 1862, and musical and other entertainments were here held until 1867. Early in that year it was again engaged for a series of

several times, passing successively under the management of Messrs. Wigan, Liston, Young, and Clifton, and of Mrs. Seymour. Many well-known artists played at this theatre—Mr. J. L. Toole, Mr. Phelps, Miss Henrietta Hodson, and Mr. and Mrs. Rousby; the last-mentioned lady having made her *début* here in 1869, as "Fiordelisa" in *The Fool's Revenge*. *'Twixt Axe and Crown* and *Joan of Arc* were first produced here. After a short career, the Queen's Theatre was closed about 1875, and converted into "co-operative stores." It has now been converted into a paper warehouse.

Opposite this place, and occupying the corner of Long Acre and Bow Street, is the shop of Messrs. Merryweather, the celebrated fire-engine manufacturers. Their business dates from the latter part of the seventeenth century; the firm being formerly known under the names of Hadley, Simpkin, and Lott. Until it was recently rebuilt, the house occupied by Messrs. Merryweather was supposed to be the only one either in Long Acre or in Bow Street standing in exactly the same

nalised himself by his strenuous opposition to the introduction of coaches into London. The sign of the alehouse, it is said, was the "Crown," for which, on the establishment of the Commonwealth, he substituted his own head, with the following witty motto :—

MR. DAVIES' SHOP, RUSSELL STREET. (*See page* 275.)

condition as when first erected. The firm has in its possession several firemen's leather helmets, dating from 1720, if not earlier, and other curious relics of former times.

A little further westwards in Long Acre is Hanover Court, formerly Phœnix Alley, celebrated as having been once the home of Taylor the "water-poet," who died in it in 1653. He kept an alehouse here, and it is on record that, as one of the privileged watermen on the Thames, he sig-

"There's many a head stands for a sign ;
Then, gentle reader, why not mine ?"

Hart Street, which runs parallel with Long Acre, between that thoroughfare and Covent Garden, was built about the year 1636–7, and derived its name from the "White Hart" Inn, which was still standing as late as the reign of George I. In it died Haines, the comic actor, in 1701. It was also at one time the abode of the celebrated Charles Macklin, who retired from the stage in middle life, under the idea of making his fortune here by establishing a tavern and coffee-house, in 1754. In the March of that year he opened a public ordinary, to be continued every day at four o'clock, price three shillings, "port, claret, or any other liquor included." An account of this dinner, given in Smith's "Historical and Literary Curiosities," presents us with an amusing picture of the manners of the day in coffee-houses and taverns. When the clock struck, a large bell suspended on the top of the house was rung for five minutes, and the dinner was ordered to be served. In ten minutes more it was put upon the table; the door was then closed, and no other guest was admitted. Macklin himself always brought in the first dish, in "a full dress suit," and with a napkin on his left arm; and when he had set it down he made a low bow and retired to a sideboard, surrounded by a bevy of waiters. For several months previous to opening he had trained his servants to communicate with him by signs, not a word being spoken by any of them while they remained in the room, for fear of interrupting the "feast of reason and the flow of soul." When the dinner was ended, and the wine set upon the table, Macklin quitted his situation, and, walking gravely up to his visitors, expressed a modest "hope that everything had been found agreeable and to their satisfaction," and then retired, making a low bow at the door. To this establishment Macklin afterwards added another, which he called "The British Inquisition," which, as stated in his advertisement, was to be on the plan of the ancient Greek, Roman, and modern French and Italian societies of liberal investigation. "Such subjects," he says in his announcement, "in arts, sciences, literature, criticism, philosophy, history, politics, and morality, as shall be found useful and entertaining to society, will there be lectured upon and freely debated. Particularly," it is added, "Mr. Macklin intends to lecture upon the comedy of the ancients, the use of their masks and flutes, their mimes and pantomimes, and the use and abuse of the stage. He will likewise lecture on the rise and progress of modern theatres, making a comparison between them and those of Greece and Rome, and between each other; he also proposes to lecture upon each of Shakespeare's plays." These discussions and discourses were to be held on the evenings of Monday and Friday, at seven o'clock; but the idea did not take. The whole establishment was a failure from the beginning; and in January, 1755, Charles Macklin became a bankrupt. After this failure he returned to the stage, doubtless a wiser man for his experience in business.

Bow Street, which forms the connecting link between Long Acre and Russell Street, and together with Endell Street and Wellington Street forms a direct communication between Oxford Street and the Strand, was built in 1637, being so called "as running in shape of a bent bow." Strype, who tells us this, also says that "the street is open and large, with very good houses, well inhabited, and resorted unto by gentry for lodgings, as are most of the other streets in this parish." This was in 1720. It ceased to be well inhabited about five years afterwards. The theatre (Covent Garden Theatre) on the west side we have described in a previous chapter. Bow Street Police Office, celebrated in the annals of crime, was established in 1749. It was formerly occupied by the novelist Fielding, who is said to have written "Tom Jones" within its walls. The office itself, as it appeared till quite recently was a mean and paltry structure, quite unworthy of being used as a temple of Justice. Its officials belong to history. The old Bow Street officers were called by fast men "Robin Redbreasts," on account of their wearing red vests; and though they were a set of brave and resolute men, they were too limited in numbers to be generally effective. Amongst the most vigilant and energetic we may mention Leadbitter, Ruthven, Goddard, and Keys. At night the only protection afforded to Londoners was a tribe of guardians who, though infinitely more in numbers, were far less useful in effect. These night guardians were generally aged and ineffective men, whose duty was to parade the streets; and the inhabitants, by rotation, had to sit up every night at the watch-house in Portugal Street, to take the charges—a pleasant task, after a man had been attending to his business all day!

Bow Street has long been celebrated all over the United Kingdom, and indeed throughout the world, as the head police-court of the metropolis, particularly since the time of Sir John Fielding, in the last century. Here are tried all extradition cases, which are taken by the chief magistrate, Sir John Bridge. The establishment consists of three magistrates, each attending two days in a week. All the magistrates belonging to this office are in the Commission of the Peace for the Counties of London, Middlesex, Surrey, Kent, Essex, and Herts. In 1880–81 a fine new building was erected on the east side of the street, to serve the purposes of both the Police Court and the Police Station. The edifice is in the Italian style of architecture, and covers a large space of ground. The old police-station was pulled down early in 1897.

Bow Street can boast of a series of illustrious names among its former inhabitants; for nearly opposite to the Police Office resided Edmund Waller the poet, from 1654 to 1656. Here, then, he was living when he wrote, in 1654, his famous panegyric upon Cromwell. William Longueville, the friend of Butler, too, lived close by. The witty Earl of Dorset resided in a house on the west side, in the years 1684 and 1685. Major Mohun, the famous actor, occupied a house on the east side, from 1671 to 1676 inclusive; Robert Harley, Earl of Oxford, the great Prime Minister of his day, was born in this street in 1661; and Grinling Gibbons, too, lived in a house on the east side (about the middle of the street), from 1678 to 1721, the period of his death. The house was distinguished by the name of "The King's Arms." In the *Postman* of the 24th of January, 1701, it is recorded that "on Thursday the house of Mr. Gibbons, the famous carver, in Bow Street, fell down; but by a special Providence none of the family were killed; but 'tis said that a young girl, which was playing in the court [King's Court?], being missing, is supposed to be buried in the rubbish."

Among other illustrious inhabitants of this street must not be forgotten Sir Godfrey Kneller, and Dr. Radcliffe, the munificent founder of the museum at Oxford which bears his name. They lived next door to each other, and were great friends, though every now and then it would appear that they had their little quarrels, as we have shown in the anecdote narrated in a previous chapter.* On reading the anecdote we feel almost irresistibly compelled to ask, with Virgil, *Tantæne animis cœlestibus iræ?* It seems that on taking his degree at Oxford Dr. Radcliffe settled in Bow Street, at that time a fashionable suburb, and soon made in fees twenty guineas a day, "through his vigorous and decisive method of practice" (says Chambers, in his "Book of Days"), "as well as his pleasantry and ready wit; many, it is said, even feigning themselves ill in order to have the pleasure of a few minutes' conversation with the facetious doctor." Even at this time his books were so few in number that one day, on being asked where was his library, he pointed to a few phials, a skeleton, and a herbal, in one corner of his apartment, exclaiming with emphasis, "There, sir, is Radcliffe's Library." The answer has all the more point because late in life he became the owner of a very fine library, which he left to the University of Oxford. We shall have more to say about Dr. Radcliffe when we

come to Kensington Palace. His fortune as a West-End physician was made in 1689, when he managed to restore to health King William just before he went to Ireland to fight the battle of the Boyne, and two years later, when he cured the young Duke of Gloucester of some fainting-fits which threatened to carry him off.

In this street, in lodgings "over against the 'Cock' Tavern," lived the dramatic poet Wycherley and his wife, the widow of the Earl of Drogheda, whom he gained by a chance introduction in a shop at Tunbridge Wells. Whilst residing here he had the honour of a visit from Charles II., who came to see him when ill, and presented him with money enough to pay the expenses of a visit to the south of France. It may perhaps be remembered that Wycherley had held a captain's commission in a regiment of which the Duke of Buckingham was colonel.

It was from the "Cock" Tavern that Sir John Coventry was on his way to his house in the neighbourhood of Pall Mall when he was severely wounded in the nose, as we shall relate when we come to speak of the neighbourhood of the Hay-market.

Mr. T. Raikes in his "Journal," under date 1842, writes:—"After dinner I went to the mock trials at the 'Garrick's Head,' in Bow Street. There is one man who imitates Brougham very well as a counsel; but the subject of debate was coarse, and the audience very vulgar."

In Bonnell Thornton's chambers in this street, "at the upper end, nearly opposite the Play-house Passage," was held in 1762, an exhibition of sign-boards, by the "Society of Sign-Painters"— of whom, by the way, Hogarth was one. It was intended as a skit upon the exhibitions then newly introduced by the Society of Arts, Manufactures, and Commerce, and its catalogue included upwards of seventy paintings, some of them curious on account of the covered satire which they were intended to convey on political events and public characters. There was, for instance, much humour in placing "The Three Coffins" as a companion to "The Three Apothecaries' Gallipots," and "The Owl in the Ivy Bush" next to "King Charles in the Oak." The exhibition caused much smart and tart writing in the newspapers at the time, and the admission was fixed at a shilling. A full account of the exhibition will be found in the appendix to Mr. Larwood's "History of Sign-Boards."

Towards the close of the last century, when Rich was in the zenith of his managerial prosperity, and the new theatre in Covent Garden had

* See *ante*, page 143.

just commenced with the reproduction of *The Beggar's Opera* a series of what would now be called blazes of triumph, there was established in the immediate vicinity a rustic-looking hostel, to accommodate a refreshment-seeking crowd finding no unoccupied nook in the taverns adjacent. This hostel was "The Wrekin" in Broad Court, on the east side of Bow Street. The original landlord was one Powell, a native of Shropshire, and he chose for his sign the name of the high hill over-shadowing the place of his birth. Hither came the actors of that date, and those who sought and valued their society of course followed in their train. The next proprietor was a gentleman named Harrold, of a good Herefordshire family, and who considerably raised the fortunes and the reputation of the house. For about half a century, under his management, "The Wrekin" was the chosen resort of the most prominent celebrities of the day; and as wine was the only refreshment supplied to those who entered the coffee-room, the visitors were exceedingly select. The Kembles—John and Charles—and the principal members of that powerful company then collected at the neighbouring theatre, would constantly avail themselves of this handy histrionic hostel to snatch a pleasant hour from the night, after the cessation of their professional duties. The tavern shared the vicissitudes of the theatre, on which it was in some degree dependent, and nearly every change of management at the one house was followed by a change in the direction of the other. Mr. Warner, the husband of the celebrated tragic actress Mrs. Warner, was at one time the landlord, and Mr. Hemming, an esteemed actor at the Haymarket and Adelphi Theatres, was another. Two famous clubs were here instituted, one called "The Rationals," and the other "The House of Uncommons." When Hemming left to become lessee of the "Café de l'Europe" in the Haymarket, he took the best of the visitors away with him. From 1842 "The Wrekin" began gradually to decline, and within the last few years its declension was so rapid that by the end of 1871 the ancient hostel was levelled with the ground, and its position occupied by a block of new houses manifestly let to respectable tenants.

Wycherley died in his house in Bow Street, in the year 1715, at the age of seventy-five. Of his death-bed we find an amusing anecdote in the "Letters" of Pope. "He had often told me, as, I doubt not, he told all his acquaintance, that he would marry as soon as his life was despaired of. Accordingly, a few days before his death, he underwent the ceremony, and joined together those two sacraments which, wise men say, should be the last we receive; for, if you observe, matrimony is placed after extreme unction in our catechism (*i.e.*, the Roman Catholic), as a kind of hint of the order of time in which they are to be taken. The old man then lay down, satisfied in the conscience of having by this one act paid his just debts, obliged a woman who (he was told) had merit, and shown an heroic resentment of the ill-usage of his next heir. Some hundred pounds which he had with the lady discharged those debts; a jointure of four hundred a year made her a recompense; and the nephew he left to comfort himself as well as he could with the miserable remains of a mortgaged estate. I saw our friend twice after this was done, less peevish in his sickness than he used to be in his health; neither much afraid of dying, nor (which in him had been more likely) much ashamed of marrying. The evening before he expired he called his young wife to the bedside, and earnestly entreated her not to deny him one request, the last he should make. Upon her assurances of consenting to it, he told her, 'My dear, it is only this, that you will never marry an old man again.' I cannot help remarking that sickness, which often destroys both wit and wisdom, yet seldom has power to remove that talent which we call humour. Mr. Wycherley showed his, even in this last compliment; though I think his request a little hard, for why should he bar her from doubling her jointure on the same easy terms?"

It seems strange at the present day to think of Bow Street as one of the most fashionable streets in London; but there can be no doubt that such must have been the character of this thoroughfare in the early part of the last century, for Dryden asserts as much in a casual manner when he writes :—

"From fops, and wits, and cits, and Bow Street beaux."

CHAPTER XXXV.
COVENT GARDEN AND ITS NEIGHBOURHOOD (*continued*).

Russell Street—Tom Davies' Bookshop—The First Meeting of Boswell and Johnson—An Anecdote of Foote, the Actor—"Will's Coffee-house"—Dryden and Addison—Pope's Youthful Visits to "Will's"—"Button's Coffee-house"—The "Lion's Head"—"Tom's Coffee-house"—The "Shakespeare's Head"—The "Albion"—Distinguished Residents in Russell Street—"The Orpheus" Music-shop—The "Rose" Tavern—The "Harp" and "The City of Lushington"—Crown Court and the Scotch National Church—Richard Steele—Gradual Decline of "Button's Coffee-house."

QUITTING Bow Street, we now enter Russell Street, the thoroughfare connecting Covent Garden Market with Drury Lane. This street was built in 1634, and so called after the Russells, Earls and Dukes of Bedford, the ground-landlords. In 1720 "it was a fine broad street, well inhabited by tradesmen;" and much the same character may be accorded to it in the present day, excepting that that portion of it which skirts the northern side of Drury Lane Theatre is considerably narrowed. Russell Street is one which will always have a memory of a character sacred to all lovers of literature, because in it Boswell was first introduced to Dr. Samuel Johnson. The old bookshop of Tom Davies on the south side of the street, where Johnson first met the Scotchman who was destined to be his biographer, became in our own day the "Caledonian" Coffee-house; and its interest is not diminished by the fact that "Bozzy," as he himself informs us, never passed by it "without feeling reverence and regret." The meeting, to use Boswell's own words, was brought about in this manner:—"At last," he writes, "on Monday, the 16th of May, when I was sitting in Mr. Davies's back parlour, after having drunk tea with him and Mrs. Davies, Johnson unexpectedly came into the shop, and Mr. Davies having perceived him through the glass door of the room in which we were sitting, advancing towards us, he rumoured his awful approach to me, somewhat in the manner of an actor in the part of 'Horatio,' when he addresses 'Hamlet' on the appearance of his father's ghost—'Look, my lord! it comes!' I found that I had a very perfect idea of Johnson's figure from the portrait of him, painted by Sir Joshua Reynolds, soon after he had published his dictionary, in the attitude of sitting in his easy-chair in deep meditation. Mr. Davies mentioned my name, and respectfully introduced me to him. I was much agitated; and recollecting his prejudice against the Scotch, of which I had heard much, I said to Davies, 'Don't tell where I come from.' 'From Scotland,' cries Davies, roguishly. 'Mr. Johnson,' said I, 'I do indeed come from Scotland, but I cannot help it.' I am willing to flatter myself that I meant this as light pleasantry, to soothe and conciliate him, and not as an humiliating abasement at the expense of my country. But however that might be, this speech was somewhat unlucky, for, with that quickness of wit for which he was remarkable, he seized the expression 'come from Scotland,' which I used in the sense of being of that country; and as if I had said that I had come away from it, or left it, retorted, 'That, sir, I find, is what a good many of your country cannot help.' This stroke stunned me a good deal; and when we had sat down I felt myself not a little embarrassed, and apprehensive of what might come next."

In the "Literary Memoirs" of Mr. Cradock, who often met Johnson, Boswell, and Foote here, we find an anecdote of Foote in connection with the shop of Tom Davies which perhaps may not be unacceptable:—"Foote by accident met an inferior person in the street very like Dr. Arne, who, when full dressed, was sometimes rather a grotesque figure, and he contrived not only to obtain some old clothes of the doctor's, but likewise one of his cast-off wigs, and introduced the man on the stage to bring in music-books, as an attendant on the Commissary. The house was all astonishment, and many began even to doubt of the absolute identity. The doctor, of course, was most horribly annoyed; but Foote put money into his pocket, which was all he cared for. Soon after he proceeded so far as to order wooden figures to be made for a puppet-show, of which Dr. Johnson and Dr. Goldsmith were to be the leading characters. Goldsmith affected to laugh, though he seriously alluded to the circumstance in a letter to me; but the great Leviathan of literature was so incensed at the report as to purchase an immense oak cudgel, which he carried with him to Tom Davies's shop, and being there asked for what purpose that was intended, he sternly replied, 'For the castigation of vice upon the stage.'" This being immediately conveyed as it was meant to be, Foote, it is stated, was really intimidated, and the scheme, as to *them*, was given up.

"Will's" Coffee-house was situated on the north side, at the corner of Bow Street; "Button's" was "on the south side, about two doors from Covent Garden;" and "Tom's" on the north side. These coffee-houses have become such classic haunts, on account of their connection with the great names of the "Augustan" period of English literature, that we may be excused if we dwell on them somewhat in detail.

Of all the coffee-houses which in the seventeenth and eighteenth centuries supplied the place in society now occupied by the modern club, none holds a higher place in the literary history of London than "Will's." It stood at the junction of Russell Street and Bow Street, and Sir Walter Scott was of opinion that the original sign of the house was a "cow;" but this is doubted by Mr. Peter Cunningham. The room in which the wits of the day used to assemble, often under the presidency of no less a person than John Dryden, was on the first floor, the ground-rooms being then occupied as a haberdasher's shop. It took its familiar appellation from Will Urwin, by whom it was kept, and whose name is preserved to us in an advertisement offering a reward for the apprehension of a runaway servant in 1674. "It was Dryden," writes Pope, "who made 'Will's' Coffee-house the great resort of the wits of his time. After his death Addison transferred this pre-eminence to 'Button's,' who had been a servant of his own; they were opposite each other in Russell Street, Covent Garden. . . . Addison passed each day alike, and much in the same way as Dryden did. Dryden employed his mornings in writing, dined *en famille*, and then went to 'Will's;' only he came home earlier at nights."

Defoe, too, in his "Journey through England," bears the following testimony to the high repute in which "Will's" Coffee-house then stood with the aristocracy of birth as well as with that of letters:— "After the play, the best of the company go to 'Tom's' and 'Will's' Coffee-house, near adjoining, where there is playing at picket, and the best of conversation till midnight. Here you will see blue and green ribbons and stars sitting familiarly, and talking with the same freedom as if they had left their quality and degrees of distance at home." And it is clear that not only literature but politics formed a subject of constant discussion in that upper room, for doubtless it will be remarked that in his first number of the *Spectator* Addison says: "There is no place of general resort wherein I do not often make my appearance; sometimes I am seen thrusting my head into a round of politicians at 'Will's,' and listening with great attention to the narratives that are made in those little circular audiences."

The *entrée* to "Will's," it seems, was not more readily granted than admission to the "Athenæum" now-a-days would be to mere pretenders to litera-

ture, or to writers of every poem of the hour: thus, the *Spectator* speaks, with something of a sneer, of some luckless wight who "came to 'Will's' Coffee-house upon the merit of having writ a posie of a ring." The coffee-house, however, appears to have been used also—just like a club of our own day—as a place where two friends could meet quietly and discuss a subject—literary, religious, or political. Thus in "The Reasons of Mr. Bays' [*i.e.*, Dryden's] Changing his Religion," Mr. B. is represented as saying, "But, if you please to give me the meeting at 'Will's' Coffee-house about three in the afternoon, we'll remove into a private room, where, over a dish of tea, we may debate this important affair with all the solitude imaginable."

"At 'Will's' Coffee-house," says Dr. Johnson in Boswell's "Life," "Dryden had a particular chair to himself, which was set by the fire in winter, and was then called his winter chair; and was carried out for him to the balcony in summer, and was then called his summer chair. Cibber could tell no more than that he remembered him a decent old man, the arbiter of critical disputes at 'Will's.'"

The position held by the wits of "Will's" Coffee-house in the republic of letters may be pretty well inferred from the first number of the *Tatler*, in which Steele and Addison write—"All accounts of gallantry, pleasure, and entertainment shall be under the article of 'White's Chocolate-house;' poetry under that of 'Will's Coffee-house;' learning under the title of the 'Grecian;' foreign and domestic news you will have from 'St. James's Coffee-house.'" The same writer complains that "the place is very much altered since Mr. Dryden frequented it; where you used to see songs, epigrams and satires in the hands of every man you met. You have now only a pack of cards; and instead of the cavils about the turn of the expression, the elegance of the style, and the like, the learned now dispute only about the truth of the game." Hence probably the truth of such a couplet as this:—

> "Rail on, ye triflers, who to 'Will's' repair,
> For new lampoons, fresh cant, or modish air."

It was to "Will's" that Pope, when a mere child, induced his friends to carry him, in order that he might gaze on the great poet whose mantle he was destined in after life so worthily to wear. "Who does not wish," writes Dr. Johnson, "that Dryden could have known the value of the homage that was paid him, and foreseen the greatness of his young admirer?" In later years Pope became a constant frequenter of "Wills,'" though not till after the illustrious Dryden's death. "Pope had now," again writes Dr. Johnson, "declared himself a poet, and thinking himself entitled to poetical conversation, began at seventeen to frequent 'Will's,' a coffee-house on the north side of Russell Street, in Covent Garden, where the wits of that time used to assemble, and where Dryden had, when he lived, been accustomed to preside."

Malone tells us that "most of the criticisms which Dryden condescended to notice were made at his favourite haunt, 'Will's' Coffee-house." There were other personages, too, who used to repair to "Will's" to meet their friends. Thus, for instance, in Pepys' "Diary," under date October 2, 1660, we find the following entry :— "At 'Will's' I met Mr. Spicer, and with him to the abbey to see them at vespers."

On the opposite side of Russell Street to "Will's" was "Button's" Coffee-house, so called after the man who established it, in 1712—one Daniel Button, who had been a servant to Joseph Addison, or rather to his wife, the Countess of Warwick. If second, it was only second to "Will's" in its literary reputation, which dated from the appearance of Addison's *Cato*, and maintained it till his death, in 1719. It was here that Addison used to retreat " whenever he suffered any vexation from the countess;" and doubt- less on other occasions also, for we know, from several independent sources of information, that he seldom let an evening pass by without looking in here along with his friends, Steele, Budgell, Philips, Carey, and Davenant. Here Pope, as he states, at one time used to meet

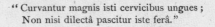

SNUFF-BOX FROM "TOM'S" COFFEE-HOUSE.   (*See p.* 278.)

Addison nearly every day; and here Ambrose Philips, as Dr. Johnson tells us, showed himself one of the *genus irritabile* by "hanging up a rod with which he threatened to chastise Pope." At " Button's " was the conventional office of the *Guardian*, whose editor erected at the entrance a lion's head with a large mouth (of which we give an engraving), to receive contributions from young and inexperienced authors.

Under the "lion's head" was inscribed the following couplet from Martial :—

" Curvantur magnis isti cervicibus ungues ;
    Non nisi dilectâ pascitur iste ferâ."

Mr. P. Cunningham traces the movements of this formidable head from " Button's " to the " Shake- speare " Tavern, under Covent Garden Piazza, and thence to " Richardson's Hotel," in the same place, from which it was removed to Woburn Abbey, being bought by the Duke of Bedford.

The origin and purpose of the lion's head above named is thus related in the *Guardian* of July 9, 1713 : " I have, I know not how, been drawn into tattle of myself, *more majorum* almost the length of a whole *Guardian*. I shall therefore fill up the remaining part of it with what still relates to my own person and my correspondents. Now I would have them all know that on the 20th instant it is my intention to erect a lion's head, in imitation of those I have described in Venice, through which all the private commonwealth is said to pass. This head is to open a most wide and vora- cious mouth, which shall take in such letters and papers as are conveyed to me by my correspondents, it being my resolution to have a particular regard to all such matters as come to my hands through the mouth of the lion. There will be under it a box, of which the key will be in my own custody, to receive such papers as are dropped into it. Whatever the lion swal- lows I shall digest for the use of the public. This head requires some time to finish, the work- men being resolved to give it several masterly touches, and to repre- sent it as ravenous as possible. It will be set up in ' Button's ' Coffee-house, in Covent Garden, who is directed to show the way to the lion's head, and to instruct any young author how to convey his works into the mouth of it with safety and secrecy."

" I think myself obliged to acquaint the public that the lion's head, of which I advertised them about a fortnight ago, is now erected at ' Button's ' Coffee-house, in Russell Street, Covent Garden, where it opens its mouth at all hours for the re- ception of such intelligence as shall be thrown into

THE LION'S HEAD AT "BUTTON'S."

it. It is reckoned an excellent piece of workmanship, and was designed by a great hand in imitation of the antique Egyptian lion, the face of it being compounded out of that of a lion and a wizard. The features are strong and well-furrowed. The whiskers are admired by all that have seen them. It is planted on the western side of the coffee-house, holding its paws under the chin, upon a box, which contains everything that he swallows. He is, indeed, a proper emblem of knowledge and action, being all head and paws." (*The Guardian*, No. 114, Wednesday, July 22, 1713.)

"Being obliged, at present, to attend a particular affair of my own, I do empower my printer to look into the arcana of the lion, and select out of them such as may be of public utility; and Mr. Button is hereby authorised and commanded to give my said printer free ingress and egress to the lion, without any hindrance, lest, or molestation whatsoever, until such time as he shall receive orders to the contrary. And, for so doing, this shall be his warrant." (*Guardian*, No. 142, August 24, 1713.)

Charles Johnson, famous for writing a play every year, was an attendant at "Button's" every day. He had, probably, thriven better in his vocation had he been somewhat leaner; he may be justly called a martyr to obesity, and may be said to have fallen a victim to the rotundity of his body. He kept a tavern in Bow Street, Covent Garden, and died about 1741. Though he was a man of inoffensive behaviour, yet he could not escape the satire of Pope, who, too ready to resent even any supposed offence, has, on some trivial pique, immortalised him in the "Dunciad."

In Russell Street, at No. 17, on the north side, was "Tom's" Coffee-house; but the house was pulled down in 1865, after having stood upwards of a century and a half. It was established about the year 1700, by a Mr. West, after whose Christian name it was called. It is mentioned in the "Journey through England," in 1714, as a place where "there was playing at piquet, and the best of conversation till midnight," and where "blue and green ribands with stars"—in other words, the bearers of the highest orders at Court—might be seen night after night "sitting and talking familiarly." Its balcony in the day-time was often crowded with members of the Upper House of Parliament, who came thither to drink tea and coffee and to be amused. In the early part of the reign of George III. there was established at "Tom's" a club, consisting of upwards of 600 members, including not only Garrick, Foote, Murphy, Dr. Dodd, George Colman, Goldsmith, Dr. Johnson, and William Bowyer, but the Duke of Montague,

Sir George (afterwards Lord) Rodney, the great Lord Clive, the Earl of Anglesey, Lord Edward Bentinck, Earl Percy, and the Duke of Northumberland. Quoting Whitehead's "Legends of London," we might add that—

"These are the men that trod our public ways,
  With brilliant wits that every fancy lov'd;
Congreve's wild, sportive flights of later days,
  And graceful Addison whom all approv'd:
While graver Johnson's wisdom spoke like truth,
  Burke's eloquence replied in tones sedate.
Here charming Goldsmith fluttered fresh as youth,
  And Swift and Gay. But see, at Fame's broad gate
The dazzling crowds our kindly memory greet;
  Their names this transient verse may not repeat."

"Tom's" continued to be used as a coffee-house down to 1814, when it passed into other uses; but many of the relics of the club still remain in private hands, including the books and lists of members and the snuff-box which was handed round among the company. This snuff-box, of which we give an engraving in page 277, is described by Mr. Timbs, in the *Illustrated London News* of 1865, as of large size and of tortoise-shell, and having on the lid in high relief, chased in silver, portraits of Charles I., Queen Anne, and the Royal Oak at Boscobel, with Charles II. hid in its branches.

At a tavern with the sign of the "Shakespeare's Head," in Russell Street, the Beefsteak Society, which we have already mentioned in our account of the Lyceum, used to meet before removing to that theatre. The sign is said by Mr. Larwood to have been "beautifully painted," and it was the work of George Lambert, scene-painter at Covent Garden Theatre.

In Russell Street was also another "Rose" Tavern, a noted place of debauchery in the Stuart times. Constant allusions to it occur in the comic writers of the age; Shadwell, for instance, in *The Scourers*, makes one of the characters observe, "Thou wilt never be his fellow . . . . oh! had you seen him scower as I did! oh! so delicately, so like a gentleman! how he cleared the 'Rose' Tavern." Mr. Larwood tells us that here, in 1712, was arranged the fatal duel between Lord Mohun and the Duke of Hamilton, of which we shall have to say more when we come to its actual scene, Hyde Park. How the character of "The Rose" for morality stood in the reign of Queen Anne, may be gathered from the following lines of the "Rake Reformed:"—

"Not far from thence appears a pendant sign,
  Whose bush declares the product of the vine;
  Where to the traveller's sight the full-blown 'Rose
  Its dazzling beauties doth in gold disclose,
  And painted beauties flock in tallied cloathes."

Hogarth has given a picture of one of the rooms in this house in his "Rake's Progress." "In 1766," adds Mr. Larwood, "the tavern was swallowed up in the enlargements of Drury Lane by Garrick; but the sign was preserved, and hung up against the front wall." An engraving of it is shown in Pennant's "London."

At the "Albion" Tavern in this street—the legitimate successor of the "Will's" and "Button's" of the last century—"the late-hour visitor," Mr. E. L. Blanchard tells us, "may occasionally see faces flitting past which have been familiar to him in association with the glare of the foot-lights; but the arrangements of that hotel are totally distinct from those of the old theatrical parlour which permitted a stranger to observe how 'Horatio' would eat a mutton chop, how 'Polonius' would crown the enjoyment of a Welsh rare-bit with a pipe, and how the thirsty 'Ghost' would evoke congenial spirits which really came when he did call for them. To mix in goodly theatrical company at the present day it is needful to be introduced to clubs like the Garrick, the Junior Garrick, or the Arundel. Such institutions have done much to alter the aspect of professional life after dark, and the marked change which has thus crept over the old haunts of the players is worth noting." The "Albion" will now be looked for in vain.

Among the temporary residents in Russell Street in olden time was John Evelyn. In his "Diary," under date September 10th, 1658, is the entry: "I came with my wife and family to London; tooke lodgings at the 3 Feathers in Russell Street, Covent Garden, for all the winter, my son being very unwell." Here, too, as he tells us, he was visited in the December following by "my Lord Count Arundel of Wardour."

Russell Street, during last century, and indeed during the earlier part of the present century, was largely inhabited by theatrical and other celebrities, of whom it would be impossible to give a full or complete list. Major Mohun; Betterton; Mrs. Barton Booth; Charles Lamb; Carr, Earl of Somerset, whose name is mixed up with the story of the poisoning of Sir Thomas Overbury; Armstrong, the poet; Joseph Taylor, one of the original performers of Shakespeare's plays—each and all of these individuals are enumerated by Mr. Peter Cunningham amongst those who have contributed to the memories of Russell Street.

In Russell Street, "next door to Isaac Bickerstaffe's Coffee-house," was the music-shop of a Mr. Peppard, which bore the appropriate sign of "The Orpheus;" and Gibbon tells us, in his "Memoirs," that, while a student at Magdalen College, Oxford, and when in doubt as to the claims of the rival Churches of England and Rome, he consulted the advice of a Mr. Lewis, a Roman Catholic bookseller in Russell Street, who recommended him to consult the priest, who received his formal abjuration of Protestantism, and admitted him into the bosom of "the one fold" in June, 1753.

In what used to be Little Russell Street formerly hung a sign of Shakespeare's head: it was painted by Clarkson, who received for it £500. Another sign—a whole-length portrait of the immortal bard, in the same street—was the work of a Royal Academician, Samuel Wale. But this had to be taken down, with many other signs, in obedience to the Act of Parliament, and was sold to a broker in Lower Grosvenor Street, at whose shop-door it stood for some years, neglected and despised, and at last was destroyed by exposure to the weather.

"The Harp," in this part of Russell Street, was long notorious as the resort of distinguished actors; and here used to be held, until only a few years ago, a society or club denominated "The City of Lushington," the members of which were presided over by a "Lord Mayor" and four "Aldermen," each of them being annually elected to those distinguished positions. Here Sims the elder flourished for many years. He was succeeded by his son, a tablet to whose memory may still be seen in the parlour of the aforesaid hostelry. In these words is he commemorated: "A tribute of respect to the memory of Sir William Sims, theatrical agent. Obiit Feb. 9th, 1841. Ætat. 54. He was for thirty-five years a distinguished member of this city, and thrice Lord Mayor. Many successful aspirants to histrionic fame are indebted to him for their advancement in the profession, and can look back with gratitude to his advice and assistance." This rattle-brained society of theatrical, commercial, mechanic, and other worthies, was most solemnly established, many years since, by the whimsical contrivance of a merry company of tipplers, that they might meet every night as citizens of "The City of Lushington," each having his own particular seat denoted as his ward, and each member, on admittance, having a particular ward assigned to him. "The uninitiated," says Mr. E. L. Blanchard, "may be advantageously told that certain burlesque ceremonies of municipal election are still continued at specified intervals, when nominal dignities are humorously conferred. The room retains all the original 'wards,' and the 'Edmund Kean corner' is scrupulously maintained as the post of honour." The title of this society,

"The City of Lushington," might lead our readers to infer that its proceedings were mixed up with a certain amount of levity and drunkenness; but this, we are credibly informed, was not the case in recent days, everything being conducted with the strictest propriety and decorum.

In Crown Court, close by, and opposite the stage entrance to Drury Lane Theatre, is the Scottish National Church, a place of worship which enjoyed great popularity under the ministry of the late Dr. Cumming, of prophetical notoriety.

At "Button's"—and, indeed, at most of the other coffee-houses—the leading company used to wear long, flowing flaxen wigs, and so did Sir Godfrey Kneller when he frequented it of an evening. John Timbs, in his "Club Life in London," tells us that "'Button's' continued in vogue until Addison's death and Steele's retirement into Wales, after which the house became gradually deserted; the coffee-drinkers went to the 'Bedford,' the dinner-parties to the 'Shakespeare.'"

Richard Steele, the celebrated wit, dramatic and essay writer, and one of the most frequent attendants at "Button's" in its palmy days, was the son of an English barrister who filled the post of secretary to the Duke of Ormond, and was born in Dublin in 1671. Through the influence of the Duke of Ormond he was sent to the Charterhouse School, in London, from whence he removed to Oxford. It was at the Charterhouse that he found Addison, a youth three years older than himself, and an intimacy was formed between them—one of the most memorable in literature. Steele commenced life by entering the army as a private soldier. His wit and brilliancy soon made him a favourite in the army, and he plunged into the fashionable vices and follies of the age, which enabled him to acquire that knowledge of life and character which proved so serviceable when he exchanged the sword for the pen. As a check on his irregular mode of life, and being thoroughly convinced of many things of which he had often repented, and which he more often repeated, he wrote for his own admonition a little work entitled "The Christian Hero;" but his gay companions did not relish this semi-religious work, and not being very deeply impressed by his own reasoning and pious examples, as a counterpoise he wrote a comedy, *The Funeral, or Grief à la Mode*, which was very successful. Steele had dedicated "The Christian Hero" to his colonel, Lord Cutts, who appointed him his secretary, and promised him a captain's command in the volunteers. It was not long, however, before Steele found that in exchanging the pen for the sword he had made a mistake; and he lost no time in following his more congenial pursuits. He wrote a number of plays, which were very successful; and through the popularity thus obtained he secured an appointment in the Stamp Office, London, which he resigned on being elected member for Stockbridge. His Parliamentary career, however, was not brilliant, for he was expelled the House for writing two alleged libels, called respectively "The Englishman" and "The Crisis," "which expulsion," says Lord Mahon, "was a fierce and most unwarrantable stretch of party violence."

The accession of George I. was a fortunate circumstance for Steele; for he not only received the honour of knighthood, but was appointed to a post of some importance at Hampton Court; and, what was far more congenial, was named Governor of the Royal Company of Comedians. And when the Rebellion of 1715 placed a number of forfeited estates at the disposal of the Government Steele was appointed a member of the Commission for Scotland. In this capacity, in 1717, he visited Edinburgh, and whilst there he is said on one occasion to have given a splendid entertainment to a multitude of decayed tradesmen and beggars collected from the streets!

Steele appears to have received fair remuneration for his literary work; and on the publication of his *Conscious Lovers*, in 1722, the king, to whom it was dedicated, gave him £500. But he was always poor, because always lavish, scheming, and unbusiness-like; yet nothing could depress the elasticity of his spirits. Being always engaged in some unsuccessful scheme or other, and with habits both benevolent and lavish, he wasted his regular income in anticipation of a greater, until absolute pecuniary distress was the result. Shortly before his death he retired into Wales, solely for the purpose of retrenching his affairs, so that he might pay his creditors. But it was too late, and before he could carry his honest intentions into effect death overtook him, and, enfeebled by dissipation and excess, he died, on September 1, 1729, at the age of fifty-eight.

It is as a witty and polished writer that Steele is best known, and especially as the originator of the *Tatler*, a paper in which Addison and some of the best writers of the time remarked on the politics of the age in which they lived. The *Spectator* and *Guardian* also received contributions from Steele's pen; and although the state of things which produced these works has passed away, yet these essays still rank as a worthy part of the standard literature of England.

After the death of Addison, the celebrity of

"Button's" Coffee-house declined, and a few years later we find its master in receipt of parish relief. His demise was thus announced in the *Daily Advertiser* at the time :—" On Sunday morning, died, after three days' illness, Mr. Button, who formerly kept 'Button's' Coffee-house, in Russell Street, Covent Garden, a very noted house for wits, being the place where the lyon produced the famous *Tatlers* and *Spectators*, written by the late Mr. Secretary Addison and Sir Richard Steele, Knt., which works will transmit their names with honour to posterity." Button lies buried, as already stated, among some of his illustrious guests, in St. Paul's Churchyard, close by.

CHAPTER XXXVI.

COVENT GARDEN AND ITS NEIGHBOURHOOD (*continued*).

καὶ δὴ καὶ ὁ τὰ συσσίτια εὑρὼν πολλῶν ἀγαθῶν αἴτιος.
Aristotle.

Club Life—Dickens's Love for Covent Garden—The "Sheridan Knowles" Tavern and the "Owls" Club—The "Whistling Oyster"—The "Shakespeare Head" Tavern—Johnson's Alamode Beef-shop—Wellington Street—Tavistock Street—Dramatic Sick Fund Association—Royal Dramatic College—A Batch of Newspaper Offices—Dr. Johnson and Dr. Perry—The Victoria Club—Royal General Theatrical Fund—Bohn's Library—The "Fleece" Inn and the "Turk's Head"—"Wright's" Coffee-house—Anecdote of Foote, the Actor—Discovery of Stone Coffins—Millar the Publisher and Fielding's "Amelia"—Sotheby and Wilkinson's Auction-rooms—Somerset House—Lancaster Place—The London Necropolis Company.

THE motto at the head of this chapter contains the opinion of one of the sages of antiquity upon the benefits which accrue to man as a "social" being through the instrumentality of the first deviser of what would now-a-days be called "Clubs" and "Club Life," but what the Athenians styled "Syssities," a system, that is, of common tables for citizens. The same institution, under a different name, flourished, so we are told, even among the hardy youth of Sparta ; and in fact, as man is not merely a gregarious but also a social animal, we may lay it down as a principle that wherever a refined and polished society has prevailed, its life has been attended by some means or other for bringing men into each other's company to discuss questions of social, political, or literary interest. With these few remarks by way of preface, we pass to some further notice of the Club Life of Covent Garden and its neighbourhood.

The Club was the natural "outcome" of the coffee-houses, which, as we have stated in a previous volume, were first introduced in St. Michael's Alley, Cornhill, by a Turkey merchant in the time of the Commonwealth. In 1663 it was ordained by Act of Parliament that all coffee-houses should be licensed by the magistrates ; and twelve years later, as Mr. Cunningham tells us, Charles II. issued a royal edict to close up the coffee-houses as "nurseries of sedition." The principle above quoted, however, asserted itself, and a few days afterwards the proclamation was cancelled.

Our modern celebrated clubs are founded upon eating and drinking, which are points wherein most men agree, and in which the learned and illiterate, the dull and the airy, the philosopher and the buffoon, can all of them bear a part. The Kit-Cat itself—of which we have already spoken in our account of Shire Lane—is said to have taken its original from the mutton pie. The Beef-steak and October Clubs were neither of them averse to eating and drinking, as is clear from their names.

Charles Dickens as a boy had an innate love for the neighbourhood of Covent Garden, as instinct with human life. With Johnson, he knew that "the full tide of life was in the Strand ;" and if so, it can scarcely be wondered at that, precocious child, he loved to sit on the shore and watch its waves breaking on its northern bank. To be taken out for a walk into the real town, especially if it were anywhere about Covent Garden or the Strand, perfectly entranced him with pleasure. But most of all he had a "profound attraction of repulsion" to St. Giles's. If he could only induce any one soever to take him through Seven Dials he was supremely happy. "Good heaven !" he would exclaim, "what wild visions of prodigies of wickedness, want, and beggary, arose in my mind out of that place !" On the same authority we learn that George Colman's "Broad Grins" seized his fancy very much, and that he was so impressed by its description of Covent Garden in the piece called *The Elder Brother*, that he stole down to the Market by himself to compare it with the book. "He remembered," says Mr. J. Forster, "as he said in telling me this, snuffing up the flavour of the faded cabbage-leaves as if it were the very breath of comic fiction." But we must pass on from the domain of poetry into the prosaic region of fact.

In Brydges Street, Covent Garden (now absorbed into Catherine Street, of which it forms a continuation), facing the entrance to Drury Lane Theatre, was a tavern bearing the sign of "The Sheridan Knowles," who is supposed by Mr. Larwood to have been the last literary celebrity to whom such an honour was paid. There the club of "Owls" used at one time to hold its meetings. Sheridan Knowles was one of its especial patrons and fre-

On the south side of Drury Lane Theatre, in a narrow court leading out of Catherine Street, called Vinegar Yard, was, until quite recently, a small tavern—or rather oyster and refreshment-rooms—dear to artists ; and, if we may trust the *Daily Telegraph*, it enjoyed a reputation of much the same kind as that which in former days attached to "Button's" or "Will's" Coffee-houses. The house rejoiced in the fanciful name of "The

THE SCOTCH NATIONAL CHURCH, CROWN COURT.   (*See page* 280.)

quenters ; and as it embraced many authors, wits, and composers, its members, it may well be imagined, were not owls of the "moping" sort, whom Gray commemorates in his "Elegy." Every panel was inscribed with the name of some dead or living dramatist.

Now-a-days the carriages of the upper ten thousand have no difficulty in finding their way to Old Drury or Covent Garden Market. The access to Drury Lane Theatre, however, was remarkably bad in old times. Walker, writing in "The Original," in 1836, says :—"Within memory, the principal carriage approach to Old Drury Lane Theatre was through that part of Drury Lane which is now a flagged foot-passage, and called Drury Court, just opposite the new church in the Strand."

Whistling Oyster," and its sign was a weirdly and grotesquely comical representation of a gigantic oyster whistling a tune, and with an intensely humorous twinkle beaming in its eye. The shop was first established by a Mr. Pearkes, in 1825. "It appears," said a writer in the *Daily Telegraph*, "that about the year 1840 the proprietor of the house in question, which had then, as it has now, a great name for the superior excellence of its delicate little 'natives,' heard a strange and unusual sound proceeding from one of the tubs in which the shell-fish lay piled in layers one over the other, placidly fattening upon oatmeal, and awaiting the inevitable advent of the remorseless knife. Mr. Pearkes, the landlord, listened, hardly at first believing his ears. There was, however, no doubt about the matter. One of the oysters was distinctly whistling ! or, at any rate, producing a sort of 'sifflement' with its shell. It was not difficult to detect this phenomenal bivalve, and in a very few minutes he was triumphantly picked out from

and the creature, breathing in his own way by the due inspiration and expiration of water, forced a small jet through the tiny orifice each time that he drew his breath, and so made the strange noise that first caught the ear of his fortunate pro-

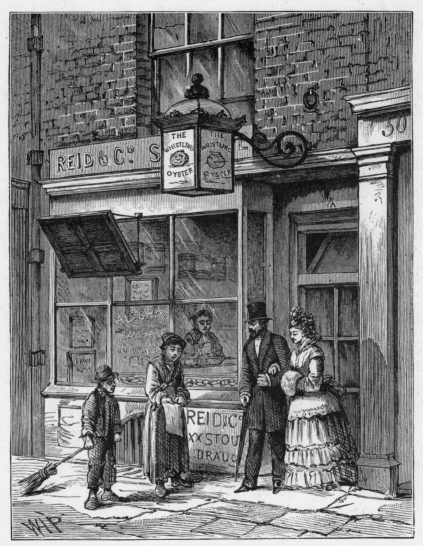

THE " WHISTLING OYSTER."

amongst his fellows, and put by himself in a spacious tub, with a bountiful supply of brine and meal. The news spread through the town, and for some days the fortunate Mr. Pearkes found his house besieged by curious crowds. That this Arion of oysters did really whistle, or do something very like whistling, is beyond all question. How he managed to do so is not upon record. Probably there existed somewhere in his shell a minute hole, such as those with which the stray oyster-shells upon the beach are usually riddled,

prietor." As for the jokes and good sayings to which the creature gave rise during its brief span of life, they would fairly fill a large folio ; and readers of *Punch* in its early volumes may even remember the famous picture of the " Whistling Oyster "—drawn, it is almost needless to add, from a purely imaginary point of view, and which those who have not been so fortunate as to have seen could behold reproduced in large upon the lamp which marked the door of the establishment in Vinegar Yard. Douglas Jerrold's suggestion was that the said oyster "had been crossed in love, and now whistled to keep up appearances, with an idea of showing that it didn't care." Thackeray used to declare that he was once actually in the shop when an American came in to see the phenomenon, as everybody else was doing, and, after hearing the talented mollusk go through its usual performance, strolled contemptuously out, declaring "it was nothing to an oyster he knew of in Massachusetts, which whistled 'Yankee Doodle' right through, and followed its master about the house like a dog." The subsequent fate of this interesting creature is a mystery —whether he was eaten alive, or ignominiously scalloped, or still more ignominiously handed over to the tender mercies of a cook in the neighbourhood to be served up in a bowl of oyster sauce as a relish to a hot beefsteak. In fact, like the "Lucy" of Wordsworth—

> "None can tell
> When th' oyster ceased to be."

But it is somewhat singular that so eccentric a creature should have existed in the middle of London, and in the middle of the nineteenth century, and that no history of his career should be on record: still more strange, we think, that he should have been set up over his master's shop as a sign, and yet that, with all its notoriety, it should have escaped the notice of Mr. Peter Cunningham, Mr. John Timbs, and even Mr. Larwood. The houses in Vinegar Yard have now been demolished.

If we may be allowed at this point to travel a little beyond the strict bounds of Covent Garden, it may be added that in Wych Street, Drury Lane, there was a "Shakespeare Head," the last haunt of the club of "Owls"—so called from the late hours they maintained. The tavern was kept at one time by Mr. Mark Lemon, afterwards the genial editor of *Punch*, assisted by his wife, formerly a singer of repute as Miss Romer. Mr. Larwood tells us that it was much frequented by actors, and that a club of *literati* used to meet on its first floor. Not far off hence was "Johnson's Alamode Beef-house," in Clare Court, close to Drury Lane, where Charles Dickens as a boy used to look in, whilst employed as a drudge at Hungerford Stairs, carrying his daily supply of bread, and "purchasing a small plate of alamode beef to eat with it," the waiter staring at the precocious boy eating his humble dinner, as if he had been a monster.

Wellington Street, strange to say, is not mentioned by Mr. P. Cunningham in his "Handbook of London," usually so exhaustive. It leads from Russell Street, in a straight line with Bow Street, across the Strand to Waterloo Bridge, and was newly made as an approach to that bridge in 1829-30. It follows as nearly as possible the line of what was once the boundary-wall separating the grounds of Exeter House from those of Wimbledon House, described in a previous chapter.

Tavistock Street, to which we have alluded in a former chapter, runs out of Wellington Street to the west, parallel with the Strand. In this street were originally the offices of the Dramatic, Equestrian, and Musical Sick Fund Association. This institution was founded in 1855, in order to assist members of these professions in sickness and in distress, and to help them to obtain employment. The offices of the Association are now in Adam Street, Adelphi. The office of the Royal Dramatic College was likewise in Tavistock Street. This institution was founded in 1858 for the relief of aged and infirm actors and actresses; but was eventually broken up, through want of support.

As we walk down the rather steep incline which leads across the Strand to Lancaster Place and Waterloo Bridge, we pass Exeter Street on the right and left of us. In this street, as we remarked in a previous chapter, Dr. Johnson lodged when he first came to town from Lichfield, and it was during his residence here that he first commenced his condensation of the speeches in Parliament for the *Gentleman's Magazine*. At the corner of Exeter Street was the office for the publication *Household Words*, and as such it was the constant haunt of Charles Dickens in his later years. Here was afterwards published the *Army and Navy Gazette*, founded and edited by Dr. W. H. Russell, and now located in York Street, Covent Garden. In Wellington Street used to be the publishing offices of a host of newspapers and magazines, and here one may still find those of the *Spectator*, the *Era*, the *Gardener's Chronicle*, and the *Morning Post* (already described). In this street, too, is the principal entrance to the Lyceum Theatre (see p. 117 *ante*). It must have been as nearly as possible on this spot that Dr. Johnson offended Dr. Percy, author of "Reliques of Ancient Poetry," by parodying the style of that charming and simple tale, "The Hermit of Warkworth," thus :—

> "I put my hat upon my head,
> And walked into the Strand,
> And there I met an other man
> With *his* hat in his hand."

"I must freely declare," says Nichols in his "Literary and Miscellaneous Memoirs," "with all my partiality for Johnson, that I think Dr. Percy had very great cause to take offence at a man who, by a ludicrous parody on a stanza of his 'Hermit,' had rendered him contemptible. It was urged that Johnson meant only to attack the metre; but he certainly turned the whole poem into ridicule. Mr. Garrick soon afterwards asked me," adds Nichols, "in a postscript to one of his letters, 'whether I had seen Johnson's criticism on the "Hermit?" it is already,' said he, 'over half the town.'"

On the eastern side of the street, occupying the corner of Exeter Street, is a handsome and substantial building of the Italian order, ambitiously styled "The Victoria Club." It has nothing, however, of royalty or aristocracy about it, and appears to have been designed mainly for betting-men. It was built about 1862; and some idea may be formed of the contrast between its members and the literary society which used to meet in the coffee-houses of the neighbourhood less than a century before it, when we add that, a few years after its foundation, the then highly intelligent committee and secretary were ignorant of its brief and unimportant history, and even of the name of its founder!

In Wellington Street used to be the offices of the Royal General Theatrical Fund. This institution was founded, in 1839, for the relief of "poor actors, actresses, singers, pantomimists, and dancers," to whom annuities are granted; aid is likewise afforded to the widows and orphans of members. It is now located in Catherine Street.

About half-way down Wellington Street, and opening into Catherine Street, is York Street. Here Mr. Henry G. Bohn, one of the most original and enterprising of modern publishers, carried on business from about the year 1835 down to 1866, when he retired, transferring his stock to Messrs. Bell and Daldy. He was one of the first publishers who tried the experiment of republishing standard works in a cheap form in "libraries" of various kinds. These amounted altogether to as many as 700 volumes, and the cost of their production could not have been very much short of £500,000. In York Street was the literary auction-room of Mr. Samuel Baker, in the middle of the last century, now represented by Messrs. Sotheby, Wilkinson, and Hodge, of whom we shall have to speak when we reach the southern part of Wellington Street. Here, too, was the "Fleece" Inn—a tavern, if we may believe Aubrey, "very unfortunate for homicides," three having happened within its walls in his time. It was afterwards turned into a private house, its former master having hanged himself! It is as well, perhaps, in this case that the timbers and walls of houses are not usually gifted with speech, or it would have been hard for its owner to find another tenant.

Another tavern in this street at one time enjoyed a different reputation to that of the "Fleece." This house bore the sign of the "Turk's Head," which was admirably painted by Cotton, and was much admired. The tavern had among its usual frequenters Bernard Lintot, the bookseller of the Strand, the rival of Tonson, and the "huge Lintot" of Pope's "Dunciad," who sang "Molly Mag" as none before or after him could sing it.

In York Street, about 1760-70, was a theatrical club which met of an evening at "Wright's Coffee-house." Foote, Holland, Powell, and many of the leading actors of the time were members; and Mr. Cradock, in his "Literary and Miscellaneous Memoirs," tells us how he went thither one evening with a young friend from the country, named Farmer, who had written on the subject of Shakespeare, and who particularly wanted to see Foote. The latter was a much kinder and more genial personage, as is clear from Cradock's narrative, than Dr. Johnson would have been if placed in a similar position. "Luckily an immediate opportunity occurred to me of introducing him, and of interesting the great satirist in his favour. Foote gravely and very handsomely said, 'I shall feel a particular pleasure in paying every attention to him as a friend of yours; he is a man of talents, and I am well acquainted with his excellent Essay on the Learning of Shakespeare;' and indeed he kept his word; for while Farmer stayed he did everything in his power to make himself agreeable and entertaining."

Foote was a man of great natural and ready wit, as would appear from the following anecdotes, which we owe to the same source:—"Mr. Howard happening to hint something about printing a second edition of his 'Thoughts and Maxims,' Foote replied directly, with a sneer, 'Right, sir, Second Thoughts are often best.' In like manner, when a gentleman, with whom he was more intimate, only quoted in jest some trifling circumstance about a game-leg, Foote maliciously replied, "Pray, sir, make no allusion to *my* weakest part; did I ever attack *your* head?' In fact, if the truth must be told, Foote at times spared neither friend nor foe. He had little regard for the feelings of others; if he thought of a witty thing that would create laughter, he said it. If Foote ever had a serious regard for any one, it was for Holland; yet at his death, or rather, indeed, after his funeral, he violated all decency concerning him. Holland was the son of a baker at Hampton, and on the stage was a close imitator of Garrick, who had such a respect for him that he played the 'Ghost' to his 'Hamlet' merely to serve him at his benefit. Holland died rather young, and Foote attended as one of the mourners. He was really grieved : and the friend from whom I had the account declared that his eyes were swollen with tears ; yet when the gentleman said to him, afterwards, ' So, Foote, you have been attending the funeral of your dear friend Holland ?' the latter instantly replied, ' Yes, we have shoved the little baker into his last oven !'"

We have said that Covent Garden in all probability served not only as a monastic garden, but also as a burial-place for the members of the abbey of St. Peter's at Westminster. This supposition is confirmed by a fact mentioned by Mr. J. H. Jesse in his "London," that "stone coffins and other relics of the dead have from time to time been discovered behind the houses on the north side of York Street."

As we cross the Strand, we might have seen until quite recently, a door or two off, on the left, the shop which once was Tonson's, and afterwards passed to Millar, then to Alderman Cadell, and about which Sir N. W. Wraxall tells us a good story. Millar gave Fielding £800 for the copyright of his "Amelia"—a high price at that time. A literary friend having expressed an opinion that it was not worth anything like that amount, and that he had better get rid of it as soon as possible, Millar resorted to a capital "trick of the trade." At his first "trade sale" he said to his brother bibliopoles that he had several works to put up, for which he would be glad if they would bid, but that every copy of "Amelia" was already bespoke. "This manœuvre had its effect," says Wraxall ; " all the booksellers were anxious to get their names put down for copies of it, and the edition, though a very large one, was immediately sold."

In that part of Wellington Street which joins the Strand to Waterloo Bridge, on the west side, on the site of part of the old Savoy, are the well-known rooms of Messrs. Sotheby, Wilkinson, and Hodge, auctioneers of literary property. The business was first established by Mr. Samuel Baker, in York Street, as stated above, in 1744. Thirty years later he was joined by Mr. G. Leigh, who appears to have conducted the business single-handed from 1777 down to 1780, when the name of Sotheby appears as his partner. In 1800 the firm was reinforced by the addition of Mr. Sotheby's son, and in 1804 the firm was styled " Leigh and S. Sotheby," their rooms being removed to " No. 145, the Strand." In 1816 the name of Leigh has disappeared from the title-pages of the

sale catalogues, which mention the name of only " Mr. Sotheby." From 1818 down to 1828 Mr. Sotheby carried on the business in Wellington Street, since which time the establishment has gone on steadily progressing. Among the most celebrated sales which have been entrusted to this firm in the last and present centuries have been the libraries or other collections of Prince Talleyrand, Professor Porson, Bishop Horsley, Joseph Addison, W. S. Rose, John Gifford, E. Malone, Dr. Hawtrey, Sir William Tite, the first Emperor Napoleon, the Chevalier d'Eon, Dr. Charles Burney, the Marquis of Lansdowne, the Earl of Bute, Sir William Dolben, Mr. H. T. Hope, the Earl of Halifax, Sir M. Sykes, Mr. John Nichols, Sir S. Romilly, Sir W. Tite, Mr. J. G. Nichols, and Lord Crauford. It may interest our readers to learn that the volumes of catalogues of sales conducted by this firm are regularly deposited in the British Museum, where about 150 volumes, all carefully priced, may be seen, giving a history of literary properties sold from 1744 down to 1828, and several hundreds more carrying the same record down to nearly the present day.

The western frontage of Somerset House, nearly opposite to Messrs. Sotheby's auction-rooms, was erected in the year 1857, from the designs of Mr. Pennethorne, and is considered one of the most successful façades in modern London. In this wing of Somerset House are the offices of the Inland Revenue Department. On the opposite side of the street, standing somewhat back from the roadway, is a terrace of large houses, called Lancaster Place, as standing on ground belonging to the Duchy of Lancaster. They are mostly cut up into chambers for artists, engineers, and lawyers. One of them is used as the chief office of the London Necropolis Company, which owns the large cemetery near Woking station. In another, the late Mr. Samuel Carter Hall for many years edited the *Art Journal*.

Passing this terrace, we are at the northern end of Waterloo Bridge, at full liberty to find our way down the steps to the Embankment, where, strictly speaking, judging from the meaning of the term, we might have expected to find the " Strand " itself, and where we certainly should have found it in very ' " Old London "—say the London of a thousand years ago. Thence we pass on to the Thames itself, to which our next chapters shall be devoted.

CHAPTER XXXVII.

THE RIVER THAMES.

"Large, gentle, deep, majestic King of Floods."—Thomson.

The Pool—Importance of the Thames in the Olden Time—King James and the Corporation of London—Scenery of the Thames from London Bridge to Westminster—The ' Folly "—A Chinese Junk—The Ancient Church of St. Mary-the-Virgin—Lilly, the Astrologer—The Thames Police—The Royal Humane Society's Reception-room—Waterloo Bridge—The Last of the Savoy Palace—Carlisle House—The Adelphi Terrace—Rousseau and Garrick—Old Hungerford Bridge—Hungerford Stairs—Warren's Blacking Warehouse and Charles Dickens—The Thames Swimming Baths—Whitehall Stairs—Cowley's Funeral—Westminster Bridge—Wordsworth's Sonnet on the Scene from the Bridge at Sunrise.

WE do not intend in this chapter to write a history of the Thames from its source to the sea ; much less to become the biographer of the rivers that fall into it : that work has been already done by Dr. Charles Mackay, in his pleasant and chatty book, "The Thames and its Tributaries." It is our business and duty to show ourselves, like Theodore Hook, "familiar with the Thames from London Bridge up to Eel Pie Island "—perhaps even a little farther. Our discourse, therefore, will be only of the Thames at and near London ; and for the present we shall keep "above bridge," simply contenting ourselves with the remark that, if the visitor from foreign lands would wish to form an adequate idea of the mercantile and commercial wealth of our great metropolis, he had better enter London not by the South-Eastern or the Chatham and Dover Railways, but by the silent highway of that noble river of which Englishmen are so proud. " The congregation of men, ships, and commerce of all nations in the ' Pool,' the din, the duskiness, the discord of order, activity, and industry, is finer," writes the author of " Babylon the Great," " than a bird's-eye view of London from the hills on the north or south, or than the royal gardens, the parks, and the palaces, that first present themselves to a stranger coming from the west. . . . This is indeed old Father Thames, in the overwhelming wonders of his wealth ; and the ships and the warehouses that we see contain the stimulus and the reward of those men who have made England the queen and London the jewel of the world." Truly indeed did Cowper write—

> " Where has commerce such a mart,
>   So rich, so throng'd, so drain'd, and so supplied
> As London—opulent, enlarg'd, and still
> Increasing London ? Babylon of old
> No more the glory of the earth than she,
> A more accomplish'd world's chief glory now ! "

The river, as the source of almost all the greatness and wealth of the metropolis, and also as one of its chief ornaments, deserves especial notice at our hands. But we are above, not below, London Bridge ; so turning our backs on the warehouses which crowd the banks on either side from Wapping to the Tower, from Limehouse and Rotherhithe to Southwark Bridge, let us make our voyage westward, by the side of our new and magnificent embankment, imagining that, as we are treating at once of London "Old" and "New," we are sailing in our barge along the channel which so many great and historic personages, from kings and queens to prisoners of State, have traversed before us.

In London certainly the river has been from earliest times "the silent highway" between the Tower and Westminster. As the Court was usually either at the Old Palace of Westminster or at Whitehall, and most of the king's liege subjects lived in and around the City proper, a boat was naturally the usual conveyance of great people, whether lords of Parliament, courtiers, or ambassadors, into the presence of the sovereign, especially at a time when as yet the Strand was unpaved, and when wagons stuck in its miry wheel-ruts in the winter season.

As a proof of the importance of the Thames in old times as a thoroughfare from London to Westminster, it was ordered that the lanes and streets leading down to it were to be kept free from all impediments, so that persons going on horseback might experience no difficulty in reaching its banks.

A capital story, showing not only the value of the Thames, but the appreciation of that value by the citizens of London, is related concerning James I. and a certain Lord Mayor in his reign. " James being in want of some twenty thousand pounds, applied to the Corporation of London for the loan of that sum. The Corporation refused. The king, whose notions of the regal power were somewhat arbitrary, sent for the Lord Mayor and certain of the aldermen, and rated them severely for their disloyalty, insisting that they should raise the money forthwith ' by hook or by crook.' ' May it please your majesty,' said the Lord Mayor, ' we cannot lend you what we have not got.' ' You must get it,' replied the king, haughtily. ' We cannot, sire,' said the Lord Mayor. ' Then I'll compel you,' rejoined the king. ' But, sire, you

WESTMINSTER FROM THE GARDENS OF SOMERSET HOUSE, 1750. (*After a View by Canaletti.*)

cannot compel us,' retorted the Lord Mayor. 'No!' exclaimed James; 'then I'll ruin you and your city for ever. I'll remove my courts of law, my Court itself, and my Parliament to Winchester or to Oxford, and make a desert of Westminster; and then think what will become of you!' 'May it please your majesty,' meekly but firmly, 'you are at liberty to remove yourself and your courts wherever you please; but, sire, there will always

Much of the scenery of the Thames in London and Westminster as it was at the commencement of the present century has been rescued from oblivion by the brothers Thomas and Paul Sandby, both Royal Academicians. Their elaborate drawings, taken from the terrace and gardens of Somerset House, exhibit on the Surrey side the landing-stairs of Kuper's Gardens, and on the Middlesex shore that part of the old Palace at

THE CHINESE JUNK.   (*See page* 290.)

be one consolation to the merchants of London: your majesty cannot take the Thames along with you.'"

The conservancy of the Thames was confirmed to the Lord Mayor and citizens of London by Henry IV., the same king whose dead body, by a strange fatality, is supposed to have been thrown into its waters. This jurisdiction was confirmed by Parliament, in 1487; and in 1538 the Common Council of London passed several regulations for the improvement of the navigation of the river, many of which are in force down to the present time, though some have been allowed to lapse, as out of date, and applicable only to a bygone state of things.*

Whitehall, then inhabited by the Duchess of Portsmouth, on the site of which afterwards the houses of Lord Farnborough and other noblemen were erected. There is also a scarce and valuable print showing the Thames at the Temple Gardens, executed and published, in 1671, under the auspices of Sir Heneage Finch, afterwards Earl of Nottingham, and reproduced in fac-simile, in 1770–71, at the charge of one of his descendants. It shows that the embanked front of the gardens was not straight, but broken by several recesses, in which are inserted stairs leading down to the water. A quantity of wherries moored at their foot proves how usual a mode of conveyance to all parts of London and Westminster the Thames was two centuries ago. The fac-simile of the print was not published, and

* See Vol. i., p. 442.

therefore it is to be found in only a few private collections. Spenser, too, gives us a "Distant View of the Temple" in the following lines :—

> "Those bricky towers,
> The which on Thamesis broad back do ride,
> Where now the student lawyers have their bowers,
> Where whilom wont the Templar Knights to bide,
> Till they decayed through pride."

One of Sandby's prints of the river-front of Somerset House shows, moored off the stairs of Somerset House, a floating coffee-house, called "The Folly," the existence of which is known to few except curious antiquaries. This was a lounge of the rich gay wits and gallants of the days of Addison and Steele, and an appendage to the coffee and chocolate houses ashore of which we have spoken in our walks round Covent Garden. This floating coffee-house appears by degrees to have attracted a disreputable company, and at last died a natural death, or was suppressed as a nuisance. Being on the water, and not on *terra firma*, there are no title-deeds or other legal documents, or entries in the parish rate-books, to help us in our inquiry as to its fate. In its appearance it somewhat resembled the modern "house-boats" which serve as clubs for rowers at Oxford and at other places on the Thames.

"The Folly"—for such the structure alluded to was named—is said by Dr. C. Mackay to have been "as bulky as a man-of-war." "The Folly" was "divided into sundry rooms, with a platform and balustrade on the top." A view of it as it rode at anchor off Somerset House is given in Strype's edition of Stow; and the humours of it are drawn to the life in Ned Ward's "London Spy." "At first," says Sir John Hawkins, in a manuscript note in his "History of Music," "it was resorted to for refreshment by persons of fashion, and Queen Mary, with some of her courtiers, had once the curiosity to visit it; but it sank gradually into a receptacle for companies of loose and disorderly people, for the purposes of drinking and promiscuous dancing, and at length becoming scandalous, the building was suffered to go to decay, and the materials thereof became firewood."

In one of Tom D'Urfey's songs, called "A Touch of the Times," published in 1719, occurs the following allusion to "The Folly :"—

> "When Drapers' smugg'd apprentices,
> With Exchange girls most jolly,
> After shop was shut up and all,
> Could sail up to 'The Folly.'"

Mr. Larwood, in his "History of Sign-Boards," tells us that "The Folly" was not an unusual sign, and that it was generally applied to a very ambitious, extravagantly furnished, or highly ornamented house. "In such a sense," he remarks, "it was already used in Queen Elizabeth's reign :—

> 'Kirby Castle and Fisher's Folly,
> Spinola's Pleasure and Megse's Glory.'

"'The Folly,' at first, was very well frequented, and the beauty and the fashion of the period used to go there on summer evenings, partake of refreshments on the platform, and enjoy the breeze on the river, then innocent of modern sewers and filth. Pepys paid it more than one visit, as he tells us in his 'Diary.' On one occasion it was honoured by a visit from Queen Mary and several members of her Court. Gradually, however, 'The Folly,' true to its name, 'took to evil courses; loose and disorderly ladies were admitted; and unrestrained drinking and dancing soon gave it an unenviable notoriety.' In this condition it was visited by 'Tom Brown,' who describes it with his usual coarse vigour, and remarks of it as follows :—'This whimsical piece of architecture was designed as a musical summer-house for the entertainment of the quality, where they might meet and ogle one another.'" He describes the company in very glowing colours, which it is not necessary to quote here, but tells us also that he found it such a confused scene of "folly" that, though not a very bashful person, he was at last compelled to return to his boat without drinking. At length the place became so scandalous that it had to be closed : it went to decay; and in the end, as we have already seen from Sir John Hawkins, "The Folly" was chopped up for firewood ! *Sic transit gloria.*

Not very far from where "The Folly" was moored a century and a half ago, there was seen anchored in our own day a wonderful vessel which had crossed the Indian Ocean and sailed round the Cape of Good Hope, and so up the whole length of the Atlantic—a veritable "Chinese junk." It made the voyage, small as it was, without suffering wreck or disaster, and arrived in the Thames in 1848. For a time it lay off Blackwall, where it was visited by thousands—among others, by Charles Dickens. Afterwards, when the London "season" began, it was brought up just above Waterloo Bridge, and moored off the Strand. Dickens describes the impression of a visit to the junk as a total, entire change from England to the Celestial Empire. "Nothing," he writes, "is left but China. How the flowery region ever came into this latitude and longitude is the first thing one asks, and it is certainly not the least of the marvels. As Aladdin's palace was transported hither and thither by the rubbing of a lamp, so the crew of Chinamen aboard the Keying devoutly believed that their good ship would turn up quite safe at the desired port if they only tied red rags enough upon the mast, rudder, and cable. Somehow they did not succeed. Perhaps they ran short of rag; at any rate they had not enough on board to keep them above water; and to the bottom they would have undoubtedly gone if it had not been for the skill and coolness of half-a-dozen English sailors, who brought them over the ocean in safety. Well, if there be any one thing in the world that this extra-ordinary craft is not at all like, that thing is a ship of any kind. So narrow, so long, so grotesque, so low in the middle, so high at each end, like a china pen-tray; with no rigging, with nowhere to go aloft; with mats for sails, great warped cigars for masts, dragons and sea-monsters disporting themselves from stem to stern, and on the stern a gigantic cock of impossible aspect, defying the world (as well he may) to produce his equal—it would look more at home on the top of a public building, or at the top of a mountain, or in an avenue of trees, or down in a mine, than afloat on the water. As for the Chinese lounging on the deck, the most extravagant imagination would never dare to suppose them to be mariners. Imagine a ship's crew without a profile amongst them, in gauze pinafores and plaited hair, wearing stiff clogs a quarter of a foot thick in the sole, and lying at night in little scented boxes, like back-gammon or chess pieces, or mother-of-pearl counters! But, by Jove! even this is nothing to your surprise when you get down into the cabin. There you get into a torture of perplexity; as, what became of all those lanterns hanging to the roof, when the junk was out at sea; whether they dangled there, banging and beating against each other, like so many jester's baubles; whether the idol Chin Tee, of the eighteen arms, enshrined in a celestial Punch's show, in the place of honour, ever tumbled out in heavy weather; whether the incense and the joss-stick still burnt before her, with a faint perfume and a little thread of smoke, while the mighty waves were roaring all around? Whether that preposterous tissue-paper umbrella in the corner was always spread, as being a convenient maritime instrument for walking about the decks with in a storm? Whether all the cool and shiny little chairs and tables were continually sliding about and bruising each other, and if not, why not? Whether anybody on the voyage ever read those two books printed in characters like bird-cages and fly-traps? Whether the mandarin passenger, He Sing, who had never been ten miles from home in his life

before, lying sick on a bamboo couch in a private china closet of his own (where he is now per-petually writing autographs for inquisitive bar-barians), ever began to doubt the potency of the Goddess of the Sea, whose counterfeit presentment, like a flowery monthly nurse, occupies the sailor's joss-house in the second gallery? Whether it is possible that the second mandarin, or the artist of the ship, Sam Sing, Esquire, R.A. of Canton, *can* ever go ashore without a walking-staff in cinnamon, agreeably to the usage of their likenesses in British tea-shops? Above all, whether the hoarse old ocean could ever have been seriously in earnest with this floating toy-shop; or had merely played with it in lightness of spirit roughly, but meaning no harm?—as the bull did with another kind of china-shop on St. Patrick's-day in the morning."

Close by the waterside, near where now stands Somerset House, formerly stood the ancient church of St. Mary the Virgin, the predecessor of the present church of St. Mary-le-Strand. It is stated by a writer in the *Sunday at Home* that no less a person than Thomas à Becket was once rector of the parish. But this statement "requires con-firmation." Another well-known rector, in more recent times, was Dr. George Horneck, author of "The Crucified Jesus," and other popular religious treatises, who was so much beloved in London that it was said his parish stretched from Whitehall to Whitechapel.

At a corner house in the Strand, with the exact locality of which we are not acquainted, though Mr. P. Cunningham fixes it as "over against Strand Bridge," lived, in 1627, William Lilly the astro-loger. He had just then privately married the widow of his master, one Gilbert Wright, in whose house he had been, up to that time, employed in menial work—cleaning the shoes and fetching tubs of water from the Thames; and having inherited her property seven years later, became the owner of house property in the neighbourhood, having, as he tells us in his autobiography, "purchased the moiety of thirteen houses in the Strand for £530." Lilly, who is the "Sidrophel" of Butler's "Hudibras," and who prophesied for the Parlia-ment and for the king, according to the times, died in 1681, and was buried in Walton Church, Surrey, where there is a monument with a Latin inscrip-tion by the antiquary Elias Ashmole, who styles this consummate impostor "*Astrologus peritissimus.*"

For several years past, down to the close of 1873, might be seen moored off the bank of the river, nearly opposite Norfolk Street, the hull—we had almost said *hulk*—of a vessel which in its time had, we believe, "done the State some service" in foreign climes. This was an old 16-gun frigate named the *Royalist*, which, having grown too old to be of any further use in the navy, had been converted into a floating police station, as the inscription in large capital letters, "Thames Police Station," painted upon its side, informed the passer-by. At the above date this vessel was removed "below bridge," to do duty in a similar capacity off East Greenwich, in place of the *Investigator*. The Thames Police have now three stations, namely: One of the floating platforms by Waterloo Bridge, originally erected as a landing-stage for passengers; another at High Street, Wapping; and the third at Blackwall.

From the Report of the Commissioner of the Metropolitan Police issued in 1896, it appears that the total number of men employed in the Thames Police was 207, including a superintendent, 59 inspectors, and 147 constables. The men selected, it need hardly be stated, have a good knowledge of "river thieves" and of those who act in collusion with them, for during a recent year, by their vigilance and good management, upwards of 450 persons were apprehended for various offences. In case of fire, too, either on board vessels or in water-side premises, the assistance rendered by the Thames Police is invaluable.

During the recent year alluded to, the Thames Police were instrumental in rescuing twenty-three persons from drowning; these, with suicides prevented, make a goodly record of lives saved by them during the year. One case, showing the keen observation kept upon river craft, deserves to be kept in mind, though it took place more than twenty years ago. About midnight of the 25th of September, 1874, a boat's crew off Wapping discovered a sailing-barge so imbedded in the mud that the tide was flowing over the decks. They hastened on board, and found her fast filling, and five persons asleep in the cabin. To rouse them was the work of a few moments; but the tide flowed so rapidly that one of the constables was waist-deep in water before the last person was rescued. Had it not been for the vigilance and timely aid of the police these five lives would in all probability have been sacrificed. In cases of accident the Thames Police invariably render prompt assistance in conveying the sufferers to the nearest hospitals, and, when necessary, in giving information to their friends.

Some idea of the very disagreeable and painful duties performed by this able and useful body of men may be gathered from the fact that during each year the number of *deaths* which come under their cognisance amount to over a hundred. These include far more males than females, and are largely made up of "suicides" and "accidentally drowned;" there are usually a few, however, about which there appears to be some doubt as to how they came in the river, and these are therefore classed under the general heading of "found drowned." Nearly all these bodies pass through the hands of the police. In many cases photography is resorted to as a means of identification of the bodies.

The building on the western portion of the landing-stage whereon stands the Thames Police Station is used by the Royal Humane Society as a place for the reception of persons rescued from drowning. This has been placed at the disposal of the Society by the Thames Conservancy, free of charge; and all the necessary appliances have been provided for rescuing bodies from the river, by means of a properly-constructed boat, and for treating them when rescued. The maintenance of this receiving-house has caused a charge on the Society's funds to the extent of about £300 per annum, for the Society's men must be always in attendance, the apparatus and baths in readiness by night and by day, and a medical officer almost within call. During the century and a quarter which has elapsed since the Society was instituted, as we learn from a recent Annual Report, it has been the means of saving upwards of forty thousand persons from premature death. In the words of the Report, we may add that "no comment is necessary upon such a statement as this: it carries with it ample evidence of the beneficent work of the Society."

> "Death may usurp on Nature many hours,
> And yet the fire of life kindle again
> The overpressèd spirits. I have heard
> Of an Egyptian had nine hours lien dead,
> By good appliance was recovered."
>
> *Shakespeare: Pericles*, Act iii., sc. 1.

Waterloo Bridge, with the contemplation of which we now resume our voyage westward—the bridges lying eastward having been dealt with in the previous volumes of this work—was considered by Canova to be "the noblest bridge in the world," the great artist backing up his enthusiasm with the assertion that it was "alone worth coming from Rome to London to see." Indeed, the lightness, grace, and symmetry of the structure are such as to give the bridge a foremost rank in buildings of the kind; although it has been eclipsed in size by subsequent erections.

This grand and useful work, which M. Dupin, his celebrated French engineer, in his "Memoir" on the public works of England, called "a colossal monument worthy of Sesostris and the Cæsars," was produced by a joint-stock company. It was erected by the late Sir John Rennie, and, together with the approaches, cost about £1,000,000.

The Act for incorporating the Company, which was designated "The Strand Bridge Company," was passed in June, 1809. Under this authority they raised the sum of £500,000, in transferable shares of £100 each, and had authority to raise a further sum of £300,000, by the issue of new shares or by mortgage, if they should find it necessary. In July, 1813, the Company obtained another Act of Parliament, by which they were authorised to raise an additional sum of £200,000; and in the session of 1816 they obtained a third Act, which received the royal assent in July, and invested the Company with additional powers. By this Act the name of the bridge was changed from that of the "Strand Bridge" to "Waterloo," in honour of that great and decisive battle. It was very natural, considering the great and important victory which the Duke of Wellington had just gained over Buonaparte, that our countrymen during the Regency should have been somewhat profuse in applying the names "Wellington" and "Waterloo" to all and every sort of thing—Wellington streets, Wellington inns, and Wellington boots; Waterloo hotels, Waterloo academies, Waterloo coaches, and Waterloo bonnets—and that, when at a later date that class of conveyance was introduced, they should have adopted "Waterloo" as the designation of a line of omnibuses, and at last of a railway station.

The design, as executed, consists of nine semi-elliptical arches, with Grecian Doric columns in front of the piers, covered by an entablature and cornice, and surmounted by a balustrade. The roadway upon the summit of the arches is level, in a line with the Strand, and is carried by a gentle declivity on a series of brick arches, some of which are used as warehouses, over the roadway on the Surrey bank of the river, to the level of the roads about the Obelisk by the Surrey Theatre. The width of the river at Waterloo Bridge was 1,326 feet at high water before its curtailment by the Victoria Embankment; and the bridge consists of nine semi-elliptical arches, of 120 feet span, and thirty-five feet high, supported on piers thirty feet thick at the foundations, diminishing to twenty feet at the springing of the arches. They are eighty-seven feet in length, with points in the form of Gothic arches as cut-waters towards the stream. The first arch on the Middlesex side spans the Embankment. The dry or land arches on the Surrey side amount to forty, thirty-nine of which are semi-circular, sixteen feet in diameter, and one semi-elliptical, over the Belvedere Road, of twenty-six feet diameter. The entire length of the bridge and causeways is 2,426 feet, made up of 1,380 feet for the entire length of the bridge and abutments, 310 feet the length of the approach from the Strand, and 766 feet the length of the causeway on the land arches of the Surrey side.

The first stone of this fine bridge was laid on the 11th of October, 1811, and the foundations of which it was a part were built in coffer-dams formed by three concentric rows of piles. In building these majestic arches such care was taken by the able engineer under whose direction the bridge was built, that on removing the centres none of the arches sank more than an inch and a half; whereas, we are told, those of the celebrated bridge of Neuilly sank in several instances so much as to entirely destroy the original curvature of the arch.

When the allied sovereigns visited this country, in 1814, this bridge was in course of erection. The Emperor Alexander I. of Russia upon several occasions visited the works, and declared it would be the finest work in masonry in the world. It was opened with great pomp upon the second anniversary of the battle of Waterloo, June 18th, 1817, by the Prince Regent, accompanied by the royal dukes, Field-Marshal the Duke of Wellington, and attended by a brilliant staff of officers who were present at the battle of Waterloo. From the centre of the bridge there is a finer view of London on the banks of the Thames than can be seen elsewhere. Looking down the river, and immediately joining the bridge, close to the Embankment, rises the noble front of Somerset House—the finest object of the kind in London, not excepting the Houses of Parliament, which appear too low. A little further on, looking like a green oasis in the midst of a dark wilderness of bricks and mortar lie the pleasant gardens of the Temple. Lower down is the new Blackfriars Bridge, rising behind which, in unrivalled grandeur, are the dome and towers of St. Paul's Cathedral, and below this the Monument, the spires of other City churches, the Tower, shipping, &c. As a commercial speculation, Waterloo Bridge proved anything but profitable to the shareholders; but it must be some consolation to them that the works were so judiciously executed as to enable them to remain intact, notwithstanding the changes in the bed of the river. A toll of one halfpenny was formerly charged for foot-passengers over the bridge, and twopence for cabs, &c. An agitation was long kept up with the view of bringing about the abolition of the tolls, and at a meeting held in 1873 for the purpose of considering the matter it was stated that during the previous six years 5,000,000 persons annually passed over this bridge, producing an income of above £21,000 per annum. The bridge was subsequently bought by the Metropolitan Board of Works, and in 1878 the toll was abolished.

In order to form an approach from the Strand to

we know nothing, nor when nor by whom it was built. Aggas in his map represents a house of some extent as standing here, and Hollar gives an elevation of it. But this shared the fate of other Church property at the Reformation, being seized by Henry VIII., and given by him to the lucky courtier from Dorsetshire, John Russell, then Controller of the Royal Household—the ancestor, it need hardly be said here, and the founder of the

HUNGERFORD SUSPENSION BRIDGE, 1850.   (*See page* 132.)

Waterloo Bridge it was found necessary to remove very many interesting remains of ancient architecture—not only those belonging to the Savoy Palace on the west, but also several walls belonging to the palace of the Duke of Somerset, with buttresses and pointed windows with Gothic tracery. All memory of these old buildings has long since perished.

But it is time that we started on our voyage westward, noting on our way a few buildings which we did not describe minutely as we passed along the Strand.

"Next to the Savoy westward," writes the author of "London in the Olden Time," "was the palace of the Bishop of Carlisle, with grounds which extended to the lane running down to the river, called Ivy Bridge. Of the history of this house

fortunes of the ducal house of Bedford. Carlisle House was afterwards known as Worcester House." At the bottom of Ivy Bridge Lane was for many years the landing-stage for the "halfpenny" steamboats plying between this place and London Bridge, one of which blew up here in August, 1847.

The Adelphi Terrace, which we pass soon after leaving Waterloo Bridge, at one time formed a conspicuous feature as seen from the river, but is so far removed by the broad Embankment with its garden, and thrown into the shade by the lofty railway station close by, that it may now be passed almost unnoticed. Northouck, in writing of the new Adelphi Buildings, tells us that Mr. Lacy, the joint patentee with Garrick in Drury Lane, formed a plan for improving the whole north bank of the river upon a plan similar to that of the

OLD WESTMINSTER BRIDGE IN 1754. (*See page 297.*)

Adelphi Terrace, and that there exists a copper-plate engraving of his design, "engraved for private distribution." Of this noble terrace we have spoken in a previous chapter, but we may be pardoned for here adding a short anecdote concerning Garrick, who lived and died in the centre house : we give it on the authority of Mr. Cradock's "Literary and Miscellaneous Memoirs." "When Jean Jacques Rousseau was in England, Garrick paid him the compliment of playing two characters on purpose to oblige him ; and as it was known that Rousseau would be present, the theatre was of course crowded to excess. Rousseau was highly gratified, but Mrs. Garrick declared that she had never spent a more unpleasant evening in her life, the recluse philosopher being so anxious to display himself, and hanging over the front of the box so much that she was obliged to hold him by the skirt of his coat to prevent him from falling over into the pit. After the performance, however, he paid a very handsome compliment to Garrick by saying, 'I have cried all through your tragedy, and laughed all through your comedy, without being at all able to understand your language.' At the end of the play Rousseau was entertained at supper at Garrick's house in the Adelphi, where many of the first literary characters of the time were invited to meet him."

Of the railway bridge which now crosses the river at this point we have already spoken in our account of the Charing Cross Railway, and a description of its predecessor, old Hungerford Suspension Bridge, will be found on page 132.

As we pass by Hungerford Bridge we can hardly help fancying that we can still see the building called "Hungerford Stairs," well known to the jolly Thames watermen of old, and of interest to English readers as one of the first abodes—we cannot call it home—of Charles Dickens, when a boy of ten. Here, at the blacking warehouse of one "Jonathan Warren, Number 80, Hungerford Stairs"—it is well to be particular—the future "Boz" was engaged, in 1822–4, as a sort of shop-drudge, at six shillings a week. He writes, in a sort of autobiographical sketch, published in his "Life," by John Forster :—

"The blacking-warehouse was the last house on the left-hand side of the way at old Hungerford Stairs. It was a crazy, break-down old house, abutting on the river, of course, and swarming with rats. Its wainscoted rooms, its rotten floors and staircases, and the old grey rats swarming down in the cellars and coming up the stairs at all times, and the dirt and decay of the place, rise up visibly before me, as if I were there again. The counting-house was on the first floor, looking over the coal-barges and the river. There was in it a recess where I used to sit and work. My work was to cover the pots of paste-blacking, first with a piece of oil-paper, and then with a piece of blue paper ; to tie them round with a string, and then to clip the paper close and neat all round, until it looked as smart as a pot of ointment from an apothecary's shop. When a certain number of grosses of pots had attained this pitch of perfection I was to paste on each a printed label, and then go on again with more pots."

Such was the intellectual occupation to which, instead of school, his parents consigned the future novelist, whilst they were living, if not in comfort, at all events in decency, in Bayham Street, Camden Town, and afterwards in Gower Street North. "No words," says Charles Dickens, "can express the agony of my soul as I sank into this companionship, and felt my hopes of growing up to be a learned and distinguished man crushed in my breast."

At this time, he remembered (as his biographer, Mr. Forster, tells us) to have spent his dinner-hour in playing about on the coal-barges, or strolling about the back streets of the Adelphi, and exploring the recesses of its dark arches, in company with his youthful companions, "Poll" Green and Bob Fagin. One of his favourite localities was the little public-house, by the waterside, called "The Fox under the Hill,"* approached by an underground passage, and outside which, as he tells us in "Copperfield," he remembered having sat "eating something on a bench, and looking at some coal-heavers dancing before the house."

The blacking warehouse at Hungerford Stairs was removed afterwards to the corner of Chandos Street and Bedford Street, Covent Garden, and young Charles Dickens removed thither along with it, as part and parcel of the establishment. He tells us that so thoroughly did he dislike his drudgery there that, after quitting Hungerford, he never went back to look at the place where his servitude had began till old Hungerford Stairs were destroyed, and that for many a long year he could not bear to pass along Chandos Street, or to smell the cement that was used in the offensive trade.

Here at Hungerford Bridge—or to give it its more common designation at the present time, Charing Cross Bridge—floating swimming-baths were erected. These baths, which were planned on an extensive scale, contained many thousand gallons of filtered water, but the venture was not a success. Yet experiments have been made which have established beyond all doubt that

---

* See *ante*, p. 101.

the Thames water can be easily and effectually filtered. When filtered it is found to contain a very large proportion of sea-water; in fact, we have heard it said that at high tide it is almost entirely sea-water, though by no means so green as at Margate. But this statement we are inclined to question. Less than half a century ago the Thames, without undergoing the process of filtering, was pure enough for the Westminster boys both to row on it and to bathe in it; so that Gray might have addressed to the river under the royal towers of Westminster the noble lines in which he apostrophises it beneath the spires of Eton and Windsor:—

> " Say, Father Thames, for thou hast seen
>   Full many a sprightly race
> Disporting on thy margent green
>   The paths of pleasure trace ;
> Who foremost now delight to cleave
>   With pliant arm thy glassy wave?
>   The captive linnet which enthral?
> What idle progeny succeed
> To chase the rolling circle's speed,
>   Or urge the flying ball?"

Immediately after passing under Charing Cross Railway Bridge the Houses of Parliament and other edifices connected with Government come full into view. Close by the western side of the railway station, and extending to Scotland Yard, appeared, until their demolition towards the close of the year 1874, the gardens and grounds of Northumberland House, the historic mansion of the Percies, about which we have already spoken in a previous chapter. Now that Northumberland House is demolished, in order to form a broad and open thoroughfare from Charing Cross to the Victoria Embankment, we obtain a partial view of the National Gallery and also of the lofty Nelson Column in Trafalgar Square, with the steeple of St. Martin's Church close at hand; a cluster of buildings which leads us to exclaim, in the words of a modern poet—

> " Behold, anent Art's palace, near a church
>   Of most surpassing beauty, and amid
> Statues of kings, a pillar ! no research
>   Need peer it out, for it will not be hid :
> Up in the broad day's lustre doth it stand,
>   A column raised to dear and dazzling fame,
> Mantling with pride the bosom of the land,
>   And stamping glory there with Nelson's name."

Further westward, towering above the cupola of the Horse Guards, and dwarfing everything else around it, stands the York Column—a poor imitation of Trajan's Column—of which we shall have more to say when we shall have extended our perambulation to the neighbourhood of Carlton Gardens. The noble "banqueting house" of

Whitehall, too, rears itself proudly on our right above the princely mansions and dwellings of the nobility which partly surround it, and whose gardens and lawns, before the formation of the Embankment, were washed by the "silver winding" Thames. All traces of the old Palace Stairs and the Privy Stairs of Whitehall which stood about here have long since disappeared; but its memory has been preserved in the pages of history. There the remains of many distinguished personages have been landed preparatory to interment. Those of Queen Elizabeth, of the poet Cowley, and of Lord Nelson, will occur at once to the reader of English history. When Elizabeth died at her palace at Sheen, or Richmond, in 1603, her coffin was brought in a barge with great state down the river to Whitehall, in order to be interred in the Abbey. The same was the case in 1667, with Abraham Cowley, on his death at Chertsey, where he spent the later years of his life, and where his house is still standing. To the latter occasion Pope gracefully alludes in the following lines :—

> " There the last numbers flow'd from Cowley's tongue.
>   Oh ! early lost ! what tears the river shed
> When the sad pomp along his banks was led !
>   His drooping swans on every note expire,
>   And on his willows hung each Muse's lyre."

Cowley's funeral is thus mentioned under date July, 1667, by John Evelyn in his Diary :—" Went to Mr. Cowley's funeral, whose corpse lay at Wallingford House, and was thence conveyed to Westminster Abbey in a hearse with six horses and all funeral decency; near a hundred coaches of noblemen and persons of quality following; amongst these all the wits in the town, divers bishops and clergymen. He was interred next Geoffrey Chaucer and near Spenser."

A good story is told, the scene of which must have been not far from Westminster Bridge, of the popular divine, Dr. Sherlock, who was being ferried across before the bridge was built, and who was being carried, in spite of the efforts of the waterman, out of his course, either up or down the river. It is epigrammatically told in verse, in the last of which the reverend gentleman observes :—

> " With the tide we must swim ;"

on which the wit who recounts the story adds, with a waggish humour—

> " To St. Paul's or to Lambeth was all one to him."

Still sailing up the stream, we shortly reach our landing-place by the arches of Westminster Bridge. The original structure, the second bridge built in London, was commenced in 1738 and finished in 1750. The Corporation of London had a notion that it would injure the trade of the City; and while the bill for its erection was under discussion in Parliament, they opposed it "tooth and nail." "For many years afterwards," writes Dr. C. Mackay in his "Thames and its Tributaries," with a playful and pardonable exaggeration, "London aldermen thought it a pollution to go over it, and passed it by with as much contempt as a dog would pass by a 'stinking brook.' So highly, however," he adds, "was the bridge esteemed by its proprietors that they procured the admission of a clause into the Act of Parliament by which the punishment of death without benefit of clergy was declared against any one who should wilfully deface and injure it. Dogs also were kept off it with as much rigour as that with which they are now excluded from Kensington Gardens." Of course this is mere badinage.

It cannot be too often impressed upon the reader that whenever mention is made in the writers of the Tudor or Stuart times of "bridges" existing in London, save and excepting London Bridge, they really mean only landing piers. From a very early date the citizens of London appear to have regarded the construction of a second bridge with intense jealousy, and from time to time any and every effort to construct a second one, though at a very remote distance, roused the fiercest opposition: an instance of which is to be found in the debate which occurred in Parliament in 1671 upon a proposal to erect a bridge at Putney, the rejection of the bill being effected by the influence of the Londoners.

The inconvenience which had been occasioned by the great resort of coaches, and other vehicles, passing and repassing at the Westminster side, induced Dr. Potter, Archbishop of Canterbury, and several noblemen, to procure an Act of Parliament in the year 1736, for building a bridge across the river Thames, from New Palace Yard, Westminster, to the opposite shore in the county of Surrey. This act, however, was not obtained without great opposition from the City of London, as well as from Southwark; and some fainter efforts in the same direction were used by the bargemen and watermen of the Thames. But private interest was obliged to give way to public advantage, and preparations were made for carrying on this great undertaking under the sanction of the Legislature. It should be mentioned here that the original design was for a wooden bridge, which idea was set aside after the severe frost of 1739-40, when the Thames was frozen over several weeks, and some of the piers for the wooden bridge were carried away. A stone bridge, from its greater durability, was then decided on, and the funds in aid of the expense were defrayed by public lotteries and Parliamentary grants.

The ballast-men of the Trinity House were employed to open a large hole for the foundation of the first pier, to the depth of five feet under the bed of the river; and this being finished and levelled at the bottom, it was kept clear by a proper inclosure of strong piles. In the meantime a strong caisson was prepared of the form and dimensions of the intended pier in the clear; this was made water-proof, and being brought over the place, was secured within the piles.

In this wooden case the first stone was laid on the 29th of January, 1738-9, by Henry, Earl of Pembroke. The caisson was above the high-water mark, and sinking gradually by the weight of the prodigious blocks of stone, the men could work below the level of the water as conveniently as on dry ground. Thus the middle pier was first formed, as were all the rest in the same manner; and when finished, the sides of the caisson being taken asunder, the stone-work appeared entire. The time occupied in building the bridge was eleven years and nine months; and the total expense, including the repairs of the piers, which sank during the erection, amounted to £389,500. The opening ceremony took place on the 17th of November, 1750.

Till the building of Westminster Bridge the only communication between Lambeth and Westminster was by the ferry-boat near the palace gate, which was the property of the Archbishop of Canterbury, and granted by patent under a rent of twenty pence. On opening Westminster Bridge, in 1750, it ceased, and £2,205 was given to the see as an equivalent. Previous to that time there were two considerable inns for the reception of travellers, who, arriving in the evening, did not choose to cross the water at such an hour, or, in case of bad weather, might prefer waiting for better.

On the 13th of November, 1750, the commissioners of the new bridge appointed a number of watchmen to guard it, and ordered thirty-two lamps of a particular size to be fixed on it. The treasurer of the bridge, we are told, "paid the rulers of the Watermen's Company, and the stewards of the chests at Westminster, £2,500, to be laid out in some of the funds secured by Parliament to maintain the poor of the said chests, instead of the money gained by the Sunday ferry for foot-passengers."

Old Westminster Bridge was long considered a triumph of engineering skill. Labelye, the architect, introduced a system of foundations which is stated to have answered very well in numerous cases, but which failed utterly here; namely, in sinking the caissons, as above stated, with the lower courses already built upon them. During the progress of the work some trifling disturbances of the bed of the river gave rise to settlements, which were easily repaired at the time. Upon the enlargement of the tideway, however, in consequence of the removal of Old London Bridge, the scouring action of the river soon carried away the substratum of several of the piers of the bridge; and, finally, after much discussion, many years' repair, great and constant expense, and occasional interruption of the carriage traffic, its demolition became a matter of necessity.

The old bridge was built of Portland stone; it was 1,223 feet in length by 44 feet in width, and there were thirteen large and two small semi-circular arches, springing about two feet above low-water mark. The centre arch was 76 feet span, the others decreasing on each side by regular intervals of 4 feet each, excepting the small arches, which were 25 feet span each. The parapet on each side was surmounted by an open balustrade. Between each arch was a semi-octagonal recess or turret, which afforded a covered shelter for foot-passengers. Owing to the sinking of the piers, however, and the generally unsafe condition of the bridge, these turrets were removed some years before the total demolition of the bridge, and some of them have been re-erected in Victoria Park, where they serve as alcoves. With regard to these turrets, Labelye, the architect, says they were not only built for their evident accommodation of passengers, desiring or obliged to stop without interfering with the roadway, or for the relief they afforded to the eye in breaking so long a line, but for the additional security they gave to the bridge, by strengthening the parts between the arches, and thereby affording so much more weight to repel the lateral pressure. Maitland, however, mentions a more serious purpose to which these recesses might have been put; he says "they might have served for places of ambush for robbers and cut-throats," but for the establishment of a guard of twelve watchmen specially appointed for the security of the passage during the night. The writer of the account of Westminster, in the "Beauties of England and Wales," mentions a peculiarity which these recesses possessed, somewhat analogous to the whispering gallery in St. Paul's Cathedral. He says, "So just are their proportions, and so complete and uniform their symmetry, that, if a person whispers against the wall on the one side of the way, he may be plainly heard on the opposite side; and parties may converse without being prevented by the interruption of the street or the noise of carriages."

The new bridge at Westminster, which occupies the place of the old one, but which is almost double the width, is a very handsome structure built chiefly of iron. It was commenced in 1855 by Mr. Page, and completed in 1862, the latter part of the work having been carried out under the direction of the late Sir Charles Barry, the well-known architect. The present bridge was constructed in two portions, the first half being erected at the western side of the original structure, and opened for traffic, after which the demolition of the old bridge was proceeded with; the remaining half —occupying the exact site of the old bridge—was added on the eastern side of the new structure. The bridge is 1,160 feet long by 85 feet wide, and is at once graceful and massive; it consists of seven arches (the centre one having a span of 120 feet), resting on granite piers, the parapet and ornamental portions having been designed to accord with the adjacent Houses of Parliament. The roadway is 53 feet wide, and each footway 15 feet; the former was divided into going and coming roads, and had tramways, or grooves, for the wheels of heavy vehicles. The cost of construction of the present bridge was £206,000.

It is well known that in 1688 the bed of the Thames between Westminster and Lambeth was made the depository of the Great Seal of England by James II. "He obtained possession of it," says Mr. Jesse, in his "London," "on the night of his flight from Whitehall, and purposely let it fall into the water as he passed across the river." Mr. Jesse adds that not long afterwards the seal was recovered by a fisherman and restored to the Government.

The following beautiful sonnet, composed by William Wordsworth in 1803, gives us a lifelike picture of London as seen from the river at Westminster at sunrise on a summer morning:—

"Earth has not anything to show more fair;
Dull would he be of soul who could pass by
A sight so touching in its majesty;
This city now doth like a garment wear
The beauty of the morning; silent, bare,
Ships, towers, domes, theatres, and temples lie,
Open unto the fields and to the sky,
All bright and glittering in the smokeless air.
Never did sun more beautifully steep
In his first splendour valley, rock, or hill;
Ne'er saw I—never felt—a calm so deep.
The river glideth at its own sweet will.
Dear God! the very houses seem asleep,
And all that mighty heart is lying still."

ALCOVE ON OLD WESTMINSTER BRIDGE.. (*See page 299.*)

CHAPTER XXXVIII.

THE RIVER THAMES (*continued*).

*"Such a stream doth run
By lovely London as beneath the sun
There's not the like."—Old Ballad.*

Poetic Effusions in Honour of the Thames—"Swan-upping"—River Waifs and Dead Houses—Watermen and Wherrymen—Authorised Rates of Charges made by Watermen—Doggett's Coat and Badge—Thomas Doggett as an Actor—Miss Benger's Apostrophies of Taylor, the "Water-Poet"—The Thames as the Great Medium of Conveyance—State Processions—Amusements on the Thames—Bathing in the Thames—Condition of the River in 1874—Depredations from Merchant Vessels—Training-vessels for the Royal Navy and Merchant Service—Mercantile Importance of the Thames.

"OF the London and Westminster of Chaucer's time," writes Mr. Matthew Browne in his pleasant work, "Chaucer's England," "there is little which the poet, however forewarned, would recognise if he were to return. The Thames, certainly, he would scarcely know, with its many bridges. The London Bridge of Peter Colechurch, with its crypt and fishpond in one of the piers, and the drawbridge arch over which rushed the insurgent commons of England under Wat Tyler, he would surely miss. And John of Gaunt's London palace of the Savoy which the insurgents burnt; would he know it? or would he know Westminster Abbey? Not Henry the Seventh's chapel, of course; nor Sir Christopher Wren's clumsy towers. Not St.

Paul's, which in his days had a spire. . . . . Not the streets; assuredly not the Strand, which in the days of the Plantagenets was really a strand sloping down to the river, with only a house here and there . . . . He would know the Tower, however, and Lambeth Palace, perhaps, and St. Mary's Overies, where his contemporary, Gower, was married by William of Wykeham."

But even the Thames has seen its changes. Three hundred years ago the river on both sides was fringed with trees and flowers to such an extent that Izaak Walton quotes the compliment of a German poet of his own time :—

"So many gardens dress'd with curious care
That Thames with royal Tiber may compare."

Indeed, this noble river has been a great theme for poets of all time, and deservedly. It is called by Pope the "silver Thames" and the "fruitful Thame;" by Spenser "the silver-streaming Thames," and by Herrick "the silver-footed Thamesis." Sir John Denham's charming lines, so descriptive of the English beauty of the Thames, often as they have been quoted, will bear being repeated here:—

than by a desire to stand well with the always vain but now aged queen, whom Horace Walpole, with his usual cynicism, describes at this period as being "an old woman with bare neck, black teeth, and false red hair."

The river and the metropolis, both so dear to Englishmen, are thus fantastically celebrated by Pope in his "Windsor Forest," from which we quote the following lines:—

THE THAMES AT LOW WATER.

"Oh! could I flow like thee, and make thy stream
My great example as it is my theme!
Though deep, yet clear; though gentle, yet not dull;
Strong without rage; without o'erflowing full."

Drayton, too, in a poem published in "England's Helicon" in 1600, thus eulogises the Thames and along with it Elizabeth under the fanciful name of "Beta:"—

"And oh! thou silver Thames, O dearest crystal flood!
Beta alone the phœnix is of all thy watery brood;
The queen of virgins only she,
And thou the queen of floods shalt be.
Range all thy swans, fair Thames, together in a rank,
And place them duly one by one upon thy stately bank."

But it is sadly to be feared that such poets were inspired less by a reverence for Father Thames

"From his oozy bed
Old Father Thames advanced his reverend head;
His tresses dropp'd with dews, and o'er the stream
His shining horns diffused a golden gleam:
Grav'd on his arm appear'd the moon that guides
His swelling waters and alternate tides:
The figur'd streams in waves of silver roll'd,
And on her banks Augusta rose in gold."

In Drayton's poem, "Polyolbion," published in 1613, in "The Seventeenth Song," we read:—

"When Thames now understood what pains the Mole did take,
How far the loving nymph adventur'd for his sake;
Although with Medway matcht, yet never could remove
The often-quick'ning sparks of his more ancient love.
So that it comes to pass, when by great Nature's guide
The ocean doth return, and thrusteth in the tide

Up towards the place where first his much-loved Mole
　　was seen,
He ever since doth flow beyond delightful Shene."

Pope, in his imitation of Spenser, has described
the alleys on the banks of the river in and about
London minutely and vividly, but in lines which
will scarcely bear quotation. And the poet Gray
describes in effect its quiet and peaceful character,
when he asks in one of his letters to Warton,
"Do you think that rivers which have lived in
London and its neighbourhood all their days, will
run roaring and tumbling about like your tramon-
tane torrents in the North?"

The following charming verses on our much-
loved river, from the first volume of *Once a Week*,
based on the quaint expression of Leland, who
speaks of London as "a praty town by Tamise
ripe," are not so well known as they deserve
to be :—

"Of Tamise ripe old Leland tells :
　I read, and many a thought up-swells
　Of Nature in her gentlest dress,
　Of peaceful homes of happiness,
　Deep-meadow'd farms, sheep-sprinkled downs,
　Fair bridges with their 'praty towns
　　　By Tamise ripe.'

＊　　＊　　＊　　＊　　＊　　＊

"Fair Oxford with her crown of towers,
　Fair Eton in her happy bowers,
　The 'reach' by Henley broadly spread,
　High Windsor, with her royal dead,
　And Richmond's lawns and Hampton's glades ;
　What shore has memories and shades
　　　Like 'Tamise ripe?'

"Not vine-clad Rhine, nor Danube's flood,
　Nor sad Ticino, red with blood,
　Not ice-born Rhone or laughing Seine,
　Nor all the golden streams of Spain ;
　Far dearer to our English eyes
　And bound with English destinies
　　　Is 'Tamise ripe.'

"High up on Danesfield's guarded post
　Great Alfred turn'd the heathen host ;
　Below the vaults of Hurley sent
　A tyrant into banishment ;
　And still more sacred was the deed
　Done on the isle by Runnymede
　　　On 'Tamise ripe.'

"And down where commerce stains the tide
　Lies London in her dusky pride,
　Deep in dim wreaths of smoke enfurl'd,
　The wonder of the modern world :
　How much to love within the walls
　That lie beneath the shade of Paul's
　　　By 'Tamise ripe'!"

The romance of the river Thames, not in its
sylvan, fishing, boating, and "swan-upping" aspect
above bridge, but in its melodramatically maritime
characteristics below bridge, was a theme which
seemed to afford unflagging delight to Charles
Dickens. Thames mud appeared to the great
novelist redolent of mysterious interest, and the
waterside scenes in "The Old Curiosity Shop,"
including the wharf where Mr. Quilp, the dwarf,
broke up his ships, where Mr. Sampson Brass so
nearly broke his shins, and where the immortal
Tom Scott so continuously stood on his head, were
rivalled in graphic vividness thirty years afterwards
by the waterside scenes and characters pictured in
"Our Mutual Friend." But with all this it is certain
that the romance of the river between London
Bridge and Greenwich has been for many years
declining, and that civilisation is all the better for
the disappearance of those picturesque features
described in 1798—not, indeed, in a work of
fiction, but in a most forcible, albeit prosaic
manner by Mr. C. Colquhoun, one of the police
magistrates of the metropolis. The lighter-buz-
zards, the "light horsemen," the sham "bum-
marees" and felonious "stevedores," the "tea-
skippers," "whisky-runners," and "rough-scullers"
—in other words, the robbers, pirates, smugglers,
and murderers who formerly infested the Pool and
the Port of London—are now but a feeble folk in
comparison with the great flotilla of river des-
peradoes denounced by Mr. Colquhoun, whose
work mainly led to the establishment of the
Thames Police. Since then "Cuckold's Point" and
"Execution Dock" have fallen out of the chart,
and, with the exception of an annual proportion of
lighter-robbing and tobacco-smuggling, the river
Thames may, in the present day, be considered as
quite respectable.

In Fitzstephen's time the Thames at London
was indeed "a fishful river," and we read of the
Thames fishermen presenting their tithe of salmon
at the high altar of the abbey church of St. Peter,
and claiming, on that occasion, the right to sit at
the Prior of Westminster's own table. At this
period the supply of fish materially contributed to
the subsistence of the inhabitants of the metropolis, and the river below the site of the present
London Bridge abounded with fish. In 1376–7
a law was passed in Parliament for the saving
of salmon and other fry of fish ; and in 1381-2
"swannes" that came through the bridge or beneath the bridge were the fees of the Constable of
the Tower.

The regulations respecting the keeping of swans
on the Thames have always been very strict, and
from a very early date the privilege of being
allowed to keep them has been very jealously
guarded. For example, we find that in the twenty-
second year of the reign of Edward IV., 1483, it

was ordered that no person not possessing a freehold of the clear yearly value of five marks should be permitted to keep any swans; and in the eleventh year of Henry VII., 1496, it was ordained that any one stealing a swan's egg should have one year's imprisonment, and be fined at the king's will; and stealing, setting snares for, or driving grey or white swans, was punished still more severely. In the time of Henry VIII. no persons having swans could appoint a new swanherd without the licence of the king's swanherd; and every swanherd on the river was bound to attend upon the king's swanherd, on warning, or else pay a fine. The Royal swanherd was obliged to keep a book of swan marks, in which no new ones could be inserted without special licence. Cygnets received the mark found on the parent bird, but if the old swans had no mark at the time of the "upping" (or marking), then the old and young birds were seized for the king, and marked accordingly. No swanherd was allowed to mark a bird, except in the presence of the king's swanherd or his deputy. When the swan made her nest on the bank of the river, instead of on one of the islands, one young bird was given to the owner of the soil, in order to induce him to protect the nest. This was called the ground bird. The Dyers' and Vintners' Companies have for several hundred years enjoyed the privilege of preserving swans on the Thames from London to some miles above Windsor, and they still continue the old custom of going with their friends and guests with the Royal swanherdsman, and their own swanherds and assistants, in the month of July or August in every year, from Lambeth, on their swan voyage, for the purpose of catching and "upping" (or marking) all the cygnets of the year. The junior warden of the Vintner's Company is called the "swan-warden"; the appointment to the office of Royal swanherd being vested in the Lord Chamberlain for the time being. Eton College has also the privilege of keeping these birds. At one period the Vintners' Company possessed over 500 swans, but the number is now much less, as, since they have ceased to be served up at great banquets and entertainments, the value of them has greatly declined.

A correspondent in a weekly journal has pictured to us in vivid colours the sad story of the "River Waifs and Dead-houses," which we here quote, as a striking contrast to the poetic and romantic views of the Thames given above:—
"Very peaceful and beautiful does the river look as we push off from one of the queer old flights of steps to be found at intervals all along the riversides. The light of the afternoon sun is gleaming down through a soft luminous mist, beneath which the face of old Father Thames looks up so smiling and placid that the idea that beneath his heaving bosom he conceals hideous secrets of death and decay, seems well nigh incredible. But he does so, nevertheless. Rarely a day passes but some poor struggling wretch goes down into those mysterious depths beneath that shining, glittering surface, never to rise again, or, if to rise, only to find a brief resting-place in one of the grim, foul little 'dead-houses'—scarcely less repulsive—dotted here and there among the dense population along the shores on either side of the great silent highway.

"Of course they are not all found; but within the London portion of the river Thames—between Chelsea and Barking, that is—there are on an average three or four of these poor waifs of humanity picked up every week.

"Yonder goes one of them, covered over with a cloth, in that small boat, threading its way through the midst of the shipping towards the foot of a long narrow stair, leading up through quaint old blocks of building overhanging the river. Following in the track of it I am soon standing before a tall iron railing, shutting in from the busy world a dreary little patch of ground, planted with old moss-covered gravestones and overrun with weeds. In the middle of this plot stands the dead-house. The depository of the dead must, of course, under any circumstances, be a dismal and unpleasant place to visit; but about many of these river-side houses there is—or one fancies there is—something peculiarly oppressive and dejecting, and any one tempted to entertain the idea of evading the responsibilities and troubles of a troublesome world by a short cut over the parapet of Waterloo Bridge would do well to take a turn round to some of them. If the thought of being brought there, friendless and unknown, bundled unceremoniously down on to a bare floor damp and blood-stained, covered with filthy-looking cloths, and laid in a 'shell,' in which temporarily, perhaps, hundreds of other piteous objects have already awaited identification or consignment to a nameless grave—if the thought of that does not act as a powerful deterrent there must, one would think, be a natural *penchant* for suicide, with which it would be hopeless to contend. There is something unutterably sad in the idea of such a termination to all the hopes and fears, the struggles and strivings of a human life; and there is something hideously grotesque in the aspect of the grizzled, crinkly-faced old beadle, as he sets about his preparations for the coroner, and chuckles at the evident shrinking of his visitor from the long black box in which, as he rolls up his sleeves, he tells him he has rather a bad subject to deal with. It is clear that he is rather proud of the indifference which long familiarity with the dead has enabled him to acquire, and he evidently enjoys the shock which he conveys in reply to a question as to what it is he is sweeping out into a corner of the ground. 'What's them? Why, somebody's toes,' says the old man ; and he adds, with a grim little smile, 'There's 'undreds o' toes down in that corner.'

"The body just brought in has been laid upon the slate shelf which runs along two sides of the building, and in the 'shell' on the floor are the remains of a young man, probably one of a score or so of poor fellows who lost their lives during the two or three days of dense fog some weeks ago, and the bodies of some of whom have ever since been floating about the still awful gloom of the bed of the river. No description of the contents of that shell can be attempted. Without some clear and specific object in doing so—such as we have here—even the mention of it would be unwarrantable. Only those who have seen a human body under such circumstances can form any conception of the duty which somebody has to perform before an inquest can be held, and they only are in a position to understand how inadequate and imperfect are the arrangements of the various metropolitan authorities for dealing with them.

"A story, which under other circumstances would be ludicrous, is told of a military officer who, some time ago, was called on to go to one of these places to identify one of his men who had been accidentally drowned in the summer time, and whose body had been recovered after many days' immersion. The officer had gone through some active service, and made light of the warning of those in charge of the mortuary as to the shock he might possibly receive. He would take just a sip of brandy if, as they said, the smell of the place was so very unpleasant ; but as to the sight of a dead body—pooh, nonsense ! He had seen too many of them. It had been necessary to place a heavy stone on the lid of the shell containing the poor fellow, and no sooner was this removed and the lid raised than, on the instant, this stout-hearted officer rushed from the place sick and pale as a ghost, and declaring that if his whole regiment were drowned he would never go near another such a sight.

"It is not surprising that the appearance of some of these melancholy objects on the river by night is often sufficient to unnerve men of the most dauntless character and whose familiarity with them would, it might be supposed, tend to render them comparatively indifferent. Veteran watermen are sometimes found to be the veriest children in dealing with them. There is an 'old stager' now on the river whose courage, under all ordinary circumstances, has been proved in a thousand different ways, but who yet dare not stay by himself for a few moments in charge of one of these stark, silent creatures. He and his comrades one night brought one to shore tied to the boat, which was left in his charge while his companions fetched a 'shell.' They had no sooner disappeared than he made his way to a neighbouring public-house, ostensibly to get a light for his lantern, but, as the joke goes, to let some of the folks there know that there was something to be seen down at his boat. His little *ruse* was successful, but his troubles were not quite over. His comrades returned with the shell, and all marched off with the body to the dead-house, which was reached by crossing a churchyard. On their arrival he was sent back to the boat, but with such terror had the sight of that object inspired this burly, really bold-hearted man, that he could not for the life of him open the gate of the churchyard, and stood inside fumbling at the handle and shaking with fear until a woman passed, and she, poor soul, took him for a ghost, and when he asked her the time of night took to her heels and ran off in frantic terror.

"It would be reasonable to suppose that with an average of some 150 to 200 of these bodies requiring attention every year there would, at proper intervals along the river-banks, and at no great distance from the river, be found not only mortuaries of the most complete and perfect construction, but every facility for conveying the bodies to them. Such, however, is by no means the case. Till within the past few months, the body of a person found drowned on the lower side of London Bridge should have been deposited in a kind of vault just between the church of St. Magnus the Martyr and the bridge. At the present time, no matter how sickening and dreadful the object found may be, it must be conveyed through the public streets to the mortuary in Golden Lane, a distance considerably over a mile. If found within that part of the river lying between the Equitable Gas Works and Chelsea College, it must be conveyed right away to Mount Street, in the neighbourhood of Hanover Square, a distance certainly not less than two miles. The idea of a corpse—it may be in an advanced stage of decomposition—being dragged from the river, laid in a filthy shell, and carried upon men's shoulders for a distance of two miles, and that, perhaps, in the height of summer, is something most revolting, and altogether discreditable to those who are responsible for it. In other cases the distance is not so great, but the accommodation for properly dealing with the dead is altogether wanting. The only dead-house for the river between Nine Elms and Waterloo Bridge is a kind of tool-house in one corner of Lambeth churchyard. Lower down the river another little tool-house, standing close under the windows of a row of cottages, is the only mortuary. Even where the places themselves are tolerably satisfactory their situations are, in some instances, most objectionable. There is a new mortuary in Pennyfields, Poplar. It is situated at the bottom of a close and narrow lane, between the workhouse on the one hand, and a densely-populated little street on the other. Often there are five or six bodies lying here at one time, and the surrounding inhabitants speak of the stench as at times something most unbearable.

"The discussion that has lately (1870) been going on as to the best method of disposing of the dead, is no doubt a very important one; but it is evident that in London at least we have not as yet given anything like sufficient attention to the disposal of the dead during the interval between death and the final solemnity, whatever it may be. This applies not only to the river district, but to all parts of London; but in no other part does it happen that bodies that have been practically buried for weeks or even months are dragged to the light of day, and have to be dealt with as in the case of an ordinary death. In no part, therefore, is it so important that mortuary accommodation of the most complete kind shall be easily accessible, and, it may be added, in no part is it so thoroughly defective. There is, of course, great difficulty in securing open spaces for these structures, and the cost would, in some cases, be very serious if provided on shore. Where this appears to be an insuperable difficulty, however, a very simple and inexpensive solution of it would be to set up a floating mortuary here and there. This would afford fresh air, plenty of water, and ready access. Something ought speedily to be done in this matter." Things have improved considerably since these words were written, but complaint is still made from time to time that the mortuary accommodation of the metropolis is inadequate.

Of the Thames watermen and wherrymen, a brief mention has been made in the second volume of this work (see pages 51 and 52): we may, however, add here a few more particulars concerning this once celebrated and now almost extinct body of men.

As may easily be imagined, they formed very much of a caste by themselves, and recognised their kinship in the craft by being ambitious of burial, when they died, in the southern side of the churchyard of St. Martin's-in-the-Fields. They were a rough, saucy, and independent lot, if we may judge from allusions to them which occur in the novels, comedies, farces, and popular songs of the last century. Their phraseology, too, was as peculiar as that of the cabmen and omnibus drivers of our own day. Peter Cunningham calls it "the water dialect or mob language," the use of which he reckons as "one of the privileges of the river assumed by the fraternity," a language of which Ned Ward and Tom Brown have both left us specimens, and of which Fielding complains so touchingly in his "Voyage to Lisbon;" and he quotes, in support of his statement, several passages from Ben Jonson, Samuel Pepys, and Wycherley. It will be remembered that in the *Spectator* (No. 383) Sir Roger de Coverley is "shocked" at the saucy language with which he is greeted by two or three young fellows, whilst taking his pleasure in a boat on the Thames; and Boswell, in his "Life of Johnson," records the fact that once when the learned doctor was in a similar situation, he gave back a wherryman railery for railery in terms which we can scarcely quote in these pages.

The Thames watermen received their licences from, and were directly amenable to, the Lord Mayor and the other members of the Thames Conservancy; and their fares were regulated by a published scale of charges a hundred years ago. A copy of the "Rates of Watermen plying on the River Thames, either with oars or skullers," dated 1770, gives a table of charges, showing that a fare could be carried with "oars" for a shilling from London Bridge to Limehouse, Shadwell Dock, or Ratcliff Cross; or from either side above London Bridge to Lambeth or Vauxhall. Eightpence was the charge for the same mode of conveyance from the Temple, Blackfriars, or Paul's Wharf to Lambeth; whilst sixpence would frank a voyager from London Bridge or St. Olave's, Tooley Street, to "Wapping Old Stairs" or Rotherhithe Church; or from Billingsgate and St. Olave's to St. Saviour's Mill, from any stairs below London Bridge and Westminster, or from Whitehall to Lambeth or Vauxhall; whilst any lady or gentleman could be ferried "over the water directly from any place between Vauxhall in the west, and Limehouse in the east, for fourpence." The charges for "skullers" for each of the above-named voyages were exactly half the sums here named. The authorised "rates of oars, down and up the river, as well for the whole fare as for company"—in other words, for a single voyager, or each person forming a party—are curious. From London to

Hampton town, Sunbury, or Walton for seven; to Weybridge or Chertsey for ten; to Staines for twelve; and all the way to Windsor for fourteen shillings. If a party was got up for the occasion the charge was a shilling for each individual for any distance beyond Kingston, even as far as Windsor.

To the above list the same little book gives in an appendix the "Rates authorised for carrying

OLD WHITEHALL STAIRS. (*See page* 297.)

Greenwich or Deptford, the charge for a single individual was eighteenpence, to Blackwall two shillings, to Woolwich half-a-crown, to Purfleet or Erith three shillings, to Grays or Greenhithe four shillings, and to Gravesend four and sixpence. When persons made the voyage in parties, each of the "company," be the latter large or small, was to be charged about a sixth of the above rates. The same regulations held good "above bridge" also: you could be taken by "oars" to Chelsea, Battersea, or Wandsworth for eighteenpence; to Putney, Fulham, or Barnes for two shillings; to Hammersmith, Chiswick, or Mortlake for half-a-crown; to Brentford, Isleworth, or Richmond for three and sixpence; to Twickenham for four shillings; to Kingston for five; to Hampton Court for six; to

goods in the tilt-boat from London to Gravesend." For this passage the charge was for each single person, ninepence; for a hogshead of liquor, two shillings; for a firkin of goods, twopence; for half a firkin, a penny; for a hundredweight of dry goods, fourpence; for a sack of corn, salt, &c., sixpence; for an "ordinary hamper," sixpence; and it is added, for the information of those whom it may concern, that "the hire of the whole tilt-boat was £1 2s. 6d." By a "tilt" boat of course is meant a boat with a covering; the term still survives, as we need hardly remind our readers, in the term "tilt" cart. It is interesting to compare these rates of transit by oars and scullers along "the silent highway" of old Father Thames with the fares charged now a-days to voyagers along

OLD WHITEHALL PALACE FROM THE RIVER. (*See page 297.*)

the same route in penny steamboats, which, with all their faults, are a good deal cheaper and swifter than their precursors.

The olden recreations on "the noble Thames" are of great celebrity. Fitzstephen tells us of the ancient Londoners fighting "battles on Easter holidays on the water, by striking a shield with a lance." There was also a kind of water tournament, in which the combatants, standing on two wherries, rowed and ran against the other, fighting with staves and swords. In Gower's time the sovereign was rowed in his tapestried barge, probably the first royal barge upon the Thames; and upon this great highway Richard II., seeing the good old rhymer, called him on board the royal vessel, and there commanded him to "make a book after his hest," which was the origin of the "Confessio Amantis." At this period a portion of London Bridge was movable, so that vessels of burthen might pass up the river, to unload at Queenhithe and elsewhere; and stairs, watergates, and palaces studded both shores. At this time, too, we are informed, boats conveyed passengers, for the sum of twopence each, from London to Gravesend.

One of the most interesting annual events in the present day in connection with the Thames watermen, and not the least popular gala day in these times, though it may hardly be compared with the Derby Day at Epsom or with the Oxford and Cambridge boat-race, is the one afforded by Thomas Doggett, comedian, on the 1st of August, to commemorate the accession of the House of Brunswick. "This scene," says Mr. J. T. Smith in his "Book for a Rainy Day," "is sure to be picturesque and cheerful should it be lit up by the glorious sun 'that gems the sea and every land that blooms.'" In 1715, the year after George I. came to the throne, Doggett, to quicken the industry and raise a laudable emulation in our young men of the Thames, whereby they not only may acquire a knowledge of the river but a skill in managing the oar with dexterity, gave an orange-coloured coat and silver badge, on which was sculptured the Hanoverian Horse, to the successful candidate of six young watermen just out of their apprenticeship, to be rowed for on the 1st of August, when the current was strongest against them, starting from the 'Old Swan,' London Bridge, to the 'Swan' at Chelsea." On the 1st of August, 1722, the year after Doggett's death, pursuant to the tenor of his will, the prize was first rowed for, and has been given annually ever since.

"They gripe their oars, and every panting breast
    Is raised by turns with hope, by turns with fear depressed."

Charles Dibdin was so amused with the sight of the contest for Doggett's prize, that in 1774 he brought out at the Haymarket a ballad opera, entitled *The Waterman: or, the First of August,* the hero in which, "Tom Tug," sings the well-known song—

"And did you ne'er hear of a jolly young waterman,
    Who at Blackfriars Bridge used for to ply?
He feather'd his oars with such skill and dexterity,
    Winning each heart and delighting each eye;"

and another when he has resolved to cast away his cares and be off to sea:—

"Then, farewell, my trim-built wherry,
    Oars and coat, and badge, farewell!
Never more at Chelsea ferry
    Shall your Thomas take a spell," &c.

However, Tom rowed for Doggett's coat and badge, which he had an eye upon, in order to obtain his love if possible by his prowess. She was seated at the "Swan Inn," Chelsea, and admired the successful candidate before she discovered him to be her suitor Thomas, then "blushed an answer to his wooing tale," and it is to be hoped lived happily with him for ever afterwards.

The old "Swan Inn" at Chelsea, we may add, was swept away about the year 1873 to make room for the Thames Embankment; but the coat and badge is still rowed for, the destination of the race being the Cadogan Pier at Chelsea. The Fishmongers' Company, of which Thomas Doggett was a member, added six guineas to the first prize; and besides this there are several other prizes awarded to the different competitors in the race. The second and third prizes are respectively five guineas and three guineas, derived from a variety of sources, among others a bequest of South Sea stock under the will of Sir William Jolliffe. The prize for the fourth man is two guineas, and for the fifth and sixth men £1 11s. 6d. and £1 6s. respectively. There are also different sums occasionally given by private individuals to the winner, or to the first, second, and third in the race. The competition is between six watermen, each being in a boat by himself with short oars or sculls; and the competitors are those who have been first and second in three trial heats from Putney to Hammersmith. The barge-master of the Fishmongers' Company is ordinarily the umpire; and the race always excites much local interest, being one of those manly sports in which the English take much pleasure.

Thomas Doggett is stated to have been a native of Dublin, and to have been born about the middle of the seventeenth century. Colley Cibber, speaking of him, says, "As an actor he was a great observer of Nature ; and as a singer he had no competitor." He was the author of the "Country Wake," a comedy published in 1696, and was a patentee of Drury Lane Theatre until 1712. He died in 1721. It may be added that Doggett was not the only actor who took an interest in the Thames watermen, for the proprietors of the old Vauxhall Gardens, and Astley the equestrian, gave wherries to be rowed for ; as did also Edmund Kean, the tragedian.

Among the most celebrated of Thames watermen in bygone days was Taylor, "the water poet," of whom we have already spoken. Miss Benger thus apostrophises both the poet and the river at once :—

> "And thou, O Thames, his lonely sighs hast caught.
> When one, the rhyming Charon of his day,
> Who tugged the oar, yet conned a merry lay,
> Full oft unconscious of the freight he bore,
> Transferred the musing bard from shore to shore.
> Too careless *Taylor !* hadst thou well divined,
> The marvellous man to thy frail skiff consigned,
> Thou shouldst have craved one tributary line,
> To blend his glorious destiny with thine !
> Nor vain the prayer !—who generous homage pays
> To genius, wins the second meed of praise."

Down to about the middle of the seventeenth century, when not only coaches, but also sedan chairs, had become pretty general, the Thames had formed the great medium of metropolitan conveyance. Its banks on either side were studded thick, as far as London extended, with the quays and "stairs" of the nobles, and wharves of the commons, while its waters were peopled with every kind of vessel, from the bucentaur-like barge of royalty, to the nutshell skiff or wherry. In 1454, Sir John Norman, Lord Mayor elect, built a magnificent barge for the use and honour of his mayoralty ; before his time it was usual for the chief magistrate and his train to go to Westminster Hall on horseback. The companies followed Norman's example, and constructed elegant vessels to accompany their mayors. The watermen were so elated by this circumstance that they caused a commemoration song to be composed on the occasion, beginning, "Row thy boat, Norman," &c.

Down to the time of the discontinuance of the "water pageant" as part of the Lord Mayor's state procession to Westminster, the officials connected with the state barge included the water-bailiff, one of his lordship's esquires, with a salary of £500 a year, a shallop, and eight men ; and in the suite were a barge-master and thirty-two City watermen. The watermen, clad in livery and wearing the badge won in the match above mentioned, have been wont to take part in the Lord Mayor's Show on the

9th of November ; and the trumpeters who formerly heralded his lordship's approach to Westminster from the prow of the gilded barge, now precede his lordship's state carriage on foot in all civic state ceremonies.

The remains of Anne of Bohemia, queen of Henry VII., who died at Richmond, were honoured with a state funeral by water, being brought with great pomp by the river to Westminster. In 1533 the mayor and citizens accompanied Anne Boleyn in their barges from Greenwich to the Tower, preparatory to her coronation at Westminster ; and this was the highway along which that unfortunate lady and more than one other of the wives of Henry VIII. made their last journey. Along it also "the seven bishops" were conveyed from Westminster to the Tower in the reign of James II. Mr. Peter Cunningham briefly reminds us that State prisoners committed from the Council Chamber to the Tower or the Fleet were invariably taken by water.

Passing up the Thames on frequent occasions might be seen in mid-stream the royal barge of Queen Elizabeth with her Majesty on board in gayest trim, on her way up the stream along with the tide going to her palace at Westminster, and possibly to land at Whitehall Stairs, or at the Westminster Palace Water Gate, at that time known, as we learn from Ralph Aggas' map, as "The Queen's Stairs."

After the great civil war, however, the royal water processions dwindled into the paltry annual pageant of the Lord Mayor's Show ; and even this, we need hardly say, has now died out. The state barge last in use by the Lord Mayor was built in 1816, and named the *Maria Wood* (from the then Lord Mayor's eldest daughter) ; it was very capacious, and richly carved and gilt.* A few of the City Companies had their own state barges, "to attend my Lord Mayor ;" as the Fishmongers, Vintners, Dyers, Stationers, Skinners, and Watermen. The barge belonging to the Goldsmiths' Company was sold in 1850.

The river state barge of the Queen has not been used since the year 1849, when Her Majesty went by water to open the new Coal Exchange. The Lords of the Admiralty have likewise their state barge ; but it is seldom or never now brought into use. Possibly water pageants may some day be revived.

The nobility, in imitation of royalty, laid aside their gilded barges ; the fashionables who dwelt near the Thames, at St. Katharine's, Bankside, Lambeth Marsh, Westminster, Whitefriars, Cole-

* See also Vol. I., p. 447.

harbour, and other such convenient localities for a water fête, preferred an inland pic-nic among the gardens or forests, to which their carriages could waft them in an hour or two ; while the busy Inns of Court, whose thousands of students and practitioners had hitherto used the facilities of the river alike for business or for pleasure, were now to be found flying along the streets with their books, briefs, and blue bags, six in a coach. The Thames, no longer the great highway of London, had become little better than a water conveyance, in the absence of bridges, between the City and the Borough ; and the small clusters of ferrymen that now lingered on at the different crossing-places, looking out hungrily for a chance fare, were but the ghosts of a departed glory, as they uplifted their voices in supplication with, " Boat, your honour ! boat, boat !"

The Thames was the usual road, and persons, a century ago, spoke of "taking the water" as we speak of taking a cab or omnibus. To quote an instance from the *Somerset House Gazette* :—" 'You do me great honour, Mr. Handel,' said my great uncle. 'I take this early visit as a great kindness.' 'A delightful morning for the water,' said Colley Cibber. 'Pray, did you come with oars or scullers, Mr. Handel?' asked Pepusch, who had lately been setting the airs to the songs in the *Beggar's Opera*."

It may interest some readers, however, to learn that when George IV. came to the throne there were still 3,000 wherries plying on the Thames, while the hackney coaches could muster only a sorry 1,200 in the whole of London. As late as the year 1829, if not more recently still, a boat was the usual conveyance from the neighbourhood of Westminster to Vauxhall ; and Mr. J. T. Smith, in his " Book for a Rainy Day," tells many anecdotes about the " Thames watermen," whose work was of course at an end as soon as new bridges were built and cheap steamboats put upon the river.

A couple of centuries ago the river was so clear and pure that the noblemen who lived upon its banks along the Strand used to bathe in it constantly. It is on record, for instance, that in the reign of Charles I. such was the practice of Lord Northampton ; and Roger North tells us, in his " Lives of the Norths," that his relative, Dudley North, used to swim on the Thames so constantly —and "above bridge," too—that "he could live in the water an afternoon with as much ease as others walk upon land." Horace Walpole, too, tells Lady Craven in one of his letters that Lord Chesterfield waggishly addressed a letter to his friend the Earl of Pembroke, who was fond of swimming in these parts, "To the Earl of Pembroke, in the Thames, over against Whitehall." Lord Byron tells us in one of his letters, in 1807, that he took a swim from Lambeth through Westminster and Blackfriars Bridges down to London Bridge apparently, or even lower, for he reckons the length of his voyage as three miles.

That a very different state of things afterwards came about in the condition or the appearance of the Thames may be inferred when we state that from the Report of the Medical Officer of Health, submitted to the Corporation of London towards the close of 1874, it appears that during the month of September of that year 2,083 vessels had been inspected in the river and the docks between Vauxhall and Woolwich, 366 of which required cleansing, 93 sick sailors had been found afloat and referred to the Seamen's Hospital at Greenwich, and of 19 samples of drinking water taken from vessels in various parts of the port for purposes of analysis, seven were found unfit for human consumption. In this matter, however, it is to be hoped that we have made some advance since 1874. The practice of carrying Asiatic crews on board British ships has revived very much since 1872, and there are now always not fewer than from 500 to 700 Lascars about Limehouse.

Those who do not know what the state of things was in the Thames in the days when shipping discharged in the stream may be astonished to read of the doings little short of piractical which were a part of the established order of things, and prevailed into the reign of George IV., when the opening of the West India Docks enabled at least a portion of the shipping to discharge their cargoes with some safety. In 1798 the depredations from merchant vessels in the river Thames were estimated by Mr. Colquhoun to amount to £506,500 a year. "Scuffle-hunters," long-shore thieves, mudlarks, "Peterboatmen," river pirates, "light horsemen," and last, but not least, the captains and mates of the vessels and the revenue officers themselves preyed upon the shipping, and "one gigantic system of plunder seems to have prevailed throughout." Not only hogsheads of sugar and puncheons of rum, but anchors, cables, and other tackle were carried off by thieves ; and mates and revenue officers seem to have had a regular scale of charges for retiring to their berths while robbery of the hold or deck was going on.

" Most of these infamous proceedings," says Mr. W. S. Lindsay, in his work on " Our Mercantile Marine," " were carried on according to a regular system, and in gangs, frequently composed of one or more receivers, together with coopers, watermen, and lumpers, who were all necessary in their different occupations to the accomplishment of the general design of wholesale plunder. They went on board the merchant vessel completely prepared with iron crows, adzes, and other implements to open and again head up the casks; with shovels to take out the sugar, and a number of bags made to contain 100 lb. each. These bags went by the name of 'black strap,' having been previously dyed black to prevent their being conspicuous in the night when stowed in the bottom of a river boat or wherry. In the course of judicial proceedings it has been shown that in the progress of the delivery of a large ship's cargo about ten to fifteen tons of sugar were on an average removed in these nocturnal expeditions, exclusive of what had been obtained by the lumpers during the day, which was frequently excessive and almost uncontrolled whenever night plunder had occurred. This indulgence was generally insisted on and granted to lumpers to prevent their making discoveries of what they called the 'drum hogsheads' found in the hold on going to work in the morning, by which were understood hogsheads out of which from one-sixth to one-fourth of the contents had been stolen the night preceding. In this manner one gang of plunderers was compelled to purchase the connivance of another to the ruinous loss of the merchant."

It was estimated that about 11,000 persons got a dishonest livelihood by taking part in the rascalities which received their first death-blow from the high walls of the West India Docks. On the manifold advantage of the dock and bonded warehouse system, which now extends to every shipping port in the kingdom, it is needless to dilate, though outsiders will thank Mr. Lindsay for the clear and interesting explanation of the course of shipping business as it is now conducted in his work above referred to.

In these days from four to five hundred boys are accommodated on the *Chichester* and *Arethusa* training ships, off Greenhithe. Other training-ships on the Thames are the *Warspite*, off Woolwich; the *Cornwall*, off Purfleet; the *Worcester*, off Greenhithe; and the *Shaftesbury* and the *Exmouth*, off Grays.

The mercantile importance of this noble stream is greater than that of any other river in the world. Its merchantmen visit the most distant parts of the globe; and the productions of every soil and of every clime are wafted home upon its bosom to answer the demands of British commerce. The frozen shores of the Baltic and North America, the sultry regions of both the Indies, and the arid coasts of Africa have alike resounded with its name; and there is not a single country, perhaps, in any quarter of the earth, bordering on the sea, that has not been visited by its sails.

CHAPTER XXXIX.

THE RIVER THAMES (*continued*).

" Cœlo gratissimus amnis."—*Virgil.*

Remarkable Frosts on the Thames—Frost Fair in 1683—Rhyming Description of " Blanket Fair."—Evelyn's Account of the Fair—Printing on the Ice—Charles II.'s Partiality to Frost Fair—The River again frozen over in 1709, 1715, 1739, 1767, 1788, and 1814—Curious Handbills printed on the Ice—Singular Feats performed on the Thames—Captain Boyton's Life-preserving Dress—Scott, the American Diver—Rise and Fall of the Tide—Projected Improvements for the Bed of the River.

HAPPILY in our latitude winter is not often so severe as to "bind in frosty chains" the river which runs through the heart of our metropolis; but still, if the old annalists and historians are to be believed, the Thames from time to time has been frozen into ice-fields, and its surface has been made the scene of frost-fairs. To mention a few instances: we are told that in the reign of Stephen, in the year 1150, "after a very wet summer there was in December so great a frost that horses and carriages crossed it upon the ice as safely as upon the dry ground, and that the frost lasted till the following month of March." Again we read that

in 1281 the Thames was frozen over, and that on the breaking up of the ice five of the arches of old London Bridge were carried away. "In 1434," says Northouck, "the Thames was so strongly frozen over, that merchandise and provisions brought into the mouth of the river were obliged to be unladen, and brought by land to the city." In 1515, too, carriages passed over on the ice from Lambeth to Westminster. At this time it is said the frost and snow were so severe that five arches of London Bridge were "borne downe and carried away with the streame." On the 21st of December, 1564, during the prevalence of a hard frost, we read of diversions on the Thames, some playing at football, and others "shooting at marks." The courtiers from the palace at White-hall mixed with the citizens, and tradition reports that Queen Elizabeth herself walked upon the ice. On the night of the 3rd of January following, however, it began to thaw, and on the 5th there was no ice to be seen on the river. In 1620 a great frost enabled the Londoners to carry on all manner of sports and trades upon the river.

wonder of this present age and a great consternation to all the spectators." The rude cut beneath the title shows the Middlesex shore, taken from the centre of the river, from Arundel House to the eastern end of the Temple; giving a view of Essex Buildings with its ugly round-headed arch, and the three groups of stairs belonging to Arundel House, Essex House, and the Temple. The street of booths holds out all sorts of signs, just like the houses in the Strand. There are men and boys

FROST FAIR ON THE THAMES IN 1683.

In a curious volume of London ballads and broadsides in the British Museum is one entitled "Great Britain's Wonder, or London's Admiration," being "a true representation of a prodigious frost which began about the beginning of December, 1683, and continued till the fourth day of February following. It held on the Thames with such violence that men and beasts, coaches and carts, went as frequently thereon as boats were wont to pass before. There was also" (continues the writer) "a street of booths built from the Temple to Southwark, where were sold all sorts of goods imaginable, namely, cloaths, plate, earthenware, meat, drink, brandy, tobacco, and a hundred sorts of commodities not here inserted: it being the

making slides, skating, and sledging in all directions; some of the sledges are of the ordinary type, like the low brewer's dray drawn by heavy horses; some are more artistic, made up like gondolas; some are apparently genuine boats, with sails; in two places are carriages drawn by a single horse, and just opposite the Temple Stairs a bull is being baited. Gallants in the fashionable dresses of the day are promenading, with wigs and swords; while the ladies, true to the instinct of their sex, are "shopping" briskly. In a corner are five men playing at skittles; one of them is smoking a pipe. The doggerel verses below the cut tell how

"The Thames is now both fair and market too,
Where many thousands daily do resort.

* * * * *

There you may see the coaches swiftly run,
As if beneath the ice were waters none,
And shoals of people everywhere there be,
Just like the herrings in the brackish sea.
And there the quaking watermen will stand ye,
'Kind master, drink you beer, or ale, or brandy;
Walk in, kind sir, this booth it is the chief,
We'll entertain you with a slice of beef.'
Another cries, 'Here, master, they but scoff ye;
Here is a dish of famous new-made coffee.'

* * * * *

entitled "A True Description of Blanket Fair upon
the River Thames in the Time of the Great Frost,
in the Year of our Lord 1683," gives a representation
of the ox being roasted, and also of the "hunting
the fox," Reynard being pursued by two men with
clubs and five queer-looking dogs: in this one of
the carriages has two horses; the verses are just
a shade above those already quoted, but running
in the same descriptive vein, as will be seen from
the following specimen:—

FROST ON THE THAMES, 1814.

There you may also this hard frosty winter
See on the rocky ice a WORKING-PRINTER,
Who hopes by his own art to reap some gain
Which he perchance does think he may obtain.
Here also is a lottery, music too,
Yea, a cheating, drunken, lewd, and debauch'd crew;
Hot codlins, pancakes, ducks, and goose, and sack,
Rabbit, capon, hen, turkey, and a wooden jack.

* * * * *

There on a sign you may most plainly see 't,
Here's the first tavern built in Freezeland Street.
There is bull-baiting and bear-baiting too.

* * * * *

There roasted was a great and well-fed ox
And there with dogs hunted the common fox."

Another rough print in the same collection,
taken from almost the very same point of view,

"The art of printing there was to be seen,
Which in no former age had ever been;
And goldsmiths' shops well furnished with plate;
But they must dearly pay for 't that would ha' it,
And coffee-houses in great numbers were
Scattered about in this cold-freezing fair.
There might you sit down by a char-cole fire
And for your money have your heart's desire,
A dish of coffee, chocolate, or tea:
Could man desire more furnishèd to be?"

In the same collection is a ballad, of a few
weeks' later date, "The Thames uncas'd; or, the
Waterman's Song upon the Thaw;" the last stanza
runs thus:—

" Meantime, if ought of honour you've got,
Let the printers have their due,

Who printed your names on the river Thames,
    While their hands with the cold look'd blue ;
There's mine, there's thine, will for ages shine,
    Now the Thames again does flow ;
Then let's gang hence, to our boats' commence,
    For the frost is over now."

In another ballad, printed and sold on the ice about this time, entitled "Blanket Fair, or History of Temple Street, being a Relation of the Merry Pranks played on the River Thames during the Great Frost," we read—

"I'll tell you a story as true as 'tis rare,
    Of a river turn'd into a Bartlemy Fair.
      Since old Christmas last,
      There has bin such a frost,
That the Thames has by half the whole nation bin crost.
O scullers ! I pity your fate of extreams,
Each landman is now become free of the Thames."

On the 1st of January, 1684, John Evelyn tells us that whole streets of booths were set out on the Thames, and that he crossed the river on the ice on foot upon the 9th in order to dine with the Archbishop of Canterbury at Lambeth, and again, in his coach, from Lambeth to the Horseferry at Millbank, upon the 5th of February. On the 6th he observes that the ice had " now become so thick as to beare not onely streetes of boothes in which they roasted meate, and had divers shops of wares quite acrosse as in a towne, but coaches, carts, and horses passed over. At this time there was a foot-passage quite over the river, from Lambeth-stairs to the Horse-ferry at Westminster ; and hackney coaches began to carry fares from Somerset House and the Temple to Southwark. On January 23rd, the first day of Hilary Term, they were regularly employed in hire, where the watermen were accustomed to be found. In this arrangement the means of conveyance only, and not the ordinary way, was altered ; since the use of boats to Westminster was almost universal at the period, as the rough paving of the streets rendered riding through them in coaches very uneasy." By the 16th the number of persons keeping shops on the ice had so greatly increased that Evelyn says, "the Thames was filled with people and tents selling all sorts of wares as in the City ;" and by the 24th the varieties and festivities of a fair appear to have been completely established. " The frost," he states, " continuing more and more severe, the Thames before London was still planted with boothes in formal streets, all sorts of trades, and shops furnish'd and full of commodities, even to a printing presse, where the people and ladys tooke a fancy to have their names printed, and the day and yeare set down, when printed on the Thames. This humour took so universally, that 'twas estimated

the printer gained about £5 a day for printing a line onely at sixpence a name, besides what he got by ballads, &c." In a poem commemorative of this frost, published at the time, there occurs the following passage relating to the printers ; the concluding four lines of which have been used in some of the verses produced at every frost fair, from that in 1684 to the last in 1814 :—

"—— To the Print-house go,
Where men the Art of Printing seem to know :
Where, for a Teaster, you may have your name
Printed, hereafter for to shew the same ;
And sure, in former ages, ne'er was found
A Press to Print where men so oft were drown'd !" *

Evelyn also quaintly tells us how that " coaches plied from Westminster to the Temple, and from several other staires, to and fro, as in the streetes : sleds [sledges], sliding with skeetes [skates], a bull-baiting, horse and coach races, puppet-plays and interludes, cookes, tippling, and other lewd places ; so that it seem'd to be a bacchanalian triumph, or carnival on the water." This traffic and festivity were continued until February 5th, when the same authority states that " it began to thaw, but froze again. My coach crossed from Lambeth to the horse-ferry at Millbank, Westminster. The booths were almost taken downe ; but there was first a map or land-skip cut in copper, representing all the manner of the camp, and the several actions, sports and pastimes thereon, in memory of so signal a frost. . . . London, by reason of the excessive coldness of the aire hindering the ascent of the smoke, was so fill'd with this fuliginous steame of the sea-coale, that hardly could one see across the streetes ; and this filling the lungs with its gross particles, exceedingly obstructed the breath, so as no one could scarcely breathe. There was no water to be had from the pipes and engines ; nor could the brewers and divers other tradesmen work ; and every moment was full of disastrous accidents." It was during the continuance of this fair that Evelyn saw a " human salamander," when he dined at Sir Stephen Fox's, and " after dinner came a fellow who ate live charcoal, glowingly ignited, quenching them in his mouth, and then champing and swallowing them down. There was also a dog which," Evelyn quaintly remarks, " seemed to do many rational actions."

The very curious original drawing of this fair, engraven on a reduced scale in Smith's " Antiquities of London," represents the Thames, looking

---

* " Thamesis's Advice to the Painter from her Frigid Zone ; or, Wonders on the Water." London : Printed by G. Groom, on the River of Thames. Small folio half-sheet, 74 lines.

from the western side of the Temple Stairs, appearing on the left, towards London Bridge, which is faintly shown in the view at the back with all the various buildings standing upon it. "The time when the view was taken," says the author of that work, "was the day previous to the first thaw, as the original is dated in a contemporaneous hand at the top of the right-hand corner, 'Munday, February the 4th, 1683-4.' The drawing consists of a spirited though unfinished sketch, on stout and coarse paper in pencil, slightly shaded with Indian ink; which was the well-known style of an artist of the seventeenth century, peculiarly eminent for his views, namely, Thomas Wyck—usually called Old Wyck, to distinguish him from his son John—who spent the greater part of his life in England. This sketch is preserved in the 'Illustrated Pennant's London,' formerly belonging to Mr. John Charles Crowle, in the Print Room of the British Museum. On the right of the view is an oblique prospect of the double line of tents which extended across the centre of the river, called at the time Temple Street, consisting of taverns, toy shops, &c., which were generally distinguished by some title or sign, as the 'Duke of York's Coffee-house,' 'the Tory booth,' 'the booth with a phenix on it, and insured to last as long as the foundation stands,' 'the Half-way House,' 'the Bear Gardenshire Booth,' 'the Roast Beef Booth,' 'the Music Booth,' 'the Printing Booth,' 'the Lottery Booth,' and 'the Horn Tavern Booth,' which is indicated about the centre of the view by the antlers of a stag raised above it. On the outside of this street were pursued the various sports of the fair, some of which are also shown in the annexed plate; but in the nearer and larger figures introduced in the pictorial map mentioned by Evelyn, there appear extensive circles of spectators, surrounding a bull-baiting, and the rapid revolution of a whirling-chair or car, drawn by several men by a long rope fastened to a stake, fixed in the ice. Large boats covered with tilts, capable of containing a considerable number of passengers, and decorated with flags and streamers, are represented as being used for sledges, some of them being drawn by horses, and others by watermen, in want of their usual employment. Another sort of boat was mounted on wheels, and one vessel called the 'Drum-boat' was distinguished by a drummer placed at the prow. The pastimes of throwing at a cock, sliding and skating, roasting an ox, foot-ball, skittles, pigeon-holes, cups and balls, &c., are represented in a large print as being carried on in various parts of the river; whilst a sliding-hutch propelled by a stick, a chariot moved by a screw, and stately coaches, filled with visitors, appear to be rapidly moving in various directions, and sledges with coals and wood are passing between the London and Southwark shores. The gardens of the Temple and the river itself are both filled in the large plate with numerous spectators, as they are also shown in the present view; but, in addition to its originality, the drawing now engraved is, perhaps, more pictorially interesting than the print, from the prospect being considerably more spacious and carefully executed; as it exhibits the whole line of the Bankside to St. Saviour's Church, with the Tower, the Monument, finished in 1677, the Windmill near Queenhythe, the new Bow Church, and some others of the new churches, the vacant site and ruins of Bridewell Palace, and Old London Bridge."

With our copy of this interesting drawing is introduced another equally curious relic of the same Frost Fair, from the collection of Henry Hyde, second Earl of Clarendon, and formerly in the collection of Mr. William Upcott. It consists of an impression of the specimen of printing on the ice, executed for King Charles II. and the Royal Family who visited the fair with him. The names upon the paper are Charles, King; James, Duke (of York, his brother, subsequently King James II.); Katherine, Queen (Catharine, Infanta of Portugal, Queen of Charles II.); Mary, Duchess (Mary d'Este, sister of Francis, Duke of Modena, the second duchess of James); Anne, princess (the second daughter of the Duke of York, afterwards Queen Anne); George, prince (the princess's husband, George of Denmark). The concluding name, "Hans in Kelder," was no doubt dictated by the humour of the king; it literally signifies "Jack in the Cellar," and alludes to the interesting situation of the Princess Anne. The card, which was printed with a type border, was worded as follows:—

CHARLES, KING.	MARY, DUTCHESS.
KATHERINE, QUEEN.	ANNE, PRINCESS.
JAMES, DUKE.	GEORGE, PRINCE.
HANS IN KELDER.	

London: Printed by G. Groom, on the Ice, on the River of Thames, January 31, 1684.

Charles II. seems to have been very partial to "Frost Fair." He is reported to have joined in a fox-hunt on the Thames; and a French traveller present in London at the time, states, in a small volume printed at Paris, that the king on one occasion passed a whole night upon the ice.

A contemporaneous notice of Frost Fair contained in a diary cited in *The Gentleman's Magazine* for 1814, states that on February 2nd, in 1684, an ox was roasted whole over against Whitehall, and that King Charles and the Queen ate a part of it. His Majesty appears to have taken much pleasure in viewing the lively scene from his palace, since in the poem also printed upon the ice, entitled "Thamesis's Advice to the Painter," there occur the following lines :—

> "Then draw the king, who on his leads doth stray
> To view the throng as on a Lord Mayor's day,
> And thus unto his nobles pleased to say :
> 'With these men on this ice I'd undertake
> To cause the Turk all Europe to forsake ;
> An army of these men, arm'd and complete,
> Would soon the Turk in Christendom defeat.' "

The print of Frost Fair, referred to in the diary of Evelyn, is entitled " An Exact and Lively Mapp or Representation of Boothes and all the varieties of Showes and Humours upon the Ice on the River of Thames by London, during that memorable Frost, in the 35th Yeare of the Reigne of His Sacred Majesty King Charles the Second, Anno Dm. MDCLXXXIII., with an Alphabetical Explanation of the most remarkable figures." It consists of a whole sheet copper-plate, the prospect being represented horizontally from the Temple Stairs and Bankside to London Bridge. In an oval cartouche at the top of the view, within the frame of the print, appears the title ; and on the outside, below, are the alphabetical references with the words, " Printed and sold by William Warter, Stationer, at the signe of the Talbott under the Mitre Tavern in Fleete Street, London." An impression of this plate will be found in the Royal Collection of Topographical Prints and Drawings given by George IV. to the British Museum, vol. xxvii., art. 39. There is also a variation of the same engraving in the City Library at Guildhall, divided with common ink into compartments as if intended to be used as cards, and numbered in the margin in type with Roman numerals, in three series of ten each and two extra. A descriptive list of the other prints, printed papers, and tracts relating to the Frost Fair of 1683-1684, will be found in Wilkinson's " Londina Illustrata," vol. i., whence much of the preceding notices has been derived ; another list is contained in the catalogue of the Sutherland collection of Prints and Drawings inserted as illustrations in Lord Clarendon's " Life " and " History of the Rebellion," and Burnet's " History of his Own Times."

Again the Duke of York (James II.) writes to his son-in-law—and destined supplanter—William

of Orange, under date January 4, 1683-4 :—" The weather is so very sharp and the frost so great that the river here is quite frozen over, so that for these three days past people have gone over it in several places, and many booths are built on it between Lambeth and Westminster, where they roast meat and sell drink." During the continuance of the frost at this time, which lasted until the 4th of February, about forty coaches plied on the Thames as on dry land, and the scene enacted on the glassy surface of the river in its course through London was known as " Frost " or "Blanket" fair.

In 1709 the Thames was again frozen over, but the frost was not sufficiently permanent to allow of a repetition of Frost Fair, although several persons crossed over on the ice.

In the winter of 1715–16 the frost was again so intensely severe that the river Thames was frozen over during almost the space of three months. Booths were erected on the congealed river for the sale of all kinds of commodities, and all the fun of the fair of 1684 was revived. On the 19th of January, 1716, two large oxen were roasted whole on the ice ; the vast quantities of snow which had fallen at different times in the season rendered the City almost impassable. The Prince of Wales was attracted to the fair, and a newspaper of the day intimates that the theatres were almost deserted.

The winter of the year 1739, generally known as " the hard winter," was a season of distress to the labouring part of the public. A most severe frost began on Christmas Day, and continued till the ensuing February. Its severity was beyond precedent, and the effect produced was long felt. Many persons who had lived in Hudson's Bay territory declared that they had never known it colder in that frozen region than it was in England during that winter. The Thames was soon covered with floating rocks and shoals of ice ; and when these were fixed, the river represented a snowy field rising in many places in hillocks and huge heaps of icebergs, and many artists seized the opportunity of making sketches of the strange scene thus presented " above bridge." The river Thames was so solidly frozen that great numbers of people dwelt upon it in tents, and a variety of booths was erected on it for the entertainment of the populace. A few days after it began there arose a very high wind, which did considerable damage to the shipping, that happened at that time to be very numerous. Several vessels laden with corn, others with coals, &c., were sunk by the ice ; many had holes beat in their sides by falling on their anchors : several lighters and boats were confined under the ice ; in short, a more dismal scene presented itself on the river Thames than had ever been beheld by the oldest man living. The damage done between the Medway and London Bridge was computed at £100,000, and besides many persons lost their lives from the severity of the weather. The watermen and fishermen were entirely disabled from earning their livelihood, as were the lower classes of labourers from their employment in the open air; and the calamity was rendered more severe by coals and other necessaries being advanced in their price in proportion to the intenseness and continuance of the frost. Happily for the poor, the hand of charity was liberally extended; great benefactions were given by persons of opulent fortunes, and considerable collections were made in most of the parishes in London; and from this benevolent assistance many wretched families were preserved that otherwise must have inevitably perished. During the nine weeks' continuance of the frost coaches plied upon the Thames, and festivities and diversions of all kinds were enjoyed upon the ice. Little or no novelty, however, appears to have been introduced into the amusements of this fair, and the same things were done as on the former occasion, even to the roasting of the regulation ox on the ice, a feat which appears to have been accomplished with some little ceremony, for we read that " Mr. Hodgeson, a butcher of St. James's Market, claimed the privilege of knocking down the beast as a right inherent in his family, his father having knocked down the ox roasted in the river in 1684, as he himself did that roasted in 1715 near Hungerford Stairs." The beast was fixed to a stake in the open market, and Mr. Hodgeson " came dressed in a rich laced cambric apron, a silver steel, and a hat and feathers, to perform the office." Printing-booths were again set up on the ice, and at one of these establishments, bearing the sign of the " Golden King's Head," was sold " An Account of the principal Frosts for above a Hundred Years," with a frontispiece of London Bridge at the time of the frost, which purported to have been printed on the ice. Another popular publication was " The Humble Petition of the River Thames to the Venerable Sages of Westminster Hall," in which we read that " ministers of punishment have treated him with the utmost contempt and insolence, have even made a publick shew of him, have call'd in heaps of ragamuffins to trample upon him, and, what is worst of all, have forced a numerous family, which he used to provide for, to beg in the streets." In this fair " Doll the Pippin Woman," recorded in Gay's " Trivia," lost her life :—

" Doll every day had walk'd these treacherous roads ;
Her neck grew warp'd beneath autumnal loads
Of various fruit : she now a basket bore ;
That head, alas ! shall basket bear no more.
    *   *   *   *
The crackling crystal yields, she smiles, she dies ;
Her head chopt off, from her lost shoulders flies ;
' Pippins,' she cries, but Death her voice confounds ;
And pip, pip, pip, along the ice resounds."

Towards the end of December, 1767, a violent frost began, which continued to increase, and was very severe till the 16th of January following. During its continuance, the sufferings of the poor in town and country were truly pitiable. Fuel and other necessaries of life were remarkably dear : the river Thames was frozen so hard, that the navigation was entirely stopped both above and below the bridge : many persons perished in boats and other craft that were jammed in by the ice ; and the wherries in the river were wholly unemployed. Many accidents happened in the cities of London and Westminster, and several people perished by the cold in the streets. The severity of the frost was equally felt in the country ; many persons were found dead in the snow, the roads were rendered quite impassable, and it was at the imminent hazard of their lives that the coachmen and mail-drivers performed their journeys. This was followed by a violent hurricane, by which damage was sustained, in the City and its neighbourhood, to the amount of £50,000.

Again there was a very severe frost in 1777–8, and the Thames was frozen over at Kingston. In the winter of 1788–9 the Thames was again frozen over, and a bear-hunt is stated to have taken place on the ice off Rotherhithe. During this frost the fair on the ice occupied a considerably larger space than on any previous occasion, extending as it did from Shadwell to Putney ; it included, among other amusements, a travelling menagerie of beasts which moved about from place to place.

At the beginning of January, 1811, a very severe frost set in. On the 8th, the Thames was so much frozen, that there was only a narrow channel in the centre free from ice. The banks of the river were so firmly set with ice and snow that people could walk upon it from Battersea Bridge to Hungerford Stairs.

In Hughson's "London" we read that "the year 1814 began with an immense fog which lasted about a week, during which a number of accidents occurred. On the 8th of January, however, the fog disappeared, in consequence of a change of wind ; and a frost then set in, almost as unexampled in its duration and severity as the fog had been for its density. The frost continued with little inter-mission till the 20th of March. On the 31st of January several persons walked across the Thames between London and Blackfriars Bridges; and on the 3rd of February a sheep was roasted on the ice on the same spot, and the whole space

Recollections" having spent this "bitter" winter in London, and having "walked from Blackfriars to London Bridge on the ice, dirty, and impure, and lumpy as it was." He describes it as "a dreary-looking scene." He adds, however, "The serpen-tine skaters, the promenading, the streets piled up

THE LONDON SCHOOL BOARD OFFICES, 1874. (*See page* 326.)

between the two bridges had become a complete fair. Thousands of persons were seen moving in all directions; about thirty booths were erected for the sale of porter, spirits, &c., as well as for skittles, dancing, and other diversions. Several printers had presses on the ice, and pulled off various impressions, for which they found a very rapid sale. So long a continuance of cold weather has seldom been experienced in our climate."

Cyrus Redding records in his "Fifty Years'

with snow and ice, and the well and ill-clad spec-tators, as they were then combined, were amusing novelties."

A cotemporary account states, with minute pre-cision, that on the morning of Sunday, the 30th of January, 1814, huge masses of ice quite blocked up the Thames between London and Blackfriars Bridges, and that no less than seventy persons walked across from Queenhithe to the opposite shore. On the same night the frost so welded the

THE EMBANKMENT, FROM CHARING CROSS BRIDGE, 1872.

vast mass together into one compact field as to render it almost immovable by the tide. On Tuesday the river presented a solid surface from Blackfriars Bridge to some distance below Three Crane Stairs, and "thousands perambulated the rugged plain, whereon a variety of amusements was provided. Among the more curious of these," continues the account, "was the ceremony of roasting a small sheep: for a view of this extraordinary spectacle sixpence was demanded and willingly paid. The delicate meat, when done, was sold at a shilling a slice, and termed 'Lapland mutton.' There were set up a great number of booths, ornamented with streamers, flags, and signs, and within them was a plentiful supply of favourite luxuries.

Near Blackfriars Bridge, however, a plumber named Davies, having ventured to cross with some lead in his hands, sank between two masses, and was seen no more. Two young women, too, nearly shared the same fate, but they were rescued from their perilous situation by the prompt efforts of some of the Thames watermen. From the solid obstruction the tide did not appear to ebb for some days more than half the usual mark. On Wednesday, the 2nd of February, the sports were repeated, and the Thames presented a complete 'frost fair' for a few days. The grand 'mall' or walk now extended, not as on former occasions across the river, but down the centre from Blackfriars to London Bridge; this was named the 'City Road,' and was lined on both sides by booths of all descriptions. Eight or ten printing-presses were erected, and numerous cards and broadsides were printed on the ice in commemoration of "the great frost.' Some of these frost-fair typographers showed considerable taste in their handiwork. At one of the presses was hoisted an orange-coloured standard, with the watch-word 'Orange Boven' in large letters, in allusion to the recent restoration of the Stadtholder to the Government of Holland, which had been for several years under the dominion of the French. From this press, too, were issued such papers as this:—

FROST FAIR.

'Amidst the arts which on the Thames appear,
To tell the wonders of this icy year,
Printing demands first place, which at one view
Erects a monument of That and You.'

Another paper runs thus :—

'You that walk here and do design to tell
Your children's children what this year befell,
Come buy this print, and it will then be seen
That such a year as this hath seldom been.'"

A handbill printed and sold on the ice contains the following notice :—"Whereas, you, J. Frost, have by force and violence taken possession of the River Thames, I hereby give you warning to quit immediately.—A. Thaw." Copies of the Lord's Prayer and several other pieces, both sacred and profane, were "worked off" at these icy printing-presses, and found many willing purchasers at high prices. On Thursday the number of booths and stalls, and also that of the visitors, was largely increased. Swings, book-stalls, skittles, dancing booths, merry-go-rounds, sliding barges, and all the other usual appendages of Greenwich and Bartlemy Fairs, now appeared in scores. The ice seemed to be a solid rock, and presented a truly picturesque appearance. Friday, the 4th, brought a fresh accession of booths and of pedlars to sell their wares, and the greatest rubbish that would have long remained unsold on the land was raked up from cellars and garrets and sold at double and treble its value. Books and toys labelled with the words "bought on the Thames" found purchasers on every side.

The Thames watermen, who it might have been supposed would have been ruined by the weather, reaped a considerable harvest; for every person was made to pay a toll of twopence or threepence before he was admitted into the precincts of "Frost Fair;" and some douceur was expected besides on quitting the scene. Indeed, some of them were said to have made as much in coppers as six pounds a day! On this afternoon, however, there occurred an incident which warned the most venturesome that the ice was not so solid, or at all events so safe, as it appeared; for three persons, a man and two lads, being on a piece of ice just above London Bridge, the latter suddenly became detached from the main body, and was carried by the tide through one of the arches. They laid themselves down at full length for safety, and happily were rescued by some Billingsgate fishermen. On the Wednesday, Thursday, and Friday "Frost Fair" was in full favour, and the grand walk between Blackfriars and London Bridges was crowded till after nightfall. Saturday, the 5th, augured but badly for the continuance of the "Frost Fair," for the wind veered round to the south, and there was a slight fall of snow and sleet. The visitors, however, were not to be deterred by trifles. Thousands again ventured on the surface, and still there was as much life and bustle as before on the frozen element; the footpath down the middle of the river was hard and secure, and amongst the crowd were some donkeys, which brought in to their owners considerable profit, as a donkey ride on the ice was charged a shilling.

These caused much merriment, as may very easily be supposed. Towards the evening the crowd thinned very much, for the rain began to fall and the ice to crack, threatening to float away and carry off booths, donkeys, printing-presses, and all the amusements of the last few days, to the no small dismay of stall-keepers, shop-keepers, typographers, and (unlicensed) publicans. The thaw, however, advanced rapidly, more rapidly indeed than heedlessness and indiscretion retreated. Two young men ventured on the ice above Blackfriars Bridge, notwithstanding the warnings of the watermen; the mass on which they stood was carried away, and they perished. On Sunday morning, February 6th, at an early hour the tide began to flow, and the thaw assisted the rising tide to break up the ice-field. On Monday, the thaw continuing, immense fragments of ice were in motion, floating up and down according to the set of the tide, carrying, of course, many of the barges and lighters from their moorings above bridge, and drifting them into positions where they speedily became wrecks and sunk. In two or three days more the frozen element again became fluid, and old Father Thames, under the bright rays of the sun, relaxed his "grim-visaged front," and very soon looked as cheerful and as busy as ever.

There can be little doubt, if reliance can be placed on the calculations of civil engineers, that the Thames would have been frozen over in 1838, in 1853, and again in 1894-5, if it had not been for the removal of old London Bridge, the narrow arches of which prevented the masses of ice from escaping seaward. The removal of this impediment has much increased what is called the "scour" of the river; and it is highly improbable that, however protracted, the frost will be able to coagulate the ice into one mass as it did, at all events, in the winters of 1564, 1608, 1634, 1683, 1715, 1739, 1789, and (as we have said above) in 1813-14.

The Thames "between bridges" in its normal and unfrozen state has been the scene of some curious experiments, wagers, &c. For instance, Mr. John Timbs, in his "Curiosities of London," states that in July, 1776, a man safely crossed the Thames in a butcher's tray from Somerset House for a wager; upon which feat depended £14,000. Again, towards the latter portion of his life, M. Lunardi, the first successful aëronaut in London, made several excursions on the Thames in a sort of tin life-buoy, which he named a water-balloon. This invention, however, has perhaps been improved on by Captain Paul Boyton, who, in the early part of the year of grace 1875, might have been seen making his way up and down the river between Westminster Bridge and Greenwich in a very novel manner. Dressed in an oil-skin or india-rubber suit of clothes, of sufficient capacity to allow of its being inflated, the captain could lie at full length on the surface of the water, or, placing himself partly in a sitting posture, propel himself comfortably along (canoe fashion) by means of a short paddle. Captain Boyton belonged to an American organisation, entitled the "Camden and Atlantic Life Guards," of which the mission was to save, not to slay; and he could boast that, armoured in the uniform of his invention, he had rescued seventy-one persons from the waves off the coast of New Jersey. The waterproof suit, which weighed about fifteen pounds, was in five separate parts—that is to say, head, breast, back, and two legs; and when all were inflated, it was capable of sustaining four men in addition to the wearer.

About the year 1841 an American diver, named Scott, created some sensation by leaping from the parapets of Southwark and Waterloo Bridges into the river beneath, which was nearly full of floating ice, but the poor fellow shortly afterwards killed himself by hanging from a scaffold upon the latter bridge. Now and then a theatrical clown navigates the river in a washing-tub drawn by geese; and occasionally there are wonderful stories of sharks, porpoises, and other strange things—all "very like a whale"—leaving their ocean sire and disporting themselves "above bridge."

Sometimes, by a freak of nature, the tide in the Thames falls very low; and by a very high wind from the south-west the river is occasionally *blown out*—or, in other words, the bed is left nearly dry from shore to shore—so that many an adventurous or frolicsome wight has been known to "walk across the Thames." As a rule, however, the tide in the Thames is generally regular in its ebb and flow, though a very strong wind from the north-west, if it comes at spring-tides, causes the river to rise higher on account of the volume of water which it forces up from the Northern Ocean. It is perhaps worthy of note that several times since the making of the Embankment, the tide in the Thames has risen many inches above Trinity mark, and inundated the south bank of the river along Lambeth, Bankside, and Rotherhithe, and even as far as Woolwich, causing a considerable loss of property.

Hunter in his "History of London" records the fact that in February, 1762, the tide overflowed the banks to such an extent that casks and other articles of merchandise were swept away from the wharves and quays, and the prison-yard of the Borough compter was some inches under water, and in the next month at spring-tide, the water rushed in a body into Westminster Hall. The same thing seems to have happened in the following September, when the water is said to have risen twelve feet perpendicular in five hours. The worst effects of this high tide, it appears, were felt below bridge ; the cattle being carried away—so Hunter says—in the marshes about Stratford and Bow. "From the nearest computation, 70,000 pigs were supposed to have been lost. Several persons lost their lives on the high road, and many machines (*i.e.* carriages and wagons) were overturned. The houses from Bow Bridge to Stratford were all overflowed, and the inhabitants obliged to get out of their windows." The same thing appears to have recurred in the February of the following year, and again in September, 1764. He also tells us the tide in the Thames ebbed and flowed, in 1661, three times within seven hours, its waters being thrown into the most violent agitation.

In order to maintain the flow and "scour" of the Thames, an Act of Common Council was passed in 1538 to enforce an early statute of Henry VIII. forbidding persons to throw solid matter or refuse into the river, but allowing them to scoop out and carry away the shelves of sand, gravel, &c., as ballast, or for any other purpose, and compelling the owners to keep the banks on either side in a fit and proper state of repair. From time to time, we may here remark, a variety of projects have been put forward having for their immediate object the improvement of the bed and course of the river both below and above London Bridge, and more than once it has been seriously proposed to dig an entirely new course, in a direct line from Lambeth to Rotherhithe ; but though these plans were canvassed and agitated from time to time, the vested interests which opposed them have succeeded in carrying the day, and for a brief period the subject has fallen through, only to be again and again brought forward and as often disposed of in a similar manner.

CHAPTER XL.

THE VICTORIA EMBANKMENT.

"I send, I send, here my supremest kiss
To thee, my silver-footed Tamasis ;
No more shall I re-iterate thy Strand,
Whereon so many goodly structures stand."—*R. Herrick.*

The Thames Banks in the Early Ages—Sir Christopher Wren's Plan for embanking the River—Evelyn's Suggestion with the same View—The Subject brought before Parliament by Sir F. W. Trench—Mr. James Walker's Plan—The Victoria Embankment commenced—The Work described—Land reclaimed from the Thames—The Metropolitan District Railway—Quantities of Materials used in constructing the Embankment—Offices of the London School Board—Somerset House and the New Will Depository—Special Curiosities in the Will Office—Cleopatra's Needle—The Savoy Theatre—The Buckingham Water-gate—Statue of Sir James Outram—The Avenue Theatre—Public Garden and Promenade—St. Stephen's Club.

MANY architects and geologists, from the days of Sir Christopher Wren, have been of opinion that the Thames was formerly not a river, but an estuary, the shores of which were the hills of Camberwell and Sydenham on the south, and of Highgate and Hampstead on the north, with a large sandy plain at low water, through which the river wound its tortuous way. Sir Christopher Wren especially considered that these sands being driven with the wind gradually formed sand-hills, which in the course of time, and by aid of Roman engineers, were embanked and so changed into meadows, or at all events into *terra firma*, the river being so reduced into its present channel, and wharves being built along the line of wall towards the river.

Considering that a large portion of what is commonly called London is lower in level than the high-water mark in the Thames, it is clear that the river must have been embanked from a very early period. Antiquaries have written to show that the river-walls of the Thames were the work of the native British before the advent of the Romans, who, no doubt, completed the work which was already begun ; but it is certain that they were not completed until a date subsequent to the Norman Conquest.

The plan proposed by Sir Christopher Wren for rebuilding of London after the Great Fire included "a commodious quay on the whole bank of the river from the Tower to Blackfriars ;" but unfortunately his idea was not adopted, and the opportunity was lost for ever. "The ingenious Mr. Evelyn," says Northouck, "suggested another plan with the same view, and besides lessening the most considerable declivities, he proposed further to employ the rubbish in filling up the shore of the Thames to low-water mark in a straight line from the Tower to the Temple, and form an ample quay, if it could be done without increasing the rapidity of the stream." But here again the old selfish objection of "vested interests" cropped up, and defeated the scheme, which it was reserved by Providence for Lord Palmerston, during his tenure of the Premiership, to carry through Parliament and enforce upon the citizens to their very great and manifest benefit.

During the reigns of George IV. and William IV., and in the early part of Victoria, the subject of an embankment for the river from London Bridge to Westminster was brought forward yearly in Parliament by the late Sir Frederick W. Trench, but still, as is too often the case, "nothing was done." Perhaps in the event London has been fortunate, for if the work of embanking the Thames had been taken in hand in the days of our fathers or our grandfathers, it is to be feared that it would not have been carried out upon the scale of magnificence which marks the work of Sir J. W. Bazalgette. It appears that in 1840 Mr. James Walker laid down for the Corporation a line of embankment, which has now in the main been followed.

This great work is in three divisions—namely, the "Victoria," extending from the northern end of Blackfriars Bridge to Westminster; the "Albert," from the Lambeth end of Westminster Bridge to Vauxhall; and a third section extending from Chelsea Bridge to the Cadogan Pier at Chelsea, close by Battersea Bridge.

The Victoria Embankment, of which alone we shall treat in this chapter, forms a wide and convenient line of communication between the City and the West End or more fashionable parts of London. It was commenced in February, 1864, and completed in July, 1870; and as a piece of engineering skill it is second to none of the great achievements that have marked the Victorian era. The river-side footway between Westminster Bridge and the Temple was opened to the public in 1868; but at that time the completion of the carriageway was prevented by the unfinished condition of the Metropolitan District Railway between Westminster and Blackfriars, and this obstacle was not removed until the end of May, 1870. On the 30th of May the first passenger train passed under the Embankment to the then terminal station at Blackfriars, and within six weeks from that date the carriage-way of the Embankment was formed and the northern footway paved; and the whole was thrown open to the public on the 13th of July in that year. The "opening" ceremony was performed by the Prince of Wales, accompanied by the Princess Louise, on behalf of Her Majesty, after whom this noble thoroughfare is named, and of whom a statue, by C. B. Birch, A.R.A., was placed at the Blackfriars end in 1896.

Following in an even line the general curve of the river, the Embankment rises at each end by a gentle gradient to open upon Bridge Street, Westminster, opposite the Clock Tower of the Houses of Parliament, and upon Bridge Street, Blackfriars, opposite the station of the Metropolitan District Railway. It passes beneath the Charing Cross Railway Bridge at Hungerford, and the first arch on the Middlesex side of Waterloo Bridge. It is about a mile and a quarter in length, and is 100 feet in width throughout. The carriage-way is 64 feet wide; the footway on the land side 16 feet, and that on the river side 20 feet, each planted with trees 20 feet apart. On the river side the footway is bounded by a moulded granite parapet, 3 feet 6 inches in height, and on the land side partly by walls and partly by cast-iron railings.

The wall of the Embankment is a work of extraordinary magnitude and solidity. It is carried down to a depth of $32\frac{1}{2}$ feet below Trinity high-water mark, and 14 feet below low water; and the level of the roadway is generally four feet above high water, rising at the extremities to twenty feet. The rising ground at each extremity is retained by the increased height of the wall, which is built throughout of brick, faced with granite, and founded in Portland cement concrete. The river front presents a slightly concave surface, which is plain from the base to mean high-water level, and is ornamented above that level by mouldings, stopped at intervals of about seventy feet by plain blocks of granite, bearing lamp standards of cast iron, and relieved on the river-face by bronze lions' heads, carrying mooring rings. The uniformity of line is broken at intervals by massive piers of granite (intended to be surmounted with groups of statuary), which flank recesses for steamboat landing-stages; and at other places by stairs projecting into the river, and designed as landing-places for small craft. The steamboat piers occur at Westminster, Charing Cross, and Waterloo Bridges, and those for small boats midway between Westminster and Charing Cross, and between Charing Cross and Waterloo Bridges, and both are united at the Temple Pier, opposite Essex Street.

Within the recesses for the steamboat landing-stages are placed admirably-contrived timber platforms, which rise and fall with the tide, and which carry the lower ends of gangways that are hinged to the masonry above. The gangways are formed of two wrought-iron girders, carrying a timber platform; and they move between granite walls parallel to the general line of the roadway. Upon the platforms there are waiting-rooms for passengers.

On the land side the Embankment is bounded from Westminster almost to Whitehall Place by four acres of recovered foreshore that were claimed by the Crown, but now belong to the City of West-

garden, and then a piece added to the grounds of the Temple, but upon which the Templars are not able to build. Lastly, we come to a splendid site where stand the City of London Schools, Sion College, the offices of the Thames Conservancy, and the Guildhall School of Music.

To the east of Blackfriars Bridge the Embankment roadway is prolonged to the Mansion House by Queen Victoria Street, forming one grand thoroughfare between the Houses of Parliament and the

WHITEHALL GARDENS FROM THE RIVER. (*See page* 328.)

minster. A broad and commodious approach to the Embankment occurs somewhat to the south-west of the Hungerford Railway Bridge, opening out of Whitehall Place. From there to Waterloo Bridge the Embankment is bounded by a similar foreshore, amounting to nearly eight acres, and becoming gradually narrowed from west to east. This portion is planted as an ornamental garden for the enjoyment of the public. To the east of Waterloo Bridge is what was once the river front of Somerset House, all marked and stained by water, and with huge mooring rings projecting from the masonry, but now quite inland. Next comes a space behind the Temple Railway Station, communicating with Surrey Street, Norfolk Street, and Arundel Street. Then another small portion of public ornamental

City. The eastern portion of this thoroughfare, between Cannon Street and the Mansion House, was completed and opened for public traffic in October, 1869.

The total area of the land reclaimed from the river amounts to $37\frac{1}{4}$ acres. Of this, nineteen acres are occupied by the carriage and foot ways, eight acres are devoted to garden, and the rest has been conveyed to the Crown, the Templars, and other proprietors along the line. Within the Embankment wall, and forming a portion of its structure, is placed the Low Level Intercepting Sewer, which is an integral portion of the main drainage scheme. Above it is a subway for gas and water pipes, the dimensions of the subway being 7 feet 6 inches in height and 9 feet in width;

and the diameter of the sewer varying from 7 feet 9 inches to 8 feet 3 inches. These are both situate under the footway next the river. The footways are paved with York stone, with granite curbs.

To the east of the Temple the roadways are carried over a double covered way, originally belonging to the City Gas Company, and leading to a landing-wharf, by which coals might be conveyed from the river without interference with the traffic. At this point, moreover, the subterranean engineer-

land reclaimed by the Embankment at the point between Cannon Row and Westminster Bridge, and passes under the public road as far as 'Charing Cross steamboat pier, where it diverges to the land side of the roadway to the Charing Cross Station, the roof of which rises above the surface and is enclosed by screen walls of brickwork. Immediately east of the station are three openings for ventilation of the railway, which, together with the screen walls, are partially concealed by the mounds and

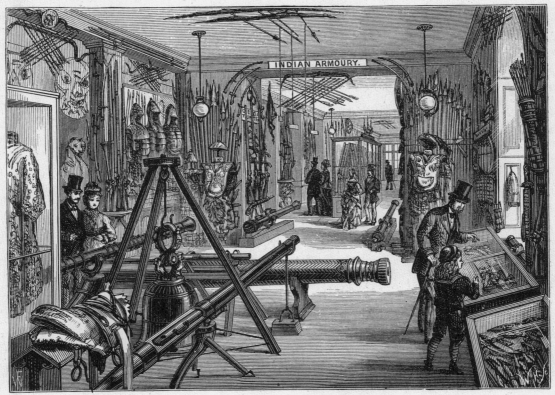

ROYAL UNITED SERVICE MUSEUM, 1876.   (*See pages* 334, 335.)

ing was of extreme complexity, for the sewers, the Fleet ditch, the subways, the Gas Company's railroad, the public railway, and a variety of gas, water, and telegraph pipes had to be interlaced in a way that almost defies description.

In connection with the steamboat pier at Westminster Bridge a subway has been constructed, communicating with the subway already existing under Bridge Street, and affording an underground thoroughfare for foot passengers between the Houses of Parliament, the railway station, the steamboat pier, and the footways in Bridge Street and on the river and land sides of the Embankment.

The Metropolitan District Railway enters the

shrubberies of the ornamental grounds. East of the openings, the railway is carried in a covered way under the ornamental grounds as far as the Waterloo steamboat pier, where it again passes under the roadway to the Temple Station, and is thence continued on the land side of the roadway to within a few feet of Blackfriars Bridge. From the east end of the Temple Gardens the concrete wall which retains the earth for the rising approach road to Blackfriars forms also the side wall of the railway. The level of the rails is generally $17\frac{1}{2}$ feet below the surface of the road, which is carried over the railway by cast-iron girders and brick arches, the upper surface of the arches being 18 inches below the surface of the road.

Mr. Peter Cunningham, writing in 1850, remarks, "I cannot conclude this too brief account of our noble river without expressing a wish that the side sewer and terrace Embankment scheme (so long ago talked about and first projected by John Martin, the painter) may be carried out before many years are over. By narrowing the current," he adds, "we shall recover a large quantity of waste ground on either side, and escape from the huge unhealthy mud-banks that disfigure the river about Scotland Yard." What would he have said had he lived to see the completion of the gigantic undertaking which forms the subject of the present chapter?

It is not easy for persons unaccustomed to deal with such matters to form any clear conception of great quantities expressed in numerical statements; but it is, nevertheless, worth while to place on record the official accounts of the cost of the work, and of the amount of various kinds of material employed in its construction. The total cost is estimated at £1,260,000, and the purchase of property at £450,000. The quantities of materials are stated to have been as follows :—Granite, 650,000 cubic feet; brickwork, 80,000 cubic yards; concrete, 140,000 cubic yards; timber (for coffer-dam, &c.), 500,000 cubic feet; caissons (for ditto), 2,500 tons; earth filling, 1,000,000 cubic yards; excavation, 144,000 cubic yards; York paving, 125,000 superficial feet; broken granite, 50,000 superficial yards.

It is but right that, in describing a work of such grandeur and national importance as the Thames Embankment, we should mention the names, not only of the principal engineer—Sir Joseph W. Bazalgette—to whom, of course, it will be a monument of enduring fame, but also of those of the contractors and resident engineers; the former were Messrs. Furness, Ritson, and Webster, and the latter Messrs. Lovick and Cooper.

The Act of Parliament under which the Metropolitan Board of Works obtained powers for the formation of new streets in connection with the Thames Embankment contains in its preamble a curious reference to the Act of William and Mary "for the relief of the orphans and other creditors of the City of London." That piece of legislation provided for the raising of a fund by the imposition of a duty on coal and on wine; and subsequent enactments continued the levy, appropriating its benefit to other requirements of metropolitan improvement. The charges on the fund set apart for making new approaches to London Bridge having been satisfied, the residue was by this Act transferred to the purposes of the Thames Embank-

ment. In 1889, however, a Bill was passed cancelling the duties. The Embankment answers a treble purpose : it serves as an effective relief to our overcrowded streets by the formation of a wide thoroughfare; it improves the navigation of the river; and it has also given an opportunity for making the low-level sewer without disturbing the Strand or Fleet Street. The importance of the improvement of the river is obvious to all, for not only has the Embankment added a handsome frontage to the side of the Thames which previously had been a public eyesore, but it has also been the means of getting rid of the unequal deposits of mud in its bed, assisting the removal of the scour of the river, and consequently improving the health of the inhabitants of London.

In those days it was difficult for the Metropolitan Board to raise capital at a less rate of interest than 4½ per cent. The importance of the work, however, had been impressed upon the ruling powers of the Government, and Parliament passed a bill by which the Board was greatly assisted in the undertaking.

Although that portion of the Embankment lying between Westminster and Waterloo Bridges is perhaps the most picturesque and varied of the whole line, that between Waterloo and Blackfriars is by no means wanting in interest and architectural effect. For the first time we have a land view of Sir W. Chambers' beautiful building, Somerset House; whilst the neighbouring Temple Gardens, "blooming in the midst of a nest of lawyers," have gained some 200 feet in depth, and thus become, on the whole, a really handsome pleasure-ground.

With this general view of the Victoria Embankment, we will at once proceed to point out some of the principal buildings that overlook it. As we pass from east to west we see, after De Keyser's Royal Hotel, the City of London School,[*] completed in 1882, and forming an admirable specimen of the Italian Renaissance, with an ornate front displaying polished columns of Aberdeen granite, and statues of Shakespeare, Milton, Newton, Bacon, and Sir Thomas More. A little way back from the Embankment is the Guildhall School of Music, opened in 1886, and behind this is the City of London School for Girls, dating from 1893. The next building on the Embankment is Sion College, a Perpendicular building with a parvised porch, flanked by the offices of the Thames Conservancy, in the same style. Of Sion College, formerly in London Wall, we have spoken before,[†] and all that need be added here

---

[*] See also Vol. I., p. 375.   [†] See also Vol. II., pp. 168-70.

is that the present building was completed in 1886. Then come the Temple Gardens, and beyond these is one of the three Embankment Gardens, backed by the offices of the London School Board, a Renaissance building of Portland stone, with bands of red brick, which had to wait until 1895 for its completion. The original architects were Messrs. Bodley and Garner; the more recent works were carried out under the supervision of Colonel Edis. In the prettily laid out Garden in front of the building is most appropriately placed a statue of the late William Edward Forster, the founder of the School Board system. Here also is Woolner's sitting figure of John Stuart Mill; and at the eastern gate are replicas of the Herculaneum "Wrestlers," while at the western end is a statue of Isambard Kingdom Brunel.

Between the Temple and Somerset House the north side of the roadway is occupied in part by the Temple Station of the Metropolitan District Railway, by the back of which is a roadway skirting the lower ends of Howard and Norfolk Streets, thus opening up communication between the Embankment and the Strand.

We now pass the Thames front of Somerset House. Of this building we have spoken generally in a previous chapter. We may, however, add here that some of the rooms under the noble balustraded terrace, which for about 600 feet overlook the Embankment, are now set apart as the national depository of wills. These documents, amounting to some tons in weight, were removed hither from Doctors' Commons at the end of the year 1874. Nearly the whole of the southern front of Somerset House, having been vacated by the Admiralty, was fitted up for their accommodation, and a range of spacious apartments some two hundred feet in length, occupying the interior of the great terrace, and also a considerable portion of the basement of Somerset House itself, has been fitted up with miles of shelving, whereon are stowed away long rows of folio volumes of formidable dimensions. The fact that in the new office at Somerset House there is a depository for the executed wills of living persons (as, indeed, there was in Doctors' Commons) must be set down in the category of "things not generally known." Known, however, or not, it is true; for any man or woman in the kingdom not incapacitated from making a will may forthwith sign, seal, and deliver here, on payment of a fee of 12s. 6d., his or her last will and testament, to be kept safely and securely until his or her death makes it operative. While in the custody of the office it is kept in a fire-proof room, and can never again be seen by the testator or testatrix. Here

the motto is plain and simple, "*Vestigia nulla retrorsum.*" It is, however, competent to the testator to annul it wholly or to vary it in part by making a fresh will or a codicil; and such fresh will or codicil he may either deposit at Somerset House or keep in his own custody. *Apropos* of this subject, what reader will not remember the Mr. Spenlow in "David Copperfield" moralising on the uncertainty of life and the duty of making a will, and then next day dying intestate?

As to the antiquity of the documents that have been brought from Doctors' Commons to Somerset House, they may be briefly summed up by saying that the original wills commence with the year 1483, the first of Edward V. The copies date from just a century earlier, viz., in the reign of Richard II. The latter are written on parchment, strongly bound, with brazen clasps. A very small volume suffices to contain the wills of a year or even of ten years before the Reformation. As we come down to more recent times the bulk of the volumes containing the wills steadily increases with the wealth and population of London and of the kingdom. Indeed, from about 1860 down to the present time the average number of volumes filled with the wills proved in the Prerogative Court of London amounts to nearly twenty a year. These wills themselves annually average, perhaps, 10,000 in the London district alone; while those of the rest of the kingdom may possibly be reckoned at 17,000 more.

It may be added that among the special curiosities of this storehouse of ancient documents are some wills which the nation, and, indeed, the world, would not willingly let perish. With a single exception, these have been transferred from Doctors' Commons to Somerset House. Here the visitor, if properly introduced, may see the wills of the painter Vandyck, of Dr. Johnson, of Lord Nelson, of William Pitt, of Edmund Burke, of Sir Isaac Newton, of Inigo Jones, of Izaak Walton, of the Duke of Wellington, of John Milton, and, above all, that of William Shakespeare. This, being of exceptional interest, has been exceptionally treated, and the three folio pages of which it consists are placed under an air-tight frame made of polished oak and plate glass. The will of the great Napoleon was to be seen for many years at old Doctors' Commons, but it was restored to the French nation in 1853, in compliance with the request of the Emperor Louis Napoleon.

It may, perhaps, be added here that in 1824 there was published a short-lived periodical, somewhat of the nature of the old *Tatlers* and *Spectators*, and partly a precursor of the *Pall Mall Gazette* and other light and chatty newspapers of our own day, called the *Somerset House Gazette*, edited by " Ephraim Hardcastle, Esq.,"—of course an assumed name.

Passing on under the northern arch of Waterloo Bridge, we enter upon the pleasantest portion of the Embankment. Here a considerable portion of land has been reclaimed from the Thames, the whole of which, except the roadway, is laid out as a garden. So high has the ground here been raised that it has fairly eclipsed Inigo Jones's watergate, at the foot of Buckingham Street. A walk 16 feet in width is carried the entire length of the ground, both on the east and west sides, and from these several other walks are carried across the area at right angles, while others are circular in form. There are three circular mounds and two of oblong form, portions of which are planted with flowers and shrubs, and the remaining parts turfed over.

About midway between Waterloo and Charing Cross Bridges rises the tall obelisk known as Cleopatra's Needle. This object of Egyptian antiquity, which is set up on the outer margin of the Embankment, immediately overlooking the river, was brought from Alexandria to this country in 1878–9, mainly through the exertions of a private gentleman, the late Sir Erasmus Wilson, F.R.S. The obelisk, 60 feet in height, stands upon a massive granite pedestal, flanked on either side by a colossal bronze sphinx. On each side of the pedestal is affixed a bronze tablet; that which faces the river bears the following inscription :—

" Through the patriotic zeal of Erasmus Wilson, F.R.S., this obelisk was brought from Alexandria in an iron cylinder; it was abandoned in the Bay of Biscay, recovered, and erected on this spot by John Dixon, C.E., in the 42nd year of the reign of Queen Victoria."

In another it is recorded that—

" This obelisk, quarried at Syeni, was erected at Heliopolis by the Pharaoh Thothmes III., about 500 B.C.,"

with other details of the ancient history of the relic.

At the lower end of Beaufort Buildings, not far from the Thames Embankment, stands the Savoy Theatre. This structure, which was built in 1881, was intended to be specially devoted to the representation of comic or satirical opera, and was opened in October of the above year with the play of " Patience," transferred from the Opera Comique. The main frontage of the theatre looks towards the river, and is constructed of red brick and Portland stone, in the Italian style of architecture. The theatre possesses several features of a novel and distinctive character; it is isolated from other buildings, and every part of the house possesses two means of egress, there being entrances and exits on all four sides. From the Strand, or northern boundary of the theatre, there is a considerable descent in the roadway along Beaufort Buildings, and with the view of providing both stage and auditorium space, excavations have been made within the building over the entire area of the interior to the depth at the north end of almost the height of the external walls themselves from the street level, with proportionate excavation at the south end. This permits of a spacious stage and stage-dock beneath it at the north end, together with a large and convenient auditorium area, including pit, stalls, lower and upper circle, and gallery. The theatre, which was planned to seat nearly 1,300 persons, was built from the designs of Mr. Phipps. Between it and the Embankment stands the Savoy Hotel, and beside it, on the west, is the huge Hôtel Cecil, the largest establishment of the kind in the country. On the east is the Examination Hall of the Royal Colleges of Physicians and Surgeons, a featureless building of red brick faced with Portland stone.

Following the course of the Embankment, under the fan-shaped connection of Charing Cross Bridge with the railway station, we now emerge upon what may be considered historic ground. Extending almost in a direct line with that portion of the Embankment which we have so far traversed, the broad roadway is continued through into Whitehall Place. Between this roadway and the railway station is Scotland Yard, for many years the head-quarters of the Metropolitan Police, about which we shall have more to say in the following chapter; and to the right of this, till its demolition to form a new opening from Charing Cross to the Embankment, stood Northumberland House. Close by the railway station is the Avenue Theatre, erected in 1881; opposite the theatre, and in Northumberland Avenue, is the apex of the triangle formed by the Hotel Métropole; then as we proceed towards Westminster we see the gigantic National Liberal Club, with its magnificent frontage to the Embankment. In the garden beneath the Club is a statue of Sir Bartle Frere, flanked by one of Wm. Tyndall, and by another of General Sir James Outram, while in the garden mentioned above, are statues of Burns and Robert Raikes, and a fountain commemorating Henry Fawcett.

Just above the railway bridge, if we had gone up the river in a steamer thirty years ago, or as now, wending our way along Sir J. W. Bazalgette's Embankment, we should have come upon a green oasis amid the surrounding streets—we refer to Whitehall Gardens. " It is," writes Dr. C. Mackay in 1840, in his "Thames and its Tributaries," "a fair lawn, neatly trimmed, and divided into compartments by little walls. . . . Just behind the house with the bow-windows, inhabited by Sir Robert Peel, is the spot where Charles the First was beheaded. In a nook close by, as if purposely hidden from the view of the world, is a very good statue of a very bad king. Unknown to the thousands of London, James the Second rears his brazen head in a corner, ashamed apparently . . . . to affront the eyes of the nation which he misgoverned."

Beyond the gardens of Montagu House, the town residence of the Duke of Buccleuch, is New Scotland Yard, designed by Mr. Norman Shaw, R.A., and completed in 1891, when it became the headquarters of the Metropolitan Police. At the junction of the Victoria Embankment with Bridge Street, close by the foot of Westminster Bridge, and facing the Clock Tower of the Houses of Parliament, stands the St. Stephen's Club. It immediately adjoins Westminster Bridge Railway Station, to which, as well as to the Houses of Parliament, it has an access under the roadway, quite protected from wind and rain. The building, which is constructed of Bath stone, with grey polished granite columns, occupies a somewhat irregularly-shaped block of land ; and it was erected in 1874, from the designs of Mr. J. Whichcord, F.S.A. The club-house, which rises from the lower basement to the full height of 100 feet, is in the Classical or Palladian style. The rooms are lofty and light. The house is well warmed throughout by an apparatus, the coils of which are cleverly concealed, and from top to bottom it is fitted up with electric bells of the newest pattern. At the top of the house is the culinary department —an arrangement by which the smell of the cook-

ing escapes without entering the club. The attic floor contains, besides accommodation for servants, a large kitchen, superintended by a French *chef de cuisine.* On the floor next the attics are two billiard-rooms, two dining-rooms, with a similar arrangement, and an occasional room for breakfasts, &c. On the next—in other words, on the first floor— are a smoking-room, a card-room, and a dining-room for members only. On the ground floor the entrance from the Embankment opens into a lofty hall paved partially with encaustic tiles and partially with inlaid polished oak, the ceiling supported by red scagliola columns, and lighted with stained-glass windows. On the left of the entrance-hall there is a small reception-room for strangers, leading into the morning-room, a lofty apartment, lighted by five large windows looking on the river and the Houses of Parliament, the ground ceiling resting on verd antique columns. To the upper floor access is gained by a spiral staircase in the Jacobean style, in plan not unlike the great staircase in the rear of Devonshire House. The windows of this staircase look out on the roof of the railway station below, and, therefore, have been filled with painted glass, in diaper work. The staircase is so arranged as to be continued down into the basement, where it leads to the secretary's office, bath-rooms, lavatories, &c. And as we read of another place that shall be nameless that "in the lowest depths there is a lower still," so in what we may call the basement of the basement there are wine and beer cellars, and strong rooms for other stores, and a place for working the hydraulic lift, by which all the provisions are raised to the top of the house without passing up the staircase.

Let us now turn our steps landward, and investigate the neighbourhood more in detail.

CHAPTER XLI.

SCOTLAND YARD AND THE METROPOLITAN POLICE.

" Stands Scotland where it did ?"—Shakespeare.

Situation and Extent—Originally the Residence of the Scottish Kings and Ambassadors when in England—Margaret Queen of Scots entertained here—Decay of the Palace—John Milton and "Beau" Fielding Residents here—Inigo Jones, Sir John Denham, and Sir Christopher Wren—Sir John Vanbrugh and his "Goose Pie"—Sir Joshua Reynolds' Encomiums on Vanbrugh's Merits—Rowe's Poetical Allusion to him—Josiah Wedgwood's Residence—The "Well's" Coffee House—Attack on Lord Herbert of Cherbury—The Palace Court or Marshalsea—The Metropolitan Police Force—Cabs and Hackney Coaches—Sedan Chairs—Care of "Tipplers"—Harrington House—"Man's" Coffee House—Whitehall Place—Middle Scotland Yard—Royal United Service Institution—Government Offices—Fife House—A "canny" Scotch Earl—Whitehall Stairs.

HAVING finished our "tour of the Thames" by way of the new Embankment, we must ask our readers to throw themselves in imagination back a century or so, and to step with ourselves mentally out of a Thames wherry alongside of the old Palace stairs

at Whitehall, at the end abutting on Scotland Yard, which lies immediately on our right as we land. To this spot, most interesting on account of its old associations, it is our intention to devote the present chapter.

It was in 1829 that Scotland Yard became the headquarters of the Metropolitan Police, though, as we have seen (p. 329), it has now ceased to be so, more commodious premises having been erected on the Victoria Embankment, close to Westminster Bridge. It is bounded on the east by what was once the garden of Northumberland House, and is now divided into Great and Middle Scotland Yard, the latter division lying close to Whitehall Yard. Both yards together constitute a poor and mean space, which certainly is no credit to the city of which it forms so important a part. How few of our readers are aware that those mean buildings cover the site of what was once a magnificent palace, built by our Saxon sovereigns for the reception of the kings of Scotland, as often as they visited this country.

Old writers describe the locality as lying a little to the south of Charing Cross, on the eastern side of the highway leading thence to Whitehall, where there stood a "palace with large pleasure-grounds extending to the river;" and where, according to Stow, "great buildings have been, for the receipt of the kings of Scotland, and other estates of that country." The old chronicler speaks of the site as "a large plot of ground enclosed with brick [walls], and called 'Scotland.'" "This property," says Mr. Newton, in his "London in the Olden Time," "was given by the Saxon King Edgar to Kenneth III., King of Scotland, for his residence, upon his annual visit to London to do homage for his kingdom to the Crown of England. It continued afterwards to be the residence of the Scottish kings when they attended the English Parliament as barons of the realm. The last of the Scottish royal family who resided here," he adds, "was Margaret, Queen of Scots, and sister to King Henry VIII., who had her abiding there when she came to England after the death of her husband," James IV., who fell at the battle of Flodden Field. She was here entertained with great splendour by her brother, as soon as he was reconciled to her second marriage with the Earl of Arran; afterwards she lived here as became a widow, in privacy, keeping up little or no semblance of state. A note in Brayley's "Londoniana" states: "The Scottish kings appear to have been anciently regarded as members of the English Parliament; and there are instances among the Tower Records of the issuing of writs to summon their attendance at Westminster. Thus in Pinkerton's 'Iconographia Scotica' is an engraving of Edward I. sitting in Parliament, with Alexander King of Scots on his right, and Llewellyn Prince of Wales on his left; and this is said to have been taken from a copy of an ancient limning formerly in the English College of Arms." It may be added that it was for their fiefs in Cumberland and Westmoreland, and not for their dominions to the north of the Tweed, that the Scottish sovereigns did homage. Besides the Scottish kings, their ambassadors also were lodged here from time to time.

The situation and extent of the mansion and grounds which occupied this site are well known to the antiquary and topographer. Concerning the details of the palace, however, we are much in the dark. There is no print of it in existence, so far as we have been able to discover; and almost all that is known about it prior to the Reformation is that it was allowed to fall into decay by Henry VIII.— most probably on account of the part which James had taken in siding with the French in the wars between the two countries.

In the reign of Elizabeth the palace had become a ruin; and upon the union of the Scottish and English crowns the *raison d'être* of the palace had ceased to exist. It was therefore dismantled, and partly demolished, its site being devoted to some of the offices of the Government, for which its proximity to Whitehall fitted it admirably.

Here John Milton lived whilst serving the Government of the Commonwealth, and acting as Latin Secretary to Oliver Cromwell, and here he lost an infant son. Here died, in the early part of the last century, that mixture of Hercules and Adonis, the eccentric "Beau Fielding," divorced from the notorious Duchess of Cleveland on the ground of bigamy, as being already the husband of the Dowager Countess of Purbeck. A full account of the career of Beau Fielding will be found in Nos. 50 and 51 of the *Tatler*, drawn by the pen of Sir Richard Steele.

Part of the remains of the Palace was, for many years, the official residence of the Surveyor of Works to the Crown. "Here," writes Mr. Peter Cunningham, "lived Inigo Jones; here died his successor, Sir John Denham, the poet of Cooper's Hill, and his successor again, Sir Christopher Wren; and here, in a fantastic house, immortalised by Swift in some ludicrous lines, lived Sir John Vanbrugh. The house of the latter was designed and built by himself, from the ruins of Whitehall, destroyed by fire in 1697."

Mr. Cunningham, in his "Life of Inigo Jones," tells us an anecdote of the great architect connected with this place, illustrative of the insecurity of the times: "Near his house in Scotland Yard, Inigo Jones, uniting with Nicholas Stone, the sculptor, buried his money in a private place. The Parliament published an order encouraging servants to

SCOTLAND YARD, ABOUT 1720.

inform of such concealments, and as four of the workmen were privy to the deposit, Jones and his friends removed it privately, and with their own hands buried it in Lambeth Marsh."

Sir John Vanbrugh, who died in 1726, was celebrated in his day not merely as an architect, but also as a comic poet and an accomplished man of letters. He was Comptroller of the Royal Works and Palaces, and his house between Scotland Yard and Whitehall, which he built for himself, was remarkable for its tiny dimensions. His friends called it a "pill-box," and Swift compared it to a goose-pie. The small size of his own house certainly was a fair object of ridicule when contrasted with the ponderous dimensions of the palace at Blenheim, and other designs by him. The epitaph on his tomb is witty and well known—

> "Lie heavy on him, earth, for he
> Laid many a heavy load on thee."

When he was made Clarencieux King-at-Arms Swift said he might now "build houses." The secret of this ridicule was that Vanbrugh was a Whig. Sir Joshua Reynolds has left the following high encomium on his merits as an architect :—"In the buildings of Vanbrugh, who was a poet as well as an architect, there is a greater display of imagination than we shall find, perhaps, in any other; and this is the ground of the effect we feel in many of his works, notwithstanding the faults with which many of them are charged. For this purpose Vanbrugh appears to have had recourse to some principles of the Gothic architecture, which, though not so ancient as the Grecian, *is more so to our imagination*, with which the artist is more concerned than with absolute truth. "To speak of Vanbrugh," adds Sir Joshua, "in the language of a painter, he had originality of invention, he understood light and shadow, and had great skill in composition. To support his principal object he produced his second and third groups in masses. He perfectly understood, in his art, what is the most difficult in ours, the conduct of the background, by which the design and invention are set off to the greatest advantage. What the background is in painting, in architecture is the real ground on which the building is erected; and no architect took greater care that his work should not appear crude and hard—that is, that it did not abruptly start out of the ground without expectation or preparation.

"This is a tribute which a painter owes to an architect who composed like a painter, and was defrauded of the due reward of his merit by the wits of his time, *who did not understand the principles of composition in poetry better than he, and who knew little or nothing of what he understood perfectly—*

the general ruling principles of architecture and painting. Vanbrugh's fate was that of the great Perrault. Both were the objects of the petulant sarcasms of factious men of letters, and both have left some of the fairest monuments which to this day decorate their several countries—the façade of the Louvre, Blenheim, and Castle Howard."

It need scarcely be remarked here, in explanation of the allusion of Sir Joshua Reynolds, that Vanbrugh was almost as celebrated for his comedies as for his architecture. Rowe thus mentions him :—

> "I'm in with Captain Vanbrugh at the present,
> A most sweet-mannered gentleman and pleasant;
> He writes your comedies, draws schemes and models,
> And builds dukes' houses upon very odd hills.
> For him, so much I dote on him, that I,
> If I was sure to go to heaven, would die."

There was, in 1767-8, at the corner of Scotland Yard, opposite the Admiralty, a large house for which Josiah Wedgwood was in treaty, in order to establish a show-room or gallery of his pottery and porcelain at the West End; but, from some reason or other, the negotiation dropped through.

Here, too, was a celebrated coffee-house named " Well's," as appears from the following advertisement in Salisbury's *Flying Post*, preserved in the first volume of Malcolm's " Manners and Customs of London :"—" Whereas, six gentlemen (all of the same honourable profession), having been more than ordinarily put to it for a little pocket-money, did, on the 14th instant, in the evening, near Kentish Town, borrow of two persons (in a coach) a certain sum of money, without staying to give bond for the repayment; and whereas, fancy was taken to the hat, peruke, cravat, sword, and cane of one of the creditors, which were all lent as freely as the money : these are therefore to desire the said six worthies, how fond soever they may be of the other loans, to un-fancy the cane again, and send it to ' Well's ' Coffee-house, in Scotland Yard, it being too short for any such proper gentlemen as they are to walk with, and too small for any of their important uses, and, withal, only valuable as having been the gift of a friend."

It was in Scotland Yard that a knight, Sir John Ayres, with the aid of four retainers, in a fit of ungrounded jealousy, waylaid Lord Herbert of Cherbury, whom he attacked with swords and daggers, though he did not succeed in wounding him, as we learn from that noble lord's " Life.

Early in the present century the Palace Court or Marshalsea was held in Scotland Yard. The court had jurisdiction of all civil suits within twelve miles of the palace. The process was short and not expensive, judgment being obtained in three weeks.

In 1829, on the formation of the new police, introduced by Sir Robert Peel to supersede the ancient " Charlies," Scotland Yard was made, as we have said, the principal station of the Metropolitan Force. The area under their jurisdiction (which excludes the City of London proper) extends from Cheshunt in the north to Chipstead in the south, and from Chadwell Heath in the east to Staines in the west. The Metropolitan Police district contains the whole of the county of Middlesex, and those parishes in the counties of Surrey, Hertford, Essex, and Kent of which any part is not more than fifteen miles in a straight line from Charing Cross, except the City of London and the Liberties. The force is also employed in Her Majesty's dockyards and military stations situated beyond the Metropolitan Police district, as well as on the Thames.

In 1896 the Metropolitan Police Force consisted of 15,271 men, made up of the Chief Commissioner, three Assistant-Commissioners, four Chief Constables, 32 superintendents, 592 inspectors, 1,870 sergeants, and 12,777 constables. The cost of maintaining this enormous force is about £1,720,000 a year, of which nearly £1,270,000 is absorbed by salaries and wages. The Police district consists of twenty-two divisions, each of them under the oversight of a superintendent, and each of them comprising sub-divisions in charge of inspectors. There are about 260 mounted officers, who patrol the outer sub-divisions and are also available for special duty at large gatherings, processions, &c. One of the most important of the agencies at New Scotland Yard is that known as the Criminal Investigation Department, which was organised in 1878 under a Director, and is now presided over by Dr. Anderson.

The office for cab licences and regulations, before its removal to Scotland Yard—it is now, of course, at New Scotland Yard—had been for many years located in Essex Street, in the Strand. We learn from a letter addressed to the Earl of Strafford in 1634, that " The Maypole " in the Strand was the place where the first stand of hackney carriages was established in London ; the enterprising gentleman who introduced them to the public was a Captain Bailey—the same, it is supposed, who had served under Raleigh in one of his expeditions to Guiana. The following is an extract from the letter :— " He hath erected, acc^g to his ability, some four hackney coaches, put his men in livery, and appointed them to stand at ' The Maypole,' in the Strand, giving them instructions at what rates to carry men into several parts of the town, where all day they may be had. Other hackney men seeing this way, they flocked to the same place, and perform their journeys at the same rate, so that sometimes there is twenty of them together, which disperse up and down, so that they and others are to be had everywhere, as watermen are to be had at the waterside. Everybody is much pleased with it, for whereas before coaches could not be had but at great rates, now a man may have one much cheaper." A strange contrast these four hackney coaches of 1634 make to the thousands of hansoms and four-wheeled cabs which now ply for hire in the great metropolis !

The use of hackney coaches was but very trifling in 1626 ; for among the many monopolies granted by the king was one which gave rise to the use of sedan chairs in London. This grant was made to Sir Sanders Duncombe, who had probably seen them at Sedan, in France, where they were first made; it is expressed in the following terms :— " Whereas the streets of our cities of London and Westminster, and their suburbs, are of late so much encumbered with the unnecessary multitude of coaches that many of our subjects are thereby exposed to great danger, and the necessary use of carts and carriages for provisions thereby much hindered ; and Sir Sanders Duncombe's petition, representing that in many parts beyond sea people are much carried in chairs that are covered, whereby few coaches are used among them ; wherefore we have granted to him the sole privilege to use, let, or hire a number of the said covered chairs for fourteen years."

This patent was soon followed by a proclamation against hackney coaches, strictly commanding, " That no hackney coach should be used in the City of London, or suburbs thereof, other than by carrying of people to and from their habitations in the country ; and that no person should make use of a coach in the City except such persons as could keep four able horses fit for his Majesty's service, which were to be ready when called for under a severe penalty."

That sedan chairs were in use in the East long before they were known in France or in London is clear from the fact that one is introduced in Sir G. Staunton's Embassy to China. And if a classical origin be sought for them, it is on record that Pliny states that his own uncle was accustomed to be carried abroad in a chair.

At the end of the seventeenth, and throughout the greater part of the eighteenth century, the sedan chair was the vehicle almost always employed by " the quality " at the West End in going backwards and forwards between each other's houses, and to Court. Even at the coronation of

William III. the peers and peeresses who desire to be present are desired, in the official programme, to come in chairs, carriages and coaches not being allowed on that day to approach the Abbey. At the coronation of George I. and George II. both were allowed.

Hackney coaches, superseding as they did the old "sedans," were, at first, often called "hackney chairs," the word *chaise* being a sort of equivalent for a "chair," and also for a "carriage." Thus, in his "Book for a Rainy Day," Mr. Smith remarks that in 1766 "hackney chairs were so numerous that their stands extended round Covent Garden, and often down the adjacent streets." Not only was the sedan chair one of the necessary social appliances of the London people in the early part of the present century, but the same may be said of the good old lumbering hackney coach. This genteel vehicle, in the natural order of events, like the heavy stage-coaches, has long ago become a thing of history. It is a sorry thing to reflect upon how the cherished objects of our youth pass away, and are superseded by modern inventions, to be in their turn associated with notions of antiquity in the minds of a generation of beings having new ideas and new habits.

Apropos of cabs and the police—or, rather, parliamentary regulations for the suppression of drunkenness—we may be pardoned for giving the following curious piece of information relating to the "Jarveys" of old, for which we are indebted to Walker's "Original :"—"I will add one more instance of change. A retired hackney-coachman, giving an account of his life to a friend of mine, stated that his principal gains had been derived from cruising at late hours in particular quarters of the town to pick up drunken gentlemen. If they were able to tell their address, he conveyed them straight home ; if not, he carried them to certain taverns, where the custom was to secure their property and put them to bed. In the morning he called to take them home, and was generally handsomely rewarded. He said there were other gentlemen who pursued the same course, and they all considered it their policy to be strictly honest. The same calling is said to have been pursued for many years in Paris. The tariff for taking the drunkard home is—or was—ten sous ; and his conductor was known as *L'Ange Gardien*."

Instead of a few dozens of chairs and hackney coaches, the people of London, writes Mr. Diprose, in his "Book about London," "are now daily whisked about the town in upwards of three thousand cabs and twelve hundred omnibuses, besides a fleet of river steamers. These conveyances annually carry more passengers than three times the number of the whole population of the United Kingdom." Since Mr. Diprose's book was published the number of public conveyances has, of course, greatly increased. There are now upwards of two thousand omnibuses, in addition to 1,100 tram-cars.

Hard by the north side of Scotland Yard, in a blind alley called Craig's Court, opening out of Charing Cross and backing upon what was once the western side of the garden of Northumberland House, is Harrington House, a dull, heavy, and gloomy mansion, belonging to the Earls of Harrington. Close by used to stand the "Northumberland" Coffee-house, one of Sheridan's favourite haunts.

Between Scotland Yard and the river-side in the rear was "Man's," or as it was sometimes styled, "Old Man's" Coffee-house ; and another, possibly a rival one, known as "Young Man's." The former is said by Mr. Peter Cunningham to have been so called after the first keeper—one Alexander Man—and to have dated from the reign of Charles II. Defoe, in his "Journey through England," mentions them among the lesser though favourite coffee-houses of the day. "The Scots," he writes, "go generally to the 'British,' and a mixture of all sorts to the 'Smyrna.' There are also other little coffee-houses much frequented in this neighbourhood—'Young Man's' for officers ; 'Old Man's' for stock-jobbers, paymasters, and courtiers ; and 'Little Man's' for sharpers."

Whitehall Place, which we cross on our way to Middle Scotland Yard, was formed about the year 1820. It is a broad thoroughfare now connecting the Embankment with Whitehall, opposite the Admiralty. Here several of the houses are used as Government offices—such as those of the Woods, Forests, and Land Revenues ; the Ecclesiastical Commissioners for England, and Church Estates Commissioners ; Parks, Palaces, and Public Buildings ; and Commissioners in Lunacy. Here, too, is the National Liberal Club, with the fine block of flats known as Whitehall Court adjoining it, and forming part of the design ; while opposite is one of the fronts of the huge caravanserai known as the Hôtel Métropole.

A portion of Middle Scotland Yard used to be occupied by the Royal United Service Institution Museum, transferred in 1895 to what was the Chapel Royal, Whitehall. This building we shall describe when we come to Whitehall, but we may here give some account of the Museum, which comprises a splendid collection of arms and accoutrements, and models illustrative of the naval architecture of various nations. Two of the models are particularly worthy of notice—that of "The Field and Battle of Waterloo," by Captain Siborne; and "The South of the Crimea and Siege of Sebastopol," by Colonel Hamilton. A smaller model, but one of equal interest to the above, gives the visitor a clear idea of Nelson's last and greatest victory, the battle of Trafalgar. There is also a Chinese cabinet, and a variety of naval and military curiosities. Here the curious visitor may see, among the articles exhibited, the jaws of a shark enclosing a tin box. The history of this tin box is thus told by Mr. John Timbs:— "A ship on her way to the West Indies fell in with and chased a suspicious-looking craft, which had all the appearance of a slaver. During the pursuit the chased vessel threw something overboard. She was subsequently captured, and taken into Port Royal to be tried as a slaver. In absence of the ship's papers and other proofs, the slaver was not only in a fair way to escape condemnation, but her captain was anticipating the recovery of pecuniary damages against his captor for illegal detention. While the subject was under discussion, a vessel came into port which had followed closely in the track in the chase above described. She had caught a shark; and in its stomach was found a tin box, which contained the slaver's papers. Upon the strength of this evidence the slaver was condemned. The written account is attached to the box." In the armoury sections are many remarkable relics, which associate us with the great and perilous events in the history of our own and other countries. From the savage's war-dress of skin and feathers to the latest improvement in armour-plated vessels—from clubs and bows and arrows to the modern quick-firing gun, the development of war material may be traced through almost every stage. There are trophies of the Crimean War and of the last campaign in China, as well as of our "little wars" with savage tribes on our frontiers; and among the most recent acquisitions under this head are some interesting objects brought back by the last Ashanti Expedition (1895–96). Here also one may see pistols which belonged to Sir Ralph Abercromby, Bolwar, and Tippo Sahib; and swords which were once wielded by Cromwell and General Wolfe. One interesting relic of a bygone system of naval warfare may be discovered in a piece of clockwork which formed part of the paraphernalia of an old-fashioned fire-ship. This mechanism was so contrived that at the end of a given time it would set fire to the vessel as it bore down on the enemy. Another means of accomplishing a somewhat similar result, though without any reference to the enemy, is shown in the nest of a family of rats, discovered on board the *Revenge*. These frugal creatures had laid by a store of

matches, which ignited and set fire to the nest, the burnt remnant of which shows what a very narrow escape the vessel had from destruction. The gradual development of the lifeboat into its present form is shown in a very interesting series of models running back to a very primitive type, and an old suggestion for lessening the danger of the Goodwin Sands is embodied in the model of a floating refuge. Here, too, are kept the sad relics of the unfortunate expedition to the Arctic regions conducted by Sir John Franklin, discovered by Sir Leopold M'Clintock, of H.M.S. *Fox*, in 1859, and equally melancholy mementoes of the *Royal George*, which sank at Spithead in 1782—an event which moved Cowper to write the fine poem, "Toll for the brave." There are also personal relics of Drake, Nelson, Captain Cook, and other naval heroes. Soldiers and sailors in uniform are admitted to the Museum free; the fee to the general public is sixpence.

The Royal United Service Institution was established in 1831 to promote naval and military art, science, and literature by means of a library, the delivery of lectures, the exhibition of inventions, the publication of a journal, and the formation of a museum; and in 1860 it received a royal charter. The annual subscription is one pound, with an entrance fee of the like amount, and the sum of ten pounds, which includes the entrance fee, constitutes a member for life. It is now housed in a new building adjoining the Museum on the south, the foundation-stone being laid by the Prince of Wales as "Admiral of the Fleet and Field Marshal" in 1893. The structure includes a large library, a commodious lecture-hall, with smoking-room, &c.

At No. 3 in Whitehall Yard (now demolished) was the office of the Comptroller-General of the Exchequer, where was formerly held "The Trial of the Pyx," a ceremony of late years performed at the Hall of the Goldsmiths' Company, as described in page 357 of the first volume of this work.

In the course of the last century the greater part of what had been the "Private" or "Privy" Gardens of Whitehall Palace became gradually covered by the houses of favoured nobles, who obtained leases from the Crown at easy rents. "Among the first of these," says Pennant, "on the site of the small beer-cellar [of which a view is preserved in No. 4 of Hollar's prints of Whitehall], is the house of the Earl of Fife." Scotch to the backbone, the noble earl who built it was resolved, it would appear, that even when in London he would never tread on other than Scottish soil; and, therefore, when he embanked the river to form a terrace commanding the water, he ordered that all the gravel necessary to form it should be brought up from his native Fifeshire. Fife House in the last century was rich in curious relics of the past, and must have been well worth a visit. Lord Fife used to show with pride a collection of Gobelin tapestry, which he had brought from Paris, and a small but select gallery of paintings, including a portrait of Charles I. when Prince of Wales, which was painted by Velasquez at Madrid. In one of the walls of this house was an archway of the Tudor style which had a direct communication with the Palace or Privy Stairs at Whitehall.

Fife House was for some years occupied by the Earl of Liverpool during his premiership; and it was within its walls that he breathed his last, in the

A SEDAN CHAIR (*see page* 333).

Speaker of the House of Commons; the last Lord Liverpool at the same time occupying Fife House, where his half-brother, the Premier, had died some seven years before.

Leading from the palace down to the river were two pairs of stairs — the one public, the other known as the "privy" stairs, for the use of the Court. The first was still in use in Pennant's time; "the other," says that writer, "is made up in the old wall adjacent to the house of the Earl of Fife, where the arch of the portal remains entire." Henry and his daughter Elizabeth, as we know, made by water such of their journeys and progresses as they did not make on horseback, though on some occasions they went mounted on a litter carried on men's shoulders. "Coaches," says Pennant,

COACHES : REIGN OF QUEEN ANNE.

month of December, 1828. The house was pulled down about the year 1862, to make room for improvements. It had for a few years been used as the receptacle of the collection forming the East India Museum, which was removed hither on the demolition of the East India House in Leadenhall street. The contents of this Museum were afterwards removed to the new India Office in Charles Street. Here, close by, in 1835, lived the Right Honourable James Abercromby, before he became

"had been introduced into England by Henry Fitzalan, Earl of Arundel, one of Elizabeth's admirers, but the spirited princess seems to have disdained their use. The author of "An Estimate of the Manners of the Times," published in 1758, asks, with reference to the Sedan chairs, of which we have spoken above, "How would he have been laughed at in the days of Elizabeth, when a great queen rode on horseback to St. Paul's, who should have foretold that in less than two centuries no man of fashion would cross the street at the west-end to dinner, without the effeminate covering and conveyance of an easy chair?"

The last occasion on which Her Majesty went by state upon the Thames was in 1849, when she opened the new Coal Exchange in the City. On that occasion she embarked and landed on her return at Whitehall Stairs, as her proud predecessor Elizabeth had often landed before her. Since that year we believe that the royal barge has been allowed to slumber in its dry-dock, and the royal bargemaster and watermen have enjoyed a sinecure.

WHITEHALL ABOUT 1650.   (*From a Copy by Smith of a Rare Print by Israel Silvestre.*)

CHAPTER XLII.

WHITEHALL.—HISTORICAL REMARKS.

"You must no more call it York Place—that is past ;
For since the Cardinal fell that title's lost ;
'Tis now the King's, and called Whitehall."
Shakespeare's Henry VIII., Act IV., sc. 1.

The most Polite Court in Europe—A School of Manners and Morals—Historical Account of Whitehall—Anciently called York Place—Name of York Place changed to Whitehall—Wolsey's Style of Living here—Visit of Henry VIII.—The Fall of Wolsey—Additions to the Palace by Henry VIII.—Queen Mary at Whitehall—The Palace attacked by Rioters—Tilting-Matches and Pageants—Queen Elizabeth's Library—The "Fortresse of Perfect Beautie"—Masques and Revels at Whitehall—The Office of "Master of the Revels"—The Tilt-yard—Charles Killigrew—Serving up the Queen's Dinner–Christian IV. of Denmark and James I.—The Gunpowder Plot—Library of James I. at Whitehall—George Villiers, Duke of Buckingham.

THE moment that we pass out of the Strand, or make our way from the Victoria Embankment into Charing Cross, and wander either westwards through Spring Gardens into St. James's Park, or in a southerly direction past Whitehall towards the venerable Abbey of Westminster, we must feel, if we know anything of the history of our country under the Tudors and the Stuarts, that we are treading on ground which is most rich in historic memories. In fact, it may be said with-out fear of contradiction that the triangular space which lies between the new Palaces of Whitehall and St. James's, and the old Palace at Westminster, is holy ground, having been the scene of more important events in English history than all which have been witnessed by the rest of the two cities of London and Westminster together. It is to be hoped, therefore, that the following chapter will not be deficient in interest. Strange indeed would it be if it were, seeing that for all this part of

London, and for this period in the annals of Great Britain, we have the most abundant stores of material provided—not merely in the gossiping Diaries of Evelyn and Pepys, but in the memoirs and correspondence of scores of statesmen, courtiers, and writers, from the Augustan era of Queen Anne down to Sir Nathaniel Wraxall, the late Duke of Buckingham, and Lord William Lennox.

Nothing can be further from our purpose than to write a complete history—either topographical or biographical—of the Palace of Whitehall. To attempt to do so would be in effect to write the history of our Tudor and Stuart sovereigns; a task which has been so well done by Miss Lucy Aikin as to render it needless for us to attempt a rival account. Whitehall was, however, as Walpole tells us, "the most polite court in Europe;" and if it was not a school of morals, at all events it was a school of manners, such as would make a "fine gentleman" or "fine lady" of the age. And therefore a few brief sketches of the palace as Englishmen find it in the reigns of Henry VIII. and Elizabeth, of James I. and Charles I., may not be a task either impossible or unattractive to our readers. It is to be feared, however, that the standard of morality was not very high among the female part of the Court at Whitehall, at the close of the reign of Charles II. Macaulay, at all events, writes :— "In that court a maid of honour who dressed in such a manner as to do full justice to a white bosom, who ogled significantly, who danced voluptuously, who excelled in pert repartee, who was not ashamed to romp with lords of the bedchamber and captains of the guards, to sing sly verses with a sly expression, or to put on a page's dress for a frolic, was more likely to be followed and admired, more likely to be honoured with royal attentions, more likely to win a rich husband, than Jane Grey or Lucy Hutchinson would have been. In such circumstances the standard of female attainments was necessarily low, and it was more dangerous to be above that standard than to be beneath it. Extreme ignorance and frivolity were thought less unbecoming in a lady than the slightest tincture of pedantry. Of the too celebrated women whose faces we still admire on the walls of Hampton Court few indeed were in the habit of reading anything more valuable than acrostics, lampoons, and translations of the Clelia and the Grand Cyrus."

It is remarked in the "New View of London," published in 1708, that "heretofore there have been many courts of our kings and queens in London and Westminster, as the Tower of London, where some believe Julius Cæsar lodged, and William the Conqueror; in the Old Jewry, where Henry VI.; Baynard's Castle, where Henry VII.; Bridewell, where John and Henry VIII.; Tower Royal, where Richard II. and Stephen; the Wardrobe, in Great Carter Lane, where Richard III. [resided]; also at Somerset House, kept by Queen Elizabeth, and at Westminster, near the Hall, where Edward the Confessor, and several other kings, kept their courts. But of later times," continues the writer, "the place for the Court, when in town, was mostly Whitehall, a very pleasant and commodious situation, looking into St. James's Park, the canal, &c., on the west, and the noble river of Thames on the east; Privy Garden, with fountain, statues, &c., and an open prospect to the statue at Charing Cross on the north." With these few words of preface let us proceed.

Whitehall was known as York Place when in the possession of Cardinal Wolsey, with whose history the palace is so intimately connected. But long before that time it had been in lay hands. We read that it was erected on lands originally belonging to one Odo, a goldsmith, and that Hubert de Burgh, Lord Chief Justice of England under John and Henry III., and who gained himself a name in the Crusades, had a mansion on this very site; having purchased the latter from the Dean and Chapter of Westminster, to whom it had been previously given or bequeathed. He left his house, about the year 1240, to the monastery of Black Friars or Dominicans, whose principal abode at that time was in Holborn. They sold it to Walter de Grey, Archbishop of York, who settled it not on his family, but on his successors in that see, as their town residence, whence it was called York Place; and it was not until it passed out of their hands into those of King Henry—how is known to every reader of a child's first History of England—that it came to be known as Whitehall; a change of name which, if not duly "recorded at the Heralds' College," is, at all events, notified by Shakespeare in the lines quoted at the head of this chapter.

To give a detailed account of all the scenes which the Palace of Whitehall witnessed in its heyday and prime, when it was the favourite abode of our Tudor and Stuart sovereigns, would really be—as we have said—to write a history of the courts and cabinets of each successive monarch from the Reformation down to the Revolution—a task which would be impossible within the limits of this book, and foreign to the purpose which we have in view. But we cannot here, in justice to our subject, forbear the due encomium to Cardinal Wolsey. We do not attempt to defend his political character, or the arrogant means by which he supported it. But he made his greatness subservient to the improvement and decoration of his country. Christ Church, Oxford, and Hampton Court are existing monuments of his liberality; and the recollection that he exhibited at his palace at Whitehall of all that was exquisite in art, refined in taste, elegant in manners, and respectable in literature, should urge us, at the same time that we pity and regret the failings of this great minister, to applaud his public spirit, and give deserved honour to the greatness of his munificence.

The sumptuous style of living adopted by Wolsey here is known to every child who has read the History of England—how he formed his domestic establishment on the model of the royal court, ranging those under his roof under three classes, to each of which a separate table was assigned, including a company of young noblemen who were placed in his household in order to receive a polite education; how he was waited on by a *chef de cuisine* with a gold chain round his neck, by yeomen of the barge, by a master of the horse and sixteen grooms of the stable, and a tribe of secretaries, grooms, and yeomen of the chamber, amounting in all to nearly a hundred and fifty persons. Such was the proud state which "my Lord Cardinal of York" kept at Whitehall, and which in the end drew down upon him the envy and wrath of his sovereign.

Here Wolsey was visited by Henry not only privately, but also in state; and we find in Shakespeare graphic pictures of the ambitious cardinal, his sensual master, and the court manners of the period in which he lived. His gentleman usher, George Cavendish, also thus writes, in his "Life and Death of Thomas Woolsey," a work reprinted in the "Harleian Miscellany." The extract, though long, is worth preserving here as a picture complete in itself:—"He lived a long season ruling all appertaining to the King by his wisdom, and all other weighty matters of foreign regions with which the King of this realm had any occasion to intermeddle. All ambassadors of foreign potentates were always despatched by his discretion, to whom they had always access for their despatch. And when it pleased the King's Majesty, for his recreation, to repair unto the Cardinal's house, as he did at divers times in the year, at which times there wanted no preparations or goodly furniture, with viands of the finest sort that might be provided for money or friendship, such pleasures were then devised for the King's comfort and consolation as might be invented or by man's wit imagined. The banquets were set

forth with masks and mummeries in so gorgeous a sort and costly manner that it was a heaven to behold. There wanted no dames or damsels meet or apt to dance with the maskers, or to garnish the place for the time with other goodly disports. Then was there all kind of music and harmony set forth, with excellent voices both of men and children. I have seen the King suddenly come in thither in a mask, with a dozen of other maskers, all in garments like shepherds, made of fine cloth of gold and fine crimson satin paned, and caps of the same, with vizors of good proportion of visnomy; their hairs and beards either of fine gold wire or else of silver, and some being of black silk: having sixteen torchbearers, besides their drums, and other persons attending upon them, with vizors, and clothed all in satin of the same colours. And at his coming, and before he came into the hall—ye shall understand that he came by water to the water-gate without any noise — where, against his coming, were laid charged many chambers, and at his landing they were all shot off, which made such a rumble in the air that it was like thunder. It made all the noblemen, ladies, and gentlemen to muse what it should mean coming so suddenly, they sitting quietly at a solemn banquet; under this sort:—First, ye shall perceive that the tables were set in the chamber of presence, banquet-wise covered, my Lord Cardinal sitting under the cloth of estate, and there having his service all alone; and then was there set a lady and a nobleman, or a gentleman and gentlewoman, throughout all the tables in the chamber on the one side, which were made and joined as it were but one table. All which order and device was done and devised by the Lord Sands, Lord Chamberlain to the King; and also by Sir Henry Guildford, Comptroller to the King. Then immediately after this great shot of guns the Cardinal desired the Lord Chamberlain and Comptroller to look what this sudden shot should mean, as though he knew nothing of the matter. They, thereupon looking out of the windows into Thames, returned again, and showed him that it seemed to them there should be some noblemen and strangers arrived at his bridge, as ambassadors from some foreign prince. With that quoth the Cardinal, ' I shall desire you, because ye can speak French, to take the pains to go down into the hall to encounter and to receive them according to their estates, and to conduct them into this chamber, where they shall see us, and all these noble personages, sitting merrily at our banquet, desiring them to sit down with us, and to take part of our fare and pastime.' Then they went incontinent down into the hall, where they received them with twenty new torches, and conveyed them up into the chamber, with such a number of drums and fifes as I have seldom seen together at one time in any masque. At their arrival into the chamber, two and two together, they went directly before the Cardinal, where he sat, saluting him very reverently; to whom the Lord Chamberlain for them said, 'Sir, forasmuch as they be strangers and can speak no English, they have desired me to declare unto your grace thus: they, having understanding of this your triumphant banquet, where was assembled such a number of excellent fair dames, could do no less, under the supportation of your good grace, but to repair hither, to view as well their incomparable beauty as for to accompany them at mumchance, and then after to dance with them, and so to have of them acquaintance. And, sir, they furthermore require of your grace license to accomplish the cause of their repair.' To whom the Cardinal answered that he was very well contented they should do so. Then the maskers went first and saluted all the dames as they sat, and then returned to the most worthiest, and there opened a cup full of gold with crowns and other pieces of coin, to whom they set divers pieces to cast at—thus perusing all the ladies and gentlemen; and some they lost, and of some they won. And thus done they returned unto the Cardinal with great reverence, pouring down all the crowns in the cup, which was about 200 crowns. 'At all,' quoth the Cardinal, and so cast the dice, and won them all at a cast, whereat was great joy made. Then quoth the Cardinal to my Lord Chamberlain, 'I pray you show them that it seemeth me that there should be amongst them some noble man, whom I suppose to be much more worthy of honour to sit and occupy this room and place than I; to whom I would gladly, if I knew him, surrender my place, according to my duty.' Then spake to them my Lord Chamberlain in French, declaring my Lord Cardinal's mind; and they, rounding him again in the ear, my Lord Chamberlain said to my Lord Cardinal, 'Sir, they confess that there is among them such a noble personage, whom, if your grace can appoint him from the other, he is content to disclose himself and to accept your place most worthily.' With that the Cardinal, taking a good advisement among them, at the last quoth he, 'Meseemeth the gentleman with the black beard should be even he.' And with that he arose out of his chair, and offered the same to the gentleman in the black beard with his cap in his hand. The person to whom he offered then his chair was

Sir Edward Neville, a comely knight of a goodly personage, that much more resembled the King's person in that mask than any other. The King, hearing and perceiving the Cardinal so deceived in his estimation and choice, could not forbear laughing, but plucked down his vizor and Master Neville's also, and dashed out with such a pleasant countenance and cheer that all noble estates there assembled, seeing the King to be there amongst them, rejoiced very much. The Cardinal eftsoons desired his Highness to take the place of estate; to whom the King answered that he would go first and shift his apparel; and so departed and went straight into my Lord's bed-chamber, where was a great fire made and prepared for him, and there new apparelled him with rich and princely garments. And in the time of the King's absence the dishes of the banquet were clean taken up, and the tables spread again with new and sweet perfumed cloths, every man sitting still until the King and his maskers came in among them again, every man being newly apparelled. Then the King took his seat under the cloth of estate, commanding no man to remove, but sit still as they did before. Then in came a new banquet before the King's Majesty and to all the rest through the tables; wherein, I suppose, were served two hundred dishes or above, of wondrous costly meats and devices subtilly devised. Thus passed they forth the whole night with banqueting, dancing, and other triumphant devices, to the great comfort of the King and pleasant regard of the nobility there assembled."

It is hoped that this long quotation will be pardoned by the reader, on account of the graphic picture which it presents to his eyes of "the inner life of Whitehall" in the days of the eighth Henry.

It was at the "masque" above described that the fickle-minded monarch first cast his admiring eyes on the ill-fated Anne Boleyn. Within a few short months Whitehall Palace was the scene where Wolsey took a final leave of "all his greatness." The profusion of rich things—hangings of cloth of gold and of silver; thousands of pieces of fine holland; the quantities of plate, even of pure gold, which covered two great tables, all of which were seized by his cruel and rapacious master—are so many proofs of his amazing wealth, splendour, and pride. It was from Whitehall Stairs that the "great Lord Cardinal" entered his barge to be rowed to Esher, after his disgrace. As every reader of history knows, the Palace passed into the possession of the Crown upon the fall of Cardinal Wolsey. It was granted by Act of Parliament to Henry VIII. "because the old Palace nigh to the Monastery of

St. Peter is now, and has long before been in a state of ruin and decay."

Henry VIII. seems to have taken a delight in his buildings at Whitehall, to which he added many sumptuous apartments. He also formed a collection of pictures, to which considerable additions were made by the unfortunate Charles I. Henry, as a sovereign, shows a strange admixture of barbarity and culture; "his cruelty could not suppress his love of the arts; and his love of the arts could not soften his savage nature. The prince who, with the utmost *sang froid*, could burn Protestants and Catholics, take off the heads of the partners of his bed one day, and celebrate new nuptials on the next, had, notwithstanding, a strong taste for refined pleasures. He cultivated architecture and painting, and invited from abroad artists of the first merit." Accordingly he commissioned Holbein to build a new gate at Whitehall with bricks of two colours, light and dark alternately, and disposed in a tesselated fashion; but of this we shall have more to say in a future chapter.

In the reign of Edward VI., it appears, there was an outdoor pulpit or preaching-place in one of the court-yards of the palace; and here Bishop Latimer, after his release from the Tower, and also many others, were in the habit of preaching, "on Sundays and holidays, to the King and the Protector, while many of all ranks resorted thither." Owing to the delicate constitution of the young king, the Parliament was held at Whitehall on one occasion during his reign.

On the last day of September, 1553, soon after her accession, Queen Mary rode in great state from the Tower, through the City, to Westminster. "The citizens received her with such respect that on her alighting at the Palace at Whitehall she publicly thanked the Lord Mayor. On the following day she was crowned with the greatest magnificence. The Lord Mayor, attended by twelve of the chief citizens, officiated as chief butler; for which service the Mayor received a gold cup and cover, weighing seventeen ounces, as his fee."

Whitehall Palace was attacked by the rioters under Sir Thomas Wyatt, and from it Elizabeth was conveyed a prisoner to the Tower, by order of her sister Mary, who had kept her "in a kind of honourable custody."

Here Lord Brooke and Sir Philip Sidney took a chief part in the tilting-matches and other pageants by which the marriage of Queen Mary with Philip of Spain was enlivened. It was this Lord Brooke (see Vol. II., p. 549) who, though no mean scholar, and an able statesman, declared that he wished to be known to posterity only as Shakespeare's friend,

Ben Jonson's master, and the patron of Lord Chancellor Egerton. In November, 1558, Elizabeth made the same royal progress in equal state, and amid even greater rejoicings than had ushered in the reign of her sister Mary.

In Elizabeth's time, it would appear, there were great doings at Whitehall on several occasions. Not only were tournaments instituted, but there were "revels and maskings, and various other mummeries." Queen Elizabeth, as every reader of history knows, was passionately fond of dancing; in this sport she would occupy herself on rainy days in her palace, dancing to the scraping of a tiny fiddle; and it is impossible not to admire her humour whenever a messenger came to her from her cousin, James VI. of Scotland; for Sir Roger Ashton assures us that, as often as he had to deliver any letters to her from his master, on lifting up the hangings he was sure to find her dancing, in order that he might be able to tell James, from his own observation, how little chance there was of his early succession to the throne.

Her library at Whitehall was well stored with books—not only in English and French, but in Greek and Italian; and her autographs show that she was skilful in penmanship. Among the other distinguished foreigners who visited her here was her lover, the Duc of Anjou, whom she received with every species of coquetry. On the 1st of January, 1581, was held in this yard "the most sumptuous tournament ever celebrated," in honour of the French commissioners sent over from France to propose the alliance. A banqueting-house, most superbly ornamented, was erected within its precincts, at the expense of more than fifteen hundred pounds. "The gallerie adjoining to Her Majestie's house at Whitehall," says Holinshed, in his "Chronicles," "whereat her person should be placed, was called, and not without cause, the Castell or fortresse of perfect Beautie!" "Romantic fooleries!" is the quiet remark of the antiquary Pennant; and it were well if every comment as terse as this were equally just. Though eight-and-forty years of age, the queen received every outward sign of flattery that the charms of fifteen could claim. The "fortresse of perfect Beautie" was assailed by Desire and his four foster-children. The combatants on both sides were persons of the first rank, and a regular summons was first sent to the possessor of the "Castell" with a song, of which this is a part :—

"Yield, yield, O yield, ye that this fort do hold,
    Which seated is in Honour's spotless field :
Desire's great force no forces can withhold,
    Then to Desire's desire, O yield, O yield !"

This ended, we are told that "two cannons were fired off, one with sweet powder, and the other with sweet water; and after these were stores of pretty scaling-ladders, and then the footmen threw floures and such fancies against the walls, with all such devices as might seem fit shot for Desire." In the end Desire was repulsed and forced to make submission; and thus ended an "amorous foolery" which the patient reader may find described at full length in Weldon's "Court of King James."

All Christmas plays were performed before the Court by the "children of the Chapel Royal;" and we read in Ben Jonson's Life that his *Cynthia's*

this masque was brought to Whitehall by the loyal barristers, who, as we know and have already explained, were of old addicted to such shows. Henry Lawes undertook the music; Inigo Jones was machinist; and Selden's antiquarian lore was called into request, in order to ensure accuracy in the costumes. The masque itself, entitled *The Triumph of Peace*, was from the courtly pen of Shirley. "At length the great day arrived. From Ely House, on Holborn Hill, the procession set forth down Chancery Lane. A hundred gentlemen of the Inns of Court, all splendidly mounted, were followed by an anti-masque of grotesque figures;

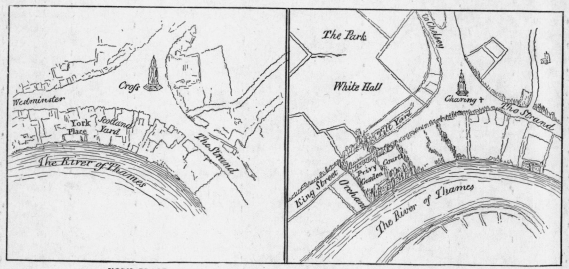

YORK PLACE.   WHITEHALL IN THE REIGN OF HENRY VIII.

(From two small Maps, printed with Fisher's Plan of Whitehall.)

Revels were put on this stage by those juvenile actors. We read also of a masque by Ben Jonson being performed at Whitehall by command of the Queen, who appeared in it herself, along with several of the ladies of her Court. Inigo Jones, it appears, contributed to the splendour of these masques, embellishing them with every grace and propriety of scenic decoration; at all events, Mr. Gerard writes to Lord Strafford: "Such a splendid scene built over the altar at Somerset House, 'The Glory of Heaven.' Inigo Jones never presented a more curious piece in any of the masques at Whitehall."

Whitehall, indeed, was the scene of many gorgeous entertainments, but none, perhaps, of its shows was more attractive than the magnificent masque got up by the Inns of Court, as "a mark of love and duty to their majesties," just at the time when Prynne, the sedition-monger, had published one of his scurrilous works. We read that in February, 1634,

then came four chariots, carrying in as many companies the masquers from the four inns. On their arrival at Whitehall *The Triumph of Peace* was acted at the Banqueting House. It was a comic allegory of the social pleasures of peace, ending with a gorgeous tableau, in which the other deities appeared, all grouped round the peaceful goddess Irene." The performance itself, which cost about £21,000, caused a perfect *furore*, and is often mentioned by writers of the time. A fortnight later Carew's masque, *The British Heaven*, was acted on the same boards at Whitehall—Lawes and Inigo Jones helping as before—by Charles I. himself, assisted by a dozen or so of his courtiers. In fact, the masque—as an intermediate step between the pastoral idyll, which is purely ideal, and the reality of the drama proper—at this time had become the favourite form which "private theatricals" assumed in the time of our last Tudor and our first Stuart sovereign, and its home was the Palace of White-

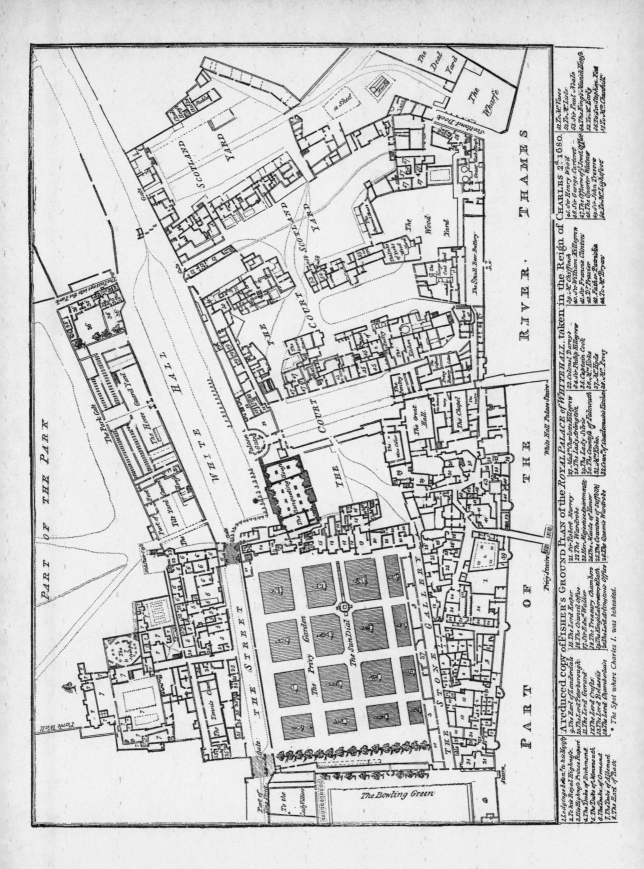

PART OF THE PARK

RIVER. THAMES.

PART OF THE

A reduced COPY of FISHER'S GROUND PLAN of the ROYAL PALACE of WHITEHALL. taken in the Reign of CHARLES 2d. 1680.

Lodgings taken in 1669.
1.To the Royal Highness.
3.His Grace Prince Rupert.
4.The Duke of Richmond.
5.The Duke of Monmouth.
6.The Duke of Ormond.
7.The Duke of Albemarl.
8.The Earl of Bath.

11.The Earl of Lauderdale.
12.Sir Robert Murray.
13.The Lord Gerrard.
14.The Lord Crofts.
15.The Lord Roberstic.
16.The Lord Chamberlain.

15.The Lord Keeper.
16.The Council Office.
17.Sir Edw.r Walker.
18.The Treasury Chambers.
19.The English drawing room Bath.
20.The Lord Privy Seal's Office.

21.Madm. Marietta Killegrew.
22.The Wardrobe.
23.Her Majesties apartments.
24.The Maids of Honor.
25.The Countess of Falmouth.
26.The Queen's Wardrobe.

27.Madm. Marietta Killegrew.
28.The Lady Arlington.
29.The Lady Scroo.
30.Mrs. Kirke.
31.Mr. Hyde.
32.Sir Ny. Armorer's Kitchin.

33.Colonel Darcy.
34.Mr. Chiffinch.
35.Captain Cook.
36.Mr. Kirke.
37.Mr. Hyde.
Sir.Mr. Perry.

39.Mr. Progers.
40.Sir William Killegrew.
41.Sir Francis Clinton.
42.Dr. Frazier.
43.Father Patrick.
44.To Mr. Bryan.

45.To. Mr. Laws.
46.Sir Henry Wood.
47.Sir George Carteret.
48.The Officers of Jewell Office.
49.The King's Wardrobe.
50.Dr. Frazier.
51.Sir John Prewen.
52.The Countess of Falmouth.

52.To. Mr. Kirke.
53.Sir Paul Neale.
54.The King's Watch Dogs.
55.To. Mr. Early.
56.To.Sir Stephen Fox.
57.To. Mr. Churchill.

* The Spot where Charles I. was beheaded.

hall. The masque, as such, is styled by pleasant and witty Leigh Hunt "the only glory of King James' reign, and the greatest glory of Whitehall."

In the palace was a private theatre, with a little stage, the contrivance of Inigo Jones, whom Ephraim Hardcastle, in the *Somerset House Gazette*, does not hesitate to call "the father of scene-painting in England." Elegant masques were performed here by "his Majesty's servants," in the reign of James I. "These pieces," says Horace Walpole, "were sometimes composed at the command of the king in compliment to the nuptials of certain lords and ladies of the Court;" and he grows positively eloquent in their praise, as a "custom productive of much good, by encouraging marriage among the young nobility." Ben Jonson was the poet, Inigo Jones the inventor of the decorations, Laniere and Ferrabosco composed the symphonies, and the king, queen, and young nobility danced in the interludes. To such an extent was the splendour of these "shows" celebrated at the rival court of the Tuileries and Versailles that the same author asserts that they formed the model which was followed in the celebrated *fêtes* of Louis le Grand.

One of the officers of the Court was the "Master of the Revels," whose office was created in 1546, by Henry VIII.—a fitting compliment to the theory—we can hardly say the fiction—which made the stage-players of the date "his Majesty's servants." Mr. Frost, in his "Old Showmen of London," tells us that all the professors of the various arts of popular entertainment had to pay an annual licence duty to the Master of the Revels, whose jurisdiction extended over all wandering minstrels, and every one who blew a trumpet publicly, except (strangely enough) "the King's Players." The seal of his office, used under five sovereigns in succession, engraved on wood, was formerly in the possession of the late Mr. Francis Douce, by whose permission it was engraved for Smith's "Ancient Topography of London," where it may be seen. The legend round it was "SIGILL : OFFIC : *Jocor : Mascar : et : Revell : Dni : Regis.*

From the same authority (Frost's "Old Showmen of London") we learn that the office of Master of the Revels, which had been held by Thomas Killigrew, the Court jester, was conferred, at his death, on his son Charles. Concerning this son the *London Gazette* of 1682 has the following advertisement :— "Whereas, Mr. John Clarke, of London, bookseller, did rent of Charles Killigrew, Esq., the licensing of all ballad-singers· for five years, which time is expired at Lady-day next; these are therefore to give notice to all ballad-singers that they take out licenses at the Office of the Revels, at White-

hall, for singing and selling of ballads and small books, according to ancient custom. And all persons concerned are hereby desired to take notice of and to suppress all mountebanks, rope-dancers, prize-players, ballad-singers, and such as make show of motions and strange sights, that have not a license in red and black letters, under the hand and seal of the said Charles Killigrew, Esq., Master of the Revels to His Majesty."

"The Tilt-yard adjoining the Palace," says Pennant, "was the delight of Queen Elizabeth, who was remarkable not only for the strength of her common sense and the violence of her disposition, but for her absurd and romantic vanity." Here, in her sixty-sixth year, "with wrinkled face, red periwig, little eyes, hooked nose, skinny lips, and black teeth," to use the phrase of Hentzner in his "Travels," she could drink in the flatteries of her favourite courtiers. Essex, by the lips of his "squire," here told her of her beauty and her worth; and a Dutch ambassador here assured her Majesty that he had undertaken the voyage to see her Majesty, who "for beauty and wisdom excelled all the other beauties in the world !"

In the collection of letters made by the late Mr. E. Lodge is one from Mr. Brackenbury to Lord Talbot, in which occurs the following passage, illustrative of Queen Elizabeth's love of her Tilt-yard :—"These sports were great, and done in costly sort, to Her Majesty's great lykinge . . . The nineteenth day, being St. Elizabeth's Day, the Erle of Cumberland, the Erle of Essex, and my Lord Burley dyd chaleng all comers, six courses apeace, which was very honourablye performed." The walls of the palace, however, if they had tongues, could tell some amusing stories of Elizabeth's passions and "tantarums;" for instance, in the same collection we read, in a letter from John Stanhope to Lord Talbot, "Thys night, God wylling, she [the queen] will go to Richmond, and on Saturday next to Somersett House; and yf she could overcome her passyon agst. my Lo. of Essex for his maryage no doubt she would be much the quyëter; yett she doth use ytt more temperately than was thought for, and (God be thanked) she *doth not strike all she thretes.*" Clearly she was a "hard hitter" when the Tudor blood within her was fairly roused.

The following account of the process of "serving up the queen's dinner" we take from Hentzner's "Travels in England," published in the reign of Elizabeth :—

"While the Queen was at prayers in the ante-chapel, a gentleman entered the room, having a rod, and along with him another who had a table-cloth, which, after they had both knelt three times with the utmost veneration, he spread upon the table, and after kneeling again, they both retired. Then came two others, one with the rod again, the other with a salt-cellar, a plate, and bread: when they had knelt as the others had done, and placed what was brought upon the table, they also retired, with the same ceremonies performed by the first. At last came an unmarried lady ('we,' says Hentzner, 'were told she was a countess'), and along with her a married one, bearing a tasting-knife; the former was dressed in white silk, who, when she had prostrated herself three times in the most graceful manner, approached the table, and rubbed the plates with bread and salt, with as much awe as if the Queen had been present. When they had waited there a little while, the yeomen of the guard entered, bare-headed, clothed in scarlet, with a golden rose upon their backs, bringing in at each turn a course of twenty-four dishes, served in plate, most of it gilt; these dishes were received by a gentleman in the same order they were brought, and placed upon the table, while the lady taster gave to each of the guard a mouthful to eat of the particular dish he had brought, for fear of any poison. During the time that this guard (which consists of the tallest and stoutest men that can be found in all England, being carefully selected for this purpose) were bringing dinner, twelve trumpets and two kettledrums made the hall ring for half an hour together. At the end of all this ceremonial, a number of unmarried ladies appeared, who, with particular solemnity, lifted the meat off the table, and conveyed it into the Queen's inner and more private chamber, where, after she had chosen for herself, the rest went to the ladies of the Court. The Queen dined and supped alone, with very few attendants, and it was very seldom that anybody, native or foreigner, was admitted at that time, and then only at the intercession of some-body in power."

Bishop Goodman, in his MS. "Memoirs of the Court of James I.," in the Bodleian Library at Oxford, tells us that it was Queen Elizabeth's constant custom, even to a late period of her reign, "a little before her coronation day," to come from Richmond to London, and to dine with the Lord Admiral (the Earl of Effingham), at his house at Chelsea, and then to set out from Chelsea, when it was "dark night," for Whitehall, where the Lord Mayor and aldermen met her. "All the way long from Chelsea to Whitehall," he adds, "was full of people to see her." The vain and silly queen appears to have liked to make these entries into London by night, because the torch-light did not reveal her wrinkles so clearly as the day. "In her yearly journeys," writes the bishop, "at her coming to London, you must understand that she did desire to be seen and to be magnified; but in her old age she had not only great wrinkles, but she had a goggle throat, with a great gullet hanging out, as her grandfather, Henry VII., is painted withal."

From and after the reign of Elizabeth the Court no longer oscillated between Greenwich, the Tower, and Westminster, moving about the goods and chattels of the Crown as occasion served. Though the Tower was still theoretically the seat of all the great attributes of royalty, and was sometimes occupied by the sovereign upon occasions of extra-ordinary solemnity, yet, from this time forth, Whitehall became the settled and fixed centre of courtly splendour and magnificence, so as soon to form a history of its own.

Lord Orrery, in a letter addressed to Dr. Birch, in November, 1741, observes, "I look upon anec-dotes as debts due to the public, and which every man, when he has that kind of cash by him, ought to pay." It is with a strong feeling of the truth of this remark that we here introduce one or two anecdotes concerning the former occupants of Whitehall.

It is on record that in 1608, when Christian IV. of Denmark, brother of the queen of James I., came to London to visit his brother-in-law, both kings got drunk together, in order to celebrate their happy meeting. An account of their shameful debauch on this occasion, which may well make us blush for royalty, will be found in Mr. John Timbs's "Romance of London;" but, in mercy to the memory of James, we will not repeat its details here.

It was here that Lord Monteagle communicated to James I.'s ministers the singular letter which was the cause of the discovery of the Gunpowder Plot, and Guy Fawkes was examined in the king's bed-chamber.

John Evelyn describes the interior of the King's Library here with great minuteness:—"Sept. 2, 1680.—I had an opportunity, his Majesty being at Windsor, of seeing his private library at White-hall at my full ease. I went with the expectation of finding some curiosities, but though there are about a thousand volumes, there were few of im-portance that I had not perused before. They consisted chiefly of such works as had been dedi-cated or presented to him, a few histories, some travels and French books, abundance of mapps and sea-chartes, entertainments, and pomps, build-ings and pieces relating to the navy, and some mathematical instruments ; but what was most rare were three or four Romish Breviaries, with a good deal of miniature and monkish painting and gilding, one of which is most excellently done, both as to the figures, grotesques, and compartments, to the utmost of that curious art. There is another, in which I find written by the hand of King Henry VII. his giving it to his deare daughter Margaret (afterwards Queen of Scots), in which he desires her to pray for his soule, subscribing his name at length. There is also the processe of the philosopher's great Elixir, represented in divers pieces of excellent miniature ; but the discourse is in High Dutch, a MS. There is also another MS., in 4to, of above 300 yeares old, in French, being an ‘ Institution of Physicke,’ and in the botanical parts the plants are curiously painted in miniature ; also a folio MS. of good thicknesse, being the severall exercises, as Theames (sic), Orations, Translations, &c., of King Edward VI., all written and subscribed with his own hand very legible, and divers of the Greeke interleaved and corrected after the manner of schoolboys’ exercises, and that exceedingly well and proper, and with some Epistles to his preceptor, which show’d that young prince to have been extraordinarily advanc’d in learning, and as Cardan (who had been in England) affirmed, stupendiously knowing for his age. There is likewise his Journal, no lesse testifying his early ripeness and care about affaires of state.” A great part of this library, there is reason to fear, perished in the fire which destroyed the palace, as will be related in a following chapter.

Here George Villiers, afterwards Duke of Buckingham, came, when quite a young man, in the reign of James I., “ to make his fortune at Court ;” to which, it would seem, he brought nothing, if we may judge by what Lord Clarendon tells us, but good looks and personal graces. “ He came to Whitehall,” says his biographer, “ in a reign when the Scots were as numerous there as the English,” and was fortunate in finding a friend in Sir John Graham, who presented him to the king, in the hopes of so cutting out the other royal favourite, Somerset. In this he was successful, and young Villiers was made cupbearer to the king, and received the honour of knighthood “ in the Queen’s bed-chamber at Whitehall, with the Prince’s rapier, and sworn one of the Gentlemen of His Majesty’s

Bedchamber.” He next was promoted to the Mastership of the Horse, and other honours soon followed. Henceforth Villiers becomes the silly and pedantic king’s “ dear child and gossip, Steenie,” and his Court history is interwoven with that of the walls of old Whitehall. The duke, it may be added, lived in greater pomp than any nobleman of his time, having six horses to his carriage, which, from its singularity, “ made him the stare of the people, as did also his being carried about in a chair on men’s shoulders ;” the noise and exclamations against it were so great that the people would openly upbraid him in the streets, as the means of bringing men to so servile a condition as horses ; but in a short time chairs became common, and the carrying of them was looked upon as a profitable employment—so various and fickle are the fancies of the time ! In dress he was extravagant beyond precedent, for in a MS. in the Harleian library, quoted in Mr. Oldys’ “ Life of Raleigh,” we read : “ It was common with him at any ordinary dancing to have his cloaths trimmed with great diamond buttons, and to have diamond hatbands, cockades, and earrings, to be yoked with great and manifold knots of pearl—in short, to be manacled, fettered, and imprisoned in jewels, insomuch that at his going over to Paris, in 1625, he had twenty-seven suits of cloaths made, the richest that embroidery, lace, silk, velvet, gold, and gems could contribute ; one of which was a white uncut velvet, set all over, both suit and cloak, with diamonds, valued at fourscore thousand pounds, besides a great feather stuck all over with diamonds ; as were also his sword, girdle, hatband, and spurs.” His entertainments to the king were also of the most sumptuous order ; in them the good, easy James would take rather more than prudence dictated ; for he was one of those who “ never mixed water with his wine.” When we mention Villiers travelling with six horses, we may as well add here that the “ proud” Earl of Northumberland, Henry Percy, on his release from the Tower, where he had been confined after the conspiracy of Guido Fawkes, on hearing that Buckingham drove his coach and six —then a great novelty—ordered that if the king’s favourite used six horses, eight should be put before his own, and drove these along the Strand to Westminster, passing, of course, along the fron of Whitehall.

CHAPTER XLIII.

WHITEHALL AND ITS HISTORICAL ASSOCIATIONS (continued).

"Parte aliâ lautas ædes, magna atria regum
Cernere erit."

Charles I. and the Parliament—Cromwell and the Commonwealth—The King brought to Trial—Execution of Charles I.—The Site of the Execution—Andrew Marvell's Lines on the Occasion—Who was the Executioner of Charles I.?—The Actual Scene of the Execution—Pennant's Opinion—The King's Bearing—A Singular Coincidence—Who struck the Fatal Blow?—Varying Statements upon this Point.

WHEN the Banqueting House of Whitehall was first erected, it was little thought that James was constructing a passage from it for his son and successor, Charles I., to the scaffold. It would be unpardonable to pass over an event of this magnitude slightly. Rapin has laid down what has been said for and against the proceedings of the Parliament in their quarrel with Charles I., which led to the establishment of the Commonwealth, and the whole question has been thoroughly investigated by more recent writers, with the impartiality that is characteristic of the new school of historians. Mr. Nightingale, in "The Beauties of England and Wales," describes the matter as follows, from a more partial point of view:—"The unfortunate monarch was evidently the prey of two contending parties: the Independents, whose descendants still survive in the various sects now called Calvinistic Methodists; and the Presbyterians, who are now risen or degenerated into the sects of Unitarians, Arians, and General Baptists. The first of these parties was bent on the king's destruction; the latter wished to save him, and eventually brought about the restoration of Charles II., though they could not succeed in saving the life of his father. The rebellious army had the support of the Independents; but it should not therefore be concluded that the king had the cordial support of the Presbyterians, whom nothing would satisfy but the abolition of the episcopacy, though they do not seem to have wished this at the expense of their monarch's life."

On the 28th of April, 1648, the House of Commons voted:—" 1. That the government of the kingdom should be still by the King, Lords, and Commons. 2. That the groundwork for this government should be the propositions last presented to the king at Hampton Court. 3. That any member of the House should have leave to speak freely to any votes, ordinances, or declarations concerning the king, &c."

These votes did not at all accord with the designs of the Independents, who meant to abolish all kingly authority, and establish a Commonwealth; and who, although weak in the House, but strong in the field, contrived to prevent a reconciliation or treaty with the king till Cromwell should be sufficiently strong to allow them to act with the necessary vigour against their enemies—the Scots, the Royalists, and the Presbyterians. In the meanwhile Cromwell gained strength, and the Independents at length openly demanded "that the king be brought to justice, as the capital cause of all the evils in the kingdom, and of so much blood being shed." Every day gave new force to their designs, and new strength to their vengeance. They had possession of the king's person, and removed him, contrary to the instructions of the Parliament, to Hurst Castle, in Hampshire.

On the 19th of January, 1648-9, the king, who had in the meantime been removed from Hurst Castle to Windsor, was brought to St. James's. His trial was quickly hurried on, and on the 27th of January sentence of death was passed upon him. His Majesty was taken back to St. James's Palace, and the sentence was carried into effect three days afterwards upon a scaffold erected in front of the Banqueting House of Whitehall. Mr. J. H. Jesse thus minutely describes the last sad scene:—

"Colonel Hacker having knocked at his door and informed him that it was time to depart, Charles took Bishop Juxon by the hand, and bidding his faithful attendant Herbert to bring with him his silver clock, intimated to Hacker, with a cheerful countenance, that he was ready to accompany him. As he passed through the Palace Garden into the Park, he inquired of Herbert the hour of the day, bidding him at the same time keep the clock for *his* sake. The procession was a remarkable one. On each side of the king marched a line of soldiers, while before him and behind him were a guard of halberdiers, their drums beating and colours flying. On his right hand was Bishop Juxon, and on his left hand Colonel Tomlinson, both bareheaded. There is a tradition that during his walk he pointed out a tree, not far from the entrance to Spring Gardens, which he said had been planted by his brother Henry. He was subjected to more than one annoyance during his progress. On reaching the spot where the Horse Guards now stand, Charles ascended a staircase which then communicated with Whitehall Palace, and passing along the famous gallery which at that time ran across the street, was conducted to his usual bedchamber, where he remained till summoned by Hacker to the scaffold."

"This day," according to a contemporary MS.,

queting House upon planks, made purposely to the scaffold. He was not long there, and what he spoke was to the two bishops, Dr. Juxon and Dr. Morton. To Dr. Juxon he gave his hat and cloak. He prayed with them, walked twice or thrice about the scaffold, and held out his hands to the people.

QUEEN ELIZABETH. (*From the Portrait by Zucchero,* 1575.)

"his Majesty died upon a scaffold at Whitehall. His children were with him last night. To the Duke of Gloucester he gave his 'George;' to the Lady Elizabeth his ring off his finger. He told them his subjects had many things to give *their* children, but that was all he had to give them. This day, about one o'clock, he came from St. James's in a long black cloak and grey stockings. The Palsgrave came through the Park with him. He was faint, and was forced to sit down and rest in the Park. He went into Whitehall the usual way out of the Park, and so came out of the Ban-

His last words, as I am informed, were, 'To your power I must submit, but your authority I deny.' He pulled his doublet off, and kneeled down to the block himself. When some officer offered to un-button him, or some such like thing, he thrust him from him. Two men, in vizards and false hair, were appointed to be his executioners. Who they were is not known. Some say he that did it was the common hangman; others, that it was one Captain Foxley, and that the hangman refused. The Bishop of London had been constantly with him since sentence was given. Since he died they have made proclamation that no man, upon pain of I know not what, shall presume to proclaim his son Prince Charles as King; and this is all I have yet heard of this sad day's work."

It has often been denied that the *front* of White-hall was the actual scene of the execution of King Charles I. But the fact that the sad scene was witnessed by Archbishop Usher from the roof of Wallingford House, which stood on the spot now occupied by the Admiralty, establishes the precise

observed by his own servant and others that stood near him, he had fainted away. So they presently carried him down and laid him upon his bed." The warrant for the execution, too, expressly commanded that the bloody deed should take place " in the open street before Whitehall." Mr. J. W. Croker denied that this was the actual scene, on the ground that "the street in front of the Banqueting House did not then exist." The contemporary prints, however, show that Croker was in error in

OLD VIEW OF WHITEHALL YARD. (*See page* 335.)

locality. "The Archbishop," says his biographer, "lived at my Lady Peterborough's house, near Charing Cross; and on the day that King Charles was put to death he got upon the leads, at the desire of some of his friends, to see his beloved sovereign for the last time. When he came upon the leads the King was in his speech; he stood motionless for some time, and sighed, and then, lifting up his tears to heaven, seemed to pray very earnestly. But when his Majesty had done speaking, and had pulled off his cloak and doublet, and stood stripped in his waistcoat, and that the villains in vizards began to put up his hair, the good Bishop, no longer able to endure so horrible a sight, grew pale and began to faint; so that if he had not been

this assertion, for the high road from Charing Cross to Westminster ran then, as now, under the very windows of the Banqueting Hall. Mr. J. H. Jesse confirms, by the evidence of his own eyes, the assertion of George Herbert (who attended the king to the last), that "a passage was broken through the wall by which the king passed unto the scaffold." He writes:—

"Having curiosity enough to visit the interior of the building, the walls of which were then [at the renovation of the Banqueting House] laid bare, a space was pointed out to the writer between the upper and lower centre windows, of about seven feet in height and four in breadth, the bricks of which presented a broken and jagged appearance, and the brickwork introduced was evidently of a different date from that of the rest of the building. There can be little doubt that it was through this passage that Charles walked to the fatal stage."

Pennant confirms the circumstantial account given above, stating that the passage broken in the wall in order to make a passage for Charles to the scaffold still remained when he wrote, forming the door to a small additional building of later date.

It is on record, and attested on all hands, that the king walked to the scaffold with a cheerful countenance and a firm and undaunted step, as one who was convinced that he died in a good cause and with a good conscience. Thus it comes to pass that one who certainly was no partisan of Charles I., or an advocate of the "divine right of kings," Andrew Marvell, penned such lines as these:

> " While round the armèd bands
> Did clasp their bloody hands,
> He nothing common did, or mean,
> Upon that memorable scene,
> Nor called the gods, with vulgar spite,
> To vindicate his hopeless right;
> But with his keener eye
> The axe's edge did try;
> Then bowed his kingly head
> Down, as upon a bed."

In a rare book, called "Gleanings," by R. Groves, published in 1651, we find noticed the following coincidence, which is certainly singular, if true :— " King Charles was beheaded in that very place where the first blood was shed in the beginning of our late troubles ; for a company of the citizens returning from Westminster, where they had been petitioning quietly for justice, were set upon by some of the Court as they passed Whitehall : in the which tumult divers were hurt and one or more were slain just by the Banqueting House, in the place where stood the scaffold on which he suffered. 'Tis further remarkable," adds the writer, "that he should end his days in a tragedie at the Banqueting House, where he had seene and caused many a comedy to be acted on the Lord's Day."

" By a signal providence," says Wheatley, "the bloody rebels chose that day for murdering their king on which the history of our Saviour's sufferings (Matt. xxvii.) was appointed to be read as a lesson. The blessed martyr had forgot that it came in the ordinary course ; and therefore, when Bishop Juxon (who read the morning office immediately before his martyrdom) named this chapter, the good prince asked him if he had singled it out as fit for the occasion : and when he was informed it was the lesson for the day, could not without a simple complacency and joy admire how suitably it concurred with his circumstances."

In this day, even those who hold that the execution of the king was unjustifiable are not likely to go so far as to endorse the exaggerated sentiments of the following epitaph, which we find in the " Eikon Basilike," published in 1648, when the irritation against the regicides was at its highest pitch :—

> " So falls the stately cedar ; while it stood,
> That was the onely glory of the wood;
> Great Charles, thou earthly god, celestial man,
> Whose life, like others, though it were a span,
> Yet in that span was comprehended more
> Than earth hath waters, or the ocean shore ;
> Thy heavenly virtues angels should rehearse,
> It is a theam too high for humane verse.
> Hee that would know thee right, then let him look
> Upon thy rare-incomparable book,
> And read it or'e and or'e, which if he do,
> Hee'll find thee king, and priest, and prophet too,
> And sadly see our losse, and though in vain,
> With fruitlesse wishes, call thee back again.
> Nor shall oblivion sit upon thy herse,
> Though there were neither monument nor verse.
> Thy suff'rings and thy death let no man name ;
> It was thy glorie, but the kingdom's shame."

A question has often been asked, who was the executioner of Charles I. ? We do not mean, who were the men at whose bidding the deed was done ? — for their names have all come down to posterity as those of "the regicides" —but, whose hand actually dealt the blow? There are undoubtedly very strong reasons for believing that it was Richard Brandon, a resident in Rosemary Lane, the entry of whose death occurs in the register of St. Mary's, Whitechapel, under date June 21st, 1649.[*] To the entry is appended a note, evidently of about the same date, to the effect that "this R. Brandon is supposed to have cut off the head of Charles the First." This man is stated to have been the son of Gregory Brandon, who beheaded Lord Strafford, and may therefore be said to have claimed the gallows as his inheritance. Besides, in the " Confessions of Richard Brandon, the Hangman " (1649), we meet with the following passage :—" He [Brandon] likewise confessed that he had thirty pounds for his pains, all paid him in half-crowns within an hour after the blow was given, and that he had an orange stuck full of cloves and a handkercher out of the king's pocket, so soon as he was carried from the scaffold, for which orange he was proffered twenty shillings by a gentleman in Whitehall, but refused the same, and afterwards sold it for ten shillings in Rosemary Lane." If this indeed be true, it follows that the man who struck the fatal blow did not long survive the deed. He was buried in Whitechapel churchyard ; and it was with

---

* See Vol. II., p. 143.

great difficulty that his interment was effected, so strong was the popular loathing against him. Various authorities, however, at different times, have charged with the deed Dun (styled in one of Butler's poems "Squire Dun"), Gregory Brandon, William Walker, Richard Brandon, Hugh Peters, Colonel Joyce, William Hewlett, and lastly, Lord Stair. Against some of these the accusation is utterly groundless. According to Sir Nathaniel Wraxall, George Selwyn, "that insatiable amateur of executions," told the story of King Charles's execution from information which he professed to have obtained from the Duchess of Portsmouth, who, he said, "always asserted, on the authority of Charles the Second, that the king, his father, was not beheaded by either Colonel Joyce or Colonel Pride, as was then commonly believed; but that the real name of the executioner was *Gregory* Brandon; that this man had worn a black crape stretched over his face, and had no sooner taken off the king's head than he was put into a boat at Whitehall Stairs, together with the block, the black cloth that covered it, the axe, and every other article that had been stained with the royal blood. Being conveyed to the Tower, all the implements used in the decapitation had been immediately reduced to ashes. A purse containing one hundred broad pieces of gold was then delivered to Brandon, and he was dismissed. He survived the transaction many years, but divulged it a short time before he died. This account," Wraxall adds, "as coming from the Duchess of Portsmouth, challenges great respect."

By Lilly's Life it would appear that the man who acted as the executioner of Charles I. was Lieut.-Colonel Joyce; but whether it was Joyce's or Brandon's hand that shed the king's blood, it is impossible to say with absolute certainty, and the question must be classed with the many that have to be regarded as insoluble.

CHAPTER XLIV.

WHITEHALL AND ITS HISTORICAL ASSOCIATIONS (*continued*).

" Lucent genialibus altis
Aurea fulcra toris, epulæque ante ora paratæ
Regifico luxo."—*Virg. Æn.* vi.

A Singular Prophecy—The Ill-fated Bust of Charles I.—Charles I. as a Patron of the Fine Arts—Relics of the "Martyr King"—"Touching" for the King's Evil—Anecdote of "Archy," the King's Jester, and Archbishop Laud—The Restoration of Charles II.—Charles II. and Lady Castlemaine—Loose Life of the Court—Catharine of Braganza—Dr. South and Lord Lauderdale—Visits of John Evelyn to White-hall—Sir William Penn—The Duke of Monmouth—The Last Hours and Death of Charles II.—The Last of the Stuarts—Whitehall as the Focus of Political Intrigue, and the Chief Staple of News—Serious Conflagrations at Whitehall.

MANY are the tales and anecdotes to which the life and death of King Charles gave rise, but among them, perhaps, few are more singular than the subjoined "prophecy," referred to by Howell in a letter to Sir Edward Spencer, dated February 20th, 1647–8 :—" Surely the witch of Endor is no fable ; the burning Joan of Arc at Rouen, and the Marchioness d'Ancre, of late years, in Paris, are no fables : the execution of Nostradamus for a kind of witch, some fourscore years since, who, among other things, foretold that the '*Senate of London will kill their King.*'"

Mr. Timbs, in his "Romance of London," relates a strange story of the ill-fated bust of Charles I. carved by Bernini, on the authority of a pamphlet on the character of Charles I., by Zachary Grey, LL.D. :—" Vandyke having drawn the king in three different faces—a profile, three-quarters, and a full face—the picture was sent to Rome for Bernini to make a bust from it. He was unaccountably dilatory in the work ; and upon this being complained of, he said that he had set about it several times, but there was something so unfortunate in the features of the face that he was shocked every time he examined it, and forced to leave off the work ; and if there was any stress to be laid on physiognomy, he was sure the person whom the picture represented was destined to a violent end. The bust was at last finished, and sent to England. As soon as the ship that brought it arrived in the river, the king, who was very impatient to see the bust, ordered it to be carried immediately to Chelsea. It was conveyed thither, and placed upon a table in the garden, whither the king went with a train of nobility to inspect the bust. As they were viewing it, a hawk flew over their heads with a partridge in its claws which he had wounded to death. Some of the partridge's blood fell upon the neck of the bust, where it remained without being wiped off. This bust was placed over the door of the king's closet at Whitehall, and continued there until the palace was destroyed by fire."

It is generally stated that Charles I. showed himself a most liberal patron of the arts. That this may have been true to some extent, cannot be doubted; but it may be desirable here to record the fact that among the State Papers there is, or was some years ago, a long bill sent in by Vandyke, for work done, and docketed by the king's own hand. The picture of his Majesty dressed for the chase, for which Vandyke charged £200, is assessed by the King at £100 instead, and in many other instances there is even a greater reduction made. Other pictures the King marked with a cross, which is explained by a note at the back by Endymion Porter, to the effect that as they were to be paid for by the Queen, his Majesty had left them for his wife to reduce at her own pleasure.

It may be added that, in spite of having done so much work for royalty, Vandyke died poor, and that his daughter was allowed a small pension—which, by the way, was most irregularly paid—on account of sums owing to her father's estate by Charles I. We are accustomed to rank Charles II. with bad paymasters, but it is to be feared that his father obtained his reputation as an art patron at much too cheap a rate.

It is also stated that King Charles I. possessed numerous portraits, drawn by Holbein, of several personages of the Court of Henry VIII., from the highest down to Mrs. Jack or Jackson, the nurse of King Edward VI. These drawings, it is said, the King exchanged for a single picture; but how they came back into the possession of the Crown is not clear. Mr. J. T. Smith, in his "Book for a Rainy Day," says that they were discovered at Kensington Palace, and taken from their frames and bound in two volumes. It would be interesting to know whether they are still in existence.

A vignette of the Bible used by King Charles I. upon the scaffold, and presented by him to Dr. Juxon, the Bishop of London, who attended him in his last moments, will be found in Smith's "Historical and Literary Curiosities."

The shirt, stained on the wrist with some drops of blood, in which Charles I. was beheaded, also his watch, which he gave at the place of execution to Mr. John Ashburnham, his white silk drawers, and the sheet that was thrown over his body, were long preserved in the vestry of Ashburnham Church, in Sussex, having been, as the "Beauties of England and Wales" informs us, "bequeathed, in 1743, by Bertram Ashburnham, Esq., to the clerk of the parish and his successors for ever, to be exhibited as curiosities." These relics of the "martyr king," we may add, have somehow found their way back into the hands of the Ashburnham family, and are now very carefully preserved at Ashburnham Place, the seat of the earls of that name. This mansion

was built by John Ashburnham, who was "page of the bed-chamber" to both Charles I. and Charles II., and who died in 1671. He attended his sovereign to the last, till he fell on the scaffold, and thus obtained possession of the articles worn by the king on that mournful occasion. Horsfield tells us that "the superstitious of the last, and even of the present age, have occasionally resorted to these relics for the cure of the king's evil."

With reference to the supposed efficacy of the touch of royalty in curing diseases, we may state that, under the Stuarts, there might be seen in the gazettes occasional advertisements announcing when and where a gracious king would next cure his subjects of scrofula by a touch of his royal finger. As may readily be supposed, the Palace at Whitehall was the place most frequently chosen for the "touching" or the "healing." Here is one of the notices issued by command of Charles I. :—
"Whitehall, May 16, 1644.—His Sacred Majesty having declared it to be his Royal will and purpose to continue the healing of his people for the Evil during the month of May, and then to give over till Michaelmas next, I am commanded to give notice thereof, that the people may not come up to town in the interim, and lose their labour."

Charles II. is said to have "touched" 92,000 people for the king's evil—about twenty a day for his whole reign. The practice was continued by James II., for Evelyn, in his "Diary," under date of 1687, writes, "I saw his Majesty touch for the evil." The word "touching" gives us a most inadequate idea of the deliberate solemnity of this ceremonial in the days of the Stuarts. Imagine the king seated in a chair of state upon his throne, under a rich canopy, in a spacious hall of the palace. Each surgeon led his patients in turn to the foot of the throne, where they knelt, and while a chaplain in full canonicals intoned the words, "He put His hands upon them and healed them," the king stroked their faces with both hands at once. When all had been thus "touched," they came up to the throne again in the same order, and the king hung about the neck of each, by a blue ribbon, a golden coin, while the chaplain chanted, "This is the true Light who came into the world." And the whole concluded with the reading of the epistle for the day and prayers for the sick.

The following description of the process of "touching" for the king's evil we take from Oudert's MS. Diary :—"A young gentlewoman, Elizabeth Stephens, of the age of sixteen, came to the Presence Chamber in 1640, to be 'touched for the Evil,' with which she was so afflicted that, by her own and her mother's testimony, she had not seen with her left eye for above a month. After prayers read by Dr. Sanderson, she knelt down to be 'touched,' with the rest, by the King. His Majesty then touched her in the usual manner, and put a ribbon with a piece of money hanging to it about her neck. Which done, his Majesty turned to the Duke of Richmond, the Earl of Southampton, and the Earl of Lindsey, to discourse with them. And the young gentlewoman said of her own accord, openly, 'Now, God be praised, I can see of this sore eye,' and afterwards declared that she did see more and more by it, and could by degrees endure the light of the candle." The Bourbon kings of France were supposed to possess a like power of healing, in virtue of their descent from St. Louis. On the day after their coronation at Rheims they went in procession to the Abbey of St. Rémy, in that city, in the garden of which convent they touched all those afflicted with the evil that were brought to them, making the sign of the cross with their fingers on the forehead of the sick person, saying, "Le Roi vous touche ; Dieu vous guérisse."

The form of prayer for the healing, we may add, is still to be seen in old Prayer-books, bound up with the rest of the occasional services. It was not dropped out till the reign of George I.

A capital story is told about "Archy," the king's fool, and Archbishop Laud, in connection with the Court of Whitehall. It is thus told in "The Book of Table Talk," published by Charles Knight :— "When news arrived from Scotland of the bad reception which the king's proclamation respecting the Book of Common Prayer had met with there, Archibald, the king's fool, happening to meet the Archbishop of Canterbury, who was going to the council-table, said to his grace, 'Wha's feule now? doth not your grace hear the news from Striveling about the Liturgy?'" But the poor jester soon learned that Laud was not a person whom even his jester's coat and privileged folly permitted him to tamper with. The primate immediately laid his complaint before the Council. How far it was attended to, the following order of Council, issued the very day on which the offence was committed, will show :—'At Whitehall, the 11th of March, 1637. It is this day ordered by his Majesty, with the advice of the Board, that Archibald Armstrong, the King's Fool, for certain scandalous words of a high nature spoken by him against the Lord Archbishop of Canterbury his Grace, and proved to be uttered by him by two witnesses, shall have his coat pulled over his head and be discharged of the King's service and banished the Court ; for which the Lord Chamberlain of the King's household is prayed and required to give order to be executed.'

And immediately the same was put into execution." Thus was poor Archy degraded and dismissed from his Majesty's service. "What was this," asks Leigh Hunt, "but to say that the fool was fool no longer? 'Write me down an ass,' says 'Dogberry,' in the comedy. 'Write down that Archy is no fool,' says King Charles in Council. 'He has called the Archbishop one ; and therefore we are all agreed, his Grace included, that the man has proved himself to be no longer entitled to the appellation.'" Archy, it appears, had on a previous occasion, when called upon to say grace before meat, incurred the displeasure of Archbishop Laud, by saying, "Great laud to the king, and little Laud to the devil."

In a pamphlet printed in 1641, entitled "Archy's Dream : sometime Jester to His Majestie, but exiled the Court by Canterburie's malice, with a relation for whom an odde chair stood void in hell," the following reason is given for Archy's banishment from Court :—"A certain nobleman asking him what he would do with his handsome daughters, he replied that he knew very well what to do with *them*, but he had sons whom he knew not what to do with ; he would gladly make scholars of them, but that he feared the archbishop would cut off their ears."

In the "Strafford Letters" will be found, as Mr. Jesse reminds us in his work on "London," several interesting notices of Archbishop Laud passing between his palace at Lambeth and the royal palace at Whitehall. For example, in one of his letters to the earl, alluding to his health as not so good as it was formerly, he expresses a regret that "in consequence of his elevation to the see of Canterbury he has now simply to glide across the river in his barge, when on his way either to the Court or the Star Chamber ; whereas, when Bishop of London, there were five miles of rough road between Fulham Palace and Whitehall, the jolting over which in his coach he describes as having been very beneficial to his health."

On his restoration, May 29th, 1660, King Charles II. was brought back hither "in military fashion" through London, by way of the Strand, "all the streetes and windows even to Whitehall being replenished with innumerable people of all conditions." It must have been indeed a gay sight to have seen the king returning to the palace of his ancestors, and the demonstrations of joy on the occasion are described as having been extravagant in the extreme. Space will not permit us to enter into the details of the enthusiastic reception on the part of the Londoners, or of the seven hours' ride through the streets to Whitehall ; all this will be found described with picturesque minuteness in the pages of Sir Edward Walker's "Manner of the Most Happy Return in England of our most gracious Sovereign Lord, King Charles the Second," and also at page 702 of Whitelock's "Memorials."

notice of each other; only at first entry he put off his hat, and she made him a very civil salute; but afterwards they took no notice one of another; but both of them now and then would take their child, which the nurse held in her arms, and dandle it."

THE HOLBEIN GATEWAY, WHITEHALL. *From a Drawing by G. Vertue.* (*See page* 362.)

On the 23rd of August, 1662, the King and Queen came by water from Hampton Court, and landed at "Whitehall Bridge," as the Stairs were often called. On this occasion Pepys draws our attention to the presence of the celebrated Lady Castlemaine, and also of her husband. "But that which pleased me most was that my Lady Castlemaine stood over against us on a piece of Whitehall. But methought it was strange to see her lord and her upon the same place, walking up and down and taking no

Pepys tells us distinctly that the removal of Lord Clarendon from place and power was "certainly designed in my Lady Castlemaine's chamber," and he adds that he saw "several of the gallants of Whitehall" staying to see the Lord Chancellor pass by, and talking to her in her "birdcage."

The loose life led by the Court of Charles II. at Whitehall—or, indeed, wherever it may have been quartered—is a matter of historic notoriety. A good insight into these royal escapades is given by

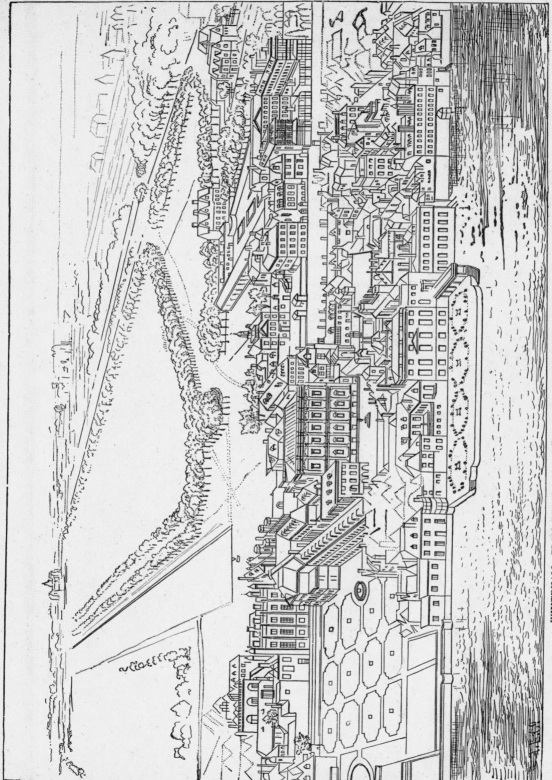

WHITEHALL, FROM THE RIVER. (*From a Copy by Smith of a View taken shortly after the Fire.*)

quaint old Pepys, who, writing in his "Diary" under date April 25th, 1663, says: "I did hear that the Queene is much grieved of late at the King's neglecting her, he not having supped with her once this quarter of a year, and almost every night with Lady Castlemaine, who hath been with him this St. George's Feast at Windsor." It is said by several retailers of Court gossip that the king spent in Lady Castlemaine's apartments the whole of the week previous to the arrival of his wife, Catherine of Braganza.

Here, probably, and not, as usually supposed, at the house of Sir Samuel Morland, at Vauxhall, Charles II. first spent his hours in dalliance with Barbara Palmer, afterwards Countess of Castle-maine and Duchess of Cleveland, of whom we shall have more to say anon, when we reach the neighbourhood of St. James's Palace. Her apart-ments, or lodgings, according to the privately-printed "Memoir" of the lady by Mr. G. S. Stein-man, were on that part of Whitehall which bordered on the Holbein Gateway, on the south side of a detached pile of buildings leading to the Cock-pit, not far from the top of King Street.

Pepys, in his "Diary," notes the fact that on more than one Sunday he "observed how the Duke and Mrs. Palmer" (the subsequent Duchess) "did talk to one another very wantonly" in the chapel, during service-time, "through the hangings that part the king's closet and the closet where the ladies sit." Her presence here was indeed a standing insult to Charles's poor queen, Catharine of Braganza, to whom her ladyship must have caused many a heartfelt pang as a wife.

But if such was the case with Lady Castlemaine. it would seem, however, that the maids of honour and the other ladies of the Court of Whitehall were left very much to their own devices under the Stuart *régime*, and were not subject to any very strict control. "What mad freaks the mayds of honour at the Court do have!" writes Pepys in his "Diary." "That Mrs. Jennings, one of the Duchess's maids, the other day dressed herself up like an orange-wench, and went up and down and cried oranges, till, falling down by some accident, her fine shoes were discovered, and she put to a great deal of shame: so that such as these tricks and worse among them, thereby few will venture upon them for wives."

To the lax and immoral Court the Queen seems to have shown herself a marked exception. "To Whitehall," writes Pepys in his "Diary" in June, 1664, "where Mr. Pearce showed me the Queene's bed-chamber and her closet, where she had nothing but some pretty pious pictures, and books of

devotion; and her holy water at her head as she sleeps; with a clock at her bedside, wherein burns a lamp that tells her the hour of the night at any time." Poor lonely Catherine of Braganza! it was probably at a very late hour of the night, or rather a very early hour of the morning, that the hands of her clock pointed to when Charles entered that room, after "supping with Lady Castlemaine" and other rivals of the Queen in his royal affections. No wonder that Charles did not find it compatible with his gallantries that his wife should be living at Whitehall, and, therefore, that he should have quietly disposed of her in lodgings at Somerset House, as we have seen in a previous chapter.

King Charles II., and his religious instructors, too, have been the theme of numerous *bon mots*. One of these has reference to Dr. South, who once, preaching before the king and his profligate Court at Whitehall, perceived in the middle of his sermon that sleep had taken possession of all his hearers. The doctor stopped, and changing his tone of voice, called three times to Lord Lauderdale, who, start-ing up, "My lord," said South, with great com-posure, "I am sorry to interrupt your repose, but I must beg you will not snore so loud, lest you awaken his Majesty."

In the year 1682 the Russian, Moroccan, and East Indian ambassadors all happened to be in London at the same time, and Evelyn, in his "Diary," gives us an amusing account of an even-ing which he spent in the company of those from Africa at the rooms of the Duchess of Portsmouth, in Whitehall.

It was at Whitehall, as Pepys tells us in his "Diary," that he found his friend Mr. Coventry chatting over a map of America with Sir William Penn.

In February, 1686, as he tells us in his "Diary," John Evelyn "came to lodge at Whitehall, in the Lord Privy Seal's lodgings."

Here James Walters, Duke of Monmouth, the natural son of Charles II., was allowed to assume the airs, and indeed all but the name, of royalty, and would stand with his hat on his head, as Macaulay remarks, when the Howards and the Seymours stood uncovered.

It was at the Court at Whitehall that Sidney, Lord Godolphin, the veteran statesman and courtier, was brought up as a page.

Having been the residence of so many of our English sovereigns in succession, the walls of Whitehall have witnessed many curious and inte-resting scenes, some also over which perhaps it would be well if a veil could be drawn. Foremost among such scenes may be reckoned the death of

Charles II., the details of which, gathered from Evelyn, and Burnet, and some other sources, have been worked up by Macaulay into a most effective picture, which has also employed the pencil of at least one modern painter of eminence.

"The palace," writes Macaulay, "had seldom presented a gayer or more scandalous appearance than on the evening of Sunday, the 1st of February, 1685. Some grave persons, who had gone thither, after the fashion of that age, to pay their duty to their sovereign, and who had expected that on such a day his Court would wear a decent aspect, were struck with astonishment and horror. The great gallery of Whitehall, an admirable relic of the magnificence of the Tudors, was crowded with revellers and gamblers. The king sat there chatting and toying with three women, whose charms were the boast and whose vices were the disgrace of three nations. Barbara Palmer, Duchess of Cleveland, was there, no longer young, but still retaining some traces of that superb and voluptuous loveliness which twenty years before overcame the hearts of all men. There, too, was the Duchess of Portsmouth, whose soft and infantine features were lighted up with the vivacity of France. Hortensia Mancini, Duchess of Mazarin, and niece of the great Cardinal, completed the group. . . . . While Charles flirted with his three sultanas, Hortensia's French page, a handsome boy, whose vocal performances were the delight of Whitehall, and were rewarded by numerous presents of rich clothes, ponies, and guineas, warbled some amatory verses. A party of twenty courtiers were seated at cards round a large table, on which gold was heaped in mountains. In the midst of this scene the king complained that he felt unwell; he was carried off to his chamber in a swoon, but recovered a little on being bled, or 'blooded,' as the phrase then went. He was laid on his bed, where, during a short time, the Duchess of Portsmouth hung over him with the familiarity of a wife. But the alarm had been given. The Queen and the Duchess of York were hastening to the room. The favourite concubine was forced to retire to her own apartments. Those apartments had been thrice pulled down and thrice rebuilt by her lover, to gratify her caprice. The very furniture of the chimney was massy silver. Several fine paintings, which properly belonged to the Queen, had been transferred to the dwelling of the mistress. The sideboards were piled with richly-wrought plate. In the niches stood cabinets, the masterpieces of Japanese art. On the hangings, fresh from the looms of Paris, were depicted, in tints which no English tapestry could rival, birds of gorgeous plumage,

landscapes, hunting-matches, the lordly terrace of Saint Germains, the statues and fountains of Versailles. In the midst of this splendour, purchased by guilt and shame, the unhappy woman gave herself up to an agony of grief which, to do her justice, was not wholly selfish.

"And now the gates of Whitehall, which ordinarily stood open to all comers, were closed; but persons whose faces were known were still permitted to enter. The ante-chambers and galleries were soon filled to overflowing, and even the sick room was crowded with peers, privy councillors, and foreign ministers; all the medical men of note in London were summoned. The Queen was for a time assiduous in her attendance. The Duke of York scarcely left his brother's bedside. The primate and four other bishops were then in London; they remained in London all day, and took it by turns to sit up at night in the king's room."

The services of the bishops, however, were not required. Macaulay remarks of the Duchess of Portsmouth that "a life of frivolity and vice had not extinguished in her all sentiments of religion, or all that kindness which is the glory of her sex." It was by her suggestion that a Roman Catholic priest, Father Huddleston, the same who had aided Charles in his escape after the battle of Worcester, was sent for, to offer the consolations of religion. The courtiers were all ordered to withdraw, except Duras, Lord Feversham, and Granville, Earl of Bath, both of whom were Protestants, and faithful friends. The rest shall be told in Macaulay's words:—"Even the physicians withdrew. The back door was then opened, and Father Huddleston entered. A cloak had been thrown over his sacred vestments, and his shaven crown was concealed by a flowing wig. 'Sir,' said the Duke [of York], 'this good man once saved your life. He now comes to save your soul.' Charles faintly answered, 'He is welcome.' Huddleston went through his part better than had been expected. He knelt by the bed, listened to the confession, pronounced the absolution, and administered extreme unction. He asked if the king wished to receive the Lord's Supper. 'Surely,' said Charles, 'if I am not unworthy.' The host was brought in. Charles feebly strove to rise and kneel before it. The priest bade him lie still, and assured him that God would accept the humiliation of his soul, and would not require the humiliation of his body. The king found so much difficulty in swallowing that it was necessary to open the door and procure a glass of water. This rite ended, the monk held up a crucifix before the penitent, charged him to fix his last thoughts on the sufferings of the Redeemer, and withdrew. The whole ceremony had occupied about three quarters of an hour, and during that time the courtiers who filled the outer room had communicated their suspicions to each other by whispers and significant glances. The door was at length thrown open, and the crowd again filled the chamber of death.

"It was now late in the evening. The king seemed much relieved by what had passed. His natural children were brought to his bedside, the Dukes of Grafton, Southampton, and Northumberland, sons of the Duchess of Cleveland; the Duke of St. Albans, son of Eleanor Gwynn; and the Duke of Richmond, son of the Duchess of Portsmouth. Charles blessed them all, but spoke with peculiar tenderness to Richmond. One face which should have been there was wanting. The eldest and beloved child was an exile and a wanderer; his name was not once mentioned by his father.

"During the night Charles earnestly recommended the Duchess of Portsmouth and her boy to the care of James. 'And do not,' he good-naturedly added, 'let poor Nelly starve.' The Queen sent excuses for her absence by Halifax. She said that she was too much disordered to resume her post by the couch, and implored pardon for any offence she might unwittingly have given. 'She ask my pardon, poor woman!' cried Charles; 'I ask hers, with all my heart.'

"The morning light began to peep through the windows of Whitehall, and Charles desired the attendants to pull aside the curtains, that he might have one more look at the day. He remarked that it was time to wind up a clock which stood near his bed. These little circumstances were long remembered, because they proved beyond dispute that while he declared himself a Roman Catholic he was in full possession of his faculties. He apologised to those who had stood round him all night for the trouble which he had caused. He had been, he said, a most unconscionable time dying, but he hoped they would excuse it. This was the last glimpse of that exquisite urbanity so often found potent to charm away the resentment of a justly incensed nation. Soon after dawn the speech of the dying man failed. Before ten his senses were gone. Great numbers had repaired to the churches at the hour of morning service. When the prayer for the king was read, loud groans and sobs showed how deeply his people felt for him. At noon on Friday, the 6th of February, he passed away without a struggle."

Since the time of Œdipus no royal line has equalled that of the Stuarts in its calamities. The first James of Scotland, adorned with the graces of poetry and chivalry, a wise legislator, a sagacious and resolute king, perished in his forty-fourth year. His son, the second James, was killed, in his thirtieth year, at the siege of Roxburgh Castle, by the bursting of a cannon. The third James, after the battle of Sauchieburn, in which his rebellious subjects were countenanced and aided by his own son, was stabbed, in his thirty-sixth year, beneath a humble roof, by a pretended priest. That son, the chivalrous madman of Flodden, compassed his own death and that of the flower of his kingdom, while only forty years of age, by a foolish knight-errantry. At an age ten years younger, his only son, James V., died of a broken heart. Over the suffering and follies—if we may not say crimes—and over the mournful and unwarrantable doom of the beauteous Mary, the world will never cease to debate. Her grandson expiated at Whitehall, by a bloody death, the errors chiefly induced by his self-will and his pernicious education. The second Charles, the "Merry Monarch," had a fate as sad as any of his ancestors; for though he died in his bed, his life was that of a heartless voluptuary, who had found in his years of seeming prosperity neither truth in man nor fidelity in woman. His brother, the bigot James, lost three kingdoms, and disinherited the dynasty, for his blind adherence to a faith that failed to regulate his life. The Old Pretender was a cipher, and the Young Pretender, after a youthful flash of promise, passed a useless life, and ended it as a drunken dotard. The last of the race, Henry, Cardinal York, died in 1804, a spiritless old man, and a pensioner of that House of Hanover against which his father and brother had waged war with no advantage to themselves, and with the forfeiture of life and lands, of liberty and country, to many of the noblest and most chivalrous inhabitants of our island.

Happy had it been for Charles II. if he had demeaned himself as well in his prosperous as in his adverse fortune. The recorded facts are highly honourable to him and the companions of his exile; while Cromwell, as the Queen of Bohemia said, was like the beast in the Revelation, that all kings and nations worshipped. Charles's horses, and some of them were favourites, were sold at Brussels, because he could not pay for their keep; and during the two years that he resided at Cologne he never kept a coach. So straitened were the exiles for money that even the postage of letters between Sir Richard Browne and Hyde was no easy burthen; and there was a mutiny in the ambassador's kitchen, because the maid "might not be trusted with the government, and the buying the meat, in which she was thought too lavish." Hyde writes that he had not been master of a crown for many months; that he was cold for want of clothes and fire; and for all the meat which he had eaten for three months he was in debt to a poor woman who was no longer able to trust. "Our necessities," he says, "would be more insupportable, if we did not see the king reduced to greater distress than you can believe or imagine." Of Charles, in prosperity, a few days before his death, Evelyn draws a fearful picture. Writing on the day when James was proclaimed, he says, "I can never forget the inexpressible luxury and profaneness, gaming, and all dissoluteness and, as it were, total forgetfulness of God (it being Sunday evening), which this day se'nnight I was witness of; the King sitting and toying with his concubines, Portsmouth, Cleaveland, and Mazarine, &c.; a French boy singing love-songs in that glorious gallery; whilst about twenty of the great courtiers and other dissolute persons were at basset round a large table, a bank of at least £2,000 in gold before them, upon which two gentlemen who were with me made reflections with astonishment. Six days after, all was in the dust!"

Whitehall, when Charles II. dwelt there, was the focus of political intrigue as well as of gaiety. "Half the jobbing and half the flirting of the metropolis," writes Macaulay, "went on under his roof. Whoever could make himself agreeable to the prince, or could secure the good offices of the mistress, might hope to rise in the world without rendering any service to the Government, without being even known by sight to any minister of state. This courtier got a frigate, and that a company; a third, the pardon of a rich offender; a fourth, a lease of Crown land on easy terms. If the king notified his pleasure that a briefless lawyer should be made a judge, or that a libertine baronet should be made a peer, the gravest counsellors, after a little murmuring, submitted. Interest, therefore, drew a constant press of suitors to the gates of the palace, and those gates always stood wide. The king kept open house every day, and all day long, for the good society of London, the extreme Whigs only excepted. Hardly any gentleman had any difficulty in making his way to the royal presence. The "levee" was exactly what the word imports. Some men of quality came every morning to stand round their master, to chat with him while his wig was combed and his cravat tied, and to accompany him in his early walk through the Park. All persons who had been properly introduced might, without any special invitation, go to see him dine, sup, dance, and play at hazard, and might have the pleasure of hearing him tell stories, which indeed he told remarkably well, about his flight from Worcester, and about the misery which he had endured when he was a State prisoner in the hands of the canting meddling preachers of Scotland. Bystanders whom his Majesty recognised often came in for a courteous word. This proved a far more successful kingcraft than any that his father or grandfather had practised. It was not easy for the most austere republican of the school of Marvell to resist the fascination of so much good humour and affability; and many a veteran Cavalier in whose heart the remembrance of unrequited sacrifices and services had been festering during twenty years, was compensated in one moment for wounds and sequestrations by his sovereign's kind nod, and 'God bless you, my old friend!'

"Whitehall naturally became the chief staple of news. Whenever there was a rumour that anything important had happened or was about to happen, people hastened thither to obtain intelligence from the fountain-head. The galleries presented the appearance of a modern club-room at an anxious time. They were full of people inquiring whether the Dutch mail was in; what tidings the express from France had brought; whether John Sobiesky had beaten the Turks; whether the Doge of Genoa was really at Paris. These were matters about which it was safe to talk aloud. But there were subjects concerning which information was asked and given in whispers. Had Halifax got the better of Rochester? Was there to be a Parliament? Was the Duke of York really going to Scotland? Had Monmouth really been summoned from the Hague? Men tried to read the countenance of every minister as he went through the throng to and from the royal closet. All sorts of auguries were drawn from the tone in which his Majesty spoke to the Lord President, or from the laugh with which his Majesty honoured a jest of the Lord Privy Seal; and in a few hours the hopes and fears inspired by such slight indications had spread to all the coffee-houses from St. James's to the Tower."

Notwithstanding the thirst for news and love of Court gossip, the Stuart kings appear to have lived here very much in public; so much so, indeed, that, if we may trust Macaulay, the "newswriters" of the reign of Charles II. would occasionally obtain admission into the gallery at Whitehall Palace, in order to tell their country friends how the king and duke looked, and what games the courtiers played at.

The sources from which Macaulay drew his information about the state of the Court are too numerous to recapitulate. Among them are the Despatches of Barillon, Van Citters, Ronquillo, and Adda; the Travels of the Grand Duke Cosmo; the Works of Roger North, the Diaries of Pepys and Evelyn, and the Memoirs of Grammont.

the labour of cutting a candle from a pound, burnt it off, and threw the rest carelessly by before the flame was out. It burnt violently till four next morning, and destroyed the Duchess of Portsmouth's lodgings, with all the stone gallery and buildings behind and down to the Thames." Six

THE KING STREET GATEWAY, WHITEHALL. (*See page 263.*)

The royal family of Stuart would seem to have been as unfortunate in their domestic servants as in their fate; for Northouck tells us that twice within a few years, in the reign of William and Mary, the Palace of Whitehall suffered serious damage by fire; firstly in April, 1691, when a large part of it was destroyed "through the negligence of a maid-servant, who, about eight o'clock at night," says the very circumstantial Northouck, "to save

years later, we learn from the same authority, by "the carelessness of a laundress," all the body of the Palace, with the new gallery, council-chamber, and several adjoining apartments, shared the same fate. It was with the greatest difficulty that the Banqueting Hall was saved. "The king," adds Northouck, "sent message after message from Kensington, for its preservation;" though it is hard to see how even royal "messengers" could have been of as much use as a few rude fire-engines.

Another event connected with Whitehall in the reigns of the Stuarts, should be mentioned here—namely, that within its walls the devotion of the "Sacred Heart," devised by Sister Marguerite Mary Alacoque at Paray-le-Monial, in France, was first publicly preached and taught in England, by Father Colombiere, the confessor of the Duchess of York—Mary of Modena, afterwards queen of James II.

SIR HENRY LEE OF DITCHLEY. *From a Portrait by Basire.* (*See page* 364.)

CHAPTER XLV.

WHITEHALL.—THE BUILDINGS DESCRIBED.

"*Donec templa refeceris.*"—*Horace.*

Description of the Old Palace—Additions made by Henry VIII.—The Holbein Gateway—Westminster Gate—Knights of the Tilt-yard—Inigo Jones' Design for a New Palace—Residence of the Ladies and Gentlemen of the Court—An Ingenious Design for Rebuilding Whitehall—Description of the Banqueting House—The Chapel Royal—Rubens' Painted Ceiling—"Maunday" Thursday—The Statue of James II.

ALTHOUGH the present remains of Whitehall are comparatively modern, not reaching farther back than the time of the Tudors, yet we know, as recorded above, that a stately palace stood on this spot as early as the reign of Henry III., when the Chief Justice of England, Hubert de Burgh, Earl of Kent, resided in it. At his death he left it to the "Black" Friars of Holborn, who sold it to the

Archbishop of York; and his successors in that metropolitan see made it their town residence for nearly three centuries. The last of the archbishops who tenanted it was Cardinal Wolsey, under whom it became one of the most sumptuous palaces in England.

The ancient palace of Whitehall, if we include its precincts, was of great extent, stretching from close to where now stands Westminster Bridge nearly up to Scotland Yard. It comprised a hall, chapel, banqueting-house, and other apartments, as "Henry VIII.'s Gallery," the "Boarded Gallery," the "Matted Gallery," the "Shield Gallery," the "Stone Gallery," the "Adam and Eve Gallery" (so named from the picture by Mabuse), and the "Vane Room." Some idea of the extent of the palace early in the sixteenth century may be formed from the following description of it, which occurs in the Act of Parliament by which it was given to the royal tyrant. Here it is styled "one great mansion-place and house, being a parcel of the possessions of the Archbishopric of York, situate in the town of Westminster, not much distant from the same ancient palace." And referring to Cardinal Wolsey, it adds that "he had lately, upon the soil of the said mansion-place and house, and upon ground thereunto belonging, most sumptuously and curiously built and edified many and distinct beautiful, costly, and pleasant lodgings, buildings, and mansions for his grace's singular pleasure, comfort, and commodity, to the honour of his highness and the realm; and thereunto adjoining had made a park, walled and environed with brick and stone; and then devised and ordained many and singular commodious things, pleasures, and other necessaries, apt and convenient to appertain to so noble a prince for his pastime and pleasure." And it must be owned that if the prints of the period are to be trusted, this description is not overdrawn. By the same Act of Parliament it was directed to be called "The King's Palace at Westminster" for ever. Its limits were defined on the one side by the "street leading from Charing Cross unto the Sanctuary Gate at Westminster," and on the other by "the water of the Thames." At this time it consisted of "a mansion with two gardens and three acres of land." Henry VIII., as we have shown in a preceding chapter, added very considerably to the buildings; and he likewise ordered a tennis-court, a cock-pit, and bowling-greens to be formed, "with other conveniences for various kinds of diversion." Here Holbein painted the portraits of Henry VII. and Henry VIII., with their queens, and also the "Dance of Death." Here, too—or, rather, across the roadway in front, leading from Charing Cross to Westminster—he built his famous gateway.

Holbein had been induced to come over to England through the reputation of the taste and generosity of Henry VIII. He was introduced to the king by the instrumentality of Sir Thomas More, at his house at Chelsea, where a number of the painter's works had been recently ranged round the walls. Taken immediately into the king's service, Holbein had apartments assigned to him in the old palace at Whitehall, for which he designed, at the king's request, in 1546, the gateway above alluded to. It stood in front of the palace, opposite the Tilt-yard, and was flanked on either side by a low brick building of a single storey in height. Its position was a little nearer to Westminster Abbey than the north-west corner of York House. The edifice was constructed of small square stones and flint boulders, of two distinct colours, "glazed and disposed in a tessellated manner." On each front there were four busts or medallions, "naturally coloured and gilt," which are stated to have resisted all influences of the weather. They were of terra-cotta, as large as life, or even a little larger, and represented some of the chief characters of the age. Among them were Henry VII., Henry VIII., and Bishop Fisher. These busts were believed by some persons to have been the work of an Italian artist named Torregiano; but Mr. Cunningham, in an article on the subject in the *Gentleman's Magazine* for June, 1866, inclines to the opinion that they were executed by John de Maiano, the sculptor of the medallions on Hampton Court Gateway. On either side of the archway were lofty embattled octagonal turrets, the faces of which, between the windows, were likewise ornamented with busts, &c. The rooms above the archway were long used as the State Paper Office.

The Holbein Gateway, as it was generally called, was removed in 1749-50, in order to widen the street and approaches to Westminster. After its demolition most of the glazed bricks and stone dressings of this historical building, rich in two centuries of associations with our kings, from Henry VIII. to William III., "were sold to repair the high roads."

Mr. J. T. Smith, in his "Antiquities of Westminster," in alluding to this gateway, says: "It is scarcely to be supposed that, in the time of Hubert de Burgh's residence here, there was anything like that noble space which the width of the street opposite Whitehall now (1807) affords. On the contrary, the probability seems to be that there was not, and it is far more likely that it did not at that time exceed the breadth of the present King Street.

Passing by Whitehall the street was continued along a street of this same width, which originally had on its eastern side the wall of part of the garden, or orchard, or other ground, if we may trust honest John Stow, belonging to Whitehall, as may be seen in the plan made in 1680, by John Fisher, a surveyor at that time, and which was afterwards engraved by Vertue. On the western side this street had the wall of that enclosure since converted into St. James's Park ; but when Henry VIII. had acquired possession of Whitehall in 1531, by exchanging with the abbot and convent of Westminster, he procured to himself this enclosure, part of which he converted into the before-mentioned park, and on the rest he erected a tennis-court, a cock-pit, a bowling-alley, a long stone gallery— which was for some time occupied by the late Duke of Dorset, and subsequently by Lord Whitworth— and other buildings, many of which are wholly, or in part, still (1807) remaining."

This building, it appears, the king connected with the palace on the opposite side by two gateways across the street ; one of them at about the middle of King Street, which was demolished in 1723 ; the other, nearer to Charing Cross, adjoining the north-east corner of the gallery abovementioned, was the gateway designed by Hans Holbein. This latter gate, it is stated in the " New View of London" (1708), was termed "Cock-pit Gate," and it is said to have been "an extraordinarily beautiful gate." The writer thus describes it : " It is built of square stone, with small squares of flint boulder, very neatly set. It has also battlements, and four lofty towers ; and the whole is enriched with busts, roses, portcullises, and queen's arms, both on the north and south sides. There are no gates hung at present, but the hinges show there have been. This is an aperture from the Cock-pit into the broad part of Charing Cross, before Whitehall Gate." We have given views of both these gates, copied from old prints published while they were standing. The Holbein Gateway is shown on page 354, and the King Street Gateway on page 360.

On the taking down of this latter gate it was begged and obtained by William, Duke of Cumberland, son of George II., and then Ranger of Windsor Park and Forest, with the view of reerecting it at the end of the Long Walk, in the Great Park at Windsor. The stones were accordingly removed, but the re-building of it at Windsor appears to have been abandoned. Some of the material, however, we are told, was, by the Duke's direction, worked up in several different buildings erected by the Duke in the Great Park. " A

medallion from it," adds Mr. J. T. Smith, " is in one of the fronts of a keeper's lodge, near Virginia Water. A similar medallion, part of it also, is in another cottage, built about the year 1790, in the Great Park, and accessible from the road from Peascod Street, by the barracks. Other stones form the basement as high as the dado or moulding, and also the cornice, of the inside of a chapel at the Great Lodge, which chapel was begun in the Duke's lifetime, but was unfinished at his death." The busts were, in number, four on each side ; they had ornamented mouldings round them, and were of baked clay, in proper colours, and glazed in the manner of Delft ware, which had preserved them entire. Mr. Smith, in the " Antiquities of Westminster," says that after the gate was taken down three of the busts fell into the hands of a man who kept an old iron shop in Belton Street, St. Giles's, to whom, it is supposed, they had been sold after having been stolen when the gate was taken down. This man had them in his possession some three or four years, when they were bought, about the year 1765, by a Mr. Wright, who employed Flaxman, the sculptor, then a boy, to repair them. They were in terra cotta, coloured and gilt. The dress of one of the busts was painted dark red, and the ornaments gilt, among which were alternately the Rose and H, and the Crown and R, in gold. Mr. Wright resided at Hatfield Priory, near Witham, in Essex, and the above-mentioned busts, when Mr. Smith wrote, were in the possession of his greatgrandson, Mr. John Wright, who, in a letter to " Sylvanus Urban," says, " I remember some years ago (after reading an account of the busts in the ' Antiquities of Westminster '), scraping off some of the paint, and I found them glazed and coloured. I suppose the reason they were painted over was that a good deal of the enamel had worn off, or was damaged in some way, so Flaxman thought it better to paint them."

Maitland, in his " History of London" (1739), speaks of Holbein's gateway as still standing. He calls it " the present stately gate, opposite the Banqueting House." He adds, that soon after becoming possessed of Whitehall, " Henry, for other diversions, erected, contiguous to the aforesaid gate, a tennis-court, cock-pit, and places to bowl in ; the former of which only," he adds, " are now remaining, the rest being converted into dwellinghouses, and offices for the Privy Council, Treasury, and Secretaries of State."

The Cockpit gateway is described in the work above referred to as "an ancient piece of building, opening out of the Cock-pit into King Street, in the north part of Westminster," and is often styled

"Westminster Gate;" the writer adds that "the structure is old, with the remains of several figures, the queen's arms, roses, &c., whereby it was enriched. It hath four towers, and the south side is adorned with pilasters and entablature of the Ionic order." It was lower than the Holbein Gateway, and not anything like so handsome; its towers were semi-circular projections, pierced with semi-circular lights, and on the top of the towers were semi-circular domelets. Altogether, if we may judge from the prints of the gate published by Kip, and also in the "Vetusta Monumenta" by the Society of Antiquaries, it was one of the ugliest structures in the metropolis. This was removed in 1723, as it blocked up the road which was then the sole access from Charing Cross to the Houses of Parliament and the Courts of Law.

In this gateway were the lodgings of the beautiful and intriguing Countess of Buckingham, the mother of George Villiers, Duke of Buckingham. She died here in 1632, and her body was conveyed hence along King Street to the Abbey to be laid beside that of her murdered son. King's Gate was converted by Henry into a passage connecting Whitehall with the park, the tennis-court, bowling-green, and tilting-yard.

The Tilt-yard stood a little to the south of "the Horse Guard Yard," adjoining the north gate of King Street; having a gate into the park, close to which was an old staircase, used, no doubt, by Elizabeth and her courtiers on State occasions, and leading to the Royal gallery. In Sydney's "State Papers" there is to be found an amusing account of the diversions of Queen Bess, which shows that even when not far short of her seventieth year, she could pursue the pleasures of out-door sports among her courtiers with the energy of youth or of middle age. "Her Majesty says she is very well. This day she appoints a Frenchman to do feats upon a rope in the conduit court: to-morrow she hath commanded the bears, the bull, and the ape to be baited in the Tilt-yard. Upon Wednesday she will have 'solemne dauncing.'"

The chief heroes of the Tilt-yard were Sir Henry Lee, of Ditchley, Knight of the Garter, and "the faithful and devoted knight of this romantic Princess," and George, Earl of Cumberland. The former had made a vow to present himself at the Tilt-yard annually on the 27th of November, till disabled by age, and so gave rise to a school of knights of the Tilt-yard, embracing about twenty-five of the most celebrated members of the Court, including Sir Christopher Hatton, and Robert, Earl of Leicester. In due course of time Sir Henry resigned his post in favour of the Earl of Cumber-

land. In 1590, it is on record that "with much form and in the true spirit of chivalry and romance, in the presence of the Queen and of the whole Court, he armed the new champion with his own hands, and mounted him on his horse. He then offered his own armour at the foot of a crowned pillar near her Majesty's feet; after which he clothed himself in a coat of black velvet pointed under the arm, and instead of a helmet, covered his head with a buttoned cap of the country fashion," as Walpole tells us in his "Miscellaneous Antiquities." Sir Henry died at the age of eighty, and was buried at Quarendon, near Aylesbury, where the inscription on his tomb recorded the fact that—

"In courtly jousts his sovereign's knight he was;
Six princes did he serve."

In the reign of James I., the old Palace of Whitehall had become so ruinous, the greater part having been destroyed by fire in 1619, that it was determined to rebuild it. Dr. Mackay, in his "Thames and its Tributaries," says that the King "entrusted the design to Inigo Jones, who built the edifice now known as the Banqueting House, . . . which was intended as a part, and a very small one, of a more magnificent conception. The palace was to have consisted of four fronts, each with an entrance between two towers. Within these were to have been one large central court and five smaller ones, and between two of the latter a handsome circus, with an arcade below, supported by pillars in the form of caryatides. The whole length of the palace was to have been 1,152 feet, and its depth 872 feet; but the times which succeeded those of James were not favourable for such designs and expenses as these, and so the palace was never completed." The original drawings, bold in their conception, are preserved at Worcester College, Oxford; and the building, as designed by Inigo Jones, has been frequently engraved. The building was actually commenced, but in consequence of the civil wars, the Banqueting House was the only portion of the design completed. This splendid fragment, which exists before our eyes, has often excited lamentations that the design of Inigo Jones was never completed; yet Horace Walpole, an incomparable critic on all writings, characters, and buildings but his own, throws strong doubts on its probable excellence. "Several plates of the intended new Palace of Whitehall," he writes, "have been given, but, I believe, from no finished design of Inigo Jones. . . . The strange kind of cherubims on the towers at the end are preposterous ornaments; and, whether of Inigo's design or not, bear no relation to the rest. The great towers in the front are too near, and evidently borrowed from what he had seen in Gothic, than in Roman, buildings. The circular court is a picturesque thought, but without meaning or utility." It is true that he equally doubts the published design to be the final one; for he continues:—" The four great sheets are evidently made up from general hints; nor could such a source of invention and taste as the mind of Inigo Jones ever produce such sameness." On this passage Dr. Croly remarks in a note on Pope's "Windsor Forest:"—"Whether the design were regal or not, the situation showed a regal sense. The position on the Thames was fit for the sea-king; its command of the rising country in front gave it the brightness and the beauty of the English landscape, before that fine space was overrun with graceless buildings. The sovereign of England has now a new palace near the Thames, but without communication with it; and near the country, but without a prospect. Yet the architecture has been needlessly criticised; with some striking errors, it has many beauties. Blackened by smoke and buried in fog, what architecture can struggle against its location? A happier site would discover in it details of elegance, novelty, and grandeur."

"At the time of the execution of King Charles," says Pennant, "contiguous to the Banqueting House was a large building with a long roof and a small cupola rising out of the middle, which is shown in Hollar's etching. Under this cupola there was an entrance and an unsightly gateway."

Directly behind the Banqueting House, very near the river, was a chapel belonging to the Palace; but no engravings of it are known to exist; and all trace of its site has disappeared. It must have stood as nearly as possible on the site of Fife House. The screen of the Queen's Chapel here, we are told, was removed by Sir William Chambers to his residence at Whitton, near Hounslow, where he set it up as a summer-house in his garden.

The Stone Gallery ran along the east, between the garden and the river, following as nearly as possible the line of the terrace which afterwards formed "Privy Gardens." The "lodgings belonging to his Majesty" faced the river, close to the "Privy Stairs." Those of the Duke of York adjoined them on the south, commanding also a view of the river. Those of Prince Rupert, the Duke of Monmouth, the ladies of the Court, of the maids of honour, the "Countess of Castlemaine," and the "Countess of Suffolk" were situated between the river-side and the Stone Gallery. Nell Gwynne,

not having the honour of belonging to the establishment of Catherine of Braganza, was obliged to keep to her apartments in Pall Mall.

"The intended Palace at Whitehall," says one writer, "if it had been carried out would have been the most truly magnificent and beautiful fabric of any of the kind in Europe. His Majesty did not send to Italy and Flanders for architects as he did for Albano and Vandyck; he had Inigo Jones. A higher compliment to both English royalty and English art could not well be paid." As it is, we can only regret that the same chance of leaving behind him a memorial worthy of his genius was not given to Inigo Jones that was given to Sir Christopher Wren.

It is not generally known that in the early part of the last century an ingenious speculator proposed to improve Westminster by carrying out the design of Inigo Jones for rebuilding Whitehall. The expense he estimated at little over half a million, and he proposed, as a means of raising that sum, that the city of Westminster should be incorporated, to consist of a mayor, recorder, and twenty-four aldermen; that the profits arising to the said corporation, after defraying its own necessary expenses, should, for seven years, be appropriated to carry on the intended new palace; that duties should be laid upon new improved rents within the city of Westminster; that all officers who held two or more offices above the annual value of £300, should pay a certain poundage, as should likewise all such as had any right or title to any house, office, or lodging within the said new projected Palace; and, lastly, that all improvements of any part of the ground of Whitehall, and the benefit arising to Her Majesty from all new inventions or forfeitures should for a term of years be appropriated to the same purpose. This plan, which might ultimately have much benefited the locality, it is superfluous to add, was never carried into effect.

The Banqueting House, so called from having been placed on the side of the apartments so called erected by Elizabeth, was begun in 1619, and finished in two years. It is divided into three storeys, of which the lowest or basement storey consists of a rustic wall, with small square windows. Above this springs a range of columns and pilasters of the Ionic order; between the columns are seven windows, with alternate arched and triangular pediments; over these is placed the proper entablature, on which is raised a second series of the Corinthian order, consisting also of columns and pilasters, their capitals being connected with festoons of flowers, with masks and other ornaments in the centre. From the entablature of this series rises a balustrade, with attic pedestals in their places crowning the whole. The building consists chiefly of one room, of an oblong form, a double cube of 55 feet. The stone for building it was drawn from the quarries at Portland, under authority of the sign-manual of James I.

lection of drawings and pictures was exhibited in the Royal Banqueting House, and in consequence realised, when subsequently put up for auction, the very large sum of £26,000. Rubens's painted ceiling is divided by a rich framework of gilded mouldings into nine compartments, the subjects

INTERIOR OF THE OLD CHAPEL ROYAL (BANQUETING HOUSE), WHITEHALL (1876).

Charles I. commissioned Rubens to paint the ceiling, and by the agency of this great artist the King was enabled to secure the noble cartoons of Raffaelle, which are preserved at the South Kensington Museum. Charles also collected a considerable number of paintings by the best masters, but these were seized by order of Parliament, who sold many of the paintings and statues, and ordered the "superstitious pictures" to be burnt. After Sir P. Lely's death, his noble col-

being what are called allegorical, the centre one representing the apotheosis of James I., or his supposed translation into the celestial regions. The king, supported by an eagle, is borne upwards, attended by figures as the representatives of Religion, Justice, &c. His Majesty appears seated on his throne, and turning with horror from War and other such-like deities, and resigning himself to Peace and her natural attendants, Commerce and the Fine Arts—a curious commentary on the Puritan age which followed so soon after the execution of the ceiling. On either side of this central compartment are oblong panels, on which the painter has endeavoured to express the peace and plenty, the harmony and happiness, which he presumed to have signalised the reign of its boldness and success. These paintings have been more than once re-touched, on one occasion by no less an artist than Cipriani; and though there is an immense distance between this artist and Rubens, there is no apparent injury done to the work. The Banqueting House cost £17,000.

THE OLD CHAPEL ROYAL, WHITEHALL, EXTERIOR (1876).

James I. In other compartments Rubens' patron and employer, Charles, is introduced, in scenes intended to represent his birth, and as being crowned King of Scotland; while the oval compartments at the corners are intended, by allegorical figures, to show the triumph of the Virtues, such as Temperance, &c., over the Vices. Vandyck was to have painted the sides of the apartment with the history of the Order of the Garter. The execution of particular parts is to be admired for Rubens received for his paintings upon the ceiling —about four hundred yards of work—the sum of four thousand pounds, or nearly ten pounds a yard; while Sir James Thornhill, three quarters of a century later, was paid only three pounds a yard for his decorations on the ceiling of Greenwich Hospital. Cipriani had two thousand pounds for his re-touching. This noble building was turned into a chapel by George I., and remained a Chapel Royal until 1890, when it was dismantled. Three years later it was handed over to the Royal United Service Institution for its Museum, of which we have already given some account (pp. 334-335). The clerical establishment of the Chapel Royal consisted of a Dean and Sub-Dean, a morning reader and two permanent preachers and readers, or chaplains; there were also two Select Preachers, chosen by the Bishop of London from the two chief Universities alternately. In 1812 five eagles and four other standards, captured from the French in the Peninsula, were publicly deposited in this chapel; and in January, 1816, the same ceremony was repeated in respect of the standards taken at the Battle of Waterloo, on the 18th of June preceding; but on the opening of the new military chapel in Birdcage Walk these trophies were removed thither. The front of the Banqueting House was largely repaired and beautified in 1829. The basement was until 1890 partly used for Government stores; it was then restored and furnished with a concrete floor, and now contains the heavy guns and shells, &c., belonging to the Institution to which the building has been transferred. The Banqueting Hall itself has not been altered structurally, and even the wood of the oak pews, which had, of course, to be removed when the place was converted into a Museum, was used as panelling for the bases of the walls and piers. The Banqueting House, although, as we have seen, converted into a chapel in the reign of George I., was never consecrated, which fact was mentioned in the House of Commons some years ago, when it was proposed to use the hall as a picture-gallery.

Evelyn in his "Diary" frequently mentions the service here, and on one occasion (at Easter, 1684), when the King received the communion, he adds, "Note, there was parfume burnt before the office began."

We must not omit to mention here an interesting ceremony which was performed in the Chapel Royal, Whitehall, from a remote period, namely, the distribution of the "Maundy," or royal alms, to the poor.

The custom of distributing the royal alms on "Maunday" Thursday—as the day before Good Friday is styled—has come down from the old Roman Catholic ages. Some such ceremony was performed by personages of the highest rank, both temporal and spiritual, from the Pope down to nobles and lords in their castles, in commemoration of our Redeemer, who "washed his disciples' feet" when He gave them that "new commandment," or "mandate," whence the day has its name. Queen Elizabeth performed this ceremony at her palace

at Greenwich; and the last of our sovereigns who went through it in person was James II. After him, under the Hanoverian line, it was performed by the Royal Almoner. The following cotemporary account of the ceremony in the reign of George II. may possibly raise a smile:—"On the 5th of April, 1731, it being Maunday Thursday, the King being then in his forty-eighth year, there was distributed, at the Banqueting House, Whitehall, to forty-eight poor men, and forty-eight poor women, boiled beef and shoulders of mutton, and small bowls of ale, which is called dinner; after that, large wooden platters of fish and loaves, viz., undressed, one large ling and one large dried cod; twelve red herrings and twelve white herrings, and four half-quartern loaves. Each person had one platter of this provision; after which was distributed to them shoes, stockings, linen and woollen cloth, and leathern bags, with one penny, twopenny, threepenny, and fourpennypieces of silver, and shillings, to each about four pounds in value. His Grace the Lord Archbishop of York, Lord High Almoner, also performed the annual ceremony of washing the feet of the poor in the Royal Chapel, Whitehall, as was formerly done by the kings themselves."

Gradual changes, however, have taken place in the manner of performing this ceremony. The ceremony is thus described towards the close of the reign of George III., namely, in 1814:—"In the morning the Sub-Almoner, the Secretary of the Lord High Almoner, and others belonging to the Lord Chamberlain's Office, attended by a party of the Yeomen of the Guard, distributed to seventy-five poor women and seventy-five poor men, being as many as the King was years old, a quantity of salt fish, consisting of salmon, cod, and herrings, pieces of very fine beef, five loaves of bread, and some ale to drink the King's health. . . . A procession entered of those engaged in the ceremony, consisting of a party of the Yeomen of the Guard, one of them carrying on his head a large gold dish, containing one hundred and fifty bags, with seventy-five silver pennies in each, for the poor people, which was placed in the royal closet. They were followed by the Sub-Almoner, in his robes, with a sash of fine linen over his shoulder and crossing his waist. He was followed by two boys, two girls, the secretary, and other gentlemen, all carrying nosegays. The Church Evening Service was then performed, at the conclusion of which the silver pennies were distributed, and woollen cloth, linen, shoes and stockings, to the men and women, and a cup of wine to drink the King's health."

The royal alms now are dispensed in money and clothing, the payment in kind of fish and flesh having been practically commuted. A few years ago it was thought that the ceremony would have been allowed to die out; but such has not been the case, and the gifts are distributed by the Lord High Almoner to so many men, and the like number of women, as may correspond with the number of years in the age of Her Majesty.

Although the mandate, or Maunday, is now little more than an empty ceremony, yet it is one which enshrines a lesson of true Christian charity. So far from censuring or despising such acts of condescension on the part of the royal and noble towards their poorer brethren and sisters, we ought rather to regret that so few opportunities occur in a year for bringing into contact and contrast the squalid poverty of "St. Giles's" with the wealth and luxury of "St. James's," and so leading the inmates of the latter region, in the words of the poet—

> "To learn the luxury of doing good."

We may, perhaps, be pardoned for reminding our readers here that the "Beef-eaters"—as the Yeomen of the Royal Guard who do duty on these occasions are called—are really *buffetiers*, that is, personal attendants of the sovereign, who, on high festivals, and on other state occasions, were ranged near the royal sideboard, or *buffet*.

In the open space in the rear, between the chapel and the houses in Whitehall Gardens, stands the celebrated statue of James II., which was set up in 1686, just two years before his abdication. It is of bronze, and represents the king as dressed in a Roman toga, and its elegant proportions have often been admired. It is the work of Grinling Gibbons. Indeed, it has been said to be nearly the only statue in the metropolis that will bear a rigid inspection as a work of art. It suffers, however, from the want of an open space around it sufficiently large to set it off to advantage.

As to the author of this statue, it is only fair to add that great doubts have prevailed. They would appear, however, to be negatived by the following passage in the "Autobiography of Sir John Bramston," published under the auspices of the Camden Society. "On New Year's Day, 1686," writes Sir John, "a statue in brass was to be seen, placed the day before in the yard at Whitehall, made by Gibbons at the charge of Toby Runstick, of the present king, James II." Horace Walpole, therefore, was correct in his surmise on the subject. "I am the rather inclined to attribute the statue at Whitehall to Gibbons, because I know of no other artist of that time capable of it." It is strange that so little should have been known for certain as to its author, considering that when it was first set up it was made the subject of numerous sets of verses and *jeux d'esprit*. "The figure, looking as it does towards the river," writes John Timbs, "was said to prognosticate the king's flight. This, however, is not more probable than that he is pointing to the spot where his father was executed, which is a vulgar error. It may be taken as a sign of the moderation of the Revolution of 1688 that after the accession of William III. the statue was still left standing." Possibly, however, this fact, so unlike what would have happened in Paris under like circumstances, may be ascribed to the new king being the son-in-law of James.

CHAPTER XLVI.

WHITEHALL, AND ITS HISTORICAL REMINISCENCES (*continued*).

"———— Non isto vivitur illic
Quo tu rere modo."—*Horace*.

Whitehall forsaken as a Royal Residence—Partial Restoration of the Palace—The Cock-pit—Cromwell and Sir Roger L'Estrange—Death of Oliver Cromwell—The Ultimate Fate of Cromwell's Body—The Exhumation discussed—Curious Record in an Old Parish Register—George Monk at the Cock-pit—Fashionable Life under the Stuarts—Cock-fighting—Defoe's Account—Its Prevalence in England.

In the "New View of London," published in 1708, we read, "This Palace being in the beginning of January, 1697, demolished by fire, except the Banqueting House and the Holbein Gateway, there has since been no reception of the Court in town but at St. James's Palace, . . . and Whitehall will doubtless be rebuilt in a short time, being designed one of the most famous palaces in Christendom." It was not rebuilt, however; and gradually the royal family removed from Whitehall to St. James's Palace, which thenceforward became known as the head-quarters of the English Court.

On page 355 there will be found a copy of a curious outline print giving a bird's-eye view of Whitehall Palace as it appeared after the fire of 1697. In this engraving a sort of lawn, divided into four parterres, projects into the river; while modern mansions of the classical style have taken the place of the old low semi-Gothic houses which previously figured in the foreground.

It is true that after the Restoration Charles II. had made a partial " restoration " at Whitehall. Horace Walpole, in his " Anecdotes of Painting," mentions, as a mark of Charles's taste, that he erected at Whitehall five curious sun-dials. He also collected again a considerable part of the treasures which had been dissipated, and added suites of apartments for the use of his abandoned favourites. James II., too, was occupying White-hall at the time of the unexpected invasion by the Dutch. He is reported to have caused the weather-vane, which still remains, to be erected on the roof of the palace, in order that he might judge whether or not the elements were favourable to his enemies.

Whitehall Palace, nevertheless, now exists only as a fragment. " The present Banqueting House is, indeed," says Mr. Edward M. Barry, " not one-fortieth part of the original design. Had the latter been carried out, the question of our public offices would probably have been settled for ever, and a modern prime minister would not have had the opportunity of forcing his taste on a reluctant architect."

There were two " cock-pits " in the neighbourhood of this palace ; the one on the site of the present Privy Council Office, and the other near the junction of Queen Street and Dartmouth Street with Bird-cage Walk. The two are often confounded together, but the former is the one most frequently mentioned in history in connection with distinguished persons. Philip Herbert, Earl of Pembroke, one of two brothers to whom Shakespeare's Works were dedicated, held the Cock-pit apartments at Whitehall under the Crown, and from a window of his apartment saw his sovereign, Charles I., walk from St. James's to the scaffold. At his death in January, 1649–50, Oliver Cromwell took possession of the rooms; and here, as Mr. Peter Cunningham tells us, he addressed his letter to his aged mother, Elizabeth Bourchier, giving an account of the battle of Dunbar. Here he was waited upon by a deputation from the Parliament, desiring him to " magnify himself with the title of king ;" and here Milton and Andrew Marvell, his secretaries, and Waller and Dryden, were his frequent guests. Though averse, by principle, to dramatic entertainments, Oliver Cromwell liked the organ, and took John Hingston, the organist of Charles I., into his own employ. He used often to summon him to play before him at the Cock-pit in White-hall, near which he resided. Hingston, it appears, used to have concerts at his own house, at which

Cromwell would often be present. In one of these musical entertainments Sir Roger L'Estrange happened to be a performer. As he did not leave the room when the Protector entered, his cavalier friends gave him the name of " Oliver's Fiddler," and the name was so serious an annoyance to him after the Restoration, that in 1662 he published a pamphlet, entitled " Truth and Loyalty Vindicated," in which he clears himself from the charge of Republican tendencies, and relates the affair just as it happened :— " Concerning the story of the fiddle, this, I suppose, might be the rise of it. Being in St. James's Park I heard an organ touched in a little low room of one Mr. Hingston : I went in, and found a private company of five or six persons ; they desired me to take a viole and bear a part. I did so, and that a part too not much to advance the reputation of my cunning. By-and-by, without the least colour of a design or expectation, in came Cromwell. He found us playing, and, as I remember, so he left us."

The great " Lord Protector " died at Whitehall on the 3rd of September, 1658, after a protracted illness, and amidst the raging of a terrific storm. During his last illness Cromwell became so depressed and debilitated that he would allow no barber to come near him ; and his beard, instead of being cut in a certain fashion, grew all over his face. After his death the body lay in state at Somerset House, having been carefully embalmed, and was afterwards buried with more than regal honours in Henry VII.'s Chapel in Westminster Abbey. John Evelyn, in his " Diary," under date of October 2nd, tells us how that he " saw the superb funerall of the Lord Protector. He was carried from Somerset House in a velvet bed of State drawn by six horses, houss'd by the same ; the pall held up by his new lords ; Oliver lying in effigie in royal robes, and crown'd with a crown, sceptre, and globe, like a king. The pendants and guidions were carried by the officers of the army ; and the imperial banner, acheivement, &c., by the heraulds in their coates ; a rich compareason'd horse, embroider'd all over with gold ; a knight of honor arm'd cap-a-pie, and after all, his guards, soldiers, and innumerable mourners. In this equipage they proceeded to Westminster ; but it was the joyfullest funeral I ever saw, for there were none that cried but dogs, which the soldiers hooted away with a barbarous noise, drinking and taking tobacco in the streets as they went."

The ultimate fate of Cromwell's body has at different periods given rise to much controversy from the Restoration down to the present time. It is asserted that after the Restoration it was taken out of his grave, together with the bodies of Ireton (Cromwell's son-in-law) and Bradshaw ; the latter, as President of the High Court of Justice, having pronounced sentence of death on Charles I. The three bodies are then said to have been taken in carts to the "Red Lion," in Holborn, and on the 30th of January, the anniversary of King Charles's death, to have been removed on sledges to Tyburn, where they were hanged until sunset, and then taken down and beheaded, their bodies buried in a deep pit under the gallows, and their heads stuck upon the top of Westminster Hall, where at that time sentinels walked.

A strong corroboration of the main incidents of this story is to be found in the "Fifty Years' Recollections, Literary and Personal," of the late Mr. Cyrus Redding, and resting on the authority of Horace Smith, one of the authors of "Rejected Addresses," &c. Redding writes under date about 1821 or 1822 :—"Horace Smith was acquainted with a medical gentleman who had in his possession the head of Oliver Cromwell, and in order to gratify my curiosity he gave me a note (of introduction) to him. There accompanied the head a memorandum relating to its history. It had been torn from the tomb with the heads of Ireton and Bradshaw after the accession of Charles II., under a feeling of impotent vengeance. All three were fixed over the entrance of Westminster Hall, the other bones of those three distinguished men being interred at Tyburn under the gibbet—an act well befitting the Stuart character. During a stormy night," he adds, "the head in the centre, that of Cromwell, fell to the ground. The sentry on guard beneath having a natural respect for an heroic soldier, no matter of what party, took up the head and placed it under his cloak until he went off duty. He then carried it to the Russells, who were the nearest relations of Cromwell's family, and disposed of it to them. It belonged to a lady, a descendant of the Cromwells, who did not like to keep it in her house. There was a written minute extant along with it. The disappearance of the head (off Westminster Hall) is mentioned in some of the publications of the time. It had been carefully embalmed, as Cromwell's body is known to have been two years before its disinterment. The nostrils were filled with a substance like cotton. The brain had been extracted by dividing the scalp. The membranes within were perfect, but dried up and looked like parchment. The decapitation had evidently been performed after death, as the state of the flesh over the vertebræ of the neck plainly showed. It was hacked, and the severance had evidently been done by a hand not

used to the work, for there were several other cuts beside that which actually separated the bone. The beard, of a chestnut colour, seemed to have grown after death. An ashen pole, pointed with iron, had received the head clumsily impaled upon its point, which came out an inch or so above the crown, rusty and time-worn. The wood of the staff and the skin itself had been perforated by the common wood-worm. I wrote to Horace Smith that I had seen the head, and deemed it genuine. Smith replied, ' I am gratified that you were pleased with Cromwell's head, as I was when I saw it, being fully persuaded of its identity.'" It remains, then, on record that two persons, both men of the world and of large experience, and yet so different from each other in character as Horace Smith and Cyrus Redding, were satisfied with the evidence brought before them to prove its being genuine three-quarters of a century ago. (See also post, pp. 539–542.)

In *Notes and Queries*, September, 1874, p. 205, we read that "Cromwell's body was dug up, his head put on a pike and exposed, and, after passing through several hands, was offered for sale to one of the Russells, who was a lineal descendant of Oliver Cromwell through his daughter, Lady Rich."

According to some authorities, the remains were privately conveyed from Whitehall and interred next to those of Mrs. Claypole, Oliver Cromwell's favourite daughter, in Northamptonshire, in accordance with his own wish, the funeral in Westminster Abbey being a mock ceremonial. According to others, the remains were conveyed to the field of Naseby, and interred at midnight in the very spot where he made his last victorious charge, the field being afterwards ploughed over that his enemies might not discover the spot. Another account, indorsed by Heath, the author of the "Flagellum"—who, by the way, contradicts himself, as he afterwards goes on to describe the exhumation in the abbey and the subsequent gibbeting—is that as the body was decomposed and corrupt to such an extent that it was impossible either to embalm or publicly bury it, it was encased in lead and flung into the Thames at midnight. Oldmixon adds that it was thrown into "the deepest part of the Thames." To say nothing of the intrinsic improbability of these accounts, of the fact that neither Cromwell nor his friends were likely to anticipate any indignity being offered to his remains, of the difficulty of secretly conveying the corpse either to Northamptonshire or to Naseby, of the physical impossibility of decomposition necessitating a hurried burial in the Thames—though this is certainly the best

WHITEHALL, LOOKING TOWARDS THE HOLBEIN GATEWAY. (*From a View by Maurer, 1753.*)

authenticated theory—there is, as we shall see, every reason to believe that he was actually interred near his mother and his daughter in the Abbey. First, there is the fact that none of the leading men of the day had any suspicion that the funeral procession, of which we have many elaborate accounts, was a mock ceremonial. Secondly, Cromwell would naturally desire to lie with his mother and daughter in the national mausoleum among those whom he

Cromwell, Ireton, and Bradshaw. This account is corroborated by the following passage in a work entitled "Oliver Cromwell and his Times," by Thomas Cromwell :—"When the coffin of Cromwell was broken into, a leaden canister was found lying on his breast, and within it a copper gilt plate with the arms of England impaling those of Cromwell," &c. "This copper plate is or was," says a writer in the *Gentleman's Magazine* for

WHITEHALL GARDENS. (*See page* 376.)

must have looked on as his royal predecessors. Thirdly, Noble, a trustworthy and sensible historian, distinctly says, in his memoirs of the "Protectorate House of Cromwell," that the body was deposited in Westminster Abbey, under a magnificent hearse of wax, on the spot subsequently occupied by the tomb of the Duke of Buckingham, adding that at the Restoration "they found in a vault at the east end of the middle aisle a magnificent coffin which contained the body of the late Protector, upon whose breast was a copper plate double gilt, which upon one side had the arms of the Commonwealth impaling those of the deceased." Of this Noble gives a fac-simile. He then goes on to say that he saw the receipt of the money paid to one John Lewis, a mason, for exhuming the bodies of

1867, "in the possession of the Marquis of Ripon. There can be little doubt, therefore," he adds, "that the body of Cromwell was, after his death, veritably interred in the Abbey. It is perfectly certain, moreover, that after the exhumation it was conveyed to Red Lion Square. Noble tells us that the body lay at the Red Lion from Saturday, January 26, 1660, to the Monday following; and the question is, did it ever leave the Red Lion? It is quite conceivable that Cromwell's partisans bribed the officers who were placed to watch the body, and, like the Ephesian matron in Petronius, substituted another body in its place." On the opposite side, however, we have the testimony of those who actually inspected Cromwell's head on the spikes. "Saw the heads of Cromwell, Bradshaw, and Ireton set up at the further end of the hall" (Westminster), writes Pepys; and in the diary of a M. Sainthill, a Spanish ambassador of the time, quoted in *Notes and Queries*, series 3, vol. iii., we find the following entry: "The odious carcases of Oliver Cromwell, Ireton, and Bradshawe were drawn on sledges to Tyburn, where they were hanged by the neck from the morning until four in the afternoon."

With reference to the above subject, it may be added that in the register-book of the parish of Deddington, in Oxfordshire, there is the following somewhat singular entry:—"His Majesty Charles II. came into London 29 day of May, 1660, which was 12 year of his raign, which was brought in without bloodshed, and his father was put to death the 30th January, 1648, by the tyrannical power of Oliver Cromwell, who died September 3d, 1658, and was taken up after he had been buried two years and above, and was hanged at Tiborne, and his head was sett up at Westminster; his body was buried underneath the Tyborne, 1661: which Oliver did governe for some years in England."

It may be remembered that in 1653 Cromwell returned from Westminster to Whitehall, with the keys of the House of Commons in his pocket, after having dissolved the "Long" Parliament, as he subsequently explained to the "Barebones" Parliament assembled in the Council Chamber here.

George Monk, Duke of Albemarle, was the next tenant of the Cock-pit at Whitehall, shortly before the Restoration. These apartments were confirmed to the Duke by Charles II., and he died here in 1670. We have already given our readers a good deal of information respecting the private relations of the Duke in our account of the Strand. Then came to reside here George Villiers, Duke of Buckingham, who died in 1687. After the disastrous fire in Whitehall, in 1697, the Cock-pit was converted into offices for the Privy Council; and in 1710, in the Council Chamber, Guiscard attempted to assassinate that noble collector of books and patron of men of letters— Robert Harley, Earl of Oxford. The Cock-pit retained its original name long after the change of its use, for the minutes of the Lords Commissioners of His Majesty's Treasury were dated from the "Cock-pit at Whitehall," as late as the year 1780, if not later. The "Picture of London" (1810) refers to the Council Chamber as "commonly called the Cock-pit."

Here is a graphic description of Court life at Whitehall in the gay days of our Stuart kings:— "Hyde Park, in the reign of the second Charles," wrote Grace and Philip Wharton in their "Queens of Society," "was only a country drive, a field, in fact, belonging to a publican. Sometimes the Princess Anne might be seen driving there . . . in her coach, panelled only, and without glass windows—a luxury introduced by Charles II. There they encountered Lady Castlemaine and Miss Stuart, whose quarrel as to which should first use the famous coach presented by Grammont to the King was the theme of Whitehall. Sometimes from the groves and alleys of Spring Gardens they emerged perhaps into the broad walks of St. James's Park, between the alleys of which the gay and titled resorted to *cafés*, such as those permitted in the gardens of the Tuileries. Sometimes again the Princess Anne, accompanied by the haughty Freeman (Sarah, Duchess of Marlborough) in her hood and mantle, descended White Hall Stairs and took her pleasure in her barge on the then fresh and pure waters of the Thames, beyond which were green fields and shady trees. These were all inexpensive pleasures; and both 'Mrs. Freeman' and 'Mrs. Morley' (the Princess Anne) were economical. The Princess's allowance from the Privy Purse was small, and Lord Churchill's means were moderate. More frequently, however, the two friends sat in the Princess's boudoir, then termed her 'closet,' and in that sanctum discussed passing events with bitterness—the dramatic close of the days of Charles II., who begged pardon of his surrounding courtiers for 'being so long a dying;' the accession and unpopularity of his brother James, and afterwards the event which roused even Anne from her apathy and made her malicious—the birth of the Prince whom we southrons call the Pretender."

Some account of the "diversion" carried on at the Cock-pit in former times, and of cock-fighting in general, may not be out of place here. Fitzstephen, who wrote the life of Archbishop Becket, in the reign of Henry II., is the first of our writers that mentions cock-fighting, describing it as the sport of school-boys on Shrove Tuesday. The Cock-pit, it appears, was the school, and the master was the comptroller and director of the sport. From this time, at least, the diversion, however absurd and even impious, was continued among us. It was followed, though disapproved and prohibited, in the 39th year of Edward III.; also in the reigns of Henry VIII. and Queen Elizabeth. It has been by some called a royal diversion, and, as every one knows, the Cock-pit at Whitehall was erected by a crowned head, for the more magnificent celebration of the sport. It was prohibited, however, by one of the Acts of Oliver Cromwell, March 31, 1654.

British cocks are mentioned by Cæsar; but the first actual notice of cock-fighting, as an established sport of the Londoners, occurs in Fitzstephen, who traces it back to the reign of Henry II. From Edward III. down to the days of the Regency—when the then Lord Lonsdale treated the allied sovereigns in 1814 to an exhibition of it—and, perhaps, we may say even to our own time, it has been a fashionable amusement with a certain set of individuals. Henry VIII., as everybody knows, added a cock-pit to his new palace at Whitehall; and even the learned pedant, James I., if we are correctly informed, used to go to witness the sport twice a week.

"A cock-fight," says Defoe, in his "Journey through England" (1724), "is the very model of an amphitheatre of the ancients. The cocks fight here in the area, as the beasts did formerly among the Romans, and round the circle above sit the spectators in their several rows. It is wonderful to see the courage of these little creatures, who always hold fighting on till one of them drops, and dies on the spot. I was at several of these matches, and never saw a cock run away. However, I must own it to be a remnant of the barbarous customs of this island, and too cruel for my entertainment. There is always a continued noise among the spectators in laying wagers upon every blow each cock gives, who, by the way, I must tell you, wear steel spurs (called gaffles) for their surer execution. And this noise runs, fluctuating backwards and forwards, during each battle, which is a great amusement, and I believe abundance of people get money by taking and laying odds on each stroke, and find their account at the end of the battle, but these are people that must nicely understand it. If an Italian, a German, or a Frenchman should by chance come into these cock-pits, without knowing beforehand what is meant by this clamour, he would certainly conclude the assembly to be all mad, by their continued outcries of 'six to four, ten pounds to a crown,' which is always repeated here, and with great earnestness, every spectator taking part with his favourite cock, as if it were a party cause."

That cock-fighting was the original appropriation of the pit of our theatres has been supposed by some who support their view by such quotations as the following:—

> "Let but Beatrice
> And Benedict be seen: Lo! in a trice,
> The cockpit, galleries, boxes, all are full."

In the *Gentleman's Journal*, 1692, is given an English epigram, "On a Cock at Rochester," by Sir Charles Sedley, wherein the following lines, which imply, as it would seem, as if the cock had suffered this annual barbarity by way of punishment for St. Peter's crime:—

> "May'st thou be punished for St. Peter's crime,
> And on Shrove Tuesday perish in thy prime."

Cock-fighting, it would appear, was peculiarly an English amusement in the seventeenth and eighteenth centuries. The characteristics of this brutal sport may be gathered from the remark of a contemporary writer, who, addressing a friend in Paris, tells him that it is worth while to come to England, if it be only to see an election and a cock-pit match. "There is a celestial spirit of anarchy and confusion in these two scenes that words cannot paint."

"Cocks of the game are yet cherished," says Stow, "by divers men for their pleasure, much money being laid on their heads, when they fight in pits, whereof some be costly made for that purpose."

It remains only to add that there were in the seventeenth century, in London and its suburbs, a variety of places where the sport of cock-fighting was practised: the best known were the Royal Cock-pit, in the Birdcage Walk; one in Bainbridge Street, St. Giles'; one "near Gray's Inn Lane;" one in "Pickled-egg Walk;" others at New Vauxhall Gardens, in St. George's-in-the-East, and in Old Gravel Lane, over Blackfriars Bridge. Cock-pits, therefore, in the good old Stuart times, must have been pretty evenly distributed among all classes of the community. The Royal Cock-pit, it will be remembered, afforded to Hogarth characters for what has been epigrammatically and wittily termed "one of his worst subjects, though best plates."

We have said that very little, indeed nothing, of old Whitehall remains. From the twenty-fifth volume of the "Archæologia" we learn that the last portion of it, an embattled doorway of the Tudor date and style, was removed in 1847. Fifteen years or so previously a stone apartment with a groined roof, no doubt a portion of the old palace, was discovered by Mr. Sidney Smirke, F.S.A., in the basement of Cromwell House, in Whitehall Yard; and it seems probable, on referring to Fisher's plan (of which we have given a copy on p. 343), that it formed part of the wine-cellar. Its identity was established by a doorway bearing in its spandrils the arms of Wolsey and of the see of York.

CHAPTER XLVII.

WHITEHALL:—ITS PRECINCT, GARDENS, &c.

" Magnos Senecæ prædivitis hortos."—*Juvenal.*

The Privy Gardens and King Charles's curious Sun-dials—Name changed to Whitehall Gardens—Lady Hervey and Sir Thomas Robinson—Sir Robert Peel's House—Pembroke House and Gwydyr House—The Local Government Board—The Duchess of Portland's Museum of Sculpture—Montagu House—Richmond House—The Duke of Richmond's Gallery of Art—Richmond Terrace—Beating the Bounds—Cannon Row—The Civil Service Commission—Derby Court—Manchester Buildings—A Touching Incident in connection with the Last Days of Charles I.—Parliament Street—Messrs. Nichols' Printing-office—Assassination of Mr. Drummond—The Residence of Charles James Fox—Whitehall Club—The *Whitehall Evening Post*—Curious House Signs.

THE gardens adjoining Whitehall Palace on the south and south-west were laid out in terraces, square and formal in plan, and adorned, after the fashion of the times, with statues of marble and bronze, many of which were subsequently removed to Hampton Court. "In the Privy Garden," says John Timbs, "was a dial, which was set up by Edward Gunter, Professor of Astronomy at Gresham College, and of which he published a description by command of James I., in 1624. A large stone pedestal bore four dials at the four corners, and the great horizontal concave in the centre; and, besides, east, west, north, and south dials at the sides." In the reign of Charles II. this dial was defaced by a nobleman of the court, when drunk; and Andrew Marvell wrote upon it the following epigram:—

"This place for a dial was too insecure,
   Since a guard and a garden it could not defend;
For, so near to the court, they will never endure,
   A witness to show how their time they mis-spend."

In the court-yard, facing the Banqueting House, was another curious dial, set up in 1669, by order of Charles II. It was invented by one Francis Hall, *alias* Lyne, a Jesuit and Professor of Mathematics at Liége. The dial consisted of five stages rising in a pyramidical form, and bearing several vertical and reclining dials, globes cut into planes, and glass bowls, showing besides "the houres of all kinds," and "many things also belonging to geography, astronomy, and astrology, by the sun's shadow made visible to the eye." Among the pictures were portraits of the King, the two Queens, the Duke of York, and Prince Rupert. Father Lyne published a description of this dial, which consisted of seventy-three parts, and was illustrated with seventeen plates. It would appear, from what the author of the "Curiosities of London" says, that it was subsequently set up at Buckingham House.

We read incidentally that the gardens were intersected by a brook or rivulet, which here ran into the Thames; for in 1667 there was an order made by the Court of Sewers, as to the "sluice near Sir Robert Pye's, and the outfall thereof into the river,

near the old orchard at Whitehall, now the Bowling Green." This orchard dated back as far as the reign of Henry VIII.

The site of the old palace of Whitehall, which was made extra-parochial at an early date, formerly formed part of the parish of St. Margaret's, Westminster. In order to assert the extent of the parish, the authorities, in "beating the bounds," took a boat at Parliament Stairs and rowed to the centre arch of Westminster Bridge, where there was a mark, and then landing at Privy Garden Stairs, "passed before Montagu House to the house of the Earl of Lowden" (Loudoun), afterwards the Duke of Richmond's, of which we shall have more to say presently.

Down to a comparatively recent date, the gardens above mentioned were called by the old name of the "Privy Gardens," but this has now become changed to "Whitehall Gardens"—a name given to a row of houses in the rear of the Banqueting House, which, until the formation of the Victoria Embankment, had its gardens and lawns sloping to the Thames. Whitehall Gardens were very fashionable residences in the reign of William IV. In 1835, No. 1, the present home of the National Club, was the town residence of the Marquis of Ailsa, and afterwards of the Dowager Marchioness of Exeter; and further on were the houses of Lord Farnborough (better known as Sir Charles Long) and the Earl of Malmesbury. Here, too, lived, in the time of Pitt and Fox, old Lady Townshend, who in her early days had been one of the "queens of society" in the court of George II. Here used to drop in of an evening George Selwyn and the other wits of the age; and it was said of her by Sir N. W. Wraxall, that, "in the empire of mind, she had succeeded to the place left vacant by Mrs. Hervey and Lady Mary Wortley Montagu, in the previous generation." Mr. Disraeli (afterwards Earl of Beaconsfield) lived in the house, No. 2, from 1873 down to 1879.

Lady Townshend's house was celebrated for the *bon mots* of its mistress. Lady Lepel Hervey tells a good story of her and two Sir Thomas Robinsons, who had both offended her. The one was very tall and thin, the other very plump and short. "I can't bear them ; and I can't imagine," remarked her ladyship, "why the one should be preferred to the other, one bit. I see but little difference between them ; the one Sir Thomas is as broad as the other is long." Lady Townshend's pleasantry, however, it should be remarked here, was scarcely just. The "broad" Sir Thomas was a man of merit and ability, and for some time Secretary of State, and afterwards was created Lord Grantham. The "long" Sir Thomas was a celebrated bore and butt of the day. Lord Chesterfield used to bear with his dulness for the sake of laughing at him. "One day," adds Lady Hervey, "when Sir Thomas requested his lordship to honour him with some poetic mention, Lord Chesterfield qualified his whim by the following couplet :—

'Unlike my subject will I frame my song,
    It *shall* be witty, and it *shan't* be long.'"

In No. 4, a house with a large bow window, the late Sir Robert Peel lived, before and during his premiership; and here he died, July 2nd, 1850, from the effects of a fall from his horse, a few days previously, on Constitution Hill. In this house, whilst occupied by the Peel family, there was a fine gallery of paintings by the old masters, and the best collection of modern portraits by Sir Thomas Lawrence. Those of Canning, Wellington, &c., were there, and a variety of others too many to enumerate here.

Among the other mansions built on the site of the old Privy Gardens two deserve to be mentioned here—viz., Pembroke House and Gwydyr House.

"Lord Pembroke's house at Whitehall," writes Lady Hervey, in 1762, "is taken for the Duc de Nivernois, the French Ambassador." His name will be remembered as one of the *Quarante* and an inveterate versifier ; and it is said that not a sitting of that illustrious body took place at Paris which the duke did not enliven by reading out a fable. It is to be hoped that he was more merciful to West-end society here. The mansion known as Pembroke House was afterwards occupied by the late Earl of Harrington, and passed, in or about the year 1853, into the hands of the Government, who turned it into one of the departments of the State.

At Gwydyr House for many years were the offices of the Commissioners of Revenue Inquiry, the Commissioners for Promoting the Fine Arts, and the Commissioners of the Health of Towns. Within its walls is now carried on the business of the Charity Commission for England and Wales. The Local Government Board, established in 1873,

has its offices in Whitehall. On the formation of this Board the Poor Law Board ceased to exist, and all the powers hitherto exercised by the Secretary of State and the Privy Council were transferred to this department. The powers exercised by the Local Government Board relate to the registration of births, deaths, and marriages, public health, drainage, public improvements, local government, &c., and also to the prevention of disease. Close by is one of the offices of the Board of Trade, and also that of the Commercial, Labour, and Statistical Departments of the Board.

One of the almost forgotten memories of the neighbourhood of Whitehall, is the celebrated Museum of Sculpture and Works of Art made by the Duchess of Portland. "Here," writes John Timbs, "Pennant was shown a rich pearl surmounted with a crown, which was taken out of the ear of Charles I., after his head was cut off. Here, also, was the Barberini or Portland Vase, purchased by the Duchess from Sir William Hamilton for 1,800 guineas, and subsequently deposited by the Duke of Portland in the British Museum."

Sir Christopher Wren was ordered by Queen Anne, in 1705, to erect a wall to enclose that part of the garden which contained the fountain, as a pleasure-ground to the house inhabited by the Scotch commissioners appointed to settle the terms of the union of the two kingdoms.

At the southern end of Whitehall Gardens is Montagu House, the town mansion of the Duke of Buccleuch, who inherited it from the noble family of Montagu. The old house was a low building, and, with the exception of the pictures it contained, had little or nothing to call for special remark. The building was demolished about the year 1860, when the present magnificent mansion, in the Italian style, was built upon its site, the architect being Mr. George Burn.

There is here a splendid gallery of pictures containing many examples of the first masters. One, having special reference to the locality, is Canaletti's fine view of Whitehall, showing Holbein's Gateway, Inigo Jones's Banqueting House, and the steeple of St. Martin's Church, with the scaffolding about it. Then there are a large number of portraits by Vandyck and others, formerly belonging to Sir Peter Lely, and purchased at the sale of his effects by Ralph, Duke of Montagu. There are also other fine pictures by Vandyck, and a series of family portraits.

On the site of what is now Richmond Terrace was formerly Richmond House, the town residence of the Dukes of Richmond. This mansion stood at the southern end of the Privy Gardens, and faced Whitehall and Charing Cross, on ground previously occupied by the apartments of the Duchess of Portsmouth, Louise Renée de Perrencourt, whose son by Charles II. was the first Duke of Richmond. The house was built for George, second Duke, by the famous architect Boyle, Earl of Burlington, concerning whom Pope asks, "Who builds like Boyle?"

Among those enlightened noblemen and gentle-generous invitation several young artists, whose names were afterwards known to the world, entered themselves as students. Cipriani, the painter, and Wilton, the sculptor, presided as instructors, till the students were sufficiently advanced to follow their bent unaided, and silver medals were occasionally awarded. This benefit was given to the rising school without fee or emolument. The gallery was opened in 1758, ten years before the

WESTMINSTER BRIDGE. *From Canaletti's View.* (*See page* 299.)

men who co-operated practically, and not merely by word of mouth, with George III. in his zeal for the promotion of the fine arts, Charles, the third Duke of Richmond, who held the title from 1750 down to 1806, claims a prominent notice. After his return from "the grand tour," the Duke munificently opened a school for the study of painting and sculpture at his house, at the end of Privy Gardens. Here a spacious gallery was provided, with every convenience and accommodation for the students, and a fine collection of casts, moulded from the most select antique and modern statues at Rome and Florence, was procured. These were set out as models, and young artists were invited, by public advertisement, to make the gallery a school for the study of art. In consequence of this

foundation of the Royal Academy. In 1770 it contained upwards of twenty-five statues, and among them may be noted the Apollo Belvidere, the Gladiator, the Venus de Medici, the Dancing Faun, Group of Hercules and Antæus, the Rape of the Sabines, and a variety of casts from the Trajan Column, &c. The value of such a school in London, at a time when there were no railways or other facilities for foreign travel, can hardly be exaggerated. Among the artists who owed some of their early art-training to this school, the *Somerset House Gazette* mentions John Parker, a painter of historical portraits, long resident in Rome; John Hamilton Mortimer, the pupil of Robert Edge Pine (known to his friends as "Friar Pine"), who outstripped all his compeers in the drawing of the

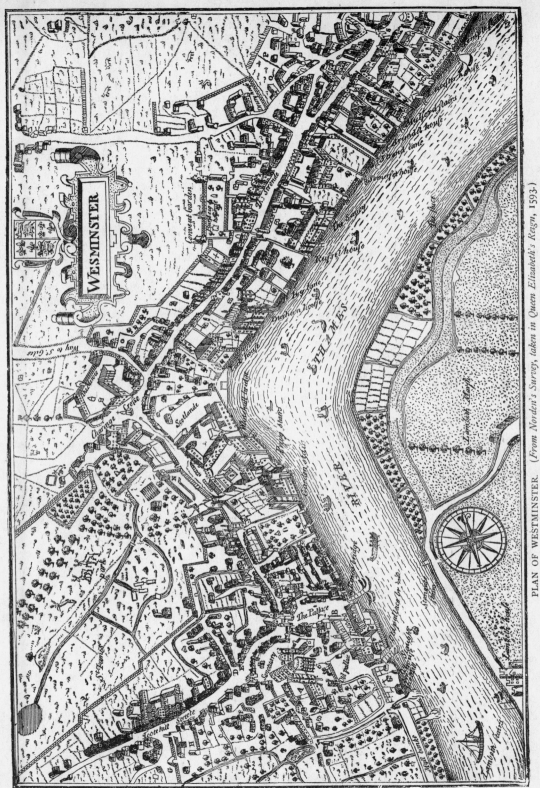

PLAN OF WESTMINSTER. (*From Norden's Survey, taken in Queen Elizabeth's Reign, 1593.*)

A. The Abbey.　B. Westminster Hall.　D. Long Ditch.　E. Thieving Lane.　F. The Amnerie.　G. Way to Tothill Fields.　H. The Lord Dacres.　K. King Street.　L. Round
Woolstaple.　M. The Park Lodgings.　N. The Tilt Yard.　O. St. Martin's-in-the-Fields.　P. Clement's Lane.　Q. New Inn.　R. St Clement D.ns.　S. Temple Bar.

antique figure, and obtained several prizes from the Society of Arts for drawings made here; Richard Cosway, the miniature painter, and William Parrs, whose productions figured on the walls at the first exhibition of the Royal Academy. This artist was a great traveller, and much patronised by the Lord Palmerston of that day. Another was John A. Grosse, a native of Geneva, and a pupil of Cipriani; another was William Parry, son of a blind Welsh harpist, who obtained several prizes for drawings made in this gallery, and afterwards was a favourite pupil of Sir Joshua Reynolds. Parry made a drawing of the Duke's gallery itself, into which he introduced several portraits: to the curious the discovery of this representation of a place so memorable would be a prize indeed. The Duke of Richmond, too, was a liberal patron of the meritorious artists of his time, as is proved by their numerous works in the Gallery at Goodwood. In other respects the Duke was often attacked for a want of hospitality and liberality; but, possibly, if he had squandered his wealth in giving costly banquets at Whitehall the artists of a century ago would have been so much the more poorly off. It would be well indeed for art, and indeed for literature also, if there were amongst us more noblemen endowed with the same generous feelings as Charles, Duke of Richmond. There is a deep truth in the old line which says:—

"Sint Mæcenates, non deerunt, Flacce, Marones."

But the house has also yet another claim to be remembered, for it was here that the first meeting of the friends of Parliamentary Reform was held, in May, 1782, a week or two before the subject was brought forward by Mr. Pitt in the House of Commons.

The mansion was burnt to the ground in December, 1791. There is an engraving of the house by Boydell; and Edwards, in his "Anecdotes," mentions the drawing of the gallery by Parry, alluded to above, which he considered curious, as being "the only representation of the place." On the site of this mansion, as already stated, has risen Richmond Terrace, a noble row of houses overlooking Montagu House and Whitehall Gardens, standing at right angles to the Thames Embankment, and having an entrance from Parliament Street through handsome iron gates.

We read in Macaulay that in the panic arising out of the perjuries of Titus Oates patrols were marched up and down the streets, and that cannon were planted round Whitehall. The same, too, was the case during the agitation respecting the bill for excluding the Duke of York from the throne.

The house No. 3 in Richmond Terrace is rich in some historical traditions of the last generation. On the formation of Lord Grey's ministry, in 1830, it was occupied by the Premier's brother-in-law, the late Mr. Edward Ellice, M.P., who had a very extensive acquaintance and influence among the Liberal party. As it was near to the Treasury and to the House of Commons, it soon became the head-quarters of the Whigs, and the chief centre of communication between the friends of the intended Reform Bill which was engrossing the attention of the public, including not only the old Whigs and modern Liberals, but also the Radicals of Birmingham. When Parliament was dissolved, in 1831, this house again became the chief centre of action, where candidates came to make inquiries for vacant constituencies, and deputations from near and distant boroughs came in search after eligible candidates, a committee for that purpose sitting there *en permanence*, under the auspices of Mr. Ellice, who here gave Parliamentary dinners and Liberal *reunions*. After the death of his wife, Lady Hannah Grey, the house passed into the hands of another leading Liberal, a son-in-law of Earl Grey, Sir Charles Wood, who, in the year 1866, was created Viscount Halifax in reward of his long official services.

It was conclusively shown, in the trial of Sir C. Burrell *v.* Nicholson, before Lord Denman, in December, 1833, that when the Palace of Whitehall was seized upon by Henry VIII., he added to its precincts the ground on the south, where Richmond Terrace now stands, the land originally being part of St. Margaret's parish, and belonging to the Abbot of Westminster. The two gardens and three acres of land which the king got from Wolsey were not enough for his Majesty.

At Richmond Terrace, on making the customary perambulation of the bounds of St. Margaret's parish every third year, a little parish apprentice usually was whipped soundly in order that the tradition might be kept up of the limits which marked off the precinct of Whitehall from the mother parish out of which it had been carved.

Extending from the back of Richmond Terrace to Bridge Street, Westminster, and about midway between the Thames and Parliament Street, is a narrow thoroughfare called Cannon (or Canon) Row, which has a little history of its own. We learn from Stow and from John Selden that Cannon Row—or, as it was often called, Channel Row—derived its name from being the residence allotted to the canons of St. Stephen's Chapel. Stow informs us that among its inhabitants in his time were "divers noblemen and gentlemen," as Sir Edward

Hobbes, John Thynne, Esq., Henry Clinton, Earl of Lincoln, and the Earl of Derby and the Duchess of Somerset, mother of the Earl of Hertford, who both occupied " stately " houses.

On the south side stands a dull and heavy building, erected in 1784 for the Ordnance Board, but soon after appropriated to the then newly-formed Board of Control. The architect was a Mr. W. Atkinson. It is now occupied by the Civil Service Commissioners.

In Cannon Row was the "Rhenish Wine House of good resort," to use Strype's quaint expression, and mentioned by Prior and Montague in terms which imply that it was well known in their day:—

" What wretch would nibble on a hanging shelf
When at Pontack's he may regale himself,
Or to the house of cleanly Rhenish go,
Or that at Charing Cross, or that in Channel Row ? "

Here stood the "stately" house built by the termagant Anne Stanhope, wife of the Protector Somerset, whose dispute about some trifling point of female precedence is said to have contributed in some degree to her husband's fall. Here, too, was Manchester House, which appears to have been cut up into tenements in the reign of Queen Anne.

Leading out of this row on the east side was formerly Derby Court, so called from the town residence of the Earl of Derby, which it adjoined. Stow describes it, in 1598, as "a stately house," then in the course of erection. It was surrendered in the time of Charles I. to the use of the Parliament, who occupied it for meetings of committees. Here died Pym, and here, as we learn from Ludlow's " Memoirs," his body was publicly exposed after his death. After the Restoration, the Stanleys removed elsewhere, and the mansion was occupied as the office of the Lord High Admiral.

A view of Westminster Bridge, whilst in the course of erection, painted by Canaletti (see page 378), shows the Middlesex bank of the river about Cannon Row and Whitehall covered with handsome mansions, most of which rise perpendicularly out of the river, with stairs and landing-places.

Between Cannon Row and the river, extending in a southerly direction, was a double row of private houses, principally occupied by bachelor members of Parliament, and known as Manchester Buildings. Their site is now covered by the Metropolitan District Railway Station and the St. Stephen's Club. They were so called because they adjoined the town residence of the Earls of Manchester, with " a very fine court which hath a handsome freestone pavement," as we learn from Strype ; and adjoining the houses of the Earls of

Derby and Lincoln. According to Mr. Peter Cunningham, a gaming-house in these buildings was once occupied by Thurtell, who murdered Mr. Weare.

Cannon Row is of historic interest on account of its connection with the very last days of the life of King Charles I. In Wood's " Athenæ Oxoniensis," we find the following touching narrative told by the King's faithful attendant, Herbert :—

" The same evening [January 28th, 1648–9], two days before his execution, the King took a ring from his finger, having an emerald set therein between two diamonds, and gave it to Mr. Herbert, and commanded him, as late as 'twas, to go with it from St. James's to a lady living then in Canon Row, on the back side of King Street, in Westminster, and to give it to her without saying anything. The night was exceeding dark, and guards were set in several places ; nevertheless, getting the word from Colonel Matthew Tomlinson, Mr. Herbert passed currently through in all places where sentinels were, but was bid stand till the corporal had the word from him. Being come to the lady's house, he delivered her the ring. 'Sir,' said she, 'give me leave to show you the way into the parlour ;' where, being seated, she desired him to stay till she returned. In a little time after she came in and put into his hands a little cabinet, closed with three seals, two of which were the King's arms, and the third was the figure of a Roman ; which done, she desired him to deliver it to the same hand that sent the ring ; which ring was left with her ; and afterwards, Mr. Herbert taking his leave, he gave the cabinet into the hands of his Majesty (at St. James's), who told him that he should see it opened next morning. Morning being over, the Bishop (Juxon) was early with the King, and, after prayers, his Majesty broke the seals, and showed them what was contained in the cabinet. There were diamonds and jewels—most part broken Georges and Garters. 'You see,' said he, 'all the wealth now in my power to give to my children.' "

Parliament Street, the line of thoroughfare which forms a direct communication between Whitehall and Westminster, was driven through the heart of the " Privy Garden " and the " Bowling Green," displacing the terraces, sun-dials, and statues, about the year 1732, in order to supersede the narrow road which led to Westminster from Charing Cross. Previously the only access from the one spot to the other was by King Street, a narrow way, muddy and ill paved, which ran parallel to Parliament Street from the corner of Downing Street to the Abbey. At the northern end it was spanned by the lofty and imposing gateway, called, from its designer, Holbein's Gate, of which we have already spoken. So bad was King Street as a thoroughfare that we are told that, when the King went to open Parliament in the winter in the early part of the eighteenth century, it was often found necessary to throw down a supply of fagots in the ruts in order to allow the royal coach to pass along. But of King Street we shall have more to say hereafter.

For thirty-six years, from 1820 down to 1856, the Messrs. Nichols issued the *Gentleman's Magazine* at their printing-office in this street. The work of editing and printing the *Gentleman's Magazine* had for many years previously been conducted by the Messrs. Nichols at their office in Red Lion Passage, Fleet Street. As far back as 1792, the writers in the *Gentleman's Magazine* were thus satirised— much to their own credit—by "Peter Pindar :"—

"And see the hacks of Nichols's Magazine
    Rush loyal to berhyme a King and Queen."

It was in Parliament Street, on the 26th of January, 1843, that Mr. E. Drummond, private secretary to Sir Robert Peel, was shot by a man named Macnaghten, who mistook him for the Premier. No. 52 in this street was for many years the residence of Charles James Fox.

At the corner of Derby Street, the short thoroughfare leading out of Parliament Street into Cannon Row, stands the Whitehall Club, which was built about the year 1866. The building, Italian in style, is constructed of stone, and consists of three storeys, besides offices in the basement. It was built from the designs of the late Mr. Parnell, at a cost of about £25,000. Over the doorway and upon the cornice is some admirable sculpture executed by Mr. Tolmie. The rooms are spacious and lofty, and well adapted to the purposes to which they are devoted.

Close by stood a small public-house, of which Charles Dickens tells us, that when a very young boy, he lounged in there and asked for a glass of ale, which the kind-hearted landlady gave him, after sundry inquiries as to his name, age, and belongings, and into the bargain a kiss, "half-admiring, half-compassionate, but all womanly and good, I am sure."

With respect to this highly historical neighbourhood, Pope, as usual, minutely accurate in details, thus writes in a spirit of prophecy, which, it is needless to say, has never yet been quite fulfilled to the letter :—

"Behold ! Augusta's glittering spires increase,
    And temples rise, the beauteous works of peace.
    I see, I see, where two fair cities bend
    Their ample bow, a new Whitehall ascend ;

There mighty nations shall enquire their doom,
    The world's great oracle in times to come :
    There kings shall sue, and suppliant states be seen
    Once more to bend before a British Queen."

And yet, after all, the seer may be regarded as not so very wide of the mark, if we interpret a "new Whitehall" to mean the new Houses of Parliament, and the new Foreign, Indian, and Colonial Offices, which have lately risen on the Park side of Whitehall, and have well nigh effaced the narrow and close *cul de sac* of Downing Street.

Before closing our remarks on Whitehall, we may state that in September, 1718, De Foe, then busy in the midst of politics, secular and religious, started the *Whitehall Evening Post*, a newspaper consisting of two leaves, in small quarto, and published on Tuesdays, Thursdays, and Saturdays. De Foe was connected with it till June, 1720, but the paper continued to exist for many years after this date. Whether it was actually published at Whitehall, or near to it, is not known, but it is probable that it was connected with the courtly locality through some of its contributors.

It must be remembered that before the middle of the eighteenth century, nearly every house in the leading streets of London and Westminster had its sign. Thus an observer in the reign of James I. remarks : "On the way from Somerset House to Charing Cross we pass the 'White Hart,' the 'Red Lion,' the 'Mairmade,' the 'iii Tuns,' 'Salutation,' the 'Graihound,' the 'Bell,' and the 'Golden Lyon;' in sight of Charing Cross, the 'Garter,' the 'Crown,' the 'Bear and Ragged Staffe,' the 'Angel,' the 'King Harry (*sic*) Head.'" It is almost needless to add that all trace and nearly every record of these house signs have long since disappeared before the onward march of the prosaic spirit of modern progress. "The houses in the West-end, in 1685, were not numbered," writes Macaulay ; "there would, indeed, have been very little advantage in numbering them, for of the coachmen, chairmen, porters, and errand-boys of London only a small proportion could read, and it was necessary to use marks which the most ignorant could understand. The shops were therefore distinguished by painted or sculptured signs, which gave a gay and grotesque aspect to the streets." If the walk from Charing Cross to Whitechapel lay through an "endless succession of 'Saracens' Heads,' 'Royal Oaks,' 'Blue Bears,' and 'Golden Lambs,' which disappeared when they were no longer required for the direction of the common people," the same, in a certain degree, must have been true of the walk from Charing Cross to Westminster Abbey.

CHAPTER XLVIII.

WHITEHALL.—THE WESTERN SIDE.

"A royal house, with learned Muses grac'd,
But by his death imperfect and defac'd."
Storer's Metrical History of Wolsey.

Wallingford House—Pope's Lines on the Death-bed Scene of Villiers, Duke of Buckingham—Wallingford House converted into the Admiralty Office—The Semaphore Telegraph—Authority and Jurisdiction of the Admiralty—Career of Lord Sandwich at the Admiralty—Funeral of Lord Nelson—Anecdote of Mr. Croker—The Horse Guards—The Commander-in-Chief's Department—Pennant's View of the Old Horse Guards—Dover House—The Treasury—Downing Street: its Political Associations, and Anecdotes of Former Occupants—The Old Foreign Office—The New Foreign, India, and Colonial Offices—Library of the India Office.

NEARLY the whole of the western side of Whitehall, between Charing Cross and Parliament Street, is occupied either by Government buildings or by other edifices of public importance. First of all we have, nearly opposite to Scotland Yard, the building known to all officers of Her Majesty's navy as the Admiralty. The present extensive building was erected in the reign of George II., from the designs of Ripley, on the site of Wallingford House, a fine mansion, built by William, Lord Knollys, Viscount Wallingford, and Earl of Banbury, in the second year of Charles I.

Wallingford House was subsequently used by the "Lord Protector" and his councillors for the purpose of holding consultations on public affairs. Here, too, was born the notorious and reprobate Villiers, Duke of Buckingham, the second of his line who bore that fatal title—the son of the royal favourite assassinated by Felton, and the man who, having squandered a princely fortune, and thrown away a splendid position, became the butt for Dryden's satire, while his death-bed served to "point a moral" for Pope:—

"In the worst inn's worst room, with mat half hung,
The floors of plaster and the walls of dung,
On once a flock-bed, but repaired with straw,
With tape-tied curtains never meant to draw,
The 'George' and 'Garter' dangling from that bed,
Where tawdry yellow strives with dirty red,
Great Villiers lies. Alas! how changed for him,
That life of pleasure and that soul of whim!
Gallant and gay in Cliefden's proud alcove—
The bower of wanton Shrewsbury and love;
Or just as gay at Council, in a ring
Of mimic statesmen and their merry King:
No wit to flatter left of all his store,
No fool to laugh at, which he valued more,
There, victor of his health, of fortune, friends,
And fame, this lord of useless thousands ends!"

Though the first line, as it has often been observed, embodies a poetical fiction, the picture as a whole is true, in spite of an error in topography. It was not at a paltry "inn" in Yorkshire, as commonly supposed, but at Kirby Mallory, in Leicestershire, at the house of one of his tenants, that Villiers, Duke of Buckingham, was suddenly struck with illness and died. From his biography by his retainer Fairfax, and from an account of his death-bed in the "Collection of Letters of Persons of Quality and Others," it is clear that, although he did not die in actual want of the necessaries of life, yet he died in comparative poverty, having wasted his fortune to a mere nothing—he who had been literally "the lord of thousands."

Wallingford House was purchased in the reign of William III., and appointed for the Admiralty Office, which had been removed thither from Duke Street, Westminster. The present edifice is very extensive. The front elevation, facing the street, has two deep wings, forming a court-yard, and in the centre is a portico formed of four lofty columns of the Ionic order; these support the pediment, within which are the Admiralty arms. The interior is very convenient, and comprises a large hall and numerous offices appropriated to the transacting of maritime concerns. The screen before the court, which was subsequently built by Robert Adam, has been much admired; it consists of a piazza of the Doric order supporting its entablature, and enriched with marine ornaments. It must be owned that the heavy structure, as a whole, is better adapted for use than for show; and it may be remarked that Pennant speaks of the Admiralty as "a clumsy pile, but properly veiled from the street by Mr. Adam's handsome screen."

During the great war against Napoleon, and subsequently, the Admiralty was surmounted by a "telegraph," as the semaphore was then called. By this "telegraph" a message could be sent, on fine days and in clear weather, to Portsmouth, and to one or two other stations, in an hour, or even in less time; and the semaphore stood on the top of the mansion until its use was entirely superseded by the electric telegraph. Hence it is that Leigh Hunt quaintly remarks, in the year 1835: "Where the poor archbishop sank down in horror at the sight of King Charles's execution, telegraphs now ply their dumb and far-seen discourses, like spirits in the guise of mechanism, and tell news of the spread of liberty and knowledge all over the world."

What would he have said if he could have looked forward only five short years and seen the machine on which he dwelt thus proudly laid quietly on the shelf, being superseded by a far more ingenious and subtle mechanism, the result of the scientific researches of Sir Charles Wheatstone and of Sir William Fothergill Cooke?

The interior of the Admiralty, although convenient and capacious, offers nothing remarkable; early part of the seventeenth century; in 1632 it was, for the first time, "put into commission," or its duty and authority confided to a Board of Commissioners, consisting of all the chief officers of state. At the Restoration the Duke of York was appointed Lord High Admiral, and he retained the office till 1684, when Charles II. took it upon himself; but James resumed it in the following year, on becoming king. The Revolution caused it again

THE HORSE GUARDS, FROM ST. JAMES'S PARK. *Temp. Charles II.* *(See page* 387.)

nor do any particular ceremonies take place within its walls; it is business, not ceremony, that is here the order of the day. It has been remarked with truth that, "without any very extravagant stretch of fancy, the Admiralty may be said to be the mighty steam-engine which sets in motion and gives energy to all the rest of the *matériel* and machinery of our naval power, and consequently contributes much to that of the whole empire."

The authority and jurisdiction now vested in the Admiralty was originally exercised by an individual, a high officer of state, called the Admiral of the King. The first upon actual record was William de Leybourne, "Admiral de la Mer du Roy d'Angleterre," in 1297. The office of High Admiral continued to be held by an individual until the to be put into commission, till 1707, when Prince George of Denmark became Lord High Admiral, with an assisting council of four members. On his death, in the following year, the Earl of Pembroke was appointed to succeed him, in similar form; but within about a twelvemonth he resigned, and from that time to the present the office has always been in commission, with the exception of a brief interval in 1827-8, during which the title of Lord High Admiral was again restored, in the person of the Duke of Clarence, afterwards William IV. The Admiralty Board consists of six members, styled the Lords (Commissioners) of the Admiralty, who are not, however, all of equal dignity and authority; for besides taking official precedence of the others, the First Lord of the Admiralty has higher privileges and emoluments than his colleagues, and he is, by virtue of his official position, a member of the Cabinet.

The Great Room used to be, during the last century, hung round with pictures of the South Sea Islands, and decorated with naval emblems and curiosities; and in the good old days, when Lord Sandwich held the office of First Lord of the Admiralty, it was the scene of many hospitable

North's ministry, in 1770, he was Secretary for Foreign Affairs, but exchanged his portfolio for that of First Lord of the Admiralty—a post for which his knowledge of maritime affairs especially fitted him. Sir N. W. Wraxall writes: "I saw, in 1782, the furniture of Lord Sandwich being carried off from the Admiralty, of which Keppel, who had been named as his successor, was just taking possession." Lord Sandwich's public career ended with the year

YORK HOUSE IN 1795. *From a View published by Colnaghi.* (*See page 387.*)

and frolicsome dinners, presided over by the elegant Miss Ray, whose murder by the Rev. Mr. Hackman, on the 7th of April, 1779, we have recorded at some length in our chapter on Covent Garden. (See *ante*, p. 260.)

Lord Sandwich, whose name is most intimately connected with the control of the Admiralty during the early part of the reign of George III., was a man of high ability as a statesman, and one to whom history has scarcely done justice. He died in April, 1792. He was educated at Eton and at Trinity College, Cambridge, and in early life had spent two years in a classical tour round the coasts of the Mediterranean, of which he published an illustrated account, at a time when "illustrated" works were less common than now. In Lord

1784, after which date he divided his time between London and his seat at Hinchinbrooke, in Huntingdonshire. He knew most ancient and modern languages, was a collector of coins, and an excellent musician. "Others," observes Mr. Cradock, who knew him well, "received great emoluments for what they performed; Lord Sandwich was always content to know that he had deserved them. He was also, in many ways, a great practical benefactor to Greenwich Hospital."

It was within the walls of Wallingford House that, in 1667, the body of the Court poet, Abraham Cowley, lay in state for a day before its interment in the Abbey hard by.

In the large room on the ground-floor, to the right as we enter, lay Nelson's body in state, on the night of January 8th, 1806, previous to its being buried the next day in St. Paul's. It had been brought from Greenwich by water to Whitehall, and thence carried to the Admiralty. The procession is described at full length in the *Gentleman's Magazine*, from which we abridge the following account :—It consisted of ten gun-boats, two and two ; boats containing the River Fencibles ; nine state barges, draped in black, containing the mourners, officials connected with the Admiralty, and also the Heralds of Arms, bearing the insignia of the deceased. The third barge, which contained the body, was covered with black velvet (the other barges being covered with black cloth), the top adorned with plumes of black feathers, and also with armorial bearings, and a viscount's coronet. The body was covered with a large sheet, and a pall of velvet adorned with six escutcheons. This part of the procession was flanked by eighteen row-boats of River Fencibles. Then came the state barges of eight of the City companies, flanked by the like number of row-boats with Harbour Marines. The funeral barge was rowed by sixteen seamen belonging to the *Victory ;* the other barges by picked men from the Greenwich pensioners. As the procession passed the Tower minute-guns were here fired. The procession arrived at Whitehall Stairs about three o'clock, having been about three hours rowing up from Greenwich, when the King's, Admiralty, Lord Mayor's, and City barges drew up in two lines, through which the barge with the body passed, the bands at the same time playing the " Dead March " in "Saul," " with other dirgeful strains, with the most impressive effect, the gun-boats firing minute-guns all the time." During the time of disembarking there was a tremendous hail-storm. In the procession from Whitehall Stairs to the Admiralty the coffin was surmounted by a rich canopy, supported by six admirals. Every necessary preparation had been made at the Admiralty for receiving the body. The Captains' Room, in which it was placed, was hung with black cloth, and lighted with wax tapers placed in sconces on the sides. The body remained in the room, guarded by the officers of the house and the undertakers, till the ceremony of its removal to St. Paul's commenced. This took place on the following day, when the remains of Nelson were conveyed by the old sailors of the *Victory,* and a large military and naval procession, on a magnificent funeral car, or open hearse, decorated with a carved imitation of the head and stern of the *Victory,* surrounded with escutcheons of the arms of the deceased, and adorned with appropriate mottoes and emblematical devices ; under an elevated canopy in the form of

the upper part of an ancient sarcophagus, with six sable plumes and the coronet of a viscount in the centre, supported by four columns representing palm-trees, with wreaths of natural laurel and cypress entwining the shafts ; the whole upon a four-wheeled carriage, drawn by six led horses, the caparisons adorned with armorial bearings.

Spacious as is the old Admiralty, it has been found, in these days of naval activity, utterly inadequate, and a large block of offices, in a modified form of the classic, with Anglo-Italian features, has been built in the rear, overlooking St. James's Park. This structure, completed in 1895, is to be supplemented by another on the north side, which will join the present buildings together at their northern extremities, and so will be formed three sides of a quadrangle enclosing the Admiralty Gardens.

A capital story in connection with the Admiralty is told by Mr. Cyrus Redding, in his " Fifty Years' Recollections :"—Mr. Croker, the Secretary of that department, happening to dine at the Pavilion at Brighton, under the Regency, entered into conversation with the Duke of Clarence. The latter liked nothing better than a sly cut at that department, and especially at Croker himself. In reply to some chance remark of the Secretary, the Duke said, " Ah ! if ever I am king, I will be my own First Lord of the Admiralty." " Does your royal highness recollect," asked Croker, " what English king was his own First Lord the last time ?" The duke shook his head, and replied in the negative. "It was James II., sir." There was a general laugh among the party, as well there might be ; but the duke was taken aback, and the regent was greatly annoyed at the remark when repeated to him afterwards.

Adjoining the Admiralty, on the south side, is the extensive range of buildings known as the Horse Guards. The building, which is heavy and tasteless, is from the designs of Kent, and was erected about the year 1753, at a cost of £30,000. The clock in the turret which surmounts the centre of the building has always enjoyed a reputation for accuracy, and used to be the grand regulator of all the timepieces in its vicinity.

The open space at the back is the Parade Ground : here are two curious pieces of ordnance —one a large howitzer or mortar captured at the siege of Cadiz, in 1810, and the other a Turkish piece, taken at Alexandria, in 1801. Under two small pavilions in front, on either side of the entrance in Whitehall, sentinels, mounted, and in uniform, do duty from ten to four o'clock every day.

The Horse Guards is somewhat appropriately placed, occupying as it does the site of the Tilt-yard (or place for military exercises), of which we have already spoken. The origin of the name is this:—Soon after the Restoration Charles II. raised a body of troops, which he designated his "Horse Guards," to whom the special duty was assigned of protecting the king's person. For this troop stables and barracks were built in the Tilt-yard, but in 1751 these were pulled down to make way for the present edifice. Accommodation for the troops quartered here is provided by two lateral pavilions, which flank the east face of the main building. Here were for many years the head-quarters of the Commander-in-Chief, the Adjutant-General, and the Quartermaster-General, whose duties are now concentrated at the War Office, in Pall Mall. The Horse Guards now furnishes accommodation mainly for the Department of the Inspector-General of Fortifications. With the War Office we shall deal in our next volume, but of the Commander-in-Chief's department it may be said that it is solely devoted to the government, discipline, and movements of the military; and that to the Commander-in-Chief is unreservedly confided the rule and governance of the whole army. He is accessible not only to every commissioned officer of the British army, but to his immediate connections; and he or his deputy (the Military Secretary) holds a *levée* at intervals during the "season." Every person desirous of attending it previously sends a letter expressing that intention, and stating the object of his visit; and as these interviews are considered strictly confidential, by endorsing it " for the *levée*," he ensures its being opened and read by the great military authority addressed, and by him only. His (or her) name is then transferred to a list, against a number which regulates the order of the applicants' reception; the ladies being always, of course, admitted first. That number is copied upon the back of each visitor's letter, which is also endorsed with a memorandum, from which the answer is orally delivered at the interview. Thus the Commander-in-Chief is at no loss, and time is not wasted in discussion. During this *levée* there is an entire absence of ceremony of every description, and the Commander-in-Chief is the only personage who appears in regimentals. The suite of rooms, also, used for the purpose consists only of three—namely, a waiting-room, a vestibule (in which the ladies abide their turn), and the audience-chamber. The first of these is a good-sized apartment, and faces Whitehall; the walls are almost covered with maps, and the chairs surrounding the

room are placed, with military precision, exactly equi-distant. The vestibule is a small circular hall, possessing nothing more remarkable than the boundary-line of the parishes of St. Martin's and St. Margaret's, Westminster, which is cut through its centre, and accompanied with suitable inscriptions. The audience-chamber, which overlooks the parade-ground in St. James's Park, partakes of the same degree of military formality that distinguishes the other rooms.

The ladies, as we have stated, are presented first. All being in readiness, the attendant in waiting, bearing a copy of the numbered list above mentioned, calls out the name of the visitor who is to be seen, and ushers her into the presence of the Commander-in-Chief. The confidential nature of the interview admits the presence of no other person—not even the private secretary. Thus there is every encouragement offered for the most minute and circumstantial detail of private interests and domestic matters, into which the head of the army fully enters, with a view to serving the applicant in proportion to the claims put forward. The ladies having all been received and dismissed, the gentlemen are then summoned, *seriatim*, in such a manner as to ensure that no moment of time shall be lost. Some of the visits are merely ceremonial; others—and by far the greater number —are made to follow up previously forwarded applications for some one or other of the few military appointments in the gift of the Commander-in-Chief.

Pennant gives an interesting view of the old Horse Guards from the Park, as the building must have appeared in 1660–70. In the background it shows the Banqueting House, the Holbein Gate, the Treasury in its ancient state, and the top of the Cock-pit adjoining. In the foreground is to be seen the " Merry Monarch," with his favourite dogs and an attendant train of courtiers. To the right of the spectator is the eastern end of the straight and formal " canal," which then almost bisected the Park. We have reproduced this print in a reduced form on page 384.

Between the Horse Guards and the Treasury stands Dover (formerly York) House, so called after the Hon. George Agar-Ellis, afterwards the accomplished Lord Dover. It is now the office of the Secretary of State for Scotland. It was built in 1774, by Payne, for Sir Matthew Fetherston-haugh, who sold it to the first Lord Melbourne, father of the late Premier. In 1789 it was bought by the Duke of York, who added the domed entrance-hall and the grand staircase, and after whom it was called York House. A print of it was published by Colnaghi in 1795, dedicated to Lord Melbourne. Of this view we have given a copy on page 385. This mansion faces the Banqueting House of Whitehall at the point where Holbein's Gate once stood, and commands a front prospect of the broad and open thoroughfare from Charing Cross to Parliament Street.

The Treasury Buildings, which occupy some 300 feet of frontage to Whitehall extending from Dover House to Downing Street, were originally part of Cardinal Wolsey's Banqueting Hall, and were re-fronted by Sir John Soane, the architect and antiquary; and it is believed that the old buttresses are still *in situ*. A new façade, in the Corinthian style, was added by the late Sir Charles Barry, R.A., about the year 1850. By these alterations and additions, the whims and conceits of Sir John Soane have disappeared, and the order, which is a reduced and simplified model of that of the Temple of Jupiter Stator, has, by the enrichment of the frieze and the addition of considerable ornament above it, been brought more into harmony with the building (or rather the building with it), which would have been impossible with less enrichment. The building, which has a short return front towards Downing Street, also contains the office of the Privy Council, of the Education Department, and of the Board of Trade. *A propos* of the first-mentioned of these offices, we may here insert the text of the oath taken by the Clerk of Her Majesty's Privy Council, on appointment, which is as follows:—"You shall swear to be a true and faithful servant unto the Queen's Majesty, in the exercise of the functions of the Clerk of the Privy Council in ordinary. You shall not know or understand of any manner of thing to be attempted, done, or spoken against Her Majesty's person, honour, crown, or dignity royal; but you shall lett or withstand the same to the uttermost of your power, and either do or cause it to be revealed, either to Her Majesty herself, or to the Privy Council. You shall keep secret all matters committed and revealed unto you, or that shall be treated of secretly in council. And if any of the said treaties or councils shall touch any of the counsellors, you shall not reveal it unto him, but shall keep the same until such time as, by the consent of Her Majesty or by the Council, publication shall be made thereof. You shall to your uttermost bear faith and allegiance to the Queen's Majesty, and shall assist and defend all jurisdictions, pre-eminences, and authorities granted to Her Majesty, and annexed to the Crown by Act of Parliament or otherwise, against all foreign princes, persons, prelates, states, or potentates.

And generally in all things you shall do as a faithful and true servant and subject ought to do to Her Majesty. So help you God, and the holy contents of this book."

The offices and official residence of the First Lord of the Treasury, where the Cabinets of Her Majesty's ministers have often been held, are, together with those of the Chancellor of the Exchequer, still located in Downing Street, in plainer buildings (partly erected for dwelling-houses), behind this handsome pile, and reaching to St. James's Park. The interior of the Treasury contains little or nothing very remarkable, excepting, perhaps, an old gilt state chair, or throne, which is placed at the head of the table in the Board-room.

Although all royal proclamations and diplomatic correspondence are dated "from our Palace at St. James's," yet for nearly the last two centuries the motive power, so to speak, of the administration of the country has had its head-quarters in Downing Street, a dull, narrow *cul de sac* running up westwards from the corner of the buildings of the Treasury. Almost the last of the houses which composed it disappeared in 1874, the work of demolition having been begun as far back as 1828; but its memory will long survive enshrined in the parliamentary history of the empire. Consequently, therefore, it must always be rich in its former associations; and probably no street in this metropolis, equally small in extent, can boast of having had such distinguished residents and tenants. Sir Robert Walpole, the Prime Minister of illustrious memory, made it his home during his long tenure of office; and he was the first Premier who did so. Lord North, as Premier, had his chambers here, occupying rooms on the first floor; and it is recorded of him that when he exchanged that post for the lesser responsibilities of a Secretary of State, he forgot that with the change of office came a change also of chambers, and walked mechanically into his old quarters instead of mounting another pair of stairs.

Different Prime Ministers have dealt differently with the official residence of the Premier in Downing Street. Some, like Pitt and Lord Grey, have made it really their home during their years of place and power; others, like Lord Melbourne and Sir Robert Peel, have used it only during the hours of business. Lord Grey took up his abode here; and it is here that R. B. Haydon has represented the earl pondering by his fireside after one of the great debates on the Reform Bill. Mr. Disraeli (afterwards Lord Beaconsfield) and Mr. Gladstone also took up their residence here as Premiers.

"Downing Street," says Mr. John Timbs, "has

a host of political associations, and anecdotes of its former occupants abound. When Sir Robert Walpole removed from his official residence here, he found an old account-book in which his father had set down his personal expenses. In three months and ten days, which he had spent in London one winter as a member of Parliament, he had expended but sixty-four pounds seven shillings and fivepence. There were in it many entries for ' Nottingham ale,' many eighteenpences for dinners, five shillings to ' Bob' Walpole, afterwards Earl of Orford, and one memorandum of ' six shillings given to Mr. Williams in exchange for a wig ;' and yet this old man—the grandfather of Horace Walpole—had a rental of £2,000 a year. He little thought, poor penurious old man that he was, that a sum which maintained him for a whole parliamentary session, would scarcely serve for one of his grandsons to buy a pair of fans for a princess at Florence !"

Here, in 1763, was the hospitable house of Sir John Cust, Speaker of the House of Commons, often mentioned by Cradock in his " Memoirs ; " and in this street Belzoni, the African explorer, and his wife lodged in 1820, on their return from Egypt and Nubia.

If we may believe Mr. Peter Cunningham, it was in this street that the Duke of Wellington and Lord Nelson met for the only time in their lives. It was at the Colonial Office, at that time " No. 14, Downing Street," in a small waiting-room on the right hand upon entering, that the two heroes—the former then plain Sir Arthur Wellesley—both wanting an interview with the Secretary of State—were accidentally brought into each other's presence. " The duke knew Nelson from his pictures : Lord Nelson, however, did not know the duke ; but he was so struck with his conversation that he stepped out of the room to inquire who he was !" This rencontre has been made the subject of a picture, which is engraved.

The " heaven-born minister," William Pitt, lived in Downing Street ; and here, as he tells us in Wraxall's " Memoirs," the first Marquis Cholmondeley waited on Pitt as head of the establishment of the Prince of Wales. " The affair," he writes, " related to a matter of accounts. I find it impossible to do justice to the perspicuity and rapidity of his (Pitt's) calculations. In the course of a few minutes he went through and settled every item, leaving me lost in admiration at his ability."

Pitt, during his tenure of office, not only kept up a house here, but made it his constant residence to such an extent that he was never willingly absent from its precincts. While his rival, Fox, could unbend himself in the society of his friends at Brooks's Club, or with his family at St. Anne's Hill, near Chertsey, Pitt could do nothing of the kind, and away from Downing Street he was miserable. When forced, from 1801 to 1804, to live in solitary grandeur at Walmer Castle, in the company of his niece, Lady Hester Stanhope, while Addington, whom he had raised to the highest posts from comparative obscurity, filled his place, he supported life only by the anticipation of a speedy return to Downing Street. His wishes were gratified. He resumed office after three years' exclusion, but in less than two more years he died, the victim of disappointed ambition.

> " Evertere domos totas optantibus ipsis
> Dî faciles."

Preliminaries of peace with France were signed at Lord Hawkesbury's office in Downing Street, on the 2nd of October, 1801 ; and on the 10th of the same month General Lauriston, Buonaparte's first aide-de-camp, arrived with the ratification. " On his arrival in town," we read, " he was greeted with immense cheering by the populace. On the same and following evening the metropolis was brilliantly illuminated."

Mr. Cyrus Redding tells an anecdote, the scene of which must have been laid in the house of the First Minister of the Crown, in the time of Earl Grey. A gentleman named Stuart, who had lately become proprietor of the Courier newspaper, and said to have made his money as a coal merchant in the City, waited on his lordship, and, without any circumlocution or " beating about the bush," offered for his acceptance the support of the paper—which up to then had been of Tory politics—in exchange for the Treasury patronage. Lord Grey looked at him with indignation, and quietly rang the bell, and when the footman entered, bade him " show that gentleman the door." It is probable that he did not know the right way to approach a minister, and that he was not worse or more corrupt than scores of members of Parliament and high-born individuals who have preferred similar requests. He merely mistook the way.

Another good story is told about Downing Street by Mr. T. Raikes, in his " Diary." In the early Reform riots, a mob ran violently into Downing Street and rushed up to the sentinel at the door of the Foreign Office, crying, " Liberty or death !" The soldier presented his musket, and said, " Hands off, you fellows ! I know nothing about liberty ; but if you come a step farther, I'll show you what death is !" It is to be hoped that the brave fellow was rewarded for his pluck and his wit too.

The general appearance of Downing Street as it was in the reign of George IV. or William IV. is thus hit off by Theodore Hook: "There is a fascination in that little *cul de sac;* an hour's inhalation of its atmosphere affects some men with giddiness, others with blindness, and very frequently with the most oblivious boastfulness." And possibly those State papers. At the offices of the Secretaries of State, when loaded with parcels of this description, he would throw open every chamber without ceremony; the Treasury and Exchequer doors could not oppose him, and even the study of archbishops has often been invaded by this important messenger of the press. His antiquated and greasy

THE NEW FOREIGN OFFICE. (*See page* 392.)

who know anything of public life and politics will confess that the wit was not far from the mark.

Between "The King's Printing-office" at Westminster and the various offices of State which centre in Downing Street, for many years there used daily to trudge a messenger or errand-carrier named John Smith, who was a favourite with several Premiers in succession, from Sir Robert Walpole down to William Pitt. What others accounted humble work became in his hands most important; and "the King's Messenger," as he styled himself, yielded to none of his Majesty's ministers in his idea of the dignity of his office, when entrusted with addresses, bills, royal speeches, and other garb corresponded with his wizard-like shape, and his immense cocked hat was continually in motion, to assist him in the bows of the old school. The recognition and nods of great men were his especial delight; but he imagined that this courtesy was due to his character, as being identified with the State, and the Chancellor and the Speaker were considered by him in no other view than persons filling departments in common with himself, for the seals of the one and the mace of the other did not, in his estimation, distinguish them more than the bag used by himself in the transmission of the despatches entrusted to his care. The imperfect intellect given to him seemed only to fit

WESTMINSTER, FROM THE ROOF OF WHITEHALL. (*From a View published by Smith, 1807.*)

him for the situation he filled. Take him out of it, he was as helpless as a child, and easily became a dupe to any one who was disposed to impose upon him. With a high opinion of his own judgment, however, he diverted himself and others by mimicking the voice and manner of his superiors, when he thought he perceived any assumption of character. Poor old John Smith, who felt as if he carried the world on his shoulders, and was as important a part of the constitution, in his own conceit, as the Prime Minister himself, died in 1818, at the age of ninety.

Downing Street—though for a century and a half the name was almost synonymous with the existing administration—has become almost entirely a thing of the past; for though two or three of the houses which were so familiar to Spencer Perceval, George Canning, and Lord Liverpool are still standing at the farther end, yet most of them have been absorbed into the large block of new public buildings which have been erected on its southern side. The clearance of Downing Street, however, as we have already shown, has been long in progress, having been commenced as far back as the year 1828, when "The Cat and Bagpipes," at its south-eastern corner, disappeared. Here, in early life, George Rose, a clerk in a Government office, afterwards Secretary of the Treasury, used to dine on a plain mutton chop.

The old Foreign Office, which stood on the south side of the street, was a brick building, with no architectural pretensions. It consisted of a centre, with two slightly projecting wings, and presented—at all events, in its latter days—anything but a fitting appearance for the use to which it was applied. It was demolished about the year 1864, in order to clear a site for the new Government offices, of which we shall presently speak. The public business of the country had been for many years carried on in the double row of mean and unsightly houses which formed the old street, when, at length, an elaborate report was presented to both Houses of Parliament, containing recommendations for the erection of a suitable block of buildings on a uniform plan, for the accommodation of ministers in the transaction of the business of the State. Nothing, however, came of these recommendations; and although the subject was from time to time brought forward in Parliament, and inquiries were made and plans suggested, nothing was done except the extension and decoration of the Whitehall front of the Treasury Buildings by Sir Charles Barry. In the meantime the question was in the way of one settlement by the fact that some of the old barns in Downing Street, and

the Foreign Office especially, were on the eve of tumbling down. By the elegant and decorative aid of beams and girders the walls were secured for a time; but at length even this standfast system was found insufficient to prevent the crumbling to pieces of the mortar and brickwork, in consequence of which the business of our diplomacy was temporarily transferred to Pembroke House, in Whitehall Gardens.

As soon as the old Foreign Office was levelled with the ground a new and stately edifice was commenced. The block of buildings extends from King Street (part of which has been merged in an enlargement of Parliament Street) on the east, to St. James's Park, near Storey's Gate, on the west; and from Downing Street on the north to Charles Street on the south. The buildings, which cover a large space of ground, surround two quadrangular courts, and are occupied by the Secretaries of State for Foreign Affairs, for India, for the Colonies, and for the Home Department. The whole exterior group of buildings was designed by Sir G. Gilbert Scott, R.A., the architect of the Foreign Office throughout; while the interior of the India Office, with the external work of the inner court belonging to that range of buildings, is the work of Sir M. Digby Wyatt, R.A.

The buildings are faced with Portland stone; granite is used for the window-columns, and granite, marble, and glass—mostly green and red—is largely employed in the decoration, in the shape of bosses and otherwise, in the friezes.

The various fronts display a large amount of carving, the execution of which was entrusted to several sculptors of eminence. The design for the buildings gave rise, from time to time, in the House of Commons, to some warm and animated discussions, which came to be familiarly called the "battles of the styles," and in which Lord Palmerston, the then Premier, vigorously defended the classical Italian or Palladian against the advocates of the Gothic. The result has been the erection of an edifice which may be said to belong to a style strictly "Palmerstonian," the architect—although chiefly celebrated for his Gothic designs—having, with a grim humour, adopted a plan which, it is stated, owed a good deal to the Premier, and which may be put down as broadly Italian, with an occasional infusion of Gothic. The Park front, as seen on approaching it from the Parade behind the Horse Guards, is at once bold and massive, the principal features being the lofty tower which separates the Foreign Office from that devoted to the Indian Department, and the grand semi-circular sweep which rounds off the angle of the building towards the Park. The niches at the angles on this side of the India Office are filled with statues of Indian statesmen. The tower on the Foreign Office side, though lower by a storey, is much more bulky than that belonging to the India Office.

In the stone-vaulted entrances through the India Office from Charles Street, and through the Foreign Office from Downing Street, are columns each of a single stone, eleven feet high; the vaulting in each case is handsome, and the groins show an incised ornament, filled in with red Parian cement. Across Downing Street, at the western end, a broad flight of steps gives access to St. James's Park; a flight of steps also leads from Charles Street into the Park.

The portion of the building which fronts Parliament Street is devoted to the Colonial and Home Departments. This part of the structure was only completed towards the commencement of the year 1875. It is adorned with statues of several eminent statesmen, including the late Lords Grenville, Liverpool, Melbourne, and Glenelg, Sir Robert Peel, Sir James Graham, Sir George Cornewall Lewis, Earl Russell, Sir George Grey, the late Earl of Derby, Earl Grey, and Sir William Molesworth.

The inner court of the Foreign Office, which is entered from Downing Street, is quite plain. Against the topmost storey, surrounding the quadrangle, stand, at certain intervals, a series of sculptured figures. Those on the Foreign Office front are emblematical of countries—Italy, France, and so on; whilst those on the other sides represent the Indian tribes—an Affghan, a Goorka, a Malay, a Mahratta, and so forth.

The principal apartments are on the first floor, and include the Cabinet-room, 70 feet long by 35 feet wide, and two spacious conference-rooms. All these rooms communicate, and afford accommodation for balls and other *réunions*. Over and below these rooms are libraries. The grand staircase occupies an area of 60 feet by 25 feet. On the India Office side there are four great staircases, but all much less in size than the Foreign Office staircase. One of these staircases has the walls ornamented with life-size statues of Indian statesmen, standing in arched niches; and upon the upper part of the wall is an oval-shaped allegorical painting brought from one of the ceilings of the old East India House in Leadenhall Street. The principal entrance to the India Office is in Charles Street. The court-yard occupies nearly a central position in the building, and affords means of light and air to a large number of the rooms on the north, east, and west sides, and to a portion of the main corridor on the south side. Above the windows of the upper storey, set within large escalop shells, are a series of busts—twenty-eight in number—of celebrated worthies, both civil and military, connected with our Indian empire, beginning with Admiral Watson and Lord Macartney, and including heroes of recent historical renown —as Havelock, Clyde, and Lawrence. At the four angles of the court are niches filled with statues; the four on the ground floor are of Lords Hastings, Minto, Amherst, and Wellesley, sculptured by Mr. Protat: those on the first floor, immediately above the others, are Cornwallis and Clive, by Mr. Nicholls; and Warren Hastings and Lord Teignmouth, by Mr. Phyffers, by whom also many of the panels have been elaborately carved.

This court is remarkable for the variety of materials employed for decorative purposes. The floor is composed of tiles, laid to a pattern. The main portion of the walling, plain and decorative, is of Portland stone. The bays of the ground floor and first storey are divided by piers faced with Doric columns of red Peterhead granite, with capitals of red Mansfield stone; whilst those on the second floor are of dark-grey Aberdeen granite, with stone capitals of the same colour; and the arches between the piers are filled with glass. In addition to these materials there are majolica and mosaic friezes and pateras, and tessellated floors and ceilings in the logias. The court is rectangular in plan, 115 feet long by 60 feet wide, and is covered by a roofing of iron and glass. Upon the floor of this court is the celebrated collection of antiquities known as the Elliott Marbles.

Some of the ceilings of the rooms in the India Office are handsomely worked in plaster, partly modelled from Indian fruits and flowers. In the committee-room there is a handsome fireplace of carved white marble, brought from the old East India House; and on the opposite wall hangs the life-size portrait of Warren Hastings which formerly occupied a conspicuous position in the old establishment. There is also a statue of Warren Hastings at the foot of the grand staircase.

In the basement floor of the building are a number of rooms and vaulted chambers. Some of these rooms are used for culinary purposes; others as engine-rooms in connection with the hot-water apparatus for heating the building, and also with the hydraulic lifts, tanks, and mains. A large part of the basement is made use of as workshops for carpenters and other branches of mechanical labour, a large number of hands being constantly employed. The space immediately beneath the pavement of the inner court of the India Office is entirely filled with racks in which are stowed away some thousands of volumes of the records from the old East India House.

At the top of this building, in a place by no means secure against fire, called the " Record Office," is a most valuable library of Oriental treasures, which contains Arabic manuscripts to the number of about 2,000 ; Persian to double that amount ; while of Sanscrit there are not less than 4,500, and many of these are gorgeously illuminated. Besides these there are 50,000 printed volumes, the greater part of which are Oriental works. On the same floor, down to the beginning of the year 1875, a series of rooms connected with each other had been set apart as the India Museum. This valuable collection, which had previously

(since its removal from Leadenhall Street) enjoyed a temporary retreat at Fife House, in Whitehall Yard, has now been transferred to South Kensington, where it has been permanently located in a part of the building occupied by the Industrial Exhibition of 1862.

The business of our Indian empire, as has been stated in a previous chapter (see Vol. II., p. 184), was formerly transacted to a very great extent at the old house of the East India Company, in Leadenhall Street. On the transfer, however, of the government of India to the Crown, in 1858, the old Board of Control in Cannon Row was abolished, and a Council of State for India was instituted. The official duties connected with the Indian Government were at the same time transferred to Westminster.